T0384013

Cybercrime and Cybersecurity in the Global South

Cybercrime and Cybersecurity in the Global South

Concepts, Strategies and Frameworks for Greater Resilience

Charlette Donalds
Corlane Barclay
Kweku-Muata Osei-Bryson

CRC Press
Taylor & Francis Group
Boca Raton London New York

CRC Press is an imprint of the
Taylor & Francis Group, an **informa** business

First edition published 2022
by CRC Press
6000 Broken Sound Parkway NW, Suite 300, Boca Raton, FL 33487-2742

and by CRC Press
4 Park Square, Milton Park, Abingdon, Oxon, OX14 4RN

© 2022 Taylor & Francis Group, LLC

CRC Press is an imprint of Taylor & Francis Group, LLC

ISBN: 978-0-367-46431-8 (hbk)
ISBN: 978-1-032-23191-4 (pbk)
ISBN: 978-1-003-02871-0 (ebk)

DOI: 10.1201/9781003028710

Typeset in Garamond
by SPi Technologies India Pvt Ltd (Straive)

To my mothers, Pauline and Alma, son, John-Michael, sister, Iesha, brother, Richard, and great friends, Janine, and George; for all your love and support over the years.

Charlette Donalds

To the special persons in my life.

Corlane Barclay

To my first grandson, Amir Kaboré, for an engaging journey on the highway of love and learning.

Kweku-Muata Osei-Bryson

Contents

Preface

Combatting cybercrime, breaches and improving cybersecurity standards continue to be top national priorities for countries with little indication that this will change in the foreseeable future. The current covid-19 pandemic has further brought increased attention to the systemic social, economic, health and security disparities and vulnerabilities that exist, particularly in less economically advantage economies. As a result, context-driven strategies, methods and frameworks are required to enable continued maturity in developing sustainable cybersecurity outcomes at different levels of an economy. We were motivated to write this book not only for scholarly pursuits but to also offer policymakers and practitioners with tangible tools and perspectives to help guide their cybersecurity initiatives, while engaging in dialogue that can advance our understanding of complexities and dynamism of the cybersecurity domain.

The Global South was chosen as the focal point because of a combination interest and pragmatism. Most books related to cybercrimes, cybersecurity and information security are contextualized to the Global North or developed economies. However, we are of the view that the Global South offers richness and diversity in both their experiences and approaches to tackling threats that are worthy of further investigation. Furthermore, there exists an opportunity to provide context-sensitive solutions and discourse that resonate with these constituents.

The book is organized into 3 parts: Assessing the Situation, which offers contributions to our understanding of the Cybersecurity situation in the Global South; Understanding User Security Compliance, which assesses employees' compliance behaviour; and, Developing Solutions for Managing Cybersecurity Risks, which focuses on practical solutions that can be adopted by Global South entities to improve cybersecurity readiness and resilience. The book's contributions include:

- Exploration of the current situation with respect to Cybersecurity risks, challenges, opportunities and capabilities.
- Experiences of the Global South economies that can enhance the learning experience.
- Evidence-based best practices in combating and preventing cyber related incidents and improving data protection practices appropriate for the Global South.

- Tools, techniques and frameworks that can improve Global South governments and MSMEs information and cybersecurity posture.

We expect that this book should be useful to a wide cross section of constituents including:

- Academics, researchers and students (undergraduate, post-graduate and doctoral), especially those engaged in academic programs that require an understanding of information security and cyber threats and those involved in understanding, developing and implementing security resilient ICT platforms.
- Global South governments that wish to improve national and/or regional legislative frameworks, capacity building and build public awareness campaigns.
- MSMEs (and other organizations), managers/owners of businesses intending to or have adopted ICTs.
- Practitioners across various industries operating in various ICT security related contexts.

The authors agree that working collaboratively and drawing on our meld of academic and industry experiences was a rewarding experience in bringing to life what started as just a conversation. Each author brought their unique perspectives and expertise to shape the discourse in a manner that brought a sense of pride during the various stages of developing the chapters and the book. We hope that the readers will sense that from reading one chapter or all the chapters of our book and find the data, analysis, and discourse meaningful whether they are a student, researcher, or practitioner.

Authors

Charlette Donalds is a full-time faculty member of the Mona School of Business & Management (MSBM), The University of the West Indies (The UWI), Mona. She holds a Ph.D. in Management Information Systems from The UWI. She has served in several capacities at the MSBM to include, Academic Director of the Masters in Computer-Based Management Information Systems and Unit Head for the Decision Sciences & Information Systems Unit. Her first book is a book of MIS cases for solving managerial problems with spreadsheets and databases. This MIS book has been the required text for a course at The UWI since 2011.

Charlette worked as an IT professional for many years before joining The UWI; thus, she has a wealth of knowledge and skill in the discipline. Of note, she has knowledge and experience in implementing, customizing and maintaining a renowned Enterprise System.

Her research areas and interests include Cybercrime, Cybersecurity, Ontology, Enterprise Systems, Knowledge Management, Technology Acceptance and Use, Information and Communication Technologies for Development (ICT4D) and Data Mining. She has published in journals including *European Journal of Information Systems, Computers in Human Behavior, Information Technology for Development* and *International Journal of Information Management.* She is a member of the Association of Information System ICT4D special interest group and the Internet Society, Cybersecurity special interest group. She serves as a reviewer for the *European Journal of Information Systems, Information Technology for Development* (journal), *The African Journal of Information Systems* and several International Information Systems Conferences.

Corlane Barclay is the principal of Smart Projects 360, https://smartprojects360.com/ which provides advisory, consultancy and research services in diverse areas of business and government operations. She is an attorney-at-law, certified Project Management Professional (PMP®) and trained legislative drafter. She has an extensive background in academia and industry working in the areas of cybersecurity, project and programme management, public policy, legal drafting and consulting. She is currently serving at the national level with responsibility for delivering diverse cybersecurity capacity development outcomes, including the drafting of Jamaica's second National Cybersecurity Strategy. She holds a Ph.D. in Information Systems from the University of the West Indies, Mona and other degrees in Management Information Systems, Accounts, Management and Law from the same University and a Graduate Diploma in Legislative Drafting from the Athabasca University, Canada.

Her research areas and interests include Project Management Performance and Success, Cybercrime, Cybersecurity, Data Protection and Privacy and Data Analytics & Data Science. She is the co-editor of two books, *Strategic Project Management: Contemporary Issues and Strategies* for *Developing Economies* and *Knowledge Discovery Process and Methods to Enhance Organizational Performance*. She has published in leading academic journals including the *European Journal of Information Systems, Information Systems Frontiers, Project Management Journal, International Journal of Production Economics* and *Information Technology for Development* in addition to technical industry press including the *ISACA Journal*. She has also served as a reviewer for leading academic journals relating to both information systems and law.

Kweku-Muata Osei-Bryson is a professor of Information Systems at Virginia Commonwealth University in Richmond, VA. He is also currently a visiting professor of Computing at The University of the West Indies, Mona and has also been visiting professor of Information Systems at the Ghana Institute of Management & Public Administration. Previously he was professor of Information Systems & Decision Sciences at Howard University in Washington, DC. He has also worked as an Information Systems practitioner in industry and government in the USA and Jamaica. He holds a Ph.D. in Applied Mathematics (Management Science & Information Systems) from the University of Maryland at College Park; an M.S. in Systems Engineering from Howard University; and a B.Sc. in Natural Sciences from the University of the West Indies at Mona.

His research areas include Analytics & Data Science, Knowledge Management, ICT for Development, Cybersecurity, Expert & Decision Support Systems, e-Commerce and Multi-Criteria Decision Making. His research has been published in various leading research journals and he is the author or editor of six books. Currently, he serves as a senior editor of *Information Technology for Development*, and the *European Journal of Information Systems*, an editor of the *African Journal of Information Systems*, a coordinating editor of *Information Systems Frontiers* and a member of the International Advisory Board of the *Journal of the Operational Research Society*.

Chapter 1

Cybersecurity and the Global South: Solution-Oriented Reflections

1.1 Introductory Discussion

The Global South is not only recognized as one of the fastest-growing regions in terms of Internet population but also as the region that accounts for the majority of Internet users. For instance, it was reported that one region of the Global South, Latin America and the Caribbean (LAC), had the fastest-growing Internet population in the world with 147 million Internet users in 2013, and which continues to grow each year (Organization of American States, 2014). By 2016, the International Telecommunication Union (ITU) reported that Global South economies accounted for the vast majority of Internet users, with 2.5 billion users compared to 1 billion in developed countries (International Telecommunication Union, 2016a). This accelerated and continued growth can be attributed to the momentous increase in mobile subscriptions and robust growth in mobile-broadband penetration (International Telecommunication Union, 2016b, 2018b). While the Internet has enabled the Global South, through the use of Information Communication Technologies (ICTs), to grow their economies, improve livelihoods, share ideas and culture, improve government and social services, collaborate in education, sciences and the arts and to do business (International Telecommunication Union, 2018a; Organization of American States, 2016), it cannot be overlooked that with increasing connectivity to and dependence on Internet-based platforms and services, so

DOI: 10.1201/9781003028710-1

too is the increased potential for cybersecurity (CS) threats, attacks and vulner-abilities. Reports in the trade press and the academic literature (albeit minimal) demonstrate these risks or threats and the impact on governments, organizations and citizens. For instance, of the 12 countries that experienced the highest percentage increases in cyberattacks in 2009 compared to 2005, 11 were from the Global South, e.g. Columbia 749%, Indonesia 675% and Zimbabwe 361% (Kim et al., 2012). Further, during a single six-month period, January–June 2016, electronic fraud alone costs the Jamaican economy some $500 million (Williams, 2016); the website of the government of St Vincent and the Grenadines was hacked in 2015 by individuals claiming to be local Islamic State group supporters; also in 2015, a mass ransomware attack on tax authorities blocked users from accessing their systems while demands for money were made; and in 2014 hackers stole US$150 million from Bank of Nova Scotia Jamaica (CARICOM Caribbean Community, 2016). At a meeting in St Lucia, Caribbean countries formally recognized that they are not adequately prepared to counteract cybercrimes and signed off on a regional Cyber Action Plan (Kentish, 2016). According to the regional plan, "preventing and combating cybercrime requires the development of strategies, legislation, criminal justice and ICT (Information and communications technology) expertise, awareness raising, and international cooperation, and involves political, private sector, and civil society leadership at the highest level" (Kentish, 2016). Even though cyber-related incidents associated with the Global South are a critical problem that warrants attention from all levels of government, organizations, individuals and scholars alike, very little research specifically focused on organizations and users in the Global South has been undertaken to further our understanding of this phenomenon. This book contributes to filling this void.

While organizations in the Global South continue to adopt ICTs to deliver services and conduct business, there remains little research about information security, CS and cybercrime issues and strategies contextualized to these developing economies. Moreover, there is even less research about security-related concerns for micro, small and medium enterprises (MSMEs) of the Global South. According to the Organization for Economic Co-operation and Development (OECD), MSMEs play a key role in national economies around the world, generating employment and contributing to innovation (The Organization for Economic Co-operation and Development, 2017). Even more pointedly, MSMEs are known to be essential to the poorest countries in the world; they serve as an important driver of economic growth that accounts for the majority of all businesses (International Monetary Fund, 2015). For instance, in the Caribbean region, the MSME sector accounts for more than 50% of private enterprises and contributes more than 50% to gross domestic product and employment as well as contributing to social development (Caribbean Development Bank, 2016). Likewise, according to researchers, African MSMEs are important to the global economy because their presence and success create "...a growing middle class with disposable income, in tandem with market opportunities for new investors" (de Sousa dos Santos, 2015).

Despite these significant contributions, MSMEs remain largely unsupported and continue to face several major constraints including inadequate access to financial resources for investment and working capital; gaps in training in business skills; high cost of infrastructure services; inadequate physical infrastructure support (for example, warehousing, factory and commercial space, industrial parks, etc.); low levels of technology usage to improve productivity; and lack of competitiveness (Caribbean Development Bank, 2016). In addition to these challenges, MSMEs in the Global South, as well as the Global North, face additional dangers from information and CS threats. Recent CS statistics show that cyberattacks on small businesses increased from 61% to 67% in 2018 over 2017 and that small businesses increasingly face the same CS risks as larger companies (Ponemon Institute, 2018). In another recent industry report, 43% of data breaches in 2018 involved small business victims (Verizon, 2019).

These cited statistics demonstrate that CS threats are just as likely for MSMEs in the Global South as those in the Global North. Arguably, these dangers are more deleterious for the Global South and even more so for Global South MSMEs since they tend to be lean, i.e. they tend to have limited access to trained IT professionals with the capacity to detect, respond to and recover from cyber incidents and limited resources to acquire and implement CS mechanisms. This claim is supported by industry statistics; according to the Ponemon Institute (2018), only 28% of small businesses rate their ability to mitigate threats, vulnerabilities and attacks as highly effective. However, the need for MSMEs in the Global South to be aware of and understand the consequences of CS cannot be understated. Furthermore, how MSMEs in the Global South can improve their cyber and information security posture is not only critical for business success and continuity but also critical for the Global South's economic development. This book seeks to address these gaps by focusing on CS challenges, potential threats and risks likely faced by MSMEs. This book also seeks to explore and design legislative frameworks and a cybercrime classification scheme appropriate for the Global South economies, among other things. Importantly, this book also explores cyber-related best practices appropriate for Global South MSMEs adoption with the aim for them to improve their cyber and information security posture. Further, this book seeks to sensitize practitioners, public and private institutions about information and CS-related challenges faced by Global South economies generally and Global South MSMEs specifically, so that stakeholders can work collaboratively to create context-specific solutions to address these challenges and improve current practices.

1.2 Contributions to the Conversation

The contributions of this book are organized into three parts: *Assessing the Situation*, *Understanding User Security Compliance Behaviour* and *Developing Solutions for Managing Cybersecurity Risks*.

1.2.1 Part I – Assessing the Situation

A survey of the environment shows that countries particularly the developing economies, alternatively referred to in the Global South, remain vulnerable to CS risks. For instance, a recent research report (IDB/OAS, 2020) reveals that the Latin American and Caribbean (LAC) region is not sufficiently prepared to handle the escalating CS risks. In other words, these countries are not cyber resilient. In order to adequately develop a feasible and effective path to becoming cyber resilient, it is important to know where you are. In this section, we present a few chapters that offer contributions to our understanding of the situation. It should be noted that we are not claiming that these chapters offer a comprehensive assessment of the situation but rather offer contributions beyond what has been presented by other researchers.

In order to adequately address a given problem, it is important to know where you are and where you need to go. Global indices (e.g. Global Cyber-Security Index, Human Development Index), though neither perfect in design nor implementation, offer the opportunity for a given country to assess its current situation and to plan for improvements. The recently presented Global Cybersecurity Index (GCI) for 2020 indicates that while many countries are making progress in their commitments to responding to CS risks and challenges, many of the countries classified as developing economies, but for few exceptions, are at the lower spectrum of the global ranking. Given the usefulness of benchmarking, Chapter 2 focuses on understanding in the context of the GCI, the ways the group of countries of the Global South differs from the remaining group of countries. We conduct data analysis using the 2020 GCI data and identified that the significant differentiators are the *Technical* and *Capacity Development* pillars of the GCI.

The increased Internet penetration creates an environment that foments the risks of escalating threats and cybercrimes such as sexual exploitation of vulnerable groups, ransomware, phishing and lottery scams. In Chapter 3, we examine the cybercrime landscape in the Caribbean, in particular the CARICOM member and associate countries, within the context of cybercrime laws and enforcement. The research underscores that while significant advances have been made in the promulgation of new and revised cybercrime laws in many of these countries, issues such as responsiveness of these laws, harmonization and regional cooperation in the investigation and prosecution of cybercrimes remain as important policy challenges in the region.

It is now acknowledged that the data protection landscape has been radically transformed since the passing of the European Union's General Data Protection Regulation (GDPR). Many countries (e.g. Jamaica, Barbados, Brazil and several states in the US) have since developed laws that are closely similar to the GDPR. In Chapter 4, we examine some of the notable fines imposed within the first year of the coming into operation of the GDPR. Our findings highlight breaches of obligations of key provisions relating to data protection principles, such as the lawfulness of processing of personal data and consent, the rights of the data subjects and security of processing, in particular. This emphasizes the importance of bolstering processing operations underpinned by privacy by design principles to reduce the risk of fines, reduced customer trust and financial viability. These findings also have implications for organizations in their prioritization of the technical and organizational safeguards during their GDPR and other data protection compliance programmes.

1.2.2 Part II – Understanding User Cybersecurity Compliance Behaviour

The CS decision problem is a complex one that involves multiple dimensions. Thus not surprisingly, the Global Security Index (ITU, 2020) involves the *Legal, Technical, Organizational, Capacity Development* and *Cooperation* dimensions. User behaviour has also been previously identified as a critical dimension because users have been recognized as key threats to achieving adequate CS because they often fail to adhere to CS best practices. According to researchers, users are often considered the *weakest link in the chain* of system security (e.g. Barrett-Maitland, et al., 2016; Warkentin and Willison, 2009). Therefore, in this section, we present chapters that focus on offering contributions to the understanding of how to improve cybersecurity compliance behaviour.

In addition to implementing technological tools, entities have adopted CS policies (CSPs) to address the rising number of employee-related CS incidents. If, however, employees do not understand the importance of or are unwilling to comply with CSPs, CS efforts may be in vain. In Chapter 5, we present an investigation of employees' actual CS compliance behaviour via an integrated CS compliance model that includes the constructs: CS awareness (CSAW), CS policy awareness (CSPA), CS training (CSTR) and top management support (TMSP). Our results suggest that (a) CSAW and CSPA are significant factors contributing to employees' actual CS compliance behaviour; (b) the support and involvement of top management have a significant impact on CSPA; and (c) CSTR influences both CSAW and CSPA.

Recent information and CS research have focused on improving individuals' security compliance behaviour. However, improved security performance remains a challenge since individuals often fail to comply with security best practices. In Chapter 6, we present an investigation of the influence of individual decision-making style (DMS) on employee's CS compliance behaviour and other antecedents of such behaviour. Our findings confirm that the individual's decision-making style, specifically, dominant orientation and dominant decision style, influence their individual CS compliance behaviour and other antecedents of such behaviour.

The studies of Donalds and Osei-Bryson (2017, 2020) have demonstrated that individual DMS impacts cybersecurity compliance behaviours. There are multiple representations of the individual DMS construct in scientific studies. In Chapter 7, we explore the relationship using different individual DMS constructs that were used in Donalds and Osei-Bryson (2017, 2020). We also allow for the exploration of moderating relationships. Our results again indicate that individual DMS influences cybersecurity compliance behaviour, but that this relationship is complex. These results also have practical use. For example, for projects which require a high level of security compliance, at the point of assignment of employees to such projects, individual DMS could be used to help identify employees who would be a good fit.

1.2.3 Part III – Developing Solutions for Managing Cybersecurity Risks

As noted earlier, a survey of the environment shows that countries particularly the developing economies remain vulnerable to CS risks. A primary lesson from these findings is that developing countries need to take urgent actions regarding developing and managing responses to cyberattacks and cybercrimes, especially at the policymaking levels. The chapters in this section of the book present some approaches that could contribute to adequately address some of the aspects of the cybersecurity problems that are faced by MSMEs and other organizations of the Global South. MSMEs/SMEs, government agencies and other organizations are often burdened with escalating security risks and dwindling resources and know-how. This calls for more targeted and structured processes and guidance to proactively manage CS risks in organizations. In Chapter 8, we present a parsimonious model for managing an organizational CS programme framework and outline critical success factors to operationalize it as means of effectively managing CS risks.

Studies continue to show that the fight against cybercrimes requires both offensive and defensive measures. This is necessary in order to gain a firm and sustainable security advantage. Security advantage is therefore defined as the ability to effectively identify, assess, plan, manage and respond to risks, including threats and vulnerabilities through a capability-based approach. In Chapter 9, we present the Cybersecurity Capability Maturity Model (CCMM), a six-step process of progressive development of CS maturity and knowledge integration that ranges from a state of limited awareness and application of security controls to pervasive optimization of the protection of critical assets.

The cybersecurity/IS-security decision problem is a complex one that involves multiple concerns of multiple stakeholders that must be taken into consideration. A useful resource to consider in addressing this problem is the Value-focused Thinking (VFT) methodology as at a minimum it can be used to elicit and structure the relevant solution objectives. However, the traditional VFT approach has several limitations, including not explicitly considering well-known organizational issues and not providing guidance on how to generate non-trivial solution alternatives. In Chapter 10, we present an enhanced VFT methodology that can be used to systematically elicit relevant cybersecurity-related objectives, and create and evaluate relevant solution alternatives. We used our proposed enhanced VFT approach to identify some limitations in a previously proposed VFT model that used the traditional VFT approach. Our aim in doing this was not to criticize the previous research but to show how the application of the traditional approach resulted in some well-known organizational and other issues not being considered.

As noted earlier, MSMEs/SMEs are crucial drivers of economic activities, particularly for developing countries. Thus, there is little doubt that the continued high occurrences of cyber incidents and crimes experienced by these businesses have had a significant economic impact both on these businesses and the economy. Adopting good cyber hygiene is necessary to minimize CS risks; however, MSMEs inconsistently apply these practices or are not aware of proper cyber-hygiene practices. In Chapter 11, we use the VFT approach as a basis to present values that are important for MSMEs in adopting good cyber-hygiene practices. The fundamental objectives underscore the crucial technical and management elements MSMEs must balance in their cyber-hygiene efforts i.e. managing *risks, reputation, ease of implementation, compliance, business continuity, partnerships and costs*. The research results can help to guide policy directions for determining CS strategies, investment priorities and setting CS and cyber-hygiene baseline standards for MSMEs, other businesses and other government agencies.

In recent years, there has been an increase in cybercrimes and its negative impacts on the lives of individuals, organizations and governments. It has been argued that a better understanding of cybercrime is a necessary condition to develop appropriate legal and policy responses to cybercrime. While a universally agreed-upon classification scheme would facilitate the development of such understanding and also collaborations, current classification schemes are insufficient, fragmented and often incompatible since each focuses on different perspectives (e.g. the role of the computer, attack, attacker's or defender's viewpoint) or uses varying terminologies to refer to the same thing, making consistent cybercrime classifications improbable. In Chapter 12, we present and illustrate a new cybercrime ontology, by classifying two real-world cybercrimes, that incorporates multiple perspectives and offers a more holistic viewpoint for cybercrime classification than prior works. Compared to other related works, our ontology is the most robust cybercrime classification scheme and should therefore prove to be a more useful tool for cybercrime stakeholders.

The increased digitalization of many businesses and services, especially during the COVID-19 pandemic, requires that Global South countries develop and implement public policies that aim to adequately address and thwart the dynamism of security threats in the cyber domain. One approach is the development and implementation of a National Cybersecurity Strategy (NCSS), which seeks to establish the government's priorities and policies as a response to potential CS threats to national and individual security. In Chapter 13, we present such an NCSS framework for consideration by GS countries.

1.3 Conclusion

The purpose of this introductory chapter is to detail the level of CS vulnerabilities and risks being experienced by developing countries, particularly countries in the Global South and make a case for the issues, concepts, models and frameworks presented in this book as being appropriate in advancing the understanding of the CS landscape and building capabilities to address these challenges over time.

Contributions of the book include the presentation and discussion of:

1. tools, techniques and or frameworks that can improve Global South governments and MSMEs information and CS posture;
2. data on the prevalence, nature, trends and impacts of cyber-related incidents in the Global South;
3. evidence-based best practices in combating and preventing cyber-related incidents and improving data protection practices appropriate for the Global South.

To the best of our knowledge, there is not another book that focuses on CS practices and challenges experienced by MSMEs in the Global South, analyses legislative frameworks of Global South economies, and discusses the GDPR regime and the potential implications on other countries' data protection landscape, among other areas as presented in this manuscript.

References

Barrett-Maitland, N., Barclay, C., & Osei-Bryson, K. M. (2016). Security in social networking services: A value-focused thinking exploration in understanding users' privacy and security concerns. *Information Technology for Development, 22*(3), 464–486.

Caribbean Development Bank. (2016). Micro, Small & Medium Enterprise Development in the Caribbean: Towards A New Frontier, 1–164. Retrieved from http://www.caribank.org/wp-content/uploads/2016/05/Study_Micro-Small-and-Medium-Enterprise-Development.pdf. Accessed February 10, 2018.

CARICOM Caribbean Community. (2016). *Caribbean to Tackle Escalating Cybercrime with Regional Approach*. Retrieved from https://caricom.org/communications/view/caribbean-to-tackle-escalating-cybercrime-with-regional-approach

de Sousa dos Santos, J. F. (2015). *Why SMEs are key to growth in Africa*. Retrieved from https://www.weforum.org/agenda/2015/08/why-smes-are-key-to-growth-in-africa/

Donalds, C., & Osei-Bryson, K. M. (2017). Exploring the impacts of individual styles on security compliance behavior: A preliminary analysis. In *SIG ICT in Global Development, 10th Annual Pre-ICIS Workshop*, Seoul, Korea.

Donalds, C., & Osei-Bryson, K. M. (2020). Cybersecurity compliance behavior: Exploring the influences of individual decision style and other antecedents. *International Journal of Information Management, 51*, 102056.

Inter-American Development Bank and Organization of American States (IDB/OAS). (2020). *Cybersecurity Risks, Progress, and the Way Forward in Latin America and The Caribbean.* Retrieved from https://publications.iadb.org/publications/english/document/2020-Cybersecurity-Report-Risks-Progress-and-the-Way-Forward-in-Latin-America-and-the-Caribbean.pdf

International Monetary Fund. (2015). *Regional Economic Outlook: Sub-Saharan Africa. World Economic and Financial Surveys, 123.* Retrieved from https://www.imf.org/external/pubs/ft/reo/2015/afr/eng/. Accessed September 11, 2018.

International Telecommunication Union. (2016a). *ICT Services Getting More Affordable—But More than Half the World's Population Still not Using the Internet.* Retrieved from http://www.itu.int/en/mediacentre/Pages/2016-PR30.aspx. Accessed January 20, 2017.

International Telecommunication Union. (2016b). Measuring the Information Society Report. Retrieved from https://www.itu.int/en/ITU-D/Statistics/Documents/publications/misr2016/MISR2016-w4.pdf. Accessed January 19, 2017.

International Telecommunication Union. (2018a). *High-speed Internet Improves Economies and Livelihoods in Least Developed Countries, Says New UN Broadband.* Retrieved from https://www.itu.int/en/mediacentre/Pages/2018-PR17.aspx. Accessed April 16, 2019.

International Telecommunication Union. (2018b). *Measuring the Information Society Report* Vol. 1. (p. 204). Retrieved from https://www.itu.int/en/ITU-D/Statistics/Documents/publications/misr2018/MISR-2018-Vol-1-E.pdf

International Telecommunication Union (ITU). (2020). *Global Cybersecurity Index 2020.* Retrieved from: https://www.itu.int/en/ITU-D/Cybersecurity/Documents/GCIv4/New_Reference_Model_GCIv4_V2_.pdf

Kentish, A. (2016). *Caribbean Nations Sign off on Cyber Crime Action Plan.* Retrieved from https://www.telesurtv.net/english/news/Caribbean-Nations-Sign-off-on-Cyber-Crime-Action-Plan-20160324-0018.html

Kim, S. H., Wang, Q.-H., & Ullrich, J. B. (2012). A Comparative study of cyberattacks. *Communications of the ACM, 55*(3), 66–773. doi:10.1145/2093548.2093568

Organization of American States. (2014). *Latin America + Caribbean Cyber Security Trends.* Retrieved from http://www.symantec.com/content/en/us/enterprise/other_resources/b-cyber-security-trends-report-lamc.pdf. Accessed February 17, 2015.

Organization of American States. (2016). *Cybersecurity: Are We Ready in Latin America and the Caribbean?* Retrieved from https://www.sbs.ox.ac.uk/cybersecurity-capacity/system/files/Cybersecurity-Are-We-Prepared-in-Latin-America-and-the-Caribbean.pdf. Accessed March 12, 2017.

Ponemon Institute. (2018). *2018 State of Cybersecurity in Small & Medium Size Businesses, 46.* Retrieved from https://keepersecurity.com/assets/pdf/Keeper-2018-Ponemon-Report.pdf?utm_campaign=2018%20Ponemon%20Nurture%20Workflow&utm_source=hs_automation&utm_medium=email&utm_content=72316430&_hsenc=p2ANqtz-__XExxs5ZzhmA10Xca0x5TMfMzBi9KjhPxg4usTMDkcf6bOKEJ_FLn3zXHsHcgx_v6agilFVu-dTRAfyCUKioN2R4A-ROdBFrHy4q273Pqsv7Y-wFw&_hsmi=72316430. Accessed August 17, 2019.

The Organization for Economic Co-operation and Development. (2017). *Enhancing the contributions of SMEs in a global and digitalised economy, 24.* Retrieved from https://www.oecd.org/mcm/documents/C-MIN-2017-8-EN.pdf.

Verizon. (2019). *2019 Data Breach Investigations Report, 78.* Retrieved from https://enterprise.verizon.com/resources/reports/2019-data-breach-investigations-report.pdf. Accessed August 17, 2019.

Warkentin, M., & Willison, R. (2009). Behavioral and policy issues in information systems security: The insider threat. *European Journal of Information Systems, 18*(2), 101–105.

Williams, A. (2016). *$500m Robbed from Bank Accounts in 6 Months … Tellers, University Students are Main Culprits.* Retrieved from http://jamaica-star.com/article/news/20160722/500m-robbed-bank-accounts-6-months-%E2%80%A6tellers-university-students-are-main

ASSESSING THE SITUATION

Chapter 2

An Exploration of Country Group Differences in the Global Cybersecurity Index

2.1 Introduction

In order to adequately address a given problem, it is important to know where you are and where you need to go. Global indices (e.g. Global Cybersecurity Index, Human Development Index), though neither perfect in design nor implementation, offer the opportunity for a given country to assess its current situation and to plan for improvements. Assessing a given country's level of cybersecurity capability could possibly be done in multiple ways, with an established one being the Global Cybersecurity Index (GCI) that has been presented by the International Telecommunications Union (ITU) since 2015. The availability of a measure such as the GCI provides several opportunities to policy-makers including an understanding of the country's strengths and weaknesses with respect to cybersecurity (CS) and also guidance for improvements via appropriate benchmarking. The 2020 version of the GCI (ITU, 2020) involves five pillars described in Table 2.1, with the overall GCI score obtained by summing the scores of the measures associated with the five pillars.

Given the usefulness of benchmarking (e.g. Samoilenko & Osei-Bryson, 2019), in this chapter we are concerned with understanding, in the context of the GCI, the

Table 2.1   Pillars of the 2020 Global Cybersecurity Index

Pillar	Description	Extract from ITU (2020)
Legal	Measures the laws and regulations on cybercrime and cybersecurity	"The development of a legal and regulatory framework to protect society and promote a safe and secure digital environment is key and should be at the outset of any national efforts in cybersecurity".
Technical	Measures the implementation of technical capabilities through national and sector-specific agencies	"Effective mechanisms and institutional structures at the national level are necessary to deal with cyber risks and incidents reliably. Computer incident response teams (CIRTs) … enable countries to respond to incidents at the national level using a centralized contact point and promote quick and systematic action, empowering countries to learn from experience and build cybersecurity resilience".
Organizational	Measures the national strategies and organizations implementing cybersecurity	"Organizational measures examine the governance and coordination mechanisms within countries that address cybersecurity. Organizational measures include ensuring that cybersecurity is sustained at the highest level of the executive and assigning relevant roles and responsibilities to various national entities, and making them accountable for the national cybersecurity posture".
Capacity Development	Measures awareness campaigns, training, education, and incentives for cybersecurity capacity development	"Securing the cyber domain through cybersecurity capacity building activities is key as it contributes to reducing issues such as digital divide and cyber risks".

(Continued)

Table 2.1   (Continued)

Pillar	Description	Extract from ITU (2020)
Cooperation	Measures partnerships between agencies, firms, and countries	"Cybersecurity remains a transnational issue due to the increasing interconnection and correlated infrastructures. The security of the global cyber ecosystem cannot be guaranteed or managed by any single stakeholder, and it needs national, regional, and international cooperation to extend reach and impact".

ways the group of countries of the Global South differs from the remaining group of countries. We focus on the following three questions:

1. RQ1: What are the pillars that most differentiate the Global South group from the group of remaining countries?
2. RQ2: Are there cut-off points in the values of these pillars that most differentiate the Global South group from the group of remaining countries?
3. RQ3: Are the scores of the GCI pillars correlated with the Human Development Index (HDI) and are the correlations different for the two groups?

Our interest in RQ3 relates to obtaining a preliminary understanding of relationships between the level of human development of a country as measured by the HDI (UNDP, 1990) and the level of commitment to CS capability (as measured by the GCI). The concept of human development can be considered to involve the ability to lead a long and healthy life, acquire knowledge and have access to the resources for a decent standard of living (UNDP, 2006). While reasonable arguments can be developed with respect to the existence of relationships between this pair of constructs, empirical analysis may offer opportunities for enhanced understanding and making inferences.

2.2 Data Analysis

2.2.1 Modelling Dataset

As noted earlier, the GCI 2020 consists of five pillars, where the score for the overall index is the sum of the scores of its individual pillars, where the score for each pillar is in the [0, 20] interval. The data for GCI 2020 (ITU, 2020), for each country in addition to including its overall GCIS and pillar scores, also include its overall GCI 2020 ranking, its region (i.e. *Americas, Africa, Arab, Asia Pacific, Commonwealth of Independent States, Europe*), and its economic development status (*Developed, Developing*). With respect to our assessment of whether a given country should be considered to be in the Global South, we considered the value of its economic development status as well as the Global South concept as expressed in Dados and Connell (2012) including its geopolitical power. Thus, all the countries of the Caribbean, Latin American, Africa were coded as being in the Global South, as were many countries in the Asia-Pacific region.

For our data analysis, our modelling set consists of those countries which had both a publicly available GCI overall score for 2020 (ITU, 2020) and an HDI score for 2019 (UNDP, 2020). For RQ1 and RQ2 we used measures for the five *GCI* pillars (i.e. *Legal, Technical, Organizational, Capacity Building, Cooperation*) as the potential predictors, and a binary target variable that indicated whether the given country could be considered to be in the Global South group (*1: Yes; 0: No*).

2.2.2 Addressing the Research Questions

To address RQ1 our analysis involved logistic regression, which returned a correct classification rate of 0.797. The corresponding results (see Figure 2.1) indicate that the *Technical* and *Capacity Development* pillars were the statistically significant predictors. It should be noted that this does not suggest that for each group of countries that there was uniformity with respect to the other pillars, but just that they were not the significant differentiators. Thus, while it is necessary to adequately address the *Legal* aspects of CS, these results suggest that for the year 2020 the major inadequacies of the countries of Global South are about the *Technical* and *Capacity Development* dimensions. It should be noted that countries of the Global South often are able to develop and approve appropriate legislation, but various reasons including inadequate resources and infrastructure fall short in the implementation of such legislation.

To address RQ2 we did Decision Tree (DT) induction (e.g. Osei-Bryson & Ngwenyama, 2014), which resulted in a correct classification rate of 0.834. The corresponding results (see Figure 2.2) again indicate that the *Technical* and *Capacity*

Results - Node: RB_Intr Diagram: GCI2020_HDI2019

File Edit View Window

Table: Effects Plot

Variable	Level	Effect	Effect Label	Coefficient	T-value	P Value	Score Code Variable
Intercept	1	Intercept	Intercept:GlobSo...	2.51705	6.646059	3.01E-11	
Technical		Technical	Technical	-0.12816	-2.3489	0.018829	Technical
CapDev		CapDev	CapDev	-0.10845	-2.00541	0.044919	CapDev

Figure 2.1   Results of regression analysis

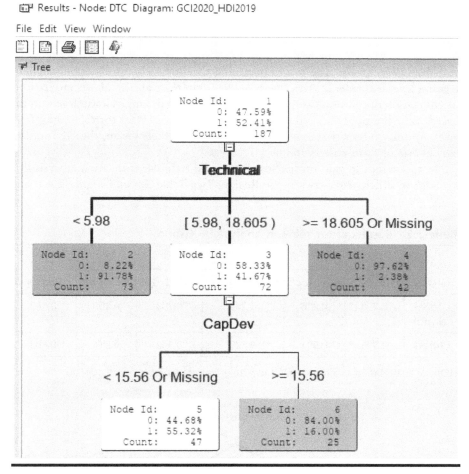

Figure 2.2   Results of decision tree induction

Development pillars were the significant predictors but also show cut-off points for these measures. Not surprisingly, the extremes of the measure for the *Technical* pillar are dominated by either the Global South group of countries or the Other group of countries. But for the interior interval of the measure for the *Technical* pillar, it is the level of *Capacity Development* that differentiates the two groups. Given the characteristics of the *Capacity Development* pillar, Global South countries whose level of *Technical* measure is within this interior interval should give emphasis to raising their level of *Capacity Development* as this may be more affordable than having a corresponding rise in the level of the *Technical* pillar.

To address RQ3 we did a correlation analysis of the *HDI* for 2019 with scores for the *GCI* and its pillars for 2020. While it might have been useful to use the *HDI* scores for 2020, at the time of writing this chapter these were not yet publicly available. However, it should also be noted that a reasonable case could be made that the level of *HDI* for the previous year could impact the *GCI* scores for a current year.

Table 2.2 provides the results of the correlation analysis for *Global South* group and the *Others* group. The reader may note that for each combination, the correlation level is smaller for the *Global South* group than for the *Others* group. One interpretation of this result is that for the *Global South* group, its lower levels on the overall *GCI* and the associated pillars may not be because of its corresponding *HDI* level. Another interpretation could be that for the Others group, the GCI indices may be related to its corresponding HDI level.

In an attempt to gain further insights we did a similar correlation analysis that focused on differences between the Regions (see Table 2.3 and Figure 2.4.), and

Table 2.2   Results of Correlation Analysis by Group

Group	Correlations					
Group	*HDI:GCI*	*HDI:Tech*	*HDI:CapDev*	*HDI:Legal*	*HDI:Org*	*HDI:Coop*
Global South	0.228	0.218	0.244	0.233	0.159	0.182
Others	0.595	0.591	0.549	0.542	0.514	0.603

HDI for 2019 (latest available); GCI for 2020 (latest available)

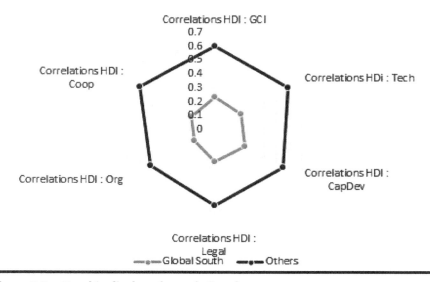

Figure 2.3   Graphic display of correlations by group

Table 2.3   Results of Correlation Analysis by Region

Region	Correlations					
	HDI:GCI	*HDI:Tech*	*HDI:CapDev*	*HDI:Legal*	*HDI:Org*	*HDI:Coop*
Africa	0.331	0.243	0.387	0.277	0.298	0.340
Americas	0.609	0.558	0.517	0.688	0.487	0.577
Arab	0.796	0.724	0.844	0.711	0.707	0.765
Asia-Pacific	0.642	0.660	0.579	0.573	0.673	0.597
CIS	0.668	0.723	0.638	0.406	0.495	0.758
Europe	0.381	0.381	0.381	0.238	0.353	0.381

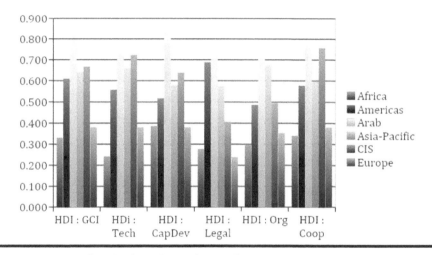

Figure 2.4   Graphic display of correlations by region

also between sub-regions of the Americas (see Table 2.4 and Figure 2.5.). These results suggest that for some pairs of Regions there are substantial differences in the correlations, including for the Asia-Pacific vs. Europe pair. Possibly surprisingly the two highest correlations are for the Arab and Commonwealth of Independent States (CIS) regions. Also interestingly the correlations for the Africa and Europe regions are the two lowest, though the reasons for these low correlations may be different. These results also suggest differences in the sub-regions of the Americas. Correlations for the Caribbean are closer to that of the African region than any other region. Further, apart from the HDI:Legal correlations are below that of Africa. In

Table 2.4   Results of Correlation Analysis by Sub-regions of the Americas

	Correlations					
SubRegion	*HDI:GCI*	*HDi:Tech*	*HDI:CapDev*	*HDI:Legal*	*HDI:Org*	*HDI:Coop*
Caribbean	0.166	0.133	−0.111	0.486	−0.008	0.210
Latin America	0.740	0.754	0.623	0.722	0.567	0.647
North America	0.991	0.622	1.000	1.000	1.000	0.974

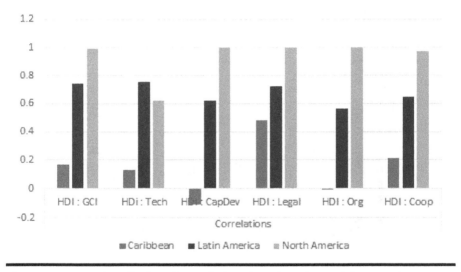

Figure 2.5   Graphic display of correlations by sub-regions of the Americas

comparing the Regions, including the sub-regions of the Americas and the other Regions where the Caribbean and African Regions have the lowest HDI:GCI correlations (Figure 2.6.). North America has the highest HDI: GCI correlation; however, that may be explained by the relatively small number of countries. Of note, these three of North America are regarded as the strongest and more mature economies in the Americas with two of them being the only countries in the Americas that are in the G7. The other high HDI:GCI groupings were the Latin America and the Arab regions followed by Asia-Pacific and CIS regions.

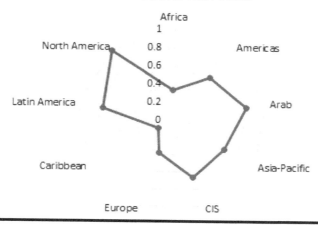

Figure 2.6   Graphic display correlations by regions (including sub-regions of the Americas)

2.3 Conclusion

In the modern age, it is necessary for countries to have adequate CS capabilities to effectively address CS risks associated with personal data breaches, cybercrimes or other malicious acts. The GCI aims to provide for appropriate assessment of such capabilities and could be used as part of a benchmarking programme. In this chapter, we have explored some of the differences between the countries of the Global South (or 'developing' countries) and the remaining countries with respect to GCI and its pillars. Even with respect to the issues of benchmarking, there are other relevant research questions apart from which we have explored that could be developed and empirically evaluated. And there are other types of issues that could be explored (e.g. Bruggemann, Koppatz, Scholl & Schuktomow, 2021). Therefore, further exploration of these GCI data is encouraged.

References

Bruggemann, R., Koppatz, P., Scholl, M., & Schuktomow, R. (2021). Global Cybersecurity Index (GCI) and the role of its 5 pillars. *Social Indicators Research*, 1–19. doi:10.1007/s11205-021-02739-y

Dados, N., & Connell, R. (2012). The Global South. *Contexts, 11*(1), 12–13.

ITU (2020): *Global Cybersecurity Index 2020*. Retrieved from: https://www.itu.int/en/ITU-D/Cybersecurity/Documents/GCIv4/New_Reference_Model_GCIv4_V2_.pdf

Osei-Bryson, K. M., & Ngwenyama, O. (2014). *Advances in Research Methods for Information Systems Research*. New York, USA: Springer. doi:10.1007/978-1-4614-9463-8.

Samoilenko, S., & Osei-Bryson, K. M. (2019). A data analytic benchmarking methodology for discovering common causal structures that describe context-diverse heterogeneous groups. *Expert Systems with Applications, 117*, 330–344.

UNDP (1990). *Concept and Measurement of Human Development*. New York: UNDP.

UNDP (2020). The 2020 Human Development Report: The Next Frontier – Human Development and the Anthropocene. http://hdr.undp.org/en/2020-report

Chapter 3

Cybercrime in the Caribbean: Risks, Challenges and Opportunities

3.1 Introduction

The threat landscape shows that security threats and breaches are escalating and morphing into more complex and damaging variants. This is further illustrated during the COVID-19 pandemic through accelerated interconnectivity and reliance on electronic and Internet-based services to carry out daily social and work demands. This development emphasizes that while there are beneficial elements to digital access and use, the harmful elements can have a devastating impact on lives and economies. A McAfee/CSIS Report reveals that the economic cost of cybercrime exceeds US$1 trillion (Smith & Lostri, 2020). A regional report (IDB/OAS, 2016) notes that in the Latin America and Caribbean regions, the cost of cybercrime amounts to approximately US$90 billion annually. It is expected that this has increased significantly since, with the estimates being multiples of these countries' gross domestic product (GDP).

The OAS report further proclaims that the Caribbean is not prepared to effectively tackle cybercrime. According to the OAS report, four out of every five countries in the region do not have national plans or strategies for cybersecurity or for protecting critical infrastructure, and a large majority of prosecutors lack the capacity to punish cybercrimes. The 2021 Global Cybersecurity Index (ITU, 2020) appears to accord with this position as many of the Caribbean countries are ranked in the 100s.

DOI: 10.1201/9781003028710-4

This means that countries such as Jamaica, Trinidad and Tobago, Barbados and Guyana are at a low level of cybersecurity development in areas that comprise technical, operational and legal measures.

There is also enough anecdotal evidence to show that it is difficult to legislate and enforce cybercrimes. According to Barclay (2017), legislating cybercrime is difficult due to the rapidly evolving nature of these forms of crime. Similarly, Broadhurst and Chang (2013) observe that given the transnational characteristics of cybercrimes, inconsistency in the laws and regulations among countries makes it difficult for countries to cooperate when investigating cross-border cybercrimes. Further, the limited resources that plague many developing economies such as those in the Caribbean make effective cybercrime law development and law enforcement very challenging.

Within the Commonwealth Caribbean, the cybercrime laws are fairly recent with many coming into operation in the early parts of the twenty-first century. Trinidad and Tobago enacted its Computer Misuse Act in 2000, while Bahamas and Barbados enacted their Computer Misuse Acts in 2003 and 2005, respectively. Jamaica enacted its first cybercrime legislation in 2009 which was later revised in 2015. Other countries have gradually enacted their cybercrime legislation during this period as it reflected an increased prominence of cybercrime and cybersecurity measures.

The purpose of this chapter is to examine the cyber threat landscape and cybercrime laws in the Caribbean, specifically the CARICOM member and associate member countries (20 countries in total) against common cybercrime model laws, including the Budapest Convention. In addition, the chapter seeks to highlight the risks, challenges and opportunities for countries within the Caribbean community. The rest of the chapter proceeds as follows: a summary of the digital access penetration in the region, followed by a discussion on the common cyber threats prevalent in the region including a discussion on the lottery scam originating in Jamaica; two cybercrime models are discussed as influencing the development of cybercrime legislation which is followed by a discussion on the respective cybercrime laws in the region. The paper closes with a discussion on the risks, challenges and opportunities that exist and concluding remarks.

3.2 Digital Access and Use in the Caribbean

Greater access to digital services and the Internet means that persons become more vulnerable or are at greater risk of computer-related crimes or cybercrimes. Within the Caribbean, digital access has been steadily increasing, particularly over the last two decades. Digital access describes the percentage of the population that has access to the Internet or social media for 2020. The data was sourced and derived (see Table 3.1 and Figures 3.1, 3.2). The data show that more than half of the countries have over 50% Internet penetration rate, with Haiti accounting for the lowest

Table 3.1 Digital Penetration in the Caribbean

Countries	Population (2021 Est.)	Internet Usage 31-Dec-20	% Population (Penetration)	Facebook 31-Dec-20	%Facebook Penetration
Anguilla	14,909	12,557	84.20	9,000	71.67
Antigua and Barbuda	103,050	81,900	79.50	62,000	75.70
Bahamas	399,285	333,143	83.40	220,000	66.04
Barbados	286,388	228,717	79.90	160,000	69.96
Belize	382,444	200,020	52.30	200,000	99.99
Bermuda	61,349	60,122	98.00	39,000	64.87
The British Virgin Islands	31,196	14,620	46.90	12,000	82.08
Cayman Islands	61,559	54,630	88.70	48,000	87.86
Dominica	73,925	49,687	67.20	39,000	78.49
Grenada	108,339	69,245	63.90	62,000	89.54
Guyana	782,225	395,007	50.50	360,000	91.14
Haiti	11,112,945	2,000,000	18.00	1,800,000	90.00
Jamaica	2,898,677	1,581,100	54.50	1,100,000	69.57
Montserrat	5,177	3,000	57.90	2,600	86.67
St Kitts and Nevis	55,345	43,618	78.80	35,000	80.24
St Lucia	179,667	142,970	79.60	92,000	64.35
St Vincent and Grenadines	110,200	76,984	69.90	61,000	79.24
Suriname	568,301	340,000	59.80	310,000	91.18
Trinidad and Tobago	1,372,598	1,003,592	73.10	700,000	69.75
Turks & Caicos	35,747	28,000	78.30	25,000	89.29

Source: https://www.internetworldstats.com/stats2.htm

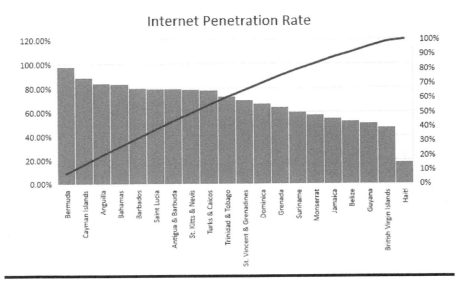

Figure 3.1   Internet penetration rate in the Caribbean

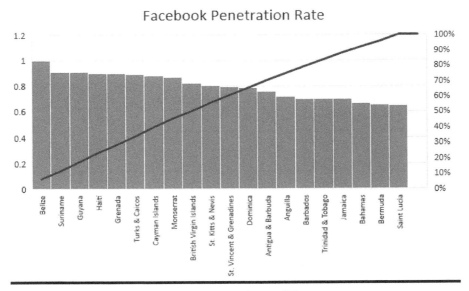

Figure 3.2   Facebook penetration rate in the Caribbean

percentage of 18%. Bermuda reports the highest Internet penetration with 98%. The data also highlight the digital divide levels among countries in the region and underscore that many countries have to make significant steps in stemming the digital divide while ensuring that their citizens are secured when accessing digital services.

There is a relatively high Facebook penetration rate across each country in the region. All countries account for more than 60% social media (Facebook) penetration rate. One significant factor this may be attributable to is the zero-rate policy, which reflects the partnership between Facebook and mobile service providers for users to access Facebook without data charges. This may be apparent in a country such as Haiti with a low Internet penetration but a relatively high Facebook penetration rate.

3.3 Cybercrime and Cyber Threat Landscape in the Caribbean

Cybercrime is any computer-related criminal act, i.e. an act that is prohibited by law. According to Barclay (2017), cybercrime or computer crime relates to any criminal act that affects the confidentiality, integrity and availability of a computer or network, or the privacy and security of a person online. The nature of the cybercrime may be categorized as either the use of the computer as a tool or target in the commission of a crime (with or without intent to cause harm) (Barclay, 2017). Examples of crimes that use the computer as a tool or as a means to commit a crime include fraud, identity theft, phishing, spamming and other malicious acts such as cyberbullying, cyberstalking and cyberwarfare. Examples of crimes where the computer is a target include malicious attacks on the computer including viruses, worms, Trojan horses and other malware. A denial of service attack is one example where the computer is used both as a tool and as a target.

Security reports (e.g. Ponemon Institute, 2021; Smith & Lostri, 2020) reveal that cyber threats are increasing in scale and impact as the threat actors seek vulnerabilities to exploit. This means that Caribbean countries are also facing escalating risks. However, an added challenge facing these countries is the limited available national statistics on the threats faced by citizens in the Caribbean. A recent report suggests that over 100 million cyberattacks occurred in the Caribbean during the first quarter of 2021 (Jamaica Gleaner, 2021). Further review of newspaper articles confirms that incidents affect all spectrum of users including both private- and public-sector organizations and individuals of all ages. Some commonly reported incidents in the Caribbean include ransomware attacks on key services, phishing, credit card fraud and abusive content. This is consistent with the global cyber landscape threat data, which also reveal additional threats such as botnets, spam, intellectual property theft, business email compromise, data breach, to name a few (e.g. FBI, 2020).

According to Smith and Lostri (2020), ransomware remains the fastest-growing part of cybercrime. Within the Caribbean, a security report (Deloitte, 2017) discloses that ransomware attacks have been rising in the Caribbean and ranks as one of the top security concerns in this region. In the region, Trinidad and Tobago and Jamaica were reported as the top countries targeted for ransomware (Jamaica Gleaner, 2021). Some notable examples of ransomware attacks were reported in 2020; a Caribbean conglomerate ANSA McAL admits that they fell victim to a ransomware attack where files and clients' personal data were leaked (Loop News, 2020) and a financial institution in Jamaica reports that one of its systems suffered a ransomware attack that resulted in the data of some members and customers being stolen (Jamaica Gleaner, 2020a). It is not known whether these organizations paid to have their data decrypted or the financial impact these incidents had on the organizations.

Phishing is a social engineering technique that is used as a gateway for other security threats such as ransomware, identity theft and fraud. As a result, threat actors rely on the use of unsolicited email, text messages and telephone calls masquerading as legitimate sources seeking personal, financial and/or login credentials. The FBI (2020) reports that Phishing scams top the number of security incidents reported for that year with an estimated US$54 million in losses. In the Caribbean, it is one of the top security incidents reported annually, according to a CIRT personnel. This includes the various forms of deception, namely pharming, vishing and smishing.

An Internet search on malware detections highlights that over half million malware are detected daily by security researchers (e.g. McAfee). These findings underline the importance of security awareness, endpoint protection, general cyber-hygiene practices and other security measures for both businesses, government agencies and individuals.

Card (credit and debit) fraud is the most prevalent financial crime committed in Jamaica. A report highlights that approximately 80%–90% of losses attributed to deposit-taking institutions were attributed to card fraud in 2018 and 2019 (Jamaica Gleaner, 2020b). Other countries in the region, for example, Trinidad and Tobago and Barbados have reported increased credit fraud incidents based on newspaper scans. As a result of these risks to financial institutions, many regional banks have taken a proactive approach to mitigate this risk, with increased customer awareness, and in the introduction of technology-enabled fraud detection tools.

Abusive content refers to any language or content that causes harm. Malicious communication, racist abuse or other forms of cyberbullying are examples of abusive content. These are global issues and have been receiving increased attention in the Caribbean, especially the impact on children, young adults and other vulnerable groups. A scan of electronic media across countries highlights similar experiences in challenges in stemming cyberbullying while seeking to understand the scale of its impact on mental health and education (particularly for children and adolescents).

Further to being at risk of cybercrimes and threats, the Caribbean, specifically Jamaica, is also home to a popular cyber threat, the Jamaican Lottery Scam. While there is limited research on this phenomenon, it is reported that it accounts for estimated annual losses of US$1 billion over the last 20 years, as reported by various US media sources (e.g. AP News, 2018). The scam involves making a call to an unsuspecting person indicating that they have won a prize in a foreign lottery or contest. The person is further told that to collect the prize, they must pay certain fees. The person is then asked to provide their banking or credit card information or to wire money via money transfer agencies. With many variations of the scam, the common trait is that the potential victim is asked to send money to receive the prize. The scammer relies on various forms of social engineering to gain credibility and convince persons to share their personal information or provide funds. A review of electronic media shows that several persons have been successfully prosecuted in both the Jamaica and United States' courts. The charges range from obtaining identity information and other breaches of the Law Reform Fraudulent Transaction Act, Jamaica, and participating in lottery scams and wire fraud, in the case of the United States. The Government of Jamaica, through its Lottery Scam Task Force, continues to track the lottery scammers; however, the scale of the scams continues to yield victims and remains a lucrative venture for scammers in Jamaica. Given the nature and scale of impact of these scammers, it is apparent that this threat group is a part of a transnational organized crime syndicate.

3.4 Cybercrime Legislative Models

The HIPCAR Project (Harmonization of ICT Policies, Legislation and Regulatory Procedures) and the Budapest Convention are discussed in section as they have influenced the cybercrime legislative development in the region. Both models are not without criticisms, however. The main criticism of the HIPCAR Project is its low adoption rate in the Caribbean. Further, opportunities for the Project to integrate discussions on the implementation processes and examine the regional and country constraints, or limitations would assist in obtaining improved support from the region (Barclay, 2014). In addition, it is observed that there were few discussions on the analysis of beneficiary countries' law-making or criminal justice processes and the level of implications these processes may have on the model legislation adoption (Barclay, 2014). These observations appear to hold given the current environment. Barclay (2017) observes that there are contending views in relation to the support of the Budapest Convention. Key criticisms are that its language has not kept pace with technological change and that it does not address new forms of offences that have come to prominence since it was drafted (Clough, 2012). Additionally, it is suggested that the categories of offences such as identity theft, grooming, spam and cyberterrorism were not contemplated by the Convention. According to Clough (2012), the Convention is unrepresentative of the countries in the world despite its influence on the drafting of cybercrime laws throughout the world. However, proponents contend that the Convention represents a significant step forward in tackling cybercrime because it commits signatories to prosecute computer-related crimes vigorously and the Convention's procedures for collecting evidence will assist law enforcement authorities in the fight against terrorism.

Taken into context, however, both models offer a sound platform for policymakers in the Caribbean to rely on as they define or refine their cybercrime laws. Other models such as the Commonwealth's Model Law on Computer and Computer Related Crime can also be integrated into the local legislative process. As a whole, the Caribbean has available resources to strengthen its cybercrime legislative profile.

3.4.1 HIPCAR Project

For close to 30 years, there has been a search for a comprehensive legal framework for combating computer-related crimes and cybercrimes for the benefit of UN beneficiary states with limited success, as according to ITU (2020), the UN has failed to adopt an agreed framework despite discussions for more than two decades. Several countries and regions have therefore attempted to develop some standards or model laws relating to cybercrime, including the EU (i.e. Budapest Convention), the Commonwealth (i.e. Commonwealth Model Law) and the HIPCAR Project in the Caribbean.

Further, due to the rapidly evolving nature of the threat landscape and cyber threats, it has become more apparent that legislating these acts is a challenging endeavour. The Caribbean community in a bid to improve regional cooperation endorsed the HIPCAR Project as a means to advance a number of legislative initiatives at the regional level, including cybercrime. The HIPCAR Project was orchestrated by the ITU, CARICOM Secretariat and the Caribbean Telecommunication Union (CTU) in response to requests from the CARICOM States and other ICT stakeholders for a more unified approach to the developing ICT policies and legislation according to online sources. The project ran between 2008 and 2013 and resulted in several outcomes, including a model cybercrime law for CARICOM.

The offences under the HIPCAR cybercrime model law relates to illegal access, illegal remaining, illegal interception, illegal data interference, data espionage, illegal system interference, illegal devices, computer-related forgery, computer-related fraud, child pornography, identity-related crimes, spam, disclosure of details of an investigation, failure to permit assistance (i.e. to permit or assist a person based on an order) and harassment utilizing means of electronic communication (ITU, 2012).

The HIPCAR model law on cybercrime and the Budapest Convention have similarities and some divergence. An examination of the model laws reveals that the HIPCAR model legislation on cybercrime includes many of the provisions of the Budapest Convention but in some areas, this regional model law goes further than the international convention. An example of provisions in the HIPCAR model law that is not part of the Budapest Convention is the criminalization of sending unsolicited emails or spam. The report explains that this difference is because regulating spam varies around the globe and there is no harmonized approach and thus is not part of the global cybercrime convention (Council of Europe, 2019).

Despite this appearance of a successful outcome of the HIPCAR Project, at least in the actual development of the model law that reflects the contributions of the respective countries, the level of adoption of the model law among the members of the Caribbean remains low. This may be explained or exacerbated by insufficient considerations by policymakers of the supportive legal and justice system processes to facilitate effective legislative development and management of cybercrime (Barclay, 2014). In other words, careful analysis and adoption of the full cycle of legislative and policy development from the drafting and operationalization of the law through to investigation, prosecutions and the levying of appropriate sanctions must be contemplated in order to ensure policy success.

3.4.2 Budapest Convention

In 2001, the Council of Europe passed the Convention on Cybercrime, which is considered the first international treaty on crimes committed via the Internet and other computer networks, dealing particularly with crimes such as infringements of copyright, computer-related fraud, child pornography and violations of network security aimed at Internet criminal behaviours and is the only global document on this issue (Council of Europe, 2001). The Convention also contains powers and procedures relating to the search of computer networks and interception. The convention mandates member countries to have unified legislation on cybercrime. The primary goal of the treaty was to create a set of standard laws concerning cybercrimes for the global community, create a common criminal policy to protect against cybercrimes and establish a framework for international cooperation between State Parties to this treaty.

Per the Council of Europe, the total number of ratifications/accessions is 48 countries to include EU and non-EU members. Notably, no member of CARICOM has ratified the Convention to date. However, in the Americas, countries such as the Dominican Republic, Canada and the United States have signed. Despite many countries in the Caribbean not signing, their cybercrime laws appear to be modelled or are closely aligned to the Convention. The HIPCAR Project may also have a contributing factor to this alignment.

The Convention consists of 4 chapters and 48 articles that consist of use of terms (definitions), Measures to be taken at the national level (substantive and procedural provisions), International cooperation, and Final provisions.

Chapter 1 provides definitions of four key terms, i.e. computer system, computer data, service provider and traffic data.

The substantive provisions comprise five categories:

a. Offences against the confidentiality, integrity and availability of computer data and systems such as illegal access to computers, illegal interception of computer data, misuse of devices, etc.;
b. Computer-related offences including computer-related forgery and computer-related fraud;
c. Content-related offences, namely offences relating to child pornography;
d. Offences related to infringements of copyright and related rights;
e. Ancillary liability and sanctions including attempt, aiding and abetting any of the other offences and corporate liability.

The procedural law describes the powers and procedures necessary to investigate and enforce. Some of the provisions include expedited preservation, production order, search and seizure and jurisdiction. The provisions also bear similarity to the HIPCAR cybercrime model law, except in several ways, where HIPCAR provides for an assistance provision for instance.

3.5 Cybercrime Legislation in the Caribbean

According to Barclay (2014), the cybercrime legislative developments in developing countries such as the Caribbean have been slow and fractured. Examples such as the ineffective or insufficient legislative support to address crimes committed at a certain time such as the 'I love you' virus launched in the Philippines, the Stuxnet virus and the lottery scam that originated in Jamaica were cited as strong support (Barclay, 2014). The results of an Internet search on the laws relating to cybercrime are shown in Table 3.2, which support these claims to the extent that the legislative development process is at various stages across the region. The data confirms that despite the presence of model laws (and the Budapest Convention), the Caribbean has more ways to go in terms of its cybercrime legislative maturity. This is as a result of a number of countries having no specific laws relating to crime, while others are still in the drafting stage.

This current environment may be attributable to several reasons. An assessment of the cybercrime environment in multiple developing countries continues to show undue delays in the passing of legislation, ineffective investigative processes to apprehend suspects, and inefficient court management that further delays the process of justice (Barclay, 2014). Arguably, this may not be unique to developing countries; however, these countries, including those in the Caribbean are usually further constrained by multiple challenges relating to capital, skilled resources and adoption of technology that has implications for effective process management of criminal justice (Barclay, 2014).

Table 3.2 Countries and Cybercrime legislation

Countries	Cybercrime Legislation
Anguilla	No dedicated law identified
Antigua and Barbuda	Electronic Crimes Act, 2013
Bahamas	Computer Misuse Act, 2003
Barbados	Computer Misuse Act, 2005
Belize	Cybercrime Act, 2020
Bermuda	No specific law identified
The British Virgin Islands	Computer Misuse and Cybercrime (Amendment) Act, 2019
Cayman Islands	Computer Misuse Act (Revised 2015)
Dominica	No dedicated law identified
Grenada	No dedicated law identified
Guyana	Cybercrime Act, 2018
Haiti	No dedicated law identified
Jamaica	Cybercrimes Act, 2015
Montserrat	No dedicated law identified; however, there is a Draft Penal Code Amdt Bill 2020 intended to address cybercrimes
St Kitts and Nevis	Electronic Crimes Act, 2009
St Lucia	No dedicated law identified; however, Criminal Code refers to computer crimes
St Vincent and Grenadines	No dedicated law identified; however, there exists a Cybercrime Bill, 2016
Suriname	No dedicated law identified
Trinidad and Tobago	Computer Misuse Act, 2000
Turks & Caicos	No dedicated law identified

The cybercrime laws in the Caribbean may be broadly categorized into four areas. First, those countries with no dedicated laws focused on cybercrime include those with non-existent cybercrime laws and others where cybercrime falls within a broader crime law framework. An example of the latter is St Lucia where their Criminal Code includes provisions related to computer fraud and searching a computer. In relation to the former, there is no evidence of specific cybercrime law in Anguilla, Bermuda or Haiti, for instance. Second, countries in which the central theme is computer misuse, such as the Bahamas, Barbados, Cayman Islands and Trinidad and Tobago. Third, countries in which the theme is on electronic crimes, namely St Kitts and Nevis. Fourth, countries whose central theme is cybercrime such as Belize, Guyana and Jamaica.

3.5.1 Computer Misuse Acts

The Computer Misuse laws in the region have been influenced in some ways by the Computer Misuse of other Commonwealth countries, such as the UK. The regional laws share similarities in that they seek to criminalize acts such as gaining unauthorized or illegal access to computer material or computer system, unauthorized modification of computer material or data, illegally intercept data or having access to devices that aid in the commission of certain offences such as access or interception. The procedural laws commonly contemplate actions required to undertake investigations and enforcements including seize and seizure. Points of departure concerning substantive provisions are Barbados which includes in its Computer Misuse Act, the criminalization of child pornography and malicious communications while the Bahamas contemplates enhanced punishment for offences involving protected computers.

3.5.2 Electronic Crimes Acts

St Kitts and Nevis' Electronic Crimes Act, revised in 2017, reflects a strong influence by the HIPCAR cybercrime model law and seeks to prohibit unauthorized access to and abuse of computers, computer systems and data. The Act criminalizes acts such as illegal access and illegal remaining, interfering with data or computer system, illegal interception, possession of illegal devices, computer-related fraud or forgery, unlawful disclosure of access code, unauthorized access to restricted computer system, child pornography, unlawful communications, data espionage, identity-related crimes and spam. Child pornography, computer-related fraud or forgery, unlawful communications, spam, and identity-related crimes reflect an evolution of the scope of cybercrime laws, particularly when compared with countries that are focused on the computer misuse theme. The penalty for conviction of an offence relating to spam includes a fine or imprisonment of up to five years.

3.5.3 Cybercrime Acts

The Cybercrime Acts in the region arguably reflect the influence of the Budapest Convention. These laws seek to combat cybercrime with the criminalization of acts such as illegal access to a computer system, illegal access to computer data, illegal data interference, illegal system interference, illegal devices and codes and computer-related fraud or forgery. Jamaica and Guyana also contemplate corporate liability offences. Jamaica's version of its Cybercrime Act is the oldest with its coming into operation in 2015, wherein there are strong similarities between the provisions of Guyana and Belize's Cybercrime Acts of 2018 and 2020, respectively. Provisions relating to revenge pornography offences and using a computer system to coerce intimidate or humiliate in the case of Belize and Guyana address contemporary concerns regarding unlawful communications. Jamaica provides a general provision in which specific acts may be inferred. A reasonable interpretation of the provision includes acts of cyberbullying, cyberstalking, revenge pornography where these acts can be seen as either obscene or is seen as a threat and can therefore result in distress and other psychological injuries (Barclay, 2017). The more current laws also reflect an extended scope of offences to include spam, phishing, revenge porn, child luring and pornography.

3.6 Risk, Challenges and Opportunities

It is apparent that policymakers are grappling with identifying appropriate measures to combat cybercrime and security incidents at the national, regional and global scale. With the growing scale and impact of cybercrime and security incidents, calls for closer attention in the identification and adoption of suitable mechanisms to stem these threats must be heeded. The research emphasizes that the region is at risk of evolving security threats, including ransomware, phishing, scams, identity theft and data breaches. There is also a notable group of persistent threat actor, namely, the Jamaican lottery scammers who continue to fleece billions of dollars from victims yearly.

The cybercrime legislative response is one way. However, the research underlined that this is not consistently adopted in the CARICOM countries despite the development of the HIPCAR cybercrime model and the Budapest Convention, and other legislative models. This suggests that there are deeper issues that prevent the wide-scale adoption of cybercrime models.

One criticism levied at the cybercrime legislative development in the Caribbean is by Barclay (2014) who shares that the inability to legislate for current threat developments indicates that the legislative development is neither comprehensive nor current to address the technological developments and advances in society nor the types of crimes that are being committed.

In addition, the presence of the legislation is only a part of a coordinated and cohesive solution that requires appropriate capacity in terms of investigation and prosecution of the crimes. Localized evidence continues to show that the countries with cybercrime legislation have a relatively limited number of successful prosecutions. This could be for several reasons, including the management of evidence and the appropriate application of the relevant cybercrime provisions.

This current state presents a good opportunity for regional cooperation in cybercrime that extends beyond cybercrime model law, although a useful and necessary tool. Mutual legal assistance, investigation, and capacity-building support are some of the possible strategies that can help to improve the regional response. Similar actions can be taken at the country level with public–private partnerships, education and awareness.

The challenge of data is also highlighted albeit, indirectly, as it is noted that often there is a lack of empirical evidence to support the necessary examination of the effectiveness of the relevant cybercrime laws and the rationale for the delays in implementation of cybercrime policies and strategies.

3.7 Conclusion

According to Barclay (2014, 2017), effective cybercrime management can influence national development, and as such, there must be effective cybercrime laws supported by an efficient and responsive process. Unfortunately, in the Caribbean, there is an insufficient/inadequate framework for an integrated formal process to inform legislative development and implementation of cybercrime (Barclay, 2014). In addition, cybercrime laws have been slow and reactive to the rapidly changing environment and countries therefore need an efficient policy development process, technology-neutral laws, regional and global partnerships and cooperation to stem transnational crimes such as cybercrime.

It must be noted that the scope of this research includes assessing specific cybercrime laws in CARICOM countries. However, it is recognized that many countries may legislate cybercrime with various offences across multiple distinct yet connected laws. Barclay (2017) in assessing Jamaica's cybercrime law regime observes that multiple statutes address the range of substantive law provisions contained in the Budapest Convention including the Copyright Act, Child Pornography Prevention Act and the Mutual Legal Assistance Act.

This research contributes to research by focusing on an underexplored area of cybercrime in the Caribbean. The research brings attention to the growing risks the region faces as it seeks to stem the digital divide and highlight the importance of a comprehensive approach to cybercrime policymaking. The research also provides value to policymakers in emphasizing the need for a collective regional approach in investigating and enforcing cybercrime while underscoring the importance of collecting and interrogating relevant cybercrime data to improve decision-making within the ecosystem. Future studies may examine approaches to resolve the challenges in the legislative development, implementation and criminal justice processes.

References

AP News. (2018), Man said to be Jamaican lottery scam kingpin gets 6 years. Accessed on July 15, 2021 at https://apnews.com/article/09ff0d2796ae4e36a4e4f76c5c808534

Barclay, C. (2014). Using frugal innovations to support cybercrime legislations in small developing states: introducing the cyber-legislation development and implementation process model (CyberLeg-DPM). *Information Technology for Development*, *20*(2), 165–195.

Barclay, C. (2017). Cybercrime and legislation: a critical reflection on the Cybercrimes Act, 2015 of Jamaica. Commonwealth Law Bulletin, 43(1), 77–107.

Broadhurst, R., & Chang, L. Y. (2013). Cybercrime in Asia: trends and challenges. In *Handbook of Asian criminology* (pp. 49–63). Springer, New York, NY.

Clough, J. (2012). The Council of Europe Convention on cybercrime: defining 'crime' in a digital world. In *Criminal Law Forum* (Vol. 23, No. 4, pp. 363–391). Springer: Springer Netherland.

Council of Europe. (2001). ETS 185, Convention on Cybercrime. Retrieved from https://www.coe.int/en/web/conventions/full-list/-/conventions/treaty/185?module=treaty-detail&treatynum=185

Council of Europe (2019) Report on the Regional Conference on Cybercrime Strategies and Policies and features of the Budapest Convention for the Caribbean Community. Retrieved from https://rm.coe.int/3148-1-1-3-final-report-dr-reg-conference-cy-policies-caribbean-comm-1/168098fb6c

Deloitte (2017). *Taking Data Hostage the Rise of Ransomware*. Retrieved from https://www2.deloitte.com/ca/en/pages/risk/articles/ransomware.html

FBI. (2020). Internet Crime Report, 2020. Retrieved from https://www.ic3.gov/Media/PDF/AnnualReport/2020_IC3Report.pdf

IDB/OAS. 2016. Cybersecurity Report, 'Cybersecurity are we ready in Latin America and the Caribbean?'

ITU. (2012). Establishment of Harmonized Policies for the ICT Market in the ACP Countries Cybercrimes/e-Crimes: Assessment Report. Retrieved from https://www.itu.int/en/ITU-D/Projects/ITU-EC-ACP/HIPCAR/Documents/FINAL%20DOCUMENTS/ENGLISH%20DOCS/cybercrimes_assessment.pdf

ITU. (2020). Global Cybersecurity Index 2020 Measuring commitment to cybersecurity. Retrieved from https://www.itu.int/en/myitu/Publications/2021/06/28/13/22/Global-Cybersecurity-Index-2020

Jamaica Gleaner. 2020a. Jamaica National hit by major cyber attack. Accessed on July 15, 2021 at https://jamaica-gleaner.com/article/news/20200320/jamaica-national-hit-major-cyber-attack

Jamaica Gleaner. 2020b. FRAUD ALARM – Women, millennials main targets of credit, debit card thieves, Accessed on July 15, 2021 at https://jamaica-gleaner.com/article/lead-stories/20201204/fraud-alarm-women-millennials-main-targets-credit-debit-card-thieves

Jamaica Gleaner. 2021. Digicel estimates 100 million hack attempts in the Caribbean. Accessed on July 15, 2021 at https://jamaica-gleaner.com/article/business/20210711/digicel-estimates-100m-hack-attempts-caribbean

Loop News. 2020. T&T's Cyber Security Team reports increase in ransomware attacks (by Nneka Parsanlal). Accessed on July 15, 2021 at https://tt.loopnews.com/content/tts-cyber-security-team-reports-increase-ransomware-attacks

Ponemon Institute/IBM Security Intelligence. 2021 Cost of Data Breach Report. Retrieved from https://www.ibm.com/security/data-breach

Smith, Z.M., & E. Lostri. (2020). *The Hidden Costs of Cybercrime.* Retrieved from https://www.mcafee.com/enterprise/en-us/assets/reports/rp-hidden-costs-of-cybercrime.pdf

Chapter 4

Privacy and Security Management: Lessons from the Enforcement of the EU General Data Protection Regulation (GDPR)

4.1 Introduction

The continued rapid technological advancements have not only resulted in increased user demands and expectations but also have significantly impacted privacy and security on a large scale. Countries have therefore sought to balance economic growth, innovation and the fundamental right of privacy through various initiatives including data protection policy and legislative schemes. The significant financial penalty imposed by France's National Data Protection Commission, Commission nationale de l'informatique et des libertés (CNIL) on Google LLC for violations of European Union General Data Protection Regulation (GDPR) (CNIL, 2019) within the first year of the coming into operation of GDPR brought into closer focus the enforcement provisions under GDPR, the reach and power of the Supervisory Authorities (SAs) and the challenges experienced by organizations in maintaining appropriate security and privacy controls. The current landscape also underlines the importance

DOI: 10.1201/9781003028710-5

of due diligence in compliance activities through ensuring the lawfulness of processing of personal data, diligent application of data protection principles to processing operations, and among other activities, the application of appropriate technical and organizational safeguards in the processing of personal data, regardless of the size of the business, customer base or income.

Since the coming into effect of GDPR, several SAs, outside of France's CNIL, have exercised their enforcement powers by conducting GDPR audit and compliance investigations, conducting investigations of complaints and imposing corrective measures. These corrective measures include reprimands, orders and the imposition of administrative fines, with the largest reported, being the €50 million imposed on Google LLC for lack of transparency, information and lack of valid consent regarding ads personalization (CNIL, 2019). Unsurprisingly, there has been a dramatic growth in the number of complaints made against organizations for alleged breaches of obligations. This is accompanied by the increased number of reported breaches as a result of organizations complying with their breach notification requirements under the Regulation. According to the European Data Protection Board, for the period up to May 2019, there were over 144,000 queries and complaints and over 89,000 data breaches (EDPB, 2019). This confirms a perceived increase in awareness about data protection rights among data subjects/individuals. The data also suggest that data subjects are neither convinced nor confident that organizations are sufficiently applying the provisions of GDPR to the processing of their personal data. Further, customers are concerned that these organizations do not have any lawful basis for processing their personal data. The perspective of the data subjects is further supported by the number of breach notifications, thereby highlighting that sufficient appropriate technical and organizational safeguards are not being employed in the processing operation concerning personal data. Consequently, it is reasonable to declare that the GDPR landscape will likely continue on this trajectory resulting in additional administrative fines and other enforcement measures levied against a growing number of organizations. It is also reasonable to expect that countries that are implementing their respective data protection/privacy laws will have similar experiences in terms of attention drawn to complaints, breaches and the imposition of fines.

The purpose of this chapter is to analyse some of the notable administrative fines or financial penalties levied under GDPR, within its first year, and discuss their potential implications on organizations as they seek to comply with the varied GDPR requirements. The administrative fines levied have implications on several areas of a data protection scheme, including the technical and organizational measures that may be adopted to ensure compliance, the complaint procedures for data subjects and the investigative powers of an SA. It is argued that the risks of administrative fines as the result of breaches of obligations, data breaches and reputational damage are too high for organizations to ignore. Therefore, it is essential that they adopt a systematic approach to understanding and complying with the Regulation and understand its impact on their business systems, processes and procedures (Barclay, 2019, 2020). Moreover, the actual imposition of administrative fines suggests a less than stellar privacy profile of the organizations concerned and highlights weaknesses and limitations in their processing of personal data. The publication of these administrative fines also presents an excellent opportunity for other organizations to learn and address their security and privacy gaps, as part of their GDPR compliance activities. The lessons also extend to jurisdictions that have implemented or are implementing their data protection regimes.

The administrative fines are examined in the context of the provisions of GDPR that were relied on during the process of investigations and the decisions made by the respective SAs. This examination reveals a common thread of exposure, risks and vulnerabilities in the types of infringements of the provisions of the Regulation for which the organizations become liable. Breaches of obligations of key provisions relating to data protection principles particularly the lawfulness of processing of personal data and consent, the rights of the data subjects and security of processing, in particular. These findings emphasize the importance of bolstering processing operations in accordance with GDPR and privacy by design principles as espoused by Cavoukian (2009) to reduce the risk of not only administrative fines but reduced customer trust and financial viability.

4.2 Infringements and the Corrective Powers of Supervisory Authorities

Strong enforcement powers are vested in the SAs under Article 58 of the Regulation (GDPR, 2016). The SAs are independent public bodies established in each Member State and are responsible for the monitoring of the application of the Regulation to ensure the objectives of the Regulation are achieved.

Where there is an infringement or likelihood of an infringement of the Regulation, an SA may rely on its range of corrective powers under Article 58(2). These include the power to issue warnings or reprimands where the processing operation of a controller or processor is likely to infringe provisions or has infringed provisions. An SA may also order a controller or processor to engage in a particular compliance activity such as to comply with a request made by a data subject, bring processing operations into compliance, communicate a data breach to the data subject concerned, or rectify or erase personal data pursuant to the Regulation, among other corrective actions. Additionally, an SA may impose an administrative fine, in addition to other corrective measures or instead of other corrective measures based on the circumstances of each infringement.

The range of administrative fines falls within two categories per Article 83 (4) to (6). An organization becomes liable to a fine of up to €10 million, or in the case of an undertaking, up to 2% of the total worldwide turnover, whichever is higher, or a fine up to €20 million, or in the case of an undertaking, up to 4% of the total worldwide turnover, whichever is higher, depending on the types of infringement. The types of infringement associated with both categories are identified in Table 4.1.

Table 4.1 GDPR Obligations and Maximum Penalties

Category I	*Category II*
fines of up to €10 million, or in the case of an undertaking, up to 2% of the total worldwide turnover, whichever is higher	*fines up to €20 million, or in the case of an undertaking, up to 4% of the total worldwide turnover, whichever is higher*
(1) Obligations of the controller and processor in relation to: (a) conditions of child's consent in respect of information services (Article 8); (b) processing which does not require identification (Article 11); (c) general obligations of a controller and processor (Articles 25–31); (d) security of personal data (Articles 32–34); (e) data protection impact assessment and prior consultation (Articles 35–36); (f) data protection officer (Articles 37–39).	(1) Basic principles of processing, including conditions of consent, in relation to – (a) principles relating to processing of personal data (Article 5); (b) lawfulness of processing (Article 6); (c) conditions of consent (Article 7); (d) processing of special categories of data (Article 9).
(2) Obligations of the certification body in relation to: (a) certification (Article 42); and (b) certification bodies (Article 43);	(2) Rights of the data subject (Articles 12–22).
(3) Obligations of the monitoring body in relation to a competent supervisory authority taking appropriate action in cases of infringement of the code of conduct by a controller or processor (Article 41(4)).	(3) Transfer of personal data to a third country or an international organization (Articles 44–49).

(Continued)

Table 4.1 (Continued)

Category I	Category II
	(4) Obligations pursuant to Member State law adopted under Chapter IX (Articles 85–91): (a) reconciliation of right to the protection of personal data with the freedom of expression and information; (b) reconciliation of public access to an official document with the right to the protection of personal data; (c) specific conditions for the processing of a national identification number or any other identifier of general application; (d) specific rules to ensure the protection of the rights and freedoms in respect of the processing of employees' personal data in the employment context; (e) safeguards in relation to the processing for archiving purposes in the public interest, scientific or historical research purposes or statistical purposes; (f) obligations of secrecy; (g) existing data protection rules of churches and religious associations.
	(5) Non-compliance to a corrective measure enforced by the supervisory authority, in accordance with Article 58(2) or failure to provide access in violation of investigative power being enforced by the supervisory authority, in accordance with Article 58(1)

Some of the acts which fall under the higher fines category include breaches relating to data protection principles, except conditions of child's consent, rights of the data subject, transfers to third countries and international organizations, and non-compliance to corrective measures enforced by an SA.

In the administering of an administrative fine, the SA must ensure that in considering the infringement, the administrative fine is *effective, proportionate and dissuasive.* In other words, the SA should take all measures necessary to guarantee the effectiveness of the Regulation (see Commission of the European Communities v Hellenic Republic). This means that the administrative fine should adequately reflect the gravity of the infringement, does not go beyond what is necessary in order to ensure compliance with obligations under the Regulation and that it has a deterrent effect. The Regulation reinforces the importance of this objective by expressly providing for the nature, gravity, duration of the actual infringement, and the general actions and attitude of the controller or processor in relation to the security and privacy of the processing of personal data, general compliance to the Regulation and other considerations as outlined under Article 83(2), in the determination of a financial penalty.

4.3 Consequences of Infringements

During the first nine months of GDPR, SAs in a few Member States, including France, Germany and Austria, have made public their imposition of administrative fines for various forms of breach of obligations, as described in Table 4.2. News and information on these fines were primarily collected from the official EU website. A closer look at these reported administrative fines reveals that the infringements fall under both categories of maximum penalties that may be attributed to the actual infringement. A breach of obligation relating to the security of processing falls under Category I fines and is the most commonly cited infringement. The other reported breaches of obligations, such as breaches of Articles 5, 6 and 12, fall under Category II. The imposition of the administrative fines highlights a wide range in value, which may be attributable to:

    a. the nature, gravity and impact of the breach;
    b. the level of cooperation with the respective SA;
    c. the size of the organization; and
    d. other factors that are outlined under Article 83(2).

The German case of the social network provider, Knuddels,[2] is illustrative of some of the best practices organizations can adopt in the event of a breach and the subsequent dealings with the SA. Knuddels was cited for fully cooperating and being transparent in where they went wrong (i.e. storing unencrypted passwords) and exhibited a willingness to follow the recommendations made by the SA and address the issues necessary to recover from the breach. It is therefore not a significant leap to advise that in the event of a breach, adopting similar tactics will likely result in a reduction in the severity of penalties. The Knuddels' decision underscores the importance of quick actions following a breach, timely breach notifications to the SA and data subjects and the influence these actions have on the SA in

Table 4.2 Summary of Notable Public Fines Under GDPR

Member State	Description of infringement (source: EU website)	GDPR Article(s) Infringed	Some Other Relevant GDPR Articles[5]	Fines imposed (Euros)
France	Lack of transparency, inadequate information and lack of valid consent regarding the ads personalization based on collective complaints made against Google LLC (CNIL, 2019).	■ Article 6 – Lawful basis for the processing of personal data ■ Article 7 – Conditions of consent ■ Article 12 – Transparent information, communication and modalities for the exercise of the rights of the data subject ■ Article 13 – Information to be provided where personal data are collected from the data subject	■ Article 5 – principles relating to the processing of data ■ Article 6 – Lawful basis for the processing of personal data ■ Article 7 – Conditions of consent ■ Article 56 – Competence of the lead supervisory authority ■ Article 77 – Right to lodge a complaint with a supervisory authority ■ Article 80 – Representation of data subjects	50,000,000.00
Portugal	Medical staff and other professionals of a hospital (Centro Hospitalar Barrero Montijo) had indiscriminate access to patient data through false profiles (Monteiro, 2019).	■ Article 5(1) (f) – integrity and confidentiality of the processing of personal data ■ Article 32 - Security of processing	■ Article 9 – processing of special categories of personal data	400,000.00

(Continued)

Table 4.2 (Continued)

Member State	Description of infringement (source: EU website)	GDPR Article(s) Infringed	Some Other Relevant GDPR Articles[5]	Fines imposed (Euros)
Germany	A social network provider was hacked in July 2018 and personal data (including passwords and email addresses) of around 330,000 users were stolen and later made public.	■ Article 32 (1) (a) – Security of processing – pseudony-mization and encryption of personal data	■ Article 5(1) (f) – integrity and confidentiality of the processing of personal data ■ Article 33 – Notification of a personal data breach to the supervisory authority ■ Article 34 – Notification of a personal data breach to the data subject ■ Article 83(2) – General conditions for imposing administrative fines	20,000.00
Austria	The use of a video surveillance system covering the public street and parking lots by a sports betting cafe.	■ Article 5 (1) (a) and (c) – Lawfulness, fairness and transparency principle ■ Article 6 (1) – Lawful basis for the processing of personal data	■ Article 2 – Material scope	5,280.00

(*Continued*)

Table 4.2 (Continued)

Member State	Description of infringement (source: EU website)	GDPR Article(s) Infringed	Some Other Relevant GDPR Articles[5]	Fines imposed (Euros)
Malta	An investigation found that the online application platform of the Lands Authority did not have the necessary technical and organizational measures to ensure the security of processing.	■ Article 32 - Security of processing	■ Article 5 – principles relating to the processing of data	5,000.00

the determination of the severity of the penalty imposed. Several provisions under Article 83(2), particularly (f) and (h) are of interest and were likely relied on during deliberations:

a. the degree of cooperation with the supervisory authority, in order to remedy the infringement and mitigate the possible adverse effects of the infringement; and

b. the manner in which the infringement became known to the supervisory authority, in particular, whether, and if so to what extent, the controller or processor notified the infringement.

The decision also has broader implications for other organizations and SAs. Some organizations continue to grapple with reporting breaches as they prefer to keep them under wraps due to fear of reputational damage or financial loss. Organizations may also view their SA as an adversary instead of viewing the relationship as an opportunity for assistance and collaboration. Moreover, SAs can confidently impose their discretionary power by taking into account multiple factors in determining the best course of action for the various types of infringements.

In addition to administrative fines, the SAs have also utilized alternative corrective measures, including imposing a temporary ban on the processing that violates the Regulation. For example, the SA in Malta imposed a temporary ban on the Lands Authority's online application platform for violating Article 32. In Austria, the SA went several steps further and imposed an immediate ban on the processing operations of the Austrian Post after investigations found that it processes special categories of data, more specifically political opinions which were derived from the use of statistical calculation methods. Presumably, the Austrian Post's processing did not fall under any of the exceptions under Article 9(2). The SA also ordered the immediate erasure of the derived data and that the Austrian Post carry out a new data protection impact assessment (DPIA) pursuant to Article 35, to rectify its record of processing.

The business impact of the breaches becomes evident in the temporary cessation of activities or the increased demands on business systems and processes as a result of the SA's orders. These have the effect of resulting in reduced income and opportunities from certain activities or portals, increased operational burdens on certain business areas and increased operational expenditures in order to comply with the orders of the SA, such as a DPIA. In addition, the affected organizations may face the risk to their reputation, reduced customer trust and reduced competitive leverage.

4.4 Issues and Challenges in Meeting the Obligations of GDPR

The number of reported complaints and breaches to the SAs emphasizes some of the obstacles faced by organizations in meeting the compliance requirements under GDPR. The resulting impact on the ecosystem of a business cannot be understated since meeting the appropriate technical and organizational safeguards will likely result in changes to the technical systems and infrastructure, business processes, policies, procedures and other governance structures. For example, the ability of an organization to meet the obligations of the rights of a data subject and the impending requests such as data subject access requests involve changes to internal processes and systems along with training and awareness activities among staff to be able to adequately address these requests and comply with the Regulation[4]. In consideration of the foregoing, it is argued that a lack of complete or rigorous assessment of the obligations under GDPR and the likely impact of these obligations on the organization's structures, i.e. the processes, systems and people lead to many of the challenges experienced by organizations in complying with the Regulation.

An examination of the reported breaches disclosed several areas of infringement, which may be categorized into:

a. data protection principle relating to the processing of personal data;
b. the lawfulness of processing of personal data;

c. conditions of consent;

d. processing of special categories of personal data;

e. transparent information, communication and modalities for the exercise of the rights of the data subject; and

f. security of processing.

4.4.1 Data Protection Principle Relating to Processing of Personal Data

Data protection principles are one of the core components of a data protection regime. These principles generally include attributes that promote fair use, transparency and accountability in the processing of personal data. These include the data subjects' consent to such processing, limiting the collection of personal data, identifying the purpose for the collection and limiting collection to only that purpose, and accuracy and completeness of the personal data being collected. The breaches under Article 5 brought into focus the deficiencies in security controls and practices in these organizations. The regulatory mechanisms therefore become necessary to help to ensure that appropriate structures are in place to ensure fair use, transparency and accountability in the processing of personal data.

While the decision of the Portugal supervisory authority (CNPD) has not been known to be made public, several online media sources reported that a hospital's staff consisting of different categories of medical professionals had access to patient data through unrestricted profiles. It was reported that doctors had unrestricted access to all patient files and that there were over 900 user profiles associated with doctors yet only close to 300 active doctors on staff. There was also evidence of maintenance of user profiles for doctors who were no longer providing services to the hospital. These actions violated the data protection principle of integrity and confidentiality, where the personal data of patient must be processed in a manner that ensures appropriate security of the personal data, including protection against unauthorized or unlawful processing and accidental loss, destruction or damage, using appropriate technical or organizational measures (Article 5 (1)(f)). The issue experienced by the hospital highlights a common security dilemma of proper access control or identity and access management (IAM). IAM refers to the technical and organizational measures adopted by an organization to manage the identity and access to data based on the respective user profiles. Several key elements include ensuring that persons who require access have access and those who should not have access do not have such access. The latter may include former employees and staff at a certain level of seniority. IAM must be seen as a continuous and evolving process (Gunter et al., 2011) to enable it to meet the changing needs of any organization. Portugal's Centro Hospitalar Barrero Montijo was therefore unable to ensure the ongoing confidentiality, integrity, availability and resilience of processing systems and services under Article 32 as a result of its poor IAM practices. The problem experienced by the hospital could be addressed with regular security audits, implementation of suitable IAM tools and training and awareness involving GDPR requirements and proper security control practice. In Austria, a sports betting café using a video surveillance system, as a controller, that covered public streets and parking lots was found to have breached several provisions of the Regulation. The Austrian DPA found that the controller breached the data protection principle of lawfulness, fairness and transparency (Article (5(1))), more specifically lawfulness and transparency. Investigations uncovered that the filmed area did not have adequate signage about the video surveillance system. Therefore, such processing lacked transparency and the necessary basis for processing. If the video surveillance system was being used only inside the cafe with clear signage of its uses and purposes, such a use would likely be within the parameters of the Regulation. Furthermore, it is likely that a competent authority responsible for safeguarding against and preventing threats to public security would lawfully be able to use a video surveillance system in a public space for that purpose in accordance with Article 2(2)(d).

4.4.2 Lawfulness of Processing of Personal Data and Conditions of Consent

Article 6 provides that for processing to be lawful, an organization must be able to demonstrate that the data subject has given consent or that the processing is necessary to meet certain obligations, including the performance of a contract to which the data subject is a party or that it is required for compliance with a legal obligation to which the organization is subject. In respect to consent, Article 7 provides for specific conditions of consent, including that consent must be freely given and the request for consent must be in an intelligible and easily accessible form, using clear and plain language.

Google LLC argued that they received the user's consent to process data for ads personalization. However, CNIL found that the consent was not validly obtained for two reasons:

1. there was not sufficient informed consent; and
2. the collected consent was not specific nor unambiguous.

The information relating to processing operations for ads personalization was described as diluted in several documents and did not enable the user to be aware of the extent of the plurality of services, websites and applications involved in the diverse processing operations. The users were provided with a pre-ticked button during their account configuration and before creating an account they were asked to check a number of boxes in order to create an account. The findings establish that Google LLC was unable to demonstrate that consent was in accordance with the Regulation because:

   a. the consent was not presented in an intelligible and easily accessible form, using clear and plain language, given the content presented to the user during account set-up of ads personalization; and

   b. the number of pages and clicks the user would have to navigate in order to complete their account set-up.

These findings have implications for service providers in the manner of the online presentation of the services being offered and the extent of such processing operations. Creative approaches will have to be employed to prevent the documents from being unwieldy, including the use of graphics, to ensure that the information is clear and intelligible, and where there are multiple services being offered, clear and specific consent options must be provided to allow the user to know which services they are giving their consent to at the onset.

4.4.3 Transparent Information, Communication and Modalities for the Exercise of the Rights of the Data Subject

Article 12 sets the context for the standard, quality and manner of information to be provided to the data subjects at the point of obtaining their personal data and in the exercise of any of their rights relating to that personal data. Therefore, an organization that is a controller must take appropriate measures to provide such information in a *concise, transparent, intelligible and easily accessible* form. Google LLC argued that the information disseminated to users met the requirements of Articles 12 and 13, in the instance where the personal data are collected from the data subject. However, CNIL found multiple issues with the information and the manner in which the information was presented, and suggest that the general structure of information did not comply with the Regulation:

1. essential information was only accessible after several steps, sometimes up to 5 or 6 actions, as in the case of users wanting to complete information on their data collected for personalization purposes or for the geo-tracking service.
2. information was not always clear or comprehensive because users were not always able to understand the extent of the processing operations carried out by Google LLC. Google LLC's processing operations were described as "particularly massive and intrusive" due to the number of services offered, the amount of data processed and combined.

Based on these findings, it became apparent why CNIL found that the information provided by Google LLC did not meet the standard of conciseness (*multiple actions were necessary to complete set-up*), transparent (*massive processing operations were associated with the services*), intelligible (*it was difficult for the user to understand the extent of processing*) or easily accessible (*multiple actions were necessary to complete set-up*).

4.4.4 Security of Processing

An organization that processes personal data must implement appropriate technical and organizational measures to ensure they meet proper security standards appropriate to their risk, thereby possessing a sound security profile. Therefore, the organization must be able to demonstrate the ability to protect and secure the processing of personal data, restore the supporting systems and processes in the event of any disaster, and conduct regular audits to identify and address risks and vulnerabilities. Article 32 provides that the technical and organizational measures may include:

- the pseudonymization and encryption of personal data, which are intended to reduce the risks of identifying the personal data or its metadata and linking the personal data to a data subject, and protecting the personal data during transit;
- the ability to ensure the ongoing confidentiality, integrity, availability and resilience of processing systems and services. These criteria depict the basic parameters required for a secure environment that must be represented in the information systems, policies and procedures of an organization. Therefore, for example, confidentiality assures a high level of assurance that data, objects, or resources are restricted from unauthorized subjects (Chapple et al., 2018);
- the ability to restore the availability and access to personal data in a timely manner in the event of a disaster i.e. natural, user-related or security-related incident, thereby ensuring business continuity.
- a process for regularly testing, assessing and evaluating the effectiveness of technical and organizational measures for ensuring the security of the processing, which endorses regular compliance checks and audits.

The chat platform provider in Germany, Knuddels lacked the appropriate technical and organizational measures to secure the passwords of its users resulting in the organization being hacked. Investigations revealed that the passwords were unencrypted thereby breaching the implementation of appropriate safeguards for the pseudonymization and encryption of personal data. Encryption, including hashing techniques, is a common method used to secure user passwords. The use and enforcement of a strong password policy framework embedded in the application combined with suitable encryption tools are appropriate measures that must be employed by organizations to meet compliance obligations. Knuddels followed the recommendations of the SA to address their security gaps and implement appropriate security controls to reduce the risk of further security breaches.

The Lands Authority in Malta was found to have lacked the necessary appropriate technical and organizational measures to ensure the security of processing on its online application platform thereby violating Article 32. A temporary ban was imposed on the portal during the investigation, underlining the alternative course of corrective measures available to the SA. Details on the type of risks and vulnerabilities existing in the online application platform were not made available in the press release, however, it is reasonable to claim that issues relating to the confidentiality, integrity, availability and resilience of the platform were basic security characteristics that if found lacking would lead to a breach of Article 32.

4.4.5 Processing of Special Categories of Personal Data

Special categories of personal data are referred to as those considered sensitive or private data on or about an individual and include genetic and biological data, and religious or political opinions. Article 9 describes those special categories as data on racial or ethnic origin, political opinions, religious or philosophical beliefs, or trade union membership, and the processing of genetic data, biometric data for the purpose of uniquely identifying a natural person, data concerning health or data concerning a natural person's sex life or sexual orientation. The processing of special categories of data is prohibited under Article 9, except in specific circumstances. This includes explicit consent to the processing and whether that processing is necessary for the purposes of preventive or occupational medicine, for the assessment of among other things, medical diagnosis or the provision of treatment in accordance with a contract with a health professional and subject to the conditions and safeguards, including an obligation of professional secrecy. As a result, the hospital in Portugal was lawfully allowed to process patients' personal data, by virtue of Article 9(2), but lacked the appropriate safeguards, such as those relating to the proper management of user profiles and general IAM.

4.5 Supplementary Matters and Considerations

In addition to the Articles infringed by the respective organizations, the respective cases also highlight other related Articles (Table 4.2). These were identified on analysis of the respective notices or news, given the nature of these cases and the issues that were discussed during the reports. It is argued that these related Articles are critical to the understanding of the issues of data protection, the nature and circumstances under consideration by the respective SAs and matters that organizations should take into consideration as they assess their compliance with the Regulation.

The decision in relation to Google LLC reinforced several important issues in the complaint and investigations process in terms of:

a. who can make a complaint; and
b. which SA is competent to handle a complaint within the context of the one-stop-shop mechanism.

4.5.1 Lodging a Complaint

A data subject has the right to lodge a complaint under article 77 or mandate a properly constituted not-for-profit body to lodge a complaint on his or her behalf under Article 80. The genesis of the financial penalty imposed on Google LLC was the result of the SA receiving complaints from two privacy advocacy groups pertaining to breaches of the Regulation. The report notes that close to 10,000 data subjects mandate the groups to refer their complaints to the SA (CNIL, 2019). Such actions emphasize the important role of these advocacy groups, the strong potential of class actions or complaints in this instance to bring attention to privacy infringements, influence actions and obtain results.

4.5.2 One-Stop-Shop Mechanism and Lead SA Competent to Handle Complaints

The question of who is the lead SA to handle a complaint, where the company has a number of establishments in different Member States, was also brought to the fore given Google LLC's global operating environment. CNIL reasons that in the absence of a main establishment allowing the identification of a lead authority, CNIL is competent to initiate the complaint and exercise its powers under Article 58. While it is being debated on whether CNIL violated the one-stop-shop mechanism (Moerel, 2019), the literal interpretation of the provision appears to support CNIL's position in light of the exception in the definition of a main establishment under Article 2(16)(a). Moreover, CNIL argues that while Google LLC indicated that Google Ireland is the headquarters of Google in the EU, in determining the decision-making power of Google Ireland, several factors were considered (CNIL, 2019):

a. at the time of the commencement of the proceedings, Google Ireland did not have any decision-making power concerning the purposes and means of processing of personal data covered by the privacy policy presented to the user during the creation of that user's account;
b. Google Ireland was not mentioned in the privacy policy dated 25 May 2018 as the entity responsible for determining the purposes and means of processing of personal data;

    c. Google Ireland did not appoint a data protection officer;

    d. in a mail to the SA, it was indicated that the transfer of responsibility of Google LLC to Google Ireland in relation to certain processing operations concerning EU citizens would be finalized on 31 January 2019.

Based on these reasons, Google Ireland could not be reasonably considered as the main establishment for Google LLC and therefore CNIL was competent to investigate the complaint. This landmark decision provides important insights to other controllers operating in similar circumstances as Google LLC, including being a controller involved in cross-border processing and having operations in multiple establishments across the EU. The ruling underlines that the place of central administration is not the sole criteria in the determination of the main establishment. Recital 36 also emphasized that such a determination must rely on objective criteria and the ability to demonstrate effective and real management activities in relation to the purposes and means of processing through stable arrangements. To put it simply, GDPR compliance documents that data subjects will rely on must reflect who is ultimately responsible and such an arrangement must coincide with the technical and organizational arrangements and structures for the processing of personal data. Given the reasons provided by CNIL, it is important for organizations to properly prepare their headquarters in a holistic manner to reflect their decision-making power. The decision shows that any lapse in the content of privacy policies or other user-dependent documents and any incomplete transfer of responsibilities will not facilitate the utilization of the one-stop-shop mechanism.

4.6 Lessons and Opportunities for Improved Business-Regulatory Alignment

The business-regulatory environment is viewed as a dynamic state in which the organization uses regulatory compliance to help achieve its strategic objectives through the utilization of appropriate financial, technical and human resources. Organizations must therefore develop a robust business-regulatory framework for their businesses in order to be able to effectively leverage their compliance with GDPR requirements into improved competitiveness and social responsibility. The number of infringements since GDPR took effect underlines the importance of improving business-regulatory alignment.

    The financial penalties imposed during the first months since GDPR came into effect are examined to help bring attention to the technical and organizational weaknesses and vulnerabilities experienced by the organizations in several Member States and to uncover other key insights. The findings and decisions from the respective SAs have significant implications for multiple stakeholders, including the data subjects, organizations who are controllers or processors, SAs and privacy groups. The data subjects across the respective Member States are continuing to see that attempts are being made to protect their data since the Regulation is being enforced in a number of different ways. The investigative and corrective roles of the SAs was also brought into focus as the SAs attempt to take a broad view of the circumstances resulting in the infringements and subsequently to these infringements, in deciding on the severity of penalties. Article 83(2) is significant not only for SAs but for organizations to take into account in their management of infringements. The decisions taken by the SAs have also underscored that they are taking their role seriously and having utilized their enforcement powers in a number of ways they are amenable to assisting organizations in minimizing breaches and recovering from breaches.

The mechanisms to make a complaint have bolstered the preservation of the right to privacy, through the provision of two principal avenues to exercise that right, including the opportunity for data subjects to mandate a properly constituted not-for-profit to make a complaint on their behalf, as in the case of Google LLC. The strength in numbers become evident as the fight is oftentimes against global powerhouses. It is therefore essential for these not-for-profits to ensure that they are properly constituted in accordance with the respective Member State laws, strengthen their understanding of the Regulation and their national data protection laws to be able to make successful complaints and improve their governance structures generally to facilitate improved efficiencies in their advocacy work.

The infringements relating to the security of processing, data protection principles, including consent and principles relating to the lawfulness, fairness and transparency, confidentiality and integrity, certain rights of the data subjects were identified as areas that required increased attention by organizations as they seek to comply with the Regulation. While it may be ideal for an organization to not experience any significant breaches, the reality is that the rapid technological advances and insufficient supporting organizational structures contribute to the likelihood of breaches. The principal consideration, outside of reducing risks of breaches, is how an organization responds to a breach will determine how best the organization can recover, from the technical, operational, financial and regulatory perspectives. The decision of the German SA in relation to Knuddels reinforced the importance of timely breach notifications and cooperation with the SA in addressing any infringement as such an approach has been proven helpful in minimizing the severity of penalties. Stated differently, the utilization of timely breach notifications and cooperation with the respective SAs aid the remediation process and reduces the risk of significant fines as a result of the infringement.

Organizations with multiple establishments in different Member States and especially where the controller is a non-EU organization must ensure that their EU headquarters can demonstrate that through key decision-making in relation to the purposes and means of processing of data is carried out by the main establishment. Such demonstration, according to objective criteria should include being the place of central administration, ensuring that governance structures such as all policies, procedures reflect the same, all appointments such as a data protection officer per

Article 37 are in place and all appropriate responsibilities are transferred. As in the case of Google LLC, lack of these elements will cause an SA to determine that there is no main establishment, which may result in the likelihood of multiple complaints made on the same issues in a number of Member States and increase the risk of administrative fines and other penalties.

As the Regulation matures, the debate continues on the applicability of the one-stop-shop mechanisms, the consistent application of administrative fines and other penalties within a Member State and across the EU and the adoption of best practices to promote business-regulatory alignment. In the meantime, one thing will remain in that the data protection regulatory landscape will continue to evolve with competing demands of data subjects, service providers, innovators and regulators. The investigative, corrective and authorization and advisory powers of the SAs provide an interesting environment for strategic insights, not only for the EU, but other jurisdictions as these countries develop or refine their own data protection schemes.

References

Barclay, C. (2019). The road to GDPR compliance: Overcoming the compliance hurdles. *ISACA Journal, 2019*(1), 24–29.

Barclay, C. (2020). What is your data protection or privacy strategy? *ISACA Journal, 2,* 21–25

Cavoukian, A. (2009). Privacy by design: The 7 foundational principles. *Information and Privacy Commissioner of Ontario, Canada, 5,* 12.

Chapple, M., Stewart, J. M., & Gibson, D. (2018). *(ISC) 2 CISSP Certified Information Systems Security Professional Official Study Guide.* Indianapolis, Indiana: John Wiley & Sons.

CNIL. (2019). *Délibération de la Formation Restreinte n° SAN – 2019-001 du 21 Janvier 2019 Prononçant Une Sanction Pécuniaire à L'Encontre de la Société Google LLC.* Retrieved on June 10, 2020 from https://www.legifrance.gouv.fr/cnil/id/CNILTEXT000038032552/

EDPB (2019). *1 Year GDPR - Taking Stock.* Retrieved on July 15, 2021 from https://edpb.europa.eu/news/news/2019/1-year-gdpr-taking-stock_en

GDPR. (2016). The General Data Protection Regulation (EU) 2016/679 of the European parliament and of the council of 27 April 2016 on the protection of natural persons with regard to the processing of personal data and on the free movement of such data, and repealing directive 95/46. *Official Journal of the European Union, 59*(1–88), 294.

Gunter, C. A., Liebovitz, D., & Malin, B. (2011). Experience-based access management: A life-cycle framework for identity and access management systems. *IEEE Security & privacy, 9*(5), 48.

Moerel, E.M.L. (2019). *CNIL's Decision Fining Google Violates One-Stop-Shop.* Available at SSRN: https://ssrn.com/abstract=3337478 or doi:10.2139/ssrn.3337478.

Monteiro, A. (2019). *First GDPR Fine in Portugal Issued Against Hospital for Three Violations.* Retrieved on July 15, 2021 from https://iapp.org/news/a/first-gdpr-fine-in-portugal-issued-against-hospital-for-three-violations/

UNDER-STANDING USER CYBERSECURITY COMPLIANCE BEHAVIOUR

Chapter 5

Cybersecurity Policy Compliance Assessment: Findings from Government Agencies in the Global South

5.1 Introduction

Governments in the Latin America and the Caribbean (LAC) region recognize the importance of information and communications technologies (ICTs) as powerful tools for sustainable socio-economic development. For instance, to realize a prosperous economy, in its most recent National Development Plan – Vision 2030 Jamaica, the government of Jamaica (GoJ) identifies a technology-enabled society as one of its key national outcomes (Planning Institute of Jamaica, 2009). Similarly, in its latest National Strategic Plan 2005–2025 the government of Barbados (GoB) highlights the importance of a state-of-the-art ICT infrastructure in realizing one of its key vision of enhancing the country's prosperity and competitiveness (Research and Planning Institute, 2005). Likewise, combining smart and resilient technology are emphasized as key enablers in Trinidad and Tobago's Vision 2030 plan, to achieve one of its key themes, improving productivity through quality infrastructure and transportation (Ministry of Planning and Development, 2017).

The reality is, however, that with the increased adoption and use of ICTs in these countries is also the increased potential of information and cybersecurity (CS)

DOI: 10.1201/9781003028710-7

threats and incidents. Indeed, recent statistics and trends reveal that government agencies and organizations in the LAC region are not immune to information and CS challenges. According to the Inter-American Development Bank (IDB) and the Organisation of American States (OAS), cyberattacks in the LAC region are increasing, especially targeting financial institutions (IDB & OAS, 2020). For instance, the 2018 Financial Stability Report, published by the Bank of Jamaica, reveals that between January and September 2018, there were 62 counts of Internet banking fraud totalling J$38.2 million in losses and that on average, Jamaican banks experience two cyberattacks per week (Wilson-Harris, 2019). Additional reports reveal that the Jamaica National Group (a large financial institution in Jamaica) reports a data security breach as a result of a cyberattack on their information systems (ISs) through ransomware, which resulted in data relating to members and customers being stolen, and disruptions in normal operations for weeks in areas such as ATM and debit cards services, online baking, online fund management and online remittance (The Gleaner, 2020). Also, a major CS ransomware attack, targeting ANSA McAl in Barbados and Trinidad and Tobago, resulted in a shutdown of Tatil and Tatil Life's information technology (IT) systems (Newsday, 2020). Another incident is the breach of the Jam-COVID web portal, which exposed local and international travelers' personal and travel data; the system was subsequently taken offline for a period (Gleaner, 2021a, 2021b).

The threat of CS incidents has prompted entities (private, public and government agencies alike) to actively use security technologies to protect IT assets; however, information security (InfoSec) and CS cannot be achieved through technological tools alone (Herath & Rao, 2009b; Stanton, Stam, Mastrangelo, & Jolton, 2005). Scholars emphasize that InfoSec and CS technological solutions should be complimented with employees' good security behaviour (Furnell & Clarke, 2012). Moreover, Donalds and Barclay (2021) identify a holistic set of factors spread across several strategic areas of organisational, risk mitigation, people and technical, that organisations should consider when seeking to improve employees' compliance with information security policies (ISPs) or CSPs. However, humans are cited as the 'weakest link' in the security chain as they often fail to comply with security best practices (Warkentin & Willison, 2009; Yeniman, Ebru Akalp, Aytac, & Bayram, 2011). In fact, a recent industry report reveals that insider, i.e. employee, threats are increasing (up some 31% in 2019 over 2018), with most being committed by negligent or careless employees (Ponemon Institute, 2020). Consequently, entities have established CSPs and procedures to mitigate intended and unintended behaviour of employees that could weaken or render technological-based solutions useless.

In general, a CSP defines rules and guidelines, roles and responsibilities for how employees, consultants, partners, etc. access online applications and Internet resources, send data over network and otherwise practice responsible security so as to protect the entity's information technology assets. However, if employees do not comply with CSPs, the entities' information assets may not be secured. There is empirical evidence that ISPs (which also outline good security practices for employees' to follow) positively influence users' computer abuse behaviour (e.g. Straub, 1990). While establishing CSPs may be a reasonable starting point for protecting organizational information assets, it is not sufficient to ensure employees' compliance with CSPs. In fact, there are reports in the extant literature that employees do not always comply with these policies; they often ignore them or circumvent the rules/guidelines outlined in the ISPs (Ifinedo, 2012; Lowry & Moody, 2015). Therefore, an understanding of what factors influence employees' compliance with their entities' CSPs is essential for helping CS managers in the LAC region diagnose deficiencies in their CS management strategies and efforts and in providing them with information to improve compliance with CSPs.

While there have been some recent works investigating factors motivating employees' security policy compliance intention behaviour (e.g. Bulgurcu, Cavusoglu, & Benbasat, 2010; Herath & Rao, 2009b; Hu, Dinev, Hart, & Cooke, 2012; Johnston, Warkentin, & Siponen, 2015; Koohang & Anderson, 2020; Sommestad, Karlzén, & Hallberg, 2019), there is a dearth of studies investigating employees self-report of actual compliance behaviour as the dependent variable (see Li et al., 2019). Chan et al. (2005) is one of the few studies that have investigated employee current behaviour and found that employees' perceptions of the information security climate positively impact security policy compliance behaviour. Khan and AlShare (2019) found that penalty, security culture and top management support (TMSP) influence employees' ISP compliance behaviour. D'Arcy and Lowry (2019) found that attitude, moral beliefs and self-efficacy influence employees' ISP compliance behaviour. As a result of these few investigations, little is known about employees' actual security compliance behaviour generally as well as employees' actual compliance behaviour in the CS context. This chapter addresses these voids in the literature by examining employees' actual compliance behaviour in the CS context.

The security literature emphasizes the need for managers to focus on InfoSec awareness (ISA), ISP awareness (ISPA) and training initiatives (see Bauer & Bernroider, 2017; Bulgurcu et al., 2010; D'Arcy, Hovav, & Galletta, 2009; Donalds & Osei-Bryson, 2020; Herath & Rao, 2009b; Puhakainen & Siponen, 2010) in order to improve employees compliance behaviour. However, there is a paucity of empirical studies that investigates the impact of ISA and ISPA on employees' actual compliance behaviour. The hypothesis that ISA and ISPA influences employees compliance intention behaviour, directly or indirectly, is empirically supported in prior research (Bulgurcu et al., 2010; Chen, Chen, & Wu, 2018; Koohang & Anderson, 2020). However, it is not yet known whether awareness of CS threats and consequences (CSAW) and awareness of the guidelines prescribed in the organization's CSP (CSPA) directly influence employees' actual compliance behaviour in the CS context. Further, cybersecurity awareness (CSAW) is cited as a key strategic objective in Jamaica's current National Cybersecurity Strategy (Government of Jamaica, 2015). In this strategy, it is posited that CS awareness and CS training (CSTR) for employees are critical factors for the successful realization of any security programme generally and Jamaica's CS plan specifically. Thus, the results of this study would be of particular interest to CS managers in Jamaica's public agencies and other similar developing countries in the LAC region and elsewhere.

Training is another approach that has been used to address the concern of IS security compliance and is also conceptualized as influencing awareness. For instance, Siponen (2000, p. 5) states that 'awareness involves education and training'; education answers the 'why' while training corresponds to the 'how', and should increase skills and competence. Notwithstanding the fact that training is touted as one of the most commonly suggested approaches to address IS security compliance (Puhakainen & Siponen, 2010), the relationship between training and IS security compliance is rarely investigated empirically. Like security awareness, security training too has received little or no attention in the CS context.

In the IS and security literatures, TMSP has emerged as a key construct. For instance, TMS is identified as (1) a critical success factor for IS implementation success and use (Sabherwal, Jeyaraj, & Chowa, 2006); (2) influencing employee behaviour and outcome (Hu et al., 2012; Liang, Saraf, Hu, & Xue, 2007); (3) a significant predictor of organization's security culture and level of policy enforcement (Knapp, Marshall, Rainer, & Ford, 2006); (4) positively related to IS security preventive efforts (Kankanhalli, Teo, Tan, & Wei, 2003); (5) significantly affecting employees belief with respect to ISPs and procedures (Hu et al., 2012); and (6) negatively associated with the likelihood of information security breaches (Kwon, Ulmer, & Wang, 2013). However, to the best of the researcher's knowledge, TMSP has not yet been investigated in the CS context and the influence of TMSP on employee CSP compliance behaviour is yet to be empirically explored.

Given the critical role of TMSP in the IS and security literatures and the influence of awareness and training on IS security behaviour, this study proposes an integrative model of CSP compliance. This model is valuable for advancing our understanding of and for devising more effective strategies to improve CS compliance in organizations in the LAC region and other developing countries in the Global South (GS). In this model, CSP compliance is employees' perceptual measures of their actions towards protecting the information assets of the entity from potential CS attacks.

This chapter seeks also to address the gaps in the literature by proposing a single integrative model to better understand employee CSP compliance behaviour with consideration towards the organizational context and behavioural interventions aimed at mitigating CSP breaches. Further, this study looks at actual compliance behaviour instead of compliance intention, which has been the focus of an emerging stream of research on individual security behaviour. Four research questions not yet investigated in the CS literature (or the InfoSec literature, for that matter) are addressed in this chapter:

    i. *What influence does CSAW have on employees' actual compliance with CSPs?*
   ii. *What influence does cybersecurity policy awareness (CSPA) have on employees' actual compliance with CSPs?*

iii. *What influence does TMSP have on employees' actual compliance with CSPs?*

iv. *What influence does CSTR have on CSAW, CSPA and employees' actual compliance with CSPs?*

Data collected via a survey of 137 employees from 10 key government agencies in one LAC country – Jamaica – are used to interrogate the research questions. The remainder of this chapter is organized as follows. The next section discusses the relevant literature followed by the conceptual foundation of the research. In the subsequent section, the research model is discussed and hypotheses to be tested are developed. The subsequent sections discuss the research design and methodology, a description of the data analysis and presentation of the research results. Finally, the findings and implications for the research are discussed.

5.2 Relevant Literature

A review of the InfoSec literature reveals that research on CS compliance has remained largely unexplored, despite the many reports of CS incidents and the operational impacts and financial costs associated with such incidents. Although it is recognized by academics and practitioners alike that employees are considered the weakest link in InfoSec and by extension CS, they are also considered to be great assets to reduce potential security risks and threats (Boss, Kirsch, Angermeier, Shingler, & Boss, 2009). However, little or no attention has been devoted to investigating factors that influence CSP compliance. That is, it is not well understood what factors influence employees' actual adherence to the CSP and procedures in organizations. Prior studies have instead focused on, albeit important security topics, such as the design, development, and alignment of the ISP (Doherty & Fulford, 2006; Siponen & Iivari, 2006); the role of organizational commitment on various security-related behaviours (Stanton, Stam, Guzman, & Caldera, 2003); the role of security climate on security policy compliance (Chan et al., 2005); IS security effectiveness (Kankanhalli et al., 2003); the influence of TMSP on an organization's security culture and level of security policy enforcement (Knapp et al., 2006); and end-user security-related behaviours (Stanton et al., 2005).

To address the issue of non-compliance with ISPs, the use of sanctions, grounded in deterrence theory (DT) (Gibbs, 1975), has been widely investigated by IS scholars. However, the results from this stream of research are mixed. For instance, Kankanhalli et al. (2003) found that greater deterrent efforts led to enhanced IS security effectiveness. D'Arcy et al. (2009) found that while severity of sanctions was significant, certainty of sanctions has no influence on IS misuse intentions. Foth (2016) found that punishment severity has no statistical significance with data protection compliance regulation yet, detection certainty was statistically significant. Khan and AlShare (2019) found that severity of penalty, celerity of penalty, TMSP and security culture are all factors that influence non-violators of their ISP. Siponen,

Pahnila, and Mahmood (2010) found that deterrents significantly influence employees' compliance with IS security policies. While Herath and Rao (2009a) and Herath and Rao (2009b) found that punishment severity has a significant impact on policy compliance intention, it has a negative effect and detection certainty has a positive and significant effect. In contrast with other DT-grounded empirical studies on compliance with IS security policies, Siponen and Vance (2010) found that formal and informal sanctions did not influence intention to violate IS security policy. Likewise, Moody, Siponen, and Pahnila (2018) found that punishments have no influence on ISP compliance intention.

Researchers and practitioners also emphasize the influence of employees' threat appraisal and coping appraisal, constituents of protection motivation theory (PMT) (Rogers, 1975), on employees' InfoSec compliance behaviour and intentions. In general, PMT explains fear appeals and how individuals cope with them. Specifically, PMT suggests that the individual's assessment of the level of security threat (threat appraisal) and his/her capability to comply with the ISP and if such compliance is effective in reducing the security threat (coping appraisal), influence compliance behaviour. Empirical results of PMT-grounded research are divergent and inconsistent. For instance, while Ifinedo (2012) found that response cost is statistically nonsignificant, perceived threat vulnerability, response efficacy and perceived threat severity are statistically significant, perceived threat severity has a negative influence. Chen and Zahedi (2016) found that perceived threat, response efficacy and self-efficacy are statistically significant with IS protective action; however, self-efficacy has a negative impact. Sommestad et al. (2019) found no support for threat severity and response cost on ISP compliance. Vance, Siponen, and Pahnila (2012) report that threat vulnerability does not influence ISP compliance; however, threat severity, response efficacy and self-efficacy are positive and significant, yet, response cost and rewards are negative and significant. However, Johnston and Warkentin (2010) found statistically significant impact of self-efficacy and response efficacy on ISP compliance.

While the use of sanctions and fear appeals are widely utilized approaches to reduce computer abuse/misuse and improve employee compliance with IS security policies, 'inconsistencies in the reported findings have yielded certain unresolved conflicts' (Cram, D'Arcy, & Proudfoot, 2019, p. 526). Moreover, scholars warn that 'one size does not fit all' for achieving employee ISP compliance (Balozian, Leidner, & Warkentin, 2017). Others suggest that behavioural interventions are also useful in addressing the IS security problem. One of the tasks of security managers is to promote positive changes in employees' security behaviour. Interventions to bring about these changes should be directed at employees' skills and knowledge pertinent to the security context. Two recommended behavioural interventions to address security breaches are as follows: improving IS security and policy awareness and/or CSAW (Donalds, & Barclay, 2021; D'Arcy et al., 2009; Government of Jamaica, 2015; Hu et al., 2012; Mitnick, 2002; Siponen, 2000) and increasing security training (Ma, Schmidt, & Pearson, 2009; Puhakainen & Siponen, 2010; Siponen, 2000;

Thomson & von Solms, 1998). The aim therefore of CSAW, CSPA and cybersecurity training (CSTR) is to persuade employees and activate their thinking processes in such a way that they internalize why it is important to comply with the CSP and enable them to take necessary actions.

In this chapter, CSAW refers to the ongoing efforts of the organization to develop employees' understanding of the potential CS threats and risks they likely face and appropriate actions to take to protect the organization's information assets. Awareness mechanisms can include posters, newsletters, security briefings, security videos, security scenarios and notices. Beyond CSAW, organizations have specific expectations of their employees with regard to the requirements of their ISPs. ISPA refers to an 'employee's knowledge and understanding of the requirements prescribed in the organization's ISP and the aims of those requirements' (Bulgurcu et al., 2010, p. 532). Therefore, CSPA refers to an employee's knowledge and understanding of his or her roles and responsibilities as prescribed in the CSP as well as the requirements of responsible security practice. The expectation is that both general CSAW and CSPA are expected to minimize security-related carelessness and maximize the effectiveness of security techniques and procedures (Hwang, Wakefield, Kim, & Kim, 2021).

Although the importance and benefits of general security awareness have long been espoused (Siponen, 2000; Straub & Welke, 1998), and more recently ISPA (Bulgurcu et al., 2010; Chen et al., 2018), there is burgeoning empirical evidence supporting these claims. Based on a review of ISA content published between 2009 and 2020, development trend analysis reveals that security education, training, and awareness (SETA) programmes are one of the most effective factors for enhancing individual employee's ISA in both the private and the public sectors (Khando, Gao, Islam, & Salman, 2021). D'Arcy et al. (2009) provide empirical evidence that user awareness of security policies, i.e. SETA programmes, can help improve security adherence. Stanton (2005) reports that a greater degree of awareness is positively associated with changing passwords more frequently and choosing better passwords, providing some support for the beneficial effects of awareness on getting employees to improve security behaviour. Consistent with findings in other studies, Bulgurcu et al. (2010) provide empirical evidence that IS awareness exerts a significant influence on an employee's attitude towards compliance, albeit indirectly. Hwang et al. (2021) found that ISA has a strong and direct statistically significant impact on employees' security compliance intention. X. Chen et al. (2018) found that ISPA and awareness of security threats impact employees' ISP compliance behaviour. Choi et al. (2013) suggest that CS counter measures (i) awareness – users' awareness of computer monitoring; (ii) users' awareness of security training programmes; and (iii) users' awareness of security policies; all influence computer misuse intention. They report that users' awareness of computer monitoring influences computer misuse intention as well as CS computing skills and that users' awareness of security policies significantly contributes to CS action skills. Donalds and Osei-Bryson (2020) found support for the impact of general CSAW on individual's CS compliance behaviour. Although there is some evidence that the direct and indirect links between security awareness (general and ISP) and individual compliance behaviour are significant, there remain gaps in the literature. For instance, actual ISP compliance and actual CSP compliance (or intention) are rarely investigated; Donalds and Osei-Bryson (2020) investigate the compliance behaviour of individuals generally, not employees specifically, and they did not investigate the influence of CSPA on individual's actual CS compliance behaviour, only general CSAW. Consequently, we examine further the role of general CS security awareness and CSPA in shaping employees' actual compliance behaviour in the CS context.

Despite the importance of security training, there is a paucity of empirical studies that analyse the impact of security training on IS security generally. Puhakainen (2006) proposed a design theory for improving security training; Thomson and von Solms (1998) and Ma et al. (2009) highlight the importance of security training; and Cox et al. (2001) suggest training via Web-based tutorial for increasing security compliance in academic environments. In an empirical vein, Goodhue et al. (1991) provide empirical evidence that training improves employees' compliance with security policies. Similarly, Stanton (2005) found that training enforcement of an acceptable use policy had beneficial effects on getting end-users to change their passwords more frequently and compose stronger passwords. D'Arcy et al. (2009) also found support that InfoSec training programmes help reduce users' misuse intention. The influence of CSTR on employees' actual CSP compliance remains unexplored, until now.

According to Boss et al. (2009), one of the noted causes of IS security failures is the lack of computer security training to develop users' security awareness. Puhakainen and Sipone (2010). found that properly designed training programmes improved employee awareness about the possible consequences of noncompliance towards established information security policies, resulting in an increased level of compliance. Ma et al. (2009) also assert that information security training is possibly one of the most important components of an effective information security programme. These reports suggest that security training influences security awareness. However, a search of the InfoSec literature reveals that the influence of security training on security and policy awareness has not yet been investigated.

TMSP is identified as one of the most critical elements in an effective IS security programme (Ma et al., 2009). For instance, by asserting that 'the realization that information security is a corporate governance responsibility (the buck stops right at the top)' as Sin number 1 of 10 deadly sins of information security management, von Solms et al. (2004, p. 372) support the view that TMSP is indeed critical to IS security. However, only a few studies investigate the effect of top management's role in the information security context. The results of a survey of IS managers reveal that organizations with stronger TMSP are engaged in more preventative security efforts than organizations with weaker TMSP (Kankanhalli et al., 2003). Puhakainen and Siponen (2010) found that one of the primary reasons why employees who ignore the policies that require encryption of emails is because of the perceived passiveness of the CEO in promoting and following the established information security policies. Using survey data Hu et al. (2012) report that top management participation in information security initiatives has a significant impact on employee security compliance intention behaviour.

While there are some empirical studies that test the effects of security awareness, IS security policy awareness and TMSP on security compliance behaviour in the InfoSec context, these antecedents are not examined in the CS context. Furthermore, the influence of training on employees' actual compliance behaviour generally or in the CS context has not been previously investigated. Moreover, employees' actual security compliance behaviour is rarely investigated. In this chapter, we undertake an investigation that integrates TMSP, CSAW, CSPA, CSTR and employees' actual CSP compliance behaviour in a single model. This model is then empirically validated in an attempt to advance our understanding of and to indicate the relevance of the factors proposed in the model for CSP compliance in a developing country in the LAC region and that may have relevance for other GS jurisdictions.

5.3 Theoretical Framework

Early InfoSec studies espouse the importance of technical measures for protecting organizations' information assets (e.g. Baskerville, 1993). While acknowledging technical measures' importance, scholars argue that InfoSec can be more effectively managed if InfoSec emphasis goes beyond technical means (see Donalds, & Barclay, 2021; Herath & Rao, 2009a; Herath & Rao, 2009b; Safa, Von Solms, & Furnell, 2016; Straub & Welke, 1998) to include ethical and human factors (Trompeter & Eloff, 2001). Given the recurring findings that employees account for a large percentage of security breaches/incidents (see Ponemon Institute, 2020) and that cyberattacks and data breaches can be potentially costly, invariably leading to market disruptions such as decreased sales revenue, higher expenses, decreased dividends, reduction in market value, decreased profit (Andoh-Baidoo & Osei-Bryson, 2007), negative impact on operational activities and reputational damage, it is only reasonable that IS security scholars focus on the human perspective of InfoSec – specifically, employee behaviour towards complying with security best practices (D'Arcy & Lowry, 2019), i.e. CSPs. Therefore, we are interested in investigating factors that motivate employees to adhere to the guidelines prescribed in their organizations' CSPs.

In this chapter, we attempt to understand some antecedents of employees' compliance with their CSPs by proposing and evaluating a model of factors that influence an employee's actual CSP compliance behaviour. Drawing on the InfoSec literatures, we adopt four main constructs – cybersecurity security awareness (CSAW), CSPA, TMSP and CSTR – as antecedents of an employee's actual CSP compliance.

The behaviour of interest in this chapter is employees' actual CS compliance behaviour with their organizational CSPs and procedures. Some widely used behavioural theories such as PMT (Gibbs, 1975) and DT (Rogers, 1975) have been used in the InfoSec context to understand why individuals behave the way they do or understand what drives their behaviours. These theories provide the basis for an examination of the relationships between deterrents or sanctions, fear appeals and behaviour or behavioural intention. However, the results from these research streams are inconsistent, divergent and mixed. Based on these results, it is reasonable to suggest that scholars and practitioners look at other factors that may influence and affect employees' course of action, i.e. their compliance with the organizational CSP. In this chapter, we propose that different behavioural interventions, other than sanctions and fear appeal, may influence employees' CSP compliance behaviour. Additionally, the extant IS literature reports that employee behaviour is also influenced by contextual factors such as national/organizational culture (Chen & Zahedi, 2016; Hovav & D'Arcy, 2012) and organizational security climate (Goo, Yim, & Kim, 2014) and TMSP (Hu et al., 2012; Puhakainen & Siponen, 2010). However, the linkages between behavioural interventions (such as CSAW, CSPA and CSTR) and the organizational context (such as TMSP) on employees' CSP compliance behaviour have not been previously explored in a single integrated model. Thus, the effects of CSAW, CSPA, CSTR and TMSP in the CS context must be accounted for to fully understand employees' actual CSP behaviour and to develop effective CSP management practices. Therefore, the fundamental argument in this chapter is that CSAW, CSP awareness and CSTR can influence employees' CSP compliance behaviour and that CSTR too can influence CSAW and CSP awareness; and, the support provided by top management can affect employees' behaviour towards CSP compliance.

5.4 Research Model and Hypotheses

Based on the literatures of security awareness, TMSP and security training, we propose a research model that explains employees' actual CSP compliance behaviour, as shown in Figure 5.1.

5.4.1 General Cybersecurity Awareness

According to researchers, most employees lack awareness of information security threats and issues (Lim, Ahmad, Chang, & Maynard, 2010). Moreover, Murray (1991) notes that one of the biggest security problems is as a result of incompetence of employees who do not understand the dangers inherent in their actions. Researchers suggest increasing employees security awareness to overcome this problem (D'Arcy et al., 2009; Donalds & Osei-Bryson, 2020; Hadland, 1998; Herath & Rao, 2009b; Murray, 1991; Puhakainen & Siponen, 2010; Siponen, Mahmood, & Pahnila, 2014). According to Hansche (2001), the goal of a security awareness programme is to heighten the importance of IS security and the possible negative effects of a security breach or failure. For instance, employees can be made aware of the critical nature of data security and their responsibility to respect and protect the privacy

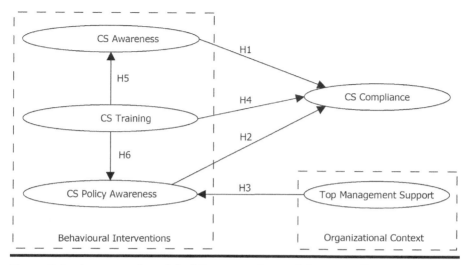

Figure 5.1   A proposed model of the antecedents of CSP compliance

of information, its integrity and confidentiality. Similarly, employees can be made aware of CS incident reporting procedure in the event a computer becomes infected by a virus or if they receive an illegitimate warning message or alert. Further, Hwang et al. (2021) suggest reduced security-related carelessness and improved effectiveness of security techniques and procedures as possible outcomes of security awareness initiatives. Therefore, the argument made by Hansche (2001) that employees who are aware of IS security issues are the single most important asset for detecting and preventing IS security incidents, is a reasonable one. Likewise, in this study we argue that employees' CSAW is crucial for detecting and preventing potential CS threats and for reporting actual CS incidents.

The argument has been made that security awareness has the potential to influence behavioural outcomes. For instance, Siponen (2000) suggests that providing security awareness is the most important factor in persuading employees to change their compliance actions. Donalds and Barclay (2021) also suggest that highlighting awareness should improve employees' security actions. Empirical evidence supports this claim as Hwang et al. (2021) found that employees' ISA has a statistically significant relationship with their security compliance intention behaviour. Stanton (2005) reports statistically significant correlations between password-related behaviours and awareness. Donalds and Osei-Bryson (2020) found statistically significant support for the impact of general CSAW on individual's CS compliance and password compliance behaviours. We therefore argue that engaging employees in CSAW should influence employees to comply with CSPs and procedures. Hence, we expect that:

H1: CSAW will positively influence CSP compliance.

5.4.2 Cybersecurity Policy Awareness

Recall, we described a CSP earlier as a resource that defines rules and guidelines, roles and responsibilities for how employees, consultants, partners, etc., access online applications and Internet resources, send data over network and otherwise practice responsible security so as to protect the entity's information technologies. A CSP can therefore be considered a crucial factor in security management practices. In the extant InfoSec literature, researchers report that ISP provision (understandable and easily accessible policies) and the promotion of the ISP are effective ways to increase employees' awareness of the ISP (Haeussinger & Kranz, 2013). According to Herath and Rao (2009a), an ISP should be made easily accessible to the employees and written in a clear understandable language since it should influence their security compliance intention or behaviour. In other words, clear and precisely presented security policies raise security knowledge and skill levels for favourable compliance behaviour (Puhakainen & Siponen, 2010). We contend, so too should a CSP. An understandable, easily accessible CSP, and the promotion of said policy should elevate employees' contextual awareness and CSP knowledge, and eventually influence employees' CSP compliance behaviour. We therefore argue that promoting the CSP, or CSPA, can influence employees' compliance behaviour by reminding them of the consequences for non-compliance, which in turn should affect their actual compliance behaviour. Thus, we hypothesize:

H2: CSP awareness will positively influence CSP compliance.

5.4.3 Top Management Support

The role of top management in the CS context is to set organizational CS goals, such as the CSPs and procedures, provide resources for their successful implementation and resolve CS issues among different stakeholders. TMSP is demonstrated via top management's actions such as the championing of initiatives, providing financial and political resources, making decisions congruent with security policies and procedures, holding lower-level managers accountable for non-compliance and communicating the seriousness and risks of non-compliance and securing legitimacy (Gomes, de Weerd-Nederhof, Pearson, & Fisscher, 2001; Hu et al., 2012). TMSP demonstrates the commitment of the organization towards an initiative. For instance, Hu et al. (2012) argue that top management's involvement in security initiatives can send a strong signal to other managers and employees about the legitimacy of the initiatives. Puhakainen and Siponen (2010) provide evidence that TMSP of established ISP affects employees' InfoSec behaviour and results in higher levels of compliance. Hwang et al. (2021) found strong and statistically significant support that top management participation strengthens the links between organizational security efforts and security awareness. In fact, the shared understanding of

InfoSec amongst employees is found to be influenced by the way they perceive the role of management and the persuasiveness of communications (Hadasch, Mueller, & Maedche, 2012).

Similar in description to a CSP, an ISP is defined as 'a set of formalised procedures, guidelines, roles and responsibilities to which employees are required to adhere to safeguard and use properly the information and technology resources of their organisations' (Lowry & Moody, 2015, p. 434). However, it has been reported that employees often do not regard ISPs as hard and fast rules to follow, instead employees often ignore or circumvent them (Lowry & Moody, 2015). According to Maeyer (2007), if managers are not engaged with the ISA programme then employees are not likely to change their ISA behaviours. There is some empirical evidence that supports the claim that management's participation in the development and implementation of security awareness programmes can motivate employees and improve their levels of security awareness (Hu et al., 2012; Hwang et al., 2021). Therefore, we argue that top management's active support of and involvement in the development and implementation of CSPA programmes and in the promoting of CSP initiatives that highlight the rules, roles and responsibilities to which employees are required to adhere, can improve employees' level of CSPA. Thus, we expect that:

H3: TMSP will positively influence CSPA.

5.4.4 Cybersecurity Training

The security literature places strong emphasis on training for enabling security compliance behaviour (Puhakainen & Siponen, 2010; Siponen, 2000; Thomson & von Solms, 1998). For instance, Mitnick and Simon (2002) argue for an ongoing IS security training programme as a means to resist social engineering. Further, Mitnick and Simon (2002) argue that the goal of the training programme is to influence employees to change their behaviours by motivating them to protect the IS asset of the company. This argument is consistent with findings of others who report security training to significantly improve ISP compliance level (Puhakainen & Siponen, 2010), reduce the number of students falling victims to phising scams (Dodge, Carver, & Ferguson, 2007) and decrease users' weak password usage and improve employees tendencies to comply with the organization's ISPs (Eminagaoglu, Ucar, & Eren, 2009). New hires should be provided CSTR and at regular intervals thereafter to improve their abilities to perform the necessary CS-related actions. For instance, employees may require training to select a strong password, i.e. passwords should be cryptic so they cannot be easily guessed but should be easily remembered and need not be written down. These abilities have been found to significantly affect compliance intention (Bulgurcu et al., 2010; Herath & Rao, 2009b). Therefore, it is likely that training results in improved abilities while the absence of training can represent a barrier to undertaking an action, resulting in reduced adherence of CSP compliance. Hence, we expect that:

H4: CSTR will positively influence CS compliance.

Prior works have highlighted that the lack of employees' ISA by way of ISPs and procedures are major causes of the mishandling of sensitive information (e.g. Abraham, 2011; Siponen, 2000). To address this issue, scholars propose, as a remedy, security training. It is advocated that security training should develop employees' security skills and competencies (Tsohou, Karyda, & Kokolakis, 2015) required to be aware of potential security risks and threats and help employees understand the rules and regulations prescribed in the ISP (D'Arcy et al., 2009). Further, security training serves to remind employees of the organizational views of information security and emphasize its importance (Herath & Rao, 2009b). Security training may include security workshops, courses, seminars, web-based tutorials and drills to educate employees and guide them towards security compliance. According to Hwang et al. (2021) disseminating security information during training begins the process in which employees' attention is captured and awareness increases. This is consistent with others' views that training can increase security awareness of existing and good IS security practices, increase understanding of and hence, participation and compliance (Hadland, 1998; Ma et al., 2009). There is some empirical evidence that employees' security awareness is elevated by SETA programmes (Ahlan, Lubis, & Lubis, 2015; Haeussinger & Kranz, 2013; Hwang et al., 2021). Therefore, we argue that CSTR will contribute substantially to developing employees' CS mindfulness and CSAW knowledge as well as help them understand and assimilate the rules outlined in the CSP and equip them with the skills and competencies geared towards compliance actions. Therefore, we hypothesize:

H5: CSTR will positively influence CSAW.
H6: CSTR will positively influence CSPA.

5.5 Research Method and Data

5.5.1 Construct Operationalization

The survey instrument was developed based on the research model shown in Figure 5.1. Measurement items for each construct are based on a 7-point Likert-like scale. We mostly adapted previously validated items from the extant literature to maximize validity and reliability of the measurement tool (Stone, 1978) (see Appendix A for the measurement items). All constructs in the model are operationalized as reflective constructs.

5.5.2 Data Collection

Data from a pilot study using employees in three GoJ agencies were used to refine the survey instrument. We made minor changes to items that showed low loading in the initial analysis. The final version of the survey was administered to 10 GoJ agencies. The researcher requested a manager from each agency to randomly distribute 40 questionnaires to employees at varying levels in the agency. Of the 400 questionnaires distributed, 166 were returned but only 137 were usable, yielding a response rate of 37%. Descriptive statistics showing the demographic profiles of the respondents are shown in Table 5.1.

5.5.3 Data Analyses and Results

The research model was analysed using the partial least-squares (PLS) structural equation modelling (SEM) analytic technique. PLS-SEM employs a component-based approach for estimation purposes (Lohmoller, 1989) and is essentially an iterative estimation procedure that integrates principal component analysis with multiple regression (Fornell & Cha, 1994; Wold, 1966). The PLS-SEM approach is appropriate for this study as it is well suited for assessing complex predictive models (Henseler, Ringle, & Sinkovics, 2009). In evaluating the research model PLS concurrently tests the psychometric properties of all variables used in the model and assesses the magnitude of the relationships and effects between the variables in the model. SmartPLS 3.3 (Ringle, Wende, & Becker, 2015) is the statistical tool used to analyse the measurement model as well as the path model for hypothesis testing.

5.5.4 Assessment of the Overall Fit of the Saturated Model

In their recent guidelines on reporting PLS results, Benitez, Henseler, Castillo, and Schuberth (2020) suggest that the overall fit of the saturated model be evaluated. The saturated model is one in which all concepts are allowed to freely correlate, whereas, the concept's operationalization is exactly as specified by the analyst (Benitez et al., 2020). These measurements are useful since they allow for the identification of possible model misfit which could be attributable to misspecifications in the common factor and/or measurement models (Benitez et al., 2020). A standardized root-mean-square residual (SRMR) measuring less than 0.08 indicates good model fit. Other tests of overall model fit are the squared Euclidean distance (d_{ULS}) and the geodesic discrepancy (d_G). Researchers recommend that all discrepancy values should be

Table 5.1 Respondent Demographics

Category	Subcategory	Count	Percentage (%)	Category	Subcategory	Count	Percentage (%)
Gender:				Job Level:			
	Male	68	50		Line Staff	81	59
	Female	69	50		Supervisor	25	18
Age:					Manager	26	19
	<30	49	36		GM/HOD	5	4
	30–49	78	57	Job Type:			
	>=50	10	7		Operational	57	42
Education:					Administrative	25	18
	High School	14	10		IT	55	40
	Diploma	22	16	Organization Tenure:			
	Undergraduate	76	55		<5 years	49	36
	Graduate	25	18		5–15 years	68	50
					>15 years	20	15

Table 5.2   Overall Model Fit Discrepancy Values of the Saturated Model

Discrepancy	Overall model fit evaluation			
	Value	HI_{95}	HI_{99}	Conclusion
SRMR	0.050	0.049	0.056	Supported
d_{ULS}	0.515	0.498	0.659	Supported
d_G	0.721	0.829	0.985	Supported

below the 95% quantile of the reference distribution (HI_{95}) (Benitez et al., 2020; Henseler, Hubona, & Ray, 2016) or below the 99% quantile (HI_{99}) before rejecting the model (Benitez et al., 2020). As displayed in Table 5.2, the SRMR and the d_{ULS} discrepancy values are below the 99% quantile (HI_{99}) of its corresponding distribution while the d_G discrepancy value is below the 95% quantile (HI_{95}) of its corresponding distribution. Therefore, the overall fit measures suggest the model has a 'good fit'.

5.5.5 Assessment of the Measurement Model

Reliability and validity tests are conducted to assess the outer model. All loadings are well above the threshold value of 0.7 and are significant at the 0.01 level, based on their *t*-values. An indicator loading above the 0.7 threshold indicates that the construct explains more than 50% of the indicator's variance (Hair, Hult, Ringle, & Sarstedt, 2014). Indicator reliability ranged from 0.709 to 0.949, greater than the recommended cut-off of 0.5 (Hair et al., 2014). The composite reliability values ranged from 0.914 to 0.973, above the recommended cut-off of 0.7 (Gefen, Straub, & Boudreau, 2000), demonstrating that the constructs have high levels of internal consistency reliability. Table 5.3 shows some quality indicators of the outer model.

Convergent validity is assessed using the average variance extracted (AVE)values (Chin, 1998; Fornell & Larcker, 1981). The AVE for each latent construct is well above 0.5 (see Table 5.3), indicating that the latent construct can account for at least 50% of the variance in the items.

Discriminant validity can be assessed using the Fornell–Larcker criterion (i.e. the square root of the AVE) and cross-loadings (Hair et al., 2014). Discriminant validity is achieved when the square root of the AVE for each construct is larger on itself than any number in the same row and column (see Table 5.4). The loadings of items on each construct are higher than all of its cross-loadings with other constructs, also establishing discriminant validity (see Table 5.5). Jointly, these tests suggest good convergent and discriminant validity.

Table 5.3 Measurement Model Indicators

Latent Construct	Item	Loading	t Value	AVE	Composite Reliability	rho_A	Cronbach's α
CS Awareness	CSAW1	0.889	25.104	0.819	0.932	0.894	0.890
	CSAW2	0.887	30.365				
	CSAW3	0.939	59.183				
CS Policy Awareness	CSPA1	0.974	133.564	0.920	0.972	0.957	0.956
	CSPA2	0.972	138.198				
	CSPA3	0.931	44.659				
CS Training	TNG1	0.933	28.726	0.835	0.953	0.958	0.935
	TNG2	0.935	32.291				
	TNG3	0.859	8.326				
	TNG4	0.927	27.981				
Top Management Support	TMS1	0.837	13.309	0.788	0.963	0.957	0.955
	TMS2	0.934	45.696				
	TMS3	0.897	31.032				
	TMS4	0.872	26.329				
	TMS5	0.928	44.887				
	TMS6	0.910	47.629				
	TMS7	0.830	13.382				
CSP Compliance	CSCP1	0.964	93.771	0.924	0.973	0.960	0.959
	CSCP2	0.966	52.529				
	CSCP3	0.954	44.588				

Although the examination of cross-loadings and the Fornell–Larker criterion are acceptable for assessing discriminant validity, according to Henseler, Ringle, and Sarstedt (2015) the heterotrait–monotrait (HTMT) ratio of correlations is a more accurate measure and the HTMT ratio should be below 1.0. Yet, others recommend a more stringent cut-off of 0.9 (Benitez et al., 2020). An examination of Table 5.6 shows that all HTMT ratio of correlations are below the more stringent cut-off of 0.9, which further support that discriminant validity has been established.

Table 5.4   Fornell–Larcker Criterion of Latent Variable Correlations

	CSPA	*CSCP*	*CSAW*	*CSTR*	*TMSP*
CS Policy Awareness (CSPA)	**0.959**				
CS Compliance (CSCP)	0.848	**0.961**			
CS Awareness (CSAW)	0.511	0.533	**0.905**		
CS Training (CSTR)	0.505	0.426	0.353	**0.914**	
Top Management Support (TMSP)	0.642	0.601	0.430	0.567	**0.888**

Note: Values on the *diagonal and bold are the square root of the AVEs.*

5.5.6 *Structural Model Assessment*

Figure 5.2 presents the estimates obtained from the PLS analysis. The results show that 44.1% of the variance in CSPA, 12.4% of the variance in general CSAW and 73.4% of the variance in CSP compliance are explained by the factors in the integrated model.

CS security training was found not to have a statistically significant impact on CSP compliance (β = –0.20); therefore, H4 is not supported. Employees' general CSAW of CS threats and their potential consequences was found to have a statistically significant effect on their CSP compliance behaviour (β = 0.137), supporting H1. Employees' awareness of CSP roles, responsibilities and requirements of the CSP was found to have a significant effect on their CSP compliance behaviour (β = 0.789); thus, H2 is supported. The support from top management is found to have a significant effect on CSPA (β = 0.525), supporting H3. It was found that CSTR concurrently influences employees' general CSAW and CSPA (β = 0.353) and (β = 0.206), respectively; thus, H5 and H6 are supported. A summary of the results is provided in Table 5.7.

Effect size f^2 has been defined as 'the increase in R^2 relative to the proportion of variance of the endogenous latent variable that remains unexplained' (Henseler et al., 2009, p. 304). Cohen (1992) suggests that effect size values of 0.02, 0.15 and 0.35 represent small, medium and large effects, respectively. According to Benitez et al. (2020) it is unlikely that most constructs will have a large effect on the model. As shown in Table 5.7, the f^2 values for the hypothesized relationships in the model range from 0.109 to 0.320 (small–medium) for the statistically significant relationships.

Table 5.5   Cross-loadings with Other Constructs

	CSPA	CSCP	CSAW	CSTR	TMSP
CSAW1	0.420	0.466	**0.889**	0.255	0.375
CSAW2	0.485	0.470	**0.887**	0.375	0.388
CSAW3	0.477	0.509	**0.939**	0.319	0.403
CSCP1	0.827	**0.964**	0.516	0.417	0.588
CSCP2	0.833	**0.966**	0.512	0.417	0.587
CSCP3	0.787	**0.954**	0.507	0.394	0.567
CSPA1	**0.974**	0.774	0.495	0.534	0.645
CSPA2	**0.972**	0.760	0.480	0.526	0.624
CSPA3	**0.931**	0.901	0.493	0.395	0.578
CSTR1	0.421	0.336	0.263	**0.933**	0.483
CSTR2	0.533	0.467	0.413	**0.935**	0.570
CSTR3	0.386	0.320	0.239	**0.859**	0.454
CSTR4	0.476	0.403	0.336	**0.927**	0.543
TMSP1	0.524	0.530	0.336	0.530	**0.837**
TMSP2	0.582	0.519	0.377	0.564	**0.934**
TMSP3	0.585	0.551	0.398	0.449	**0.897**
TMSP4	0.581	0.583	0.410	0.456	**0.872**
TMSP5	0.580	0.550	0.369	0.491	**0.928**
TMSP6	0.620	0.542	0.370	0.518	**0.910**
TMSP7	0.508	0.444	0.379	0.532	**0.830**

Table 5.6   HTMT Ratio of Correlations

	CSPA	CSCP	CSAW	CSTR
CS Policy Awareness (CSPA)	—			
CS Compliance (CSCP)	0.884			
CS Awareness (CSAW)	0.551	0.576		
CS Training (CSTR)	0.527	0.441	0.372	
Top Management Support (TMSP)	0.671	0.626	0.466	0.597

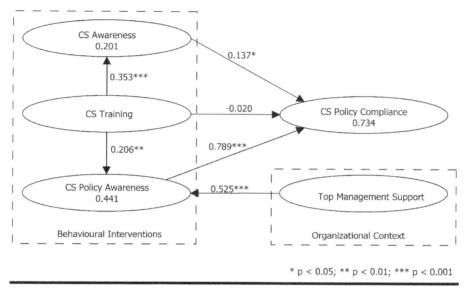

* p < 0.05; ** p < 0.01; *** p < 0.001

Figure 5.2   PLS results of the structural model

Table 5.7   Summary Results of the Structural Model Assessment

Hypothesis		β	*t-value*	*Supported*	*f²*
H1:	**CS awareness →** **CSP compliance**	*0.138*	*2.253*	**Yes**	*0.320*
H2:	**CS policy awareness →** **CSP compliance**	0.789	14.485	**Yes**	0.001
H3:	**Top management support** **→ CS policy awareness**	0.525	5.329	**Yes**	0.076
H4:	CS Training → CSP compliance	−0.020	0.297	No	0.958
H5:	**CS Training → CS** **awareness**	0.353	4.462	**Yes**	0.109
H6:	**CS Training → CS policy** **awareness**	0.206	2.500	**Yes**	0.284

5.6 Discussion, Implications and Future Research

5.6.1 Discussion of the Findings

This chapter identifies several key findings and offers several theoretical and practical implications. Despite the plethora of studies investigating employees' security behaviour, most have examined employees' security compliance intention; this is one of the few works that have focused on employees' actual security compliance behaviour. Relatedly, the extant literature has investigated employees' security compliance behaviour generally but has rarely emphasized the CS context. Another key contribution is that this work integrates CSAW, CSPA, TMSP and CSTR into one model. In the extant InfoSec literature, the antecedents of CSAW, CSPA, TMSP and CSTR were not previously studied together. Another key contribution is that this is the first study that has empirically shown the effects of CSAW, CSPA, TMSP and CSTR on employees' actual compliance behaviour in the CS context.

Our results indicate that employees' understanding or awareness of the CS policy requirements (CSPA) as well as general awareness of CS threats and possible actions to take to mitigate those threats (CSAW) significantly influence their CSP compliance behaviour. Our data suggest that CSPA has a significantly higher magnitude of impact on employees' actual CSP compliance behaviour than general CSAW, highlighting the importance of CSPA. This is consistent with Li et al.'s (2019) findings who report that employees who were aware of their organization's InfoSec policies and procedures were more likely to manage CS tasks than those who were not aware of their organization's CSPs.

Although security training has been emphasized as one of the most important component of an effective security programme, empirical evaluations of the relationship between security behaviour and training are limited. This work is one of few that has empirically evaluated the link between training and employees' security or actual CSP compliance behaviour. However, our results reveal that CSTR did not have a direct effect on employee' actual CS compliance behaviour. This finding is consistent with other literature that states that training has failed to change employees' security behaviour (Abawajy, 2014; Cone, Irvine, Thompson, & Nguyen, 2007). However, according to Ma et al. (2009) security training should consist of initial and refresher classroom and/or online courses, frequent updates, issuing of other relevant security materials such as posters, and a system of rewards and penalties for desirable and undesirable actions. Puhakainen and Siponen (2010) also suggest that security training should be based on information security theoretical underpinnings, since theoretically grounded training is usually more effective than generic training of information security technologies and policies. Puhakainen and Siponen (2010) further suggest that for training to be effective, it should be continuous and integrated into the organization's normal communication effort. Eminagaoglu et al.'s (2009) findings affirm the effectiveness of continual training for effective password usage, password quality and compliance of employees with the password policies of the company. We therefore suggest that CSTR did not directly influence employee's actual CS compliance behaviour because: (1) perhaps the CSTR offered by the GoJ agencies were too generic, i.e. they were rote and did not require employees to think about and apply CS security concepts; and (2) perhaps the CSTR may not have been frequent or continual, given the financial constraints of most GoJ government agencies.

While our results reveal that CSTR did not have a direct impact on employees' actual CSP compliance behaviour, it has indirect influence through general CSAW and CSPA. Since security awareness is highlighted as a key factor in the success of employees' security compliance behaviour and is empirically validated in prior works (e.g. Bulgurcu et al., 2010; Chen et al., 2018; Donalds & Osei-Bryson, 2020), it is reasonable to suggest that if an organization security strategy is to be successful, knowledge of what factors influence security awareness is germane. However, little is known about factors that directly influence such awareness. This study addresses this deficiency in the literature; our findings further our understanding of how employees' actual CSP compliance behaviour may be motivated and aid in the identification of CSAW antecedents. That is, we add to the InfoSec/CS nomological net by identifying CSTR as a statistically significant direct antecedent of general CSAW and CSPA.

We note that while TMSP has received much attention in the management literature, it has not received commensurate attention in the InfoSec context. We address this void in the literature and continue the discourse to improve our understanding of how top management can influence employees' behaviour, more specifically, their actual compliance behaviour with the CSP in the organization. Relating to TMSP, our results show that employees CSPA does respond to stimuli related to top management security support. Our results suggest that TMSP influence employees' compliance with the CSP by supporting CSP compliance awareness initiatives. In other words, when top management is observed by employees as drivers of CSPA initiatives, the effect is strong CSP compliance by employees. This finding is confirmed by others; for instance, Kankanhalli et al. (2003) report that organizations with stronger TMSP engaged in more preventative security efforts, such as those initiatives that would be undertaken to improve CSPA. Some InfoSec experts in the GS also identify top management support (i.e. board support) as an important driver of employees' information security actions (Donalds, & Barclay, 2021).

5.6.2 Contribution to Practice

InfoSec researchers and practitioners contend that information security and/or CS can be more effectively managed when organizations look beyond the technical means to consider organizational and human factors (Baskerville, 1993; Straub & Welke, 1998; Trompeter & Eloff, 2001). As organizations in the LAC region continue to face rising cyberattacks (IDB & OAS, 2020), it may indeed be difficult for these entities to achieve CS protection without considering the human and organizational aspects of CS. InfoSec security experts in a GS context affirmed the need for organizations to focus on risk mitigation, technical, people and organizational factors in achieving appropriate InfoSec outcomes (Donalds, & Barclay, 2021). Consistent with these arguments are our findings; that is, our results affirm that organizations should consider organizational and human-related security interventions factors. In fact, the factors in the research model explained a substantial amount of variance in employees' actual CSP compliance behaviour, as high as 73%. In other words, employees' actual CSP compliance behaviours are substantially influenced by TMSP, CSAW, CSPA and CSTR, whether directly or indirectly. Therefore, in their quest to achieve employees' compliance with the CSPs, security practitioners in the LAC and other organizations in the GS should largely promote activities aligned to these factors.

In our study, TMSP positively influences CSPA. This finding has practical significance for CS security practitioners, policy and decision-makers in the LAC region and other jurisdictions. These stakeholders should actively support CSPA by actively participating in CSPA initiatives and mobilizing or allocating the requisite funds to ensure the initiatives can be successfully realized. Further, the findings of this and other studies (El-Haddadeh, Tsohou, & Karyda, 2012; Marks & Rezgui, 2009) suggest that TMSP is crucial for positive organizational security culture/climate changes to take place, which in turn has a positive impact on CSPA development. Therefore, top management should demonstrate strong leadership throughout CSP development and implementation, including them acting as role models for employees and all other stakeholders.

The results of the study also provide evidence that general awareness of CS threats and possible consequences (CSAW), awareness of CS policies (CSPA) and CSTR; each has some effect (direct and indirect) on influencing employees' actual CSP compliance behaviour. CSAW, CSPA and CSTR are elements over which the organization has direct control; however, they also have implications for the allocation of security funds/budget. Since developing countries and by extension, GS government agencies, are characterized by limited financial and CS technical resources, CS managers and officers can use cost-effective mechanisms such as newsletter, posters, bulletins, emails, screensavers, security pop-us, etc., to remind employees of potential CS security threats and to take appropriate security actions. Free and low-cost CS learning content from reputable sources (such as NIST), to include CSTR, can also be adopted and used in the organization. Onboarding of new hires should also include CSAW and CSPA activities. Government agencies could also develop a CSTR website, requiring all employees to complete an approved annual refresher CSTR programme and new employees having to complete the CSTR programme within 30 days of hire.

Although our results provide evidence of the importance of CSTR to employees, they also reveal that CSTR may not be sufficient to directly influence employees' actual CSP compliance behaviour. In fact, the results suggest that CSAW and CSPA mediate the relationship between CSTR and actual CS compliance; thus, managers should focus CSTR activities to support CSAW and CSPA.

5.6.3 *Limitations and Future Research*

There are limitations to the study. For instance, it has been suggested that information security assurance will require a multifaceted approach encompassing both social and technical factors (Dhillon & Backhouse, 2001). Likewise, the GoJ National Cybersecurity Plan also suggests a multifaceted approach (Government of Jamaica, 2015) and InfoSec experts in the GS suggest a holistic approach focusing on risk mitigation, technical, people and organizational factors (Donalds, & Barclay, 2021) . However, this study does not consider such factors as organization climate and culture, which has been shown to influence organization phenomenon such as individual performance (Donalds, 2010) and InfoSec behaviour (Chen & Zahedi, 2016; Goo et al., 2014; Khan & AlShare, 2019). Incorporating social factors in future studies may also improve our understanding of what influences employees' actual CS compliance behaviour. The model proposed in this study was tested using employees' perceptual measures of CS compliance. However, there can be discrepancies between self-reports and actual behaviours; therefore, it is not known how well the respondents' perceptions matched their actual compliance behaviours. In a follow-up study, objective measures could be used; however, this may increase the risk of response bias.

5.7 Conclusion

Employees' compliance with CSPs remains a challenge for organizations in the LAC region. Empirical evidence indicates that a major cause of CS incidents is primarily due to employees failing to comply with CSPs and/or other InfoSec best practices. In response, scholars and practitioners have presented models that have incorporated sanctions and fear appeals to explain factors that reduce computer misuse/abuse or improve employees' compliance with IS security policies. Regardless, employees' CSP compliance remains a challenge for organizations as employees are reported as the weak link in the InfoSec chain, because they often fail to adhere to CSPs and procedures. In this study, we advance a long stream of research on information security compliance by examining actual security behaviour, i.e. actual CSP compliance, instead of behavioural intention. Further, this study augments research on employees' compliance behaviour by interrogating an integrated model which includes organizational and human-related factors to explain employees' CSP compliance behaviour. For InfoSec and CS researchers, this study makes important contributions towards understanding employees' actual CS compliance behaviour by interrogating a new CS compliance model that incorporates factors and relationships not previously tested. By testing the relationships between employees' CSTR, CSAW, CSPA and TMSP on their actual CS compliance behaviour, this study assesses the effectiveness of these influencers and offers suggestions regarding management practices that can improve employees' CSP compliance behaviour.

Our results suggest that (a) CSPA has a very strong impact on employees' actual CSP compliance behaviour; (b) general CS security awareness influences employees' actual CSP compliance behaviour; (c) TMSP has a strong impact on CSPA; and (d) CSTR influences both CSAW and CSPA. Thus, our findings suggest that employees' actual CSP compliance behaviours are influenced by human-related intervention factors, such as CSAW and CSTR initiatives, as well as the organizational context. Overall, the results provide a parsimonious model which explains a substantial amount of variance in employees' actual CSP compliance behaviour. Since GS organizations are generally constrained by limited resources, in terms of people, technology and finances, such a parsimonious model can be used by practitioners as a guide in crafting effective CS programmes that improve employees' CS policy compliance behaviour in the GS and other jurisdictions, such as the global north.

Appendix A – Description of the Constructs

Table A1 Constructs, Items & Sources

Construct	Code	Item	Source
General Cybersecurity Awareness (CSAW)	CSAW1	Overall, I am aware of the potential cybersecurity threats and their negative consequences	Bulgurcu et al. (2010)
	CSAW2	I have sufficient knowledge about the cost of potential cybersecurity problems	
	CSAW3	I understand the concerns regarding cybersecurity and the risks they pose in general	
Cybersecurity Policy Awareness (CSPA)	CSPA1	I know the rules and regulations prescribed by the cybersecurity policy of my organization	Bulgurcu et al. (2010)
	CSPA2	I understand the rules and regulations prescribed by the cybersecurity policy of my organization	
	CSPA3	I know my responsibilities as prescribed in the computer security policy to enhance cybersecurity of organization	

(Continued)

Construct	Code	Item	Source
Cybersecurity Compliance (CSCP)	CSCP1	I comply with the requirements of the cybersecurity policy of my organization	Bulgurcu et al. (2010); Herath and Rao (2009b);
	CSCP2	I carry out my responsibilities as prescribed in the cybersecurity policy of my organization when I use information and technology within my organization	
	CSCP3	I protect information and technology resources according to the cybersecurity policy of my organization	
Top Management Support (TMSP)	TMSP1	Enough resources have been provided to support the implementation of the cybersecurity plan	Kankanhalli et al. (2003); Hu et al. (2012); Knapp et al. (2006); Self-developed
	TMSP2	Senior management monitors the implementation of the cybersecurity plan	
	TMSP3	Senior management gets involved in decisions that affect the cybersecurity plan	
	TMSP4	Problems regarding the cybersecurity plan have been timely resolved whenever they occur	
	TMSP5	Enough resources have been provided to support the timely resolution of cybersecurity incidents	
	TMSP6	Processes are in place to escalate cybersecurity breaches to senior management	
	TMSP7	A senior management committee has adequate time devoted to the discussion of the implementation of the cybersecurity plan	

(Continued)

Construct	Code	Item	Source
Cybersecurity Training (CSTR)	CSTR1	Adequate cybersecurity training is provided to new and existing employees	D'Arcy et al. (2009); Chan et al. (2005); Self-developed
	CSTR2	Adequate cybersecurity training is provided to raise awareness of employees	
	CSTR3	Relevant cybersecurity training is provided to existing employees on an ongoing basis	
	CSTR4	Employees receive adequate cybersecurity training before getting a network account	

Acknowledgements

Some material in this chapter previously appeared in Donalds, C. (2015). *Cybersecurity Policy Compliance: An Empirical Study of Jamaican Government Agencies.* Paper presented at the SIG GlobDev Pre-ECIS Workshop, Munster, Germany.

References

Abawajy, J. (2014). User preference of cyber security awareness delivery methods. *Behaviour & Information Technology, 33*(3), 237–248. doi: 10.1080/0144929X.2012.708787

Abraham, S. (2011, August 4–8). Information Security Behavior: Factors and Research Directions. *Paper Presented at the Americas Conference on Information Systems*, Detroit, Michigan.

Ahlan, A. R., Lubis, M., & Lubis, A. R. (2015). Information security awareness at the knowledge-based institution: Its antecedents and measures. *Procedia Computer Science, 72*, 361–373.

Andoh-Baidoo, F. K., & Osei-Bryson, K.-M. (2007). Exploring the characteristics of internet security breaches that impact the market value of breached firms. *Expert Systems with Applications, 32*(3), 703–725. doi: 10.1016/j.eswa.2006.01.020

Balozian, P., Leidner, D., & Warkentin, M. (2017). Managers' and employees' differing responses to security approaches. *Journal of Computer Information Systems, 59*(3), 197–210. doi: 10.1080/08874417.2017.1318687

Baskerville, R. (1993). Information systems security design methods: Implications for information systems development. *ACM Computing Surveys, 25*(4), 375–414. doi: 10.1145/162124.162127

Bauer, S., & Bernroider, E. W. N. (2017). From information security awareness to reasoned compliant action: Analyzing information security policy compliance in a large banking organization. *The DATA BASE for Advances in Information Systems, 48*(3), 44–68.

Benitez, J., Henseler, J., Castillo, A., & Schuberth, F. (2020). How to perform and report an impactful analysis using partial least squares: Guidelines for confirmatory and explanatory IS research. *Information & Management, 57*(2), 103168. doi: 10.1016/j.im.2019.05.003

Boss, S. R., Kirsch, L. J., Angermeier, I., Shingler, R. A., & Boss, R. W. (2009). If someone is watching, I'll do what I'm asked: Mandatoriness, control, and information security. *European Journal of Information Systems, 18,* 151–164.

Bulgurcu, B., Cavusoglu, H., & Benbasat, I. (2010). Information security policy compliance: An empirical study of rationality-based beliefs and information security awareness. *MIS Quarterly, 34*(3), 523–548.

Chan, M., Woon, I., & Kankanhalli, A. (2005). Perceptions of information security in the workplace: Linking information security climate to compliant behavior. *Journal of Information Privacy & Security, 1*(3), 18–41.

Chen, X., Chen, L., & Wu, D. (2018). Factors that influence employees' security policy compliance: An awareness-motivation-capability perspective. *Journal of Computer Information Systems, 58*(4), 312–324. doi:10.1080/08874417.2016.1258679

Chen, Y., & Zahedi, F. M. (2016). Individuals' internet security perceptions and behaviors: Polycontextual contrasts between the United States and China. *MIS Quarterly, 40*(1), 205–222.

Chin, W. W. (1998). The Partial Least Squares Approach to Structural Equation Modeling. In G. A. Marcoulides (Ed.), *Modern Methods for Business Research* (pp. 295–358). Mahwah, NJ: Lawrence Erlbaum Associates.

Choi, M. S., Levy, Y., & Anat, H. (2013). The Role of User Computer Self-Efficacy, Cybersecurity Countermeasures Awareness, and Cybersecurity Skills Influence on Computer Misuse. *Paper Presented at the Eighth Pre-ICIS Workshop on Information Security and Privacy (WISP 2013)*, Milan, Italy.

Cohen, J. (1992). Quantitative methods in psychology: A power primer. *Psychological Bulletin, 112*(1), 155–159.

Cone, B. D., Irvine, C. E., Thompson, M. F., & Nguyen, T. D. (2007). A video game for cyber security training and awareness. *Computers & Security, 26*(1), 63–72. doi: 10.1016/j.cose.2006.10.005

Cox, A., Connolly, S., & Currall, J. (2001). Raising IS security awareness in the academic setting. *VINE, 31*(2), 11–16.

Cram, W. A., D'Arcy, J., & Proudfoot, J. G. (2019). Seeing the forest and the trees: A meta-analysis of the antecedents to information security policy compliance. *MIS Quarterly, 43*(2), 525–554. doi: 10.25300/MISQ/2019/15117

D'Arcy, J., & Lowry, P. B. (2019). Cognitive-affective drivers of employees' daily compliance with information security policies: A multilevel, longitudinal study. *Information Systems Journal, 29*(1), 43–69. doi:doi:10.1111/isj.12173

D'Arcy, J., Hovav, A., & Galletta, D. (2009). User awareness of security countermeasures and its impact on information systems misuse: A deterrence approach. *Information Systems Research, 20*(1), 79–98.

Dhillon, G., & Backhouse, J. (2001). Current direction in IS security research: Towards socio-organizational perspective. *Information Systems Journal, 11*(2), 127–153.

Dodge, R. C., Carver, C., & Ferguson, A. J. (2007). Phishing for user security awareness. *Computers & Security, 26*(1), 73–80.

Doherty, N. F., & Fulford, H. (2006). Aligning the information security policy with the strategic information systems plan. *Computers and Security, 25*(1), 55–63.

Donalds, C. (2010, May 16–18). 46P. Towards an ERP Individual Performance Model. *Paper Presented at the CONF-IRM 2010 Proceedings*, Montego Bay, Jamaica.

Donalds, C., & Barclay, C. (2021). Beyond technical measures: a value-focused thinking appraisal of strategic drivers in improving information security policy compliance. *European Journal of Information Systems*, 1–16. 10.1080/0960085X.2021.1978344.

Donalds, C., & Osei-Bryson, K.-M. (2020). Cybersecurity compliance behavior: Exploring the influences of individual decision style and other antecedents. *International Journal of Information Management, 51*. doi: 10.1016/j.ijinfomgt.2019.102056.

El-Haddadeh, R., Tsohou, A., & Karyda, M. (2012). Implementation Challenges for Information Security Awareness Initiatives in E-Government. *Paper Presented at the European Conference on Information Systems*, Barcelona.

Eminagaoglu, M., Ucar, E., & Eren, S. (2009). The positive outcomes of information security awareness training in companies – A case study. *Information Security Technical Report, 14*(4), 223–229.

Fornell, C., & Cha, J. (1994). Partial Least Squares. In R. P. Bagozzi (Ed.), *Advanced Methods of Marketing Research* (pp. 52–78). Cambridge, Mass: Blackwell Business.

Fornell, C., & Larcker, D. F. (1981). Evaluating structural equation models with unobservable variables and measurement error. *Journal of Marketing Research, 18*(1), 39–50.

Foth, M. (2016). Factors influencing the intention to comply with data protection regulations in hospitals: Based on gender differences in behaviour and deterrence. *European Journal of Information Systems, 25*(2), 91–109. doi:10.1057/ejis.2015.9.

Furnell, S., & Clarke, N. L. (2012). Power to the people? The evolving recognition of human aspects of security. *Computers & Security, 31*(8), 983–988. doi:10.1016/j.cose.2012.08.004.

Gefen, D., Straub, D. W., & Boudreau, M.-C. (2000). Structural equation modeling and regression: Guidelines for research practice. *Communications of the Association for Information System, 4*(7), 2–76.

Gibbs, J. P. (1975). *Crime, Punishment, and Deterrence*. New York: Elsevier.

Gomes, J., de Weerd-Nederhof, P., Pearson, A., & Fisscher, O. (2001). Senior management support in the new product development process. *Creativity and Innovation Management, 10*(4), 234–242.

Goo, J., Yim, M.-S., & Kim, D. J. (2014). A path to successful management of employee security compliance: An empirical study of information security climate. *IEEE Transactions on Professional Communications, 57*(4), 286–308.

Goodhue, D. L., & Straub, D. W. (1991). Security concerns of system users: A study of perceptions of the adequacy of security. *Information & Management, 20*(1), 13–27.

Government of Jamaica. (2015). *Jamaica National Cyber Security Strategy*. Ministry of Science, Technology, Energy and Mining. Retrieved from http://www.mstem.gov.jm/sites/default/files/documents/Jamaica%20National%20Cyber%20Security%20Strategy.pdf.

Hadasch, F., Mueller, B., & Maedche, A. (2012). Exploring Antecedent Environmental And Organizational Factors To User-Caused Information Leaks: A Qualitative Study. *Paper presented at the European Conference on Information Systems*, Barcelona.

Hadland, T. (1998). IS Security Management: An Awareness Campaign. *Paper presented at the UKOLUG98: New Networks, Old Information—UKOLUG's 20th Birthday Conference*, Manchester, England.

Haeussinger, F., & Kranz, J. (2013). Information Security Awareness: Its Antecedents and Mediating Effects on Security Compliant Behavior. *Paper presented at the 34th International Conference on Information Systems*, Milano, Italy.

Hair, J. F., Hult, G. T. M., Ringle, C. M., & Sarstedt, M. (2014). *A Primer on Partial Least Squares Structural Equation Modeling (PLS-SEM)*. Thousand Oaks: Sage.

Hansche, S. (2001). Designing a security awareness program: Part 1. *Information Systems Security, 9*(6), 14–22.

Henseler, J., Hubona, G., & Ray, P. A. (2016). Using PLS path modeling in new technology research: Updated guidelines. *Industrial Management & Data Systems, 116*(1), 2–20.

Henseler, J., Ringle, C. M., & Sarstedt, M. (2015). A new criterion for assessing discriminant validity in variance-based structural equation modeling. *Journal of the Academy of Marketing Science, 43*(1), 115–135.

Henseler, J., Ringle, C. M., & Sinkovics, R. R. (2009). The Use of Partial Least Squares Path Modeling in International Marketing. In R. R. Sinkovics & P. N. Ghauri (Eds.), *Advances in International Marketing* (Vol. 20, pp. 277–319): Emerald Group Publishing Limited.

Herath, T., & Rao, H. R. (2009a). Encouraging information security behaviors: Role of penalties, pressures and perceived effectiveness. *Decision Support Systems, 47*(2), 154–165.

Herath, T., & Rao, H. R. (2009b). Protection motivation and deterrence: A framework for security policy compliance in organisations. *European Journal of Information Systems, 18*(2), 106–125. doi: 10.1057/ejis.2009.6.

Hovav, A., & D'Arcy, J. (2012). Applying an extended model of deterrence across cultures: An investigation of information systems misuse in the US and South Korea. *Information & Management, 49*(2), 99–110.

Hu, Q., Dinev, T., Hart, P., & Cooke, D. (2012). Managing employee compliance with information security policies: The critical role of top management and organizational culture. *Decision Sciences, 43*(4), 615–659.

Hwang, I., Wakefield, R., Kim, S., & Kim, T. (2021). Security awareness: The first step in information security compliance behavior. *Journal of Computer Information Systems, 61*(4) 345–356.

IDB & OAS. (2020). *2020 Cybersecurity Report: Risks, Progress, and the Way Forward In Latin America and the Caribbean*. Retrieved from Inter-American Development Bank: https://publications.iadb.org/publications/english/document/2020-Cybersecurity-Report-Risks-Progress-and-the-Way-Forward-in-Latin-America-and-the-Caribbean.pdf

Ifinedo, P. (2012). Understanding information systems security policy compliance: An integration of the theory of planned behavior and the protection motivation theory. *Computers & Security, 31*(1), 83–95. doi: 10.1016/j.cose.2011.10.007.

Johnston, A. C., & Warkentin, M. (2010). Fear appeals and information security behaviors: An empirical study. *MIS Quarterly, 34*(3), 549–566.

Johnston, A. C., Warkentin, M., & Siponen, M. (2015). An enhanced fear appeal rhetorical framework: Leveraging threats to the human asset through sanctioning rhetoric. *MIS Quarterly, 39*(1), 113–134.

Kankanhalli, A., Teo, H.-H., Tan, B. C. Y., & Wei, K.-K. (2003). An integrative study of information systems security effectiveness. *International Journal of Information Management, 23*(2), 139–154.

Khan, H. U., & AlShare, K. A. (2019). Violators versus non-violators of information security measures in organizations—A study of distinguishing factors. *Journal of Organizational Computing and Electronic Commerce, 29*(1), 4–23. doi: 10.1080/10919392.2019.1552743.

Khando, K., Gao, S., Islam, S. M., & Salman, A. (2021). Enhancing employees information security awareness in private and public organisations: A systematic literature review. *Computers & Security, 106*, 1–22. doi: 10.1016/j.cose.2021.102267.

Knapp, K., Marshall, T. E., Rainer, R. K., & Ford, F. N. (2006). Information security: Management's effect on culture and policy. *Information Management & Computer Security, 14*(1), 24–36.

Koohang, A., & Anderson, J. (2020). Building an awareness-centered information security policy compliance model. *Industrial Management & Data, 120*(1), 231–247.

Kwon, J., Ulmer, J. R., & Wang, T. (2013). The association between top management involvement and compensation and information security breaches. *Journal of Information Systems, 27*(1), 219–236. doi: 10.2308/isys-50339.

Li, L., He, W., Xu, L., Ash, I., Anwar, M., & Yuan, X. (2019). Investigating the impact of cybersecurity policy awareness on employees' cybersecurity behavior. *International Journal of Information Management, 45*, 13–24. doi: 10.1016/j.ijinfomgt.2018.10.017.

Liang, H., Saraf, N., Hu, Q., & Xue, Y. (2007). Assimilation of enterprise systems: The effect of institutional pressures and the mediating role of top management. *MIS Quarterly, 31*(1), 59–87.

Lim, J. S., Ahmad, A., Chang, S., & Maynard, S. (2010). Embedding Information Security Culture Emerging Concerns and Challenges. *Paper Presented at the Pacific Asia Conference on Information Systems*, Taipei, Taiwan.

Lohmoller, J. B. (1989). *Latent Variable Path Modeling with Partial Least Squares*. New York: Springer-Verlag.

Lowry, P. B., & Moody, G. D. (2015). Proposing the control-reactance compliance model (CRCM) to explain opposing motivations to comply with organisational information security policies. *Information Systems Journal, 25*(5), 433–463. doi: 0.1111/isj.12043.

Ma, Q., Schmidt, M. B., & Pearson, J. M. (2009). An integrated framework for information security management. *Review of Business, 30*(1), 58–69.

Maeyer, D. D. (2007). Setting Up an Effective Information Security Awareness Programme. In N. Pohlmann, H. Reimer, & W. Schneider (Eds.), *ISSE/SECURE 2007 Securing Electronic Business Processes* (pp. 49–58). Vieweg. doi:10.1007/978-3-8348-9418-2_5

Marks, A., & Rezgui, Y. (2009). Comparative Study of Information Security Awareness in Higher Education Based on the Concept of Design Theorizing. *Paper Presented at the International Conference on Management and Service Science*, Wuhan, China.

Ministry of Planning and Development. (2017). Retrieved from *Socio-Economic Policy Planning Division, Trinidad and Tobago*. https://observatorioplanificacion.cepal.org/sites/default/files/plan/files/Trinidad_y_Tobago_Vision_%202030_2016_2030_tiny.pdf

Mitnick, K. D. (2002). *The Art of Deception: Controlling the Human Element of Security*. New York: Wiley Publishing.

Mitnick, K. D., & Simon, W. L. (2002). *The Art of Deception: Controlling the Human Element of Security*. USA: Wiley Publishing.

Moody, G. D., Siponen, M. T., & Pahnila, S. (2018). Toward a unified model of information security policy compliance. *MIS Quarterly, 42*(1), 285–311.

Murray, B. (1991). Running Corporate and National Security Awareness Programs. *Paper Presented at the IFIP TC11 Seventh International Conference on IS Security*, Amsterdam.

Newsday. (2020). *Responding to the Cybersecurity Threat.* Retrieved from https://newsday. co.tt/2020/10/22/responding-to-the-cybersecurity-threat/

Planning Institute of Jamaica. (2009). *Vision 2030 Jamaica: National Development Plan (978-976-8103-28-4).* Retrieved from Planning Institute of Jamaica. http://www. vision2030.gov.jm/Portals/0/NDP/Vision%202030%20Jamaica%20NDP%20 Full%20No%20Cover%20(web).pdf

Ponemon Institute. (2020). 2020 Cost of Insider Threats: Global Report. Retrieved from https://www.observeit.com/cost-of-insider-threats/

Puhakainen, P. (2006). *A Design Theory for Information Security Awareness.* (PhD), Oulu, Finland: University of Oulu, Finland. Retrieved from http://herkules.oulu.fi/ isbn9514281144/isbn9514281144.pdf

Puhakainen, P., & Siponen, M. T. (2010). Improving employees' compliance through information systems security training: An action research study. *MIS Quarterly, 34*(4), 757–778.

Research and Planning Institute. (2005). *National Strategic Plan of Barbados 2005–2025.* Retrieved from Barbados: Ministry of Finance and Economic Affairs. http://www.sice. oas.org/ctyindex/brb/plan2005-2025.pdf

Ringle, C. M., Wende, S., & Becker, J.-M. (2015). *SmartPLS* 3. Retrieved from http://www. smartpls.com

Rogers, R. W. (1975). A protection motivation theory of fear appeals and attitude change. *The Journal of Psychology, 91*(1), 93–114. doi: 10.1080/00223980.1975.9915803

Sabherwal, R., Jeyaraj, A., & Chowa, C. (2006). Information system success: Individual and organizational determinants. *Management Science, 52*(12), 1849–1864.

Safa, N. S., Von Solms, R., & Furnell, S. (2016). Information security policy compliance model in organizations. *Computers & Security, 56*(C), 70–82.

Siponen, M. T. (2000). A conceptual foundation for organizational information security awareness. *Information Management & Computer Security Journal, 8*(1), 31–41.

Siponen, M. T., & Iivari, J. (2006). Six design theories for IS security policies and guidelines. *Journal of the Association for Information Systems, 7*(7), 445–472.

Siponen, M. T., Mahmood, M. A., & Pahnila, S. (2014). Employees' adherence to information security policies: An exploratory field study. *Information & Management, 51*(2), 217–224. doi:10.1016/j.im.2013.08.006

Siponen, M. T., Pahnila, S., & Mahmood, M. A. (2010). Compliance with information security policies: An empirical investigation. *Computer, 43*(2), 64–71. doi:10.1109/ MC.2010.35

Siponen, M. T., & Vance, A. (2010). Neutralization: New insights into the problem of employee information systems security policy violations. *MIS Quarterly, 34*(3), 487–502.

Sommestad, T., Karlzén, H., & Hallberg, J. (2019). The theory of planned behavior and information security policy compliance. *Journal of Computer Information Systems, 59*(4), 344–353. doi:10.1080/08874417.2017.1368421

Stanton, J. M., Stam, K., Guzman, I., & Caldera, C. (2003). Examining the Linkages Between Organizational Commitment and Information Security. *Paper Presented at the IEEE Systems, Man, and Cybernetics Conference*, Washington, DC, USA.

Stanton, J. M., Stam, K. R., Mastrangelo, P., & Jolton, J. (2005). Analysis of end user security behaviors. *Computers & Security, 24*(2), 124–133.

Stone, E. F. (1978). *Research Methods in Organizational Behavior.* Santa Monica, CA: Goodyear.

Straub, D. W. (1990). Effective IS security: An empirical study. *Information Systems Research, 1*(3), 255–276.

Straub, D. W., & Welke, R. J. (1998). Coping with systems risk: Security planning models for management decision making. *MIS Quarterly, 22*(4), 441–469.

The Gleaner. (2020). *Jamaica National Hit by Major Cyber Attack.* Retrieved from https://jamaica-gleaner.com/article/news/20200320/jamaica-national-hit-major-cyber-attack

Thomson, M. E., & von Solms, R. (1998). IS security awareness: Educating your users effectively. *Information Management & Computer Security, 6*(4), 167–173.

Trompeter, C. M., & Eloff, J. H. P. (2001). A framework for the implementation of socio-ethical controls in information security. *Computers and Security, 20*(5), 384–391. doi: 10.1016/S0167-4048(01)00507-7.

Tsohou, A., Karyda, M., & Kokolakis, S. (2015). Analyzing the role of cognitive and cultural biases in the internalization of information security policies: Recommendations for information security awareness programs. *Compters & Security, 52*, 128–141. doi: 10.1016/j.cose.2015.04.006.

Vance, A., Siponen, M. T., & Pahnila, S. (2012). Motivating IS security compliance: Insights from habit and protection motivation theory. *Information & Management, 49*(3–4), 190–198.

von Solms, B., & von Solms, R. (2004). The 10 deadly sins of information security management. *Computers & Security, 23*(5), 371–376.

Warkentin, M., & Willison, R. (2009). Behavioral and policy issues in information systems security: The insider threat. *European Journal of Information Systems, 18*(2), 101–105.

Wilson-Harris, N. (2019, June 30). Cyber thieves run rampant - Jamaica suffering billions in losses from online crime. *The Gleaner.* Retrieved from https://jamaica-gleaner.com/article/lead-stories/20190630/cyber-thieves-run-rampant-jamaica-suffering-billions-losses-online

Wold, H. (1966). *Estimation of Principal Components and Related Models by Iterative Least Squares* (Vol. 3). New York: Academic Press.

Yeniman, Y., Ebru Akalp, G., Aytac, S., & Bayram, N. (2011). Factors influencing information security management in small-and medium-sized enterprises: A case study from turkey. *International Journal of Information Management, 31*(4), 360–365.

Chapter 6

Cybersecurity Compliance Behaviour: Exploring the Influences of Individual Decision Style and Other Antecedents

6.1 Introduction

Individual security compliance behaviour[1] has been a challenge for public and private entities alike. While individuals have been recognized by academics and practitioners as an important element in achieving security, they have also been described as the weakest link in the security chain because they often fail to comply with security best practices (Boss, Kirsch, Angermeier, Shingler, & Boss, 2009; Vroom & von Solms, 2004; Warkentin & Willison, 2009; Yeniman, Ebru Akalp, Aytac, & Bayram, 2011). Consequently, it is not surprising that individual security compliance behaviour has become a key management issue for entities as well as an important topic of investigation for researchers. Despite increased management efforts to improve security, industry statistics identify individuals' malicious, negligent or inadvertent actions as the top cause of security incidents. For instance, the Ponemon

DOI: 10.1201/9781003028710-8

Institute (2016) reports that of 874 reported security incidents, 68% were caused by negligent internal individuals (i.e. employees or contractors), 22% by malicious and/or criminal internal individuals and 10% by external individuals using stolen credentials. Besides, it is not only the volume of incidents that is important but also the actual and potential financial losses due to incidents by internal individuals. According to a recent Insider Threat Study, more than 75% of organizations surveyed estimate that the costs of remediating internal individuals' security incidents could reach US$500,000, while the other 25% anticipates costs to exceed US$500,000 and possibly up to millions of dollars (Haystax Technology, 2017). Moreover, 90% of cybersecurity professionals feel that their organizations are vulnerable to threats from internal individuals' (Cybersecurity Insiders, 2018). These statistics make it clear that individual security compliance behaviour remains a challenge. We argue that individual security compliance behaviour mitigates the risk of as well as actual security incidents.

In an attempt to safeguard critical information system (IS) assets, entities often implement technological solutions such as intrusion detection systems, comprehensive monitoring systems, anti-malware, antivirus and anti-phishing applications; however, same are rarely sufficient in providing complete protection of IS assets (Herath & Rao, 2009b; Stanton, Stam, Mastrangelo, & Jolton, 2005). Researchers note that technological solutions should ideally be combined with acceptable individual security behaviour (Furnell & Clarke, 2012). Moreover, others note that entities focusing on technical as well as non-technical means of protecting their key IS assets are likely to be more successful in their attempts to protect those assets (Pahnila, Siponen, & Mahomood, 2007; Stanton et al., 2005; Vroom & von Solms, 2004). Therefore, the onus then is on entities to utilize multi-perspective approaches to safeguard their IS assets (Herath & Rao, 2009a). This is affirmed by Donalds and Barclay (2021) who report that information security (InfoSec) experts of the Global South (GS) highlighted that organizations can achieve improvement in individual's security actions by focusing their InfoSec approaches on a holistic set of factors to include risk mitigation, people, technical and organizational.

To explain individual security compliance intention and/or actual behaviour, scholars and practitioners have proposed many different models, grounded in prominent theories, including general deterrence theory (e.g. Chen, Ramamurthy, & Wen, 2012; Kankanhalli, Teo, Tan, & Wei, 2003; Moody, Siponen, & Pahnila, 2018; Siponen, Pahnila, & Mahmood, 2007; Siponen & Vance, 2010), protection motivation theory (e.g. Crossler & Bélanger, 2014; Li et al., 2019; Safa et al., 2015; Siponen & Vance, 2014; Vance, Siponen, & Pahnila, 2012), theory of planned behaviour (e.g. Bulgurcu, Cavusoglu, & Benbasat, 2010; Herath & Rao, 2009b; Ifinedo, 2014; Moody et al., 2018), rational choice theory (e.g. Bulgurcu et al., 2010; Hu, Xu, Dinev, & Ling, 2011; Vance & Siponen, 2012) and neutralization theory (e.g. Barlow, Warkentin, Ormond, & Dennis, 2013; Siponen & Vance, 2010). The use of these theories has improved our understanding because they permit a deeper consideration of motivations of individuals behind the behaviour being investigated and propose possible interventions that can be used to positively influence the behaviour in question. However, these models/theories have primarily focused on extrinsic or perceived factors, such as subjective norms, social influence, rewards, perceived cost, perceived effectiveness and perceived susceptibility, as antecedents of individual's behaviour (Lu, 2018), and not on intrinsic factors, such as decision styles, that may also explain their behaviour.

The discussion prior highlights the fact that individual security compliance behaviour remains a challenge and the question of what other factor(s) influences individual security compliance behaviour remains an open one. Moreover, scholars argue that while the theories listed above

> can be (and will continue to be) fruitful areas for understanding the motivations of individuals, we must incorporate new avenues of exploration into our repertoire. We should expand our horizons and incorporate not only new theoretical foundations, but new methodological approaches as well. We can learn from other cognitive and behavioral sciences....
>
> (Warkentin & Willison, 2009, p. 102)

In this research, we have heeded the call to incorporate new theoretical foundations by examining not only extrinsic or perceived factors but also intrinsic factors that may influence an individual's behaviour.

The issue of security compliance relates to individuals and how s/he perceives and comprehends security threats and chooses to respond, i.e. whether to comply or not with security best practices. This type of cognitive processing relates to individuals' decision styles. However, this area of research has received very little attention from the IS security community, except for the study by Donalds and Osei-Bryson (2017). This is an important omission since decision-style theory (Rowe & Boulgarides, 1983; Rowe & Mason, 1987) suggests that decision style may explain individuals' decision behaviour. Furthermore, decision style has been found to be a significant factor in explaining decision behaviour in other contexts (e.g. Hafni & Nurlaelah, 2018; Henderson & Nutt, 1980; Martinsons & Davison, 2007). Therefore, by interrogating the relationships in the Donalds and Osei-Bryson (2017) model, we explore the question 'What influence does decision style have on individuals' security compliance behaviour and other antecedents of such behaviour?'.

To address this gap, we introduce and examine Donalds and Osei-Bryson's (2017) individual cybersecurity compliance behaviour model, which focuses on individual decision styles and other antecedents of cybersecurity compliance behaviour. By empirically validating the assertions of the Donalds and Osei-Bryson model, we aim to identify statistically significant relationships that may exist between individuals' decision styles and their cybersecurity compliance behaviour as well as other antecedents of their cybersecurity compliance behaviour. We use survey data collected from 248 individuals to explore the abductive-generated relationships in the model and analyse the data using multiple linear regression. The findings of this work suggest a new and promising area for researching the individual perspective of cybersecurity compliance behaviour. In Sections 6.2 and 6.3, we present relevant literature and outline the key details of the Donalds and Osei-Bryson model, respectively. In Section 6.4 we present the research model and hypotheses. We describe the research methodology and the steps followed in conducting this study in Section 6.5. In Section 6.6 we discuss our findings, their implications, limitations and suggestions for future research. We present our conclusion in Section 6.7.

6.2 Relevant Literature

6.2.1 Decision-Making Style and Behaviour

Individuals in organizations are required to make decisions daily. While these decisions vary vastly, such as how to predict consumer reaction to a new marketing promotion or whether to comply with established security best practices, experts argue that individuals have 'habitual response patterns' in approaching various decision situations in consistent similar ways over time (Scott & Bruce, 1995; Thunholm, 2004). Others argue that talent, skill, experience and a 'hidden factor' typically influence individuals' decisions (Rowe & Mason, 1987). According to Rowe and Mason (1987) we tend to ignore this 'hidden factor' yet it is such an important part of how humans think and act; it forms a fundamental base that accounts for everything that a person does. These 'habitual response patterns' or 'hidden factor' applied in decision-making are commonly referred to as decision-making styles (DMSs) (Rowe & Mason, 1987; Scott & Bruce, 1995; Thunholm, 2004).

Driver (1979) defines DMS as a habitual pattern individuals use in decision-making, while Harren (1979) defines it as an individual characteristic for perceiving and responding to decision-making tasks. Rowe and Boulgarides (1992) define DMS as the way an individual visualizes and thinks about situations. Further, it is the way an individual perceives and comprehends stimuli and how s/he chooses to respond. Scott and Bruce (1995) define it as the habit-based propensity exhibited by an individual to react in a certain way in a specific decision context. They explained further that DMSs are individuals' characteristic mode of perceiving and responding to decision-making tasks. Sternberg and Zhang (2001) propose a working definition of DMS as a habitual pattern or preferred way of doing something that is consistent over time and across activities. Although these definitions vary, implicit in these definitions is that an individual's decision-making behaviour approach is: 1) intrinsic to the individual; 2) considered fairly stable over time; 3) that individuals have different DMSs based on the most dominant individual characteristic of their approach to the decision situation, and 4) that DMS influences the individual's action/behaviour.

DMS is also described as a cognitive process which represents the way an individual approaches a problem (Rowe & Mason, 1987). That is, an individual's DMS reflects the way s/he visualizes, thinks and interprets situations. According to Rowe and Mason (1987) different individuals will make different decisions because they use different methods to perceive and evaluate information. For instance, some individuals prefer acting to thinking, others think quickly while others slowly, others are concerned with the rules whereas others are concerned with people's feelings. Still, others are innovative, take risks, are creative, depend more on intuition than on fact (Mech, 1993). According to Nutt (1990), DMS offers a way to understand why managers, faced with seemingly identical situations, use such different decision processes. DMS then can help us identify the different types of individual decision-makers and could help us understand how the individual thinks about situations and ultimately, their decision behaviour. Nutt (1990) also found that decision style depicts an individual's belief system, including classification categories and sorted data that are taken for granted and unconsciously applied in decision-making. Rowe and Boulgarides (1992) suggest that once we know an individual's DMS we will be able to predict outcomes in terms of decision behaviour. This type of knowledge could prove useful to the IS community in understanding why individuals make certain security/cybersecurity compliance or non-compliance decisions as well as be able to predict individuals' security/cybersecurity compliance behaviour.

Prior research has investigated the relationship between DMS and the behaviour of individuals. For instance, Henderson and Nutt (1980) found DMS to be a significant factor in explaining individuals' decision behaviour of project adoption as well as perception of risk. Bavol'ár and Orosová (2015) found statistically significant relationships between DMSs and higher and lower decision-making competencies as well as between DMSs and mental health indicators such as stress and well-being, stress and depression and well-being and depression. Pedram and Garkaz (2016) also found that different DMSs explain significant differences in how individuals' process information, in terms of volume and processing time. Fox and Spence (2005) too, found that DMS significantly influenced project managers' behaviour in regard to the use of a project management tool, specifically, the time required to complete an initial project plan as well as the accuracy of the plan. Another study investigated education leaders' DMS behaviour and found that some leaders are more likely to repeat information while others are more likely to discuss information (Larson, Foster-Fishman, & Franz, 1998). Mech (1993) found that library directors with less administrative experience were more likely to have a people-oriented DMS than directors with more administrative experience. DMS has also been found to influence academic achievement (Baiocco, Laghi, & D'Alessio, 2009; Hafni & Nurlaelah, 2018), decision-making competences (Bruine de Bruin, Del Missier, & Levin, 2012) and various other performance criteria including job satisfaction (Crossley & Highhouse, 2005) and person-job fit (Crossley & Highhouse, 2005; Singh & Greenhaus, 2004). The results of these studies support the claim that DMS is an important determinant of behaviour.

Despite prior works investigating the influence of DMS on behaviour and other outcomes, the question of how DMS influences security/cybersecurity compliance behaviour and other antecedents of such behaviour remains unanswered. In this study, we seek to address this question. Because individuals are not all alike, understanding individuals' DMSs and identifying their cognitive preferences in security/ cybersecurity compliance decision situations may improve our understanding of their security/cybersecurity compliance behaviour and perhaps help us predict outcomes in terms of said behaviour.

6.2.2 Decision-Making Style Model

Since the model we adopted for investigation in this research used the decision-style inventory (DSI) measures proposed by Rowe and Mason (1987), in this section we provide a brief overview of the associated DMSs measured by the DSI (c.f., Rowe & Boulgarides, 1983; Rowe & Mason, 1987) as well as the DSI's DMS intensity levels and associated scores (Rowe & Boulgarides, 1992). Further, Figure 6.1 shows the DMS model (adapted from, Rowe & Boulgarides, 1983; Rowe & Mason, 1987).

The decision-style model suggests that an individual's DMS is based on two key aspects, cognitive complexity and the individual's value orientation. Cognitive complexity addresses the issue of tolerance for ambiguity, specifically, whether an

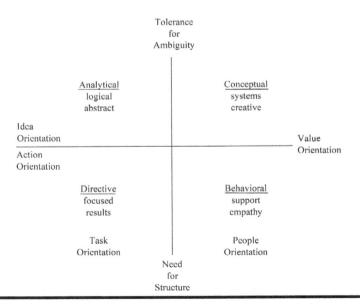

Figure 6.1   Decision-style model

(adapted from, Rowe & Boulgarides, 1983; Rowe & Mason, 1987)

individual has a high tolerance for ambiguity or a high need for structure (i.e. low tolerance for ambiguity). Values are oriented to task and technical concerns or people and social concerns. Combining these two dimensions yields four DMSs: *analytical, directive, behavioural* and *conceptual*.

Each DMS elicits specific traits and/or preferences. The *analytical* DMS has a high tolerance for ambiguity and is oriented toward task and technical concerns. *Analytical* individuals are logical in their approach, have a strong need for achievement in the form of new challenges, are slow decision-makers because they process considerable information in decision-making, prefer written reports, look for variety in their work and do well in impersonal situations like solving complex problems.

Like *analyticals*, *directive* individuals are logical in their approach and are oriented towards task and technical concerns. However, they have a low tolerance for ambiguity, emphasize speed and action thereby using limited information in decision-making, have strong need for power, tend to be aggressive, authoritarian and prefer tangible rewards over intrinsic rewards.

The *behavioural* DMS has a low tolerance for ambiguity and is strongly oriented toward people and social concerns. *Behavioural* individuals, thus, tend to be receptive to suggestions, supportive and empathetic, willing to compromise, prefer meetings/discussions to reports as well as loose controls and use intuition rather than information in decision-making.

Conceptuals are comfortable with considerable complexity (high tolerance for ambiguity) and are interested in people and social concerns. They generally prefer loose control over power, favour openness, share goals with subordinates, are high achievers but crave extrinsic rewards such as praise, recognition and independence. *Conceptuals* are generally broad and future-oriented thinkers, are very creative, value quality, take a system's perspective and typically gather information from multiple sources in decision-making.

While the DSI generates scores for the four DMSs, other combination of scores, such as for identifying individuals that have a preference for acting (*action*-oriented) or thinking (*idea*-oriented), are also possible. *Action*-oriented individuals work well with others, are concerned with achieving results and feeling internal pressure to act, s/he may engage in inadequate reflection before acting. On the other hand, *idea*-oriented individuals are creative, are more concerned with analysis, visualization, judgment, perspective and are predisposed to first engage in deep analysis and synthesis before acting in a decision situation. They usually formulate innovative solutions and prefer written communication. The Donalds and Osei-Bryson's (2017) model identifies individuals' dominant orientation (i.e. *action*-oriented or *idea*-oriented) as indirectly influencing their cybersecurity behaviour (see Figure 6.2).

The DSI is also used to identify the level of intensity of an individual's DMS. Level of intensity refers to the extent that each of the DMS is used in decision-making. There are four levels of intensity: (1) *Least preferred* – indicates that an individual rarely uses the DMS but could do so if required; (2) *Back-up* – indicates

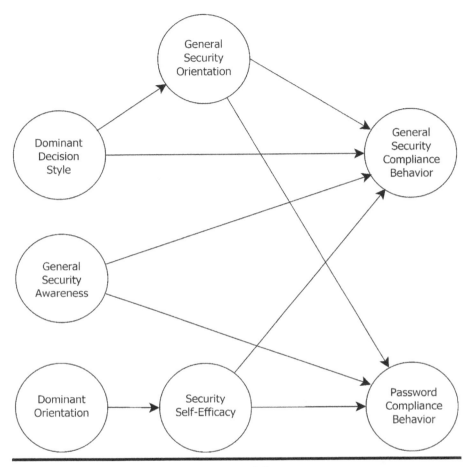

Figure 6.2   Donalds and Osei-Bryson's model

(Donalds and Osei-Bryson, 2017)

that the individual uses the DMS occasionally; (3) *Dominant* – indicates that the individual frequently uses the DMS over other DMSs; (4) *Very dominant* – indicates the highest level of intensity which describes the compulsive use of the style preferred by an individual. This level of intensity (i.e. *very dominant*) becomes the focus of individuals and will override other DMSs that have less intensity levels. Table 6.1 shows the DMS intensity levels with associated scores for interpreting an individual's style based on scores obtained using the DSI (Rowe & Boulgarides, 1992). For instance, an individual with scores of Conceptual = 85 has *Back-up* intensity, Analytic = 100 has *Dominant* intensity, Behavioural = 45 has *Least preferred* intensity and Directive = 70 has *Back-up* intensity. Based on these scores the individual has one *dominant* DMS, i.e. Analytic, two *back-up* DMSs, i.e. Conceptual and Directive, and one *least preferred* DMS, i.e. Behavioural. The Donalds and Osei-Bryson's (2017) model identifies individuals' *dominant* DMS as directly influencing

Table 6.1 DMS Intensity Levels and Scores (Rowe & Boulgarides, 1992)

Style	*Least preferred*	*Back-up*	*Dominant*	*Very Dominant*
	Intensity Level			
Directive	Below 68	68–72	83–90	Over 90
Analytic	Below 83	83–97	98–104	Over 104
Conceptual	Below 73	73–87	88–94	Over 94
Behavioural	Below 48	48–62	63–70	Over 70

their security compliance cybersecurity behaviour as well as another antecedent of such behaviour (see Figure 6.2).

The DSI aims at testing individuals' preferences when approaching a decision situation using a standard questionnaire consisting of 20 items, each with four response behaviours corresponding to the various DMSs. The respondents are asked to rank behaviours in each question using the scale 8 (most like you), 4 (moderately like you), 2 (slightly like you) and 1 (least like you). According to Rowe and Mason (1987), the DSI has a test-retest reliability of 0.7 and excellent face validity with over 90% of individuals who took the test agreeing with its findings; thus, the instrument shows good psychometric characteristics.

6.3 The Donalds and Osei-Bryson Model

The Donalds and Osei-Bryson model (see Figure 6.2), to the researchers' best knowledge, is the only model that has incorporated decision-style theory to address the phenomenon of individual cybersecurity compliance behaviour. Donalds and Osei-Bryson proposed that (1) DMS directly influences individuals' general security compliance behaviour and other antecedents of said behaviour and (2) DMS indirectly influences individual's password compliance behaviour. Descriptions/definitions for the factors in the Donalds and Osei-Bryson model are provided in Table 6.2 and the hypotheses are elaborated in Section 6.4.

The development of the Donalds and Osei-Bryson causal model can be considered to be based on the hybrid Peircian abduction framework proposed by Osei-Bryson and Ngwenyama (2011) and the hybrid process for empirically-based theory development by Kositanurit, Osei-Bryson, and Ngwenyama (2011), where the latter parallels the traditional ideal model of scientific inquiry. In Table 6.3 we have divided Kositanurit et al. (2011)'s hybrid process into two main phases. The process that was used to develop the Donalds and Osei-Bryson causal model can be considered to be equivalent to Phase 1 of Kositanurit et al. (2011)'s hybrid process, while

Table 6.2   Description of Factors in the Donalds and Osei-Bryson's Model

Factor	Description/Definition
General Security Orientation	An individual's predisposition and interest concerning practicing cybersecurity actions Donalds and Osei-Bryson, (2017); Ng, Kankanhalli, and Xu (2009).
General Security Awareness	An individual's overall awareness/mindfulness and understanding of potential issues related to cybersecurity and their ramifications Bulgurcu et al. (2010); Donalds and Osei-Bryson (2017).
Security Self-Efficacy	An individual's ability or judgment of his or her ability to perform cybersecurity actions in such a manner that minimizes the risk of security breaches/incidents Bandura (1977); Donalds and Osei-Bryson (2017).
General Security Compliance Behaviour	An individual's compliance with established security best practices/policies.
Password Compliance Behaviour	An individual's compliance with established password security best practices/policies.
Dominant Decision Style	Indicates that an individual frequently uses a particular decision-making style over other decision-making styles Rowe and Boulgarides (1992).
Dominant Orientation	Indicates an individual's preference for acting (action-oriented) or thinking (idea-oriented) Rowe and Mason (1987).

the methodology that is used in this paper to empirically evaluate Donalds and Osei-Bryson causal model can be considered to be equivalent to Phase 2.

The procedural equivalent of Phase 1 that was used in Donalds and Osei-Bryson (2017) can be summarized as follows: (1) existing theory was used to select direct and indirect predictor variables of cybersecurity compliance behaviour; (2) relevant data were collected; (3) exploratory factor analysis (EFA) was conducted on the data to identify the underlying theoretical structure of the phenomena; (4) decision tree (DT) induction was applied to generate rulesets; and (5) using abductive reasoning, hypotheses were generated from the results of the decision tree induction. For a detailed description of how the Donalds and Osei-Bryson model was generated, see Appendix C. It should be noted that the equivalent of Phase 1 has been successfully

Table 6.3 Hybrid Process for Empirically bases Theory Development (Kositanurit et al., 2011; Osei-Bryson & Ngwenyama, 2011)

Phase	Step	Description
1	1	■ 1a: Use existing theory to identify variables that are likely to be relevant to the phenomena of interest. ■ 1b: Based on Substep 1a, gather data related to the phenomena of interest.
	2	■ 2a: Use data mining approach to do automatic generation and preliminary testing of hypotheses. ■ 2b: Based on the results of Substep 2a, generate a preliminary model that appears to explain the phenomena of interest. ■ 2c: The researcher examines, and if necessary, revises the preliminary model that was generated in Substep 2b. This revision may be based on the researcher's knowledge of existing theory.
2	3	■ Design an experiment to test the logical consequences of the hypotheses. Conventional data analysis approaches may be included in the experimental design.
	4	■ 4a: Collect observations about the phenomena. ■ 4b: Conduct measurement validity. ■ 4c: Determine if hypotheses of the current model are supported based on data analysis of the given dataset.

used in previously published research (see, for example, Andoh-Baidoo, Osei-Bryson, & Amoako-Gyampah, 2013; Yeo & Grant, 2018). Yeo and Grant (2018) used DT induction, framed by the Technology, Organization, and Environment framework to investigate how information and communication technologies and financial factors affect sale revenue growth in service industries globally and to use the research findings to identify hypotheses for future research.

6.4 Research Model and Hypotheses

Our research model (see Figure 6.3) is based on the Donalds and Osei-Bryson model. Since the relationships in the Donalds and Osei-Bryson model remain a set of assertions, in this study we empirically validate said hypotheses in order to

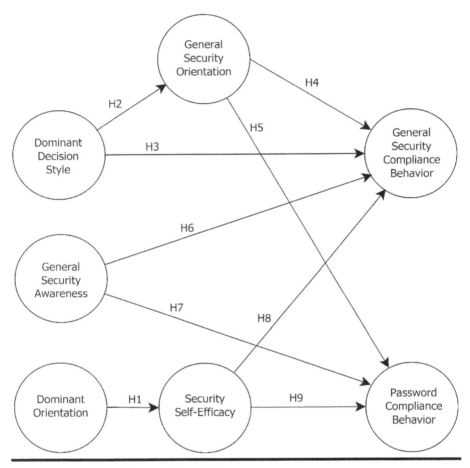

Figure 6.3   Proposed research model

determine whether they are statistically significant and can therefore offer new insights about factors not previously examined, that may influence individuals' cybersecurity behaviour. Some of the hypotheses in the Donalds and Osei-Bryson model were generated by applying decision tree induction and abductive reasoning, while others were presented in prior research. The Process column in Table 6.4 identifies which process was used to generate each hypothesis. Table 6.4 also provides literature support for the hypotheses in the Donalds and Osei-Bryson model, vis-à-vis our research model.

Table 6.4 Literature Support for the Hypotheses in the Research Model

Hypothesis			Literature Support
Label	*Link*	*Process*	
H1	Dominant Orientation → Security Self-Efficacy	Abductive Reasoning	Donalds and Osei-Bryson (2017)
H2	Dominant Decision Style → General Security Orientation	Abductive Reasoning	Donalds and Osei-Bryson (2017)
H3	General Security Orientation → General Security Compliance Behaviour	Existing Theory	Ng et al. (2009); Jayanti and Burns (1998)
H4	Dominant Decision Style → General Security Compliance Behaviour	Abductive Reasoning	Donalds and Osei-Bryson (2017)
H5	General Security Awareness → General Security Compliance Behaviour	Existing Theory	Stanton et al. (2005); Bulgurcu et al. (2010); Donalds (2015)
H6	Security Self-Efficacy → General Security Compliance Behaviour	Existing Theory	Chan, Woon, and Kankanhalli (2005); Ng et al. (2009)
H7	General Security Orientation → Password Compliance Behaviour	Existing Theory	Ng et al. (2009); Jayanti and Burns (1998)
H8	General Security Awareness → Password Compliance Behaviour	Existing Theory	Bulgurcu et al. (2010); Donalds (2015)
H9	Security Self-Efficacy → Password Compliance Behaviour	Existing Theory	Chan et al. (2005); Ng et al. (2009)

6.5 Hypotheses Development

6.5.1 Dominant Orientation

Dominant orientation indicates an individual's preference for acting (action-oriented) or thinking (idea-oriented). The reader may recall that idea-oriented individuals are described as more concerned with analysis, synthesis, creativity, visualizing, music, art and writing while action-oriented people tend to work well with others, concerned with achieving results but may engage in inadequate reflection before acting (Rowe & Mason, 1987). While dominant orientation is not present in prior IS research, it may be an important explanatory construct in cybersecurity/computer security practice.

One important concept of cybersecurity compliance behaviour is individuals' responses to the challenges of performing security tasks/actions related to established security best practices/policies. This relates to individuals' security self-efficacy. Security self-efficacy refers to individuals' assessment of his/her ability to perform cybersecurity actions/tasks so as to minimize cybersecurity threats/incidents (Bandura, 1977; Donalds and Osei-Bryson, 2017) and prior research have demonstrated the importance of self-efficacy in influencing individuals' security behaviour (e.g. D'Arcy & Lowry, 2019; Ng et al., 2009). Prior research has shown trait-based characteristics as influencing individual's security self-efficacy. For instance, Vance et al. (2012) found that habit towards compliance with IS security policies had a significant impact on self-efficacy. Habit is described as a form of routinized behaviour, that is, 'many actions occur without conscious decision to act and are performed because individuals are accustomed to performing them' (Vance et al., 2012, p. 192). Wall, Palvia and Lowry (2013) found statistical support for the influence of self-determination on self-efficacy to comply with security policy. Self-determination, another trait-based characteristic, refers to an individual's belief that his/her actions are self-guided and should therefore lead to increased intrinsic motivation to accomplish a task (Deci & Ryan, 1985; Ryan & Deci, 2000). These results show that trait-based characteristics have influenced individuals' self-efficacy. As another trait-based characteristic, we argue that dominant orientation too has the potential to influence security self-efficacy. Therefore, we propose:

H1. Dominant orientation influences security self-efficacy.

6.5.2 Dominant Decision Style

General security orientation relates to the individual's predisposition and interest concerning practicing security compliance actions. Individuals with different decision-making styles vary with respect to methods used to perceive and evaluate potential threats. Results from previous research (e.g. Ali, 1993; Singh, 1986) have indicated that individual decision-making style is linked with the individual's attitude towards risk. Cybersecurity compliance actions are aimed at addressing vulnerability conditions posed by threats (or hazards). As noted by Cardona (2004, p. 38) 'due to the fact that in many cases it is not possible to modify the hazard in order to reduce the risk, there is nothing left to do except modify the conditions of vulnerability of the exposed elements'. The individual's attitude towards risk will thus affect his/her predisposition and interest concerning practicing actions aimed at modifying 'the conditions of vulnerability'. It is therefore reasonable to infer that the individual's dominant decision style would have an impact on general security orientation. Therefore, we hypothesize:

H2. Dominant decision style influences general security orientation.

Recall, dominant decision style indicates that an individual frequently uses a particular DMS over other DMSs. There is some evidence that individuals' predominant decision styles (i.e. dominant decision styles) influence their performance or behaviour. For instance, Fox and Spence (2005) found that project managers' with directive or analytical dominant decision styles significantly outperformed other project managers with other decision styles, in regard to completing an initial project plan using a computerized project management tool as well as the accuracy or completeness of said plan. There is also evidence that individuals' dominant decision styles influence their driving style. For example, French, West, Elander and Wildin (1993) found that individuals carried their 'global' DMSs (referring to individual's dominant decision style), into the driving situation, and that in so doing put themselves at differential risk of having a road traffic accident. These results suggest a direct relationship between individual's dominant decision style and their behaviour. In this study we argue that a similar relationship exists between dominant decision style and general security compliance behaviour, thus, the following hypothesis is proposed:

H3. Dominant decision style directly influences general security compliance behaviour.

6.5.3 General Security Orientation

Analogous to general health orientation of the health belief model, which captures the individual's tendency towards performing healthy behaviour, general security orientation captures an individual's tendency or predisposition towards individual security compliance behaviour. According to Ng et al. (2009), general security orientation is an individual's security consciousness or predisposition and interest concerning practicing computer security. In one study, it was found that individuals' with greater security orientation or having higher security consciousness, caused them to be more proactive in computer security behaviour when they perceived the severity of the security threat to be high (Ng et al., 2009). In other words, the relationship between general security orientation and computer security behaviour was moderated by perceived threat severity. However, Jayanti and Burns (1998) observed that individuals with higher levels of health consciousness exhibit greater levels of preventative healthcare behaviour, suggesting a direct relationship between 'consciousness' and 'behaviour'. In this study we expect that a similar relationship exists between general security orientation and individual compliance behaviour, thus we hypothesize:

> **H4.** General security orientation directly influences general security compliance behaviour.

Organizational security policies are by their nature restrictive and, would be viewed by some employees as being unnecessarily constraining or burdensome while others would consider the cost of damage versus the cost of the restriction. It is known that while some employee-related security breaches are caused by intentional acts, others are the result of inadequate security compliance where the employee engages in naïve or undisciplined behaviour including the sharing of passwords or poor choice of passwords (Stanton et al., 2005). It is to be expected that individuals with higher levels of general security orientation would be more constantly sensitive to the possible occurrence of security incidents and their damaging effects. It can be reasonably argued that whether an employee avoids or engages in such naïve or undisciplined behaviour is in part determined by his/her general security orientation. Thus, the following hypothesis is proposed:

> **H5.** General security orientation directly influences password security compliance behaviour.

6.5.4 General Security Awareness

According to Hansche (2001), security awareness can be used to heighten the importance of IS security and the possible negative effects of a security breach or failure. Security awareness has also been espoused as important to achieving individual security compliance behaviour. For instance, Siponen (2000) argues that providing security awareness is the most important factor in persuading employees to change their compliance actions. Donalds and Barclay (2021) also argue that security awareness is necessary to realize improved security knowledge and security-related behaviours. Empirical evidence supports these claims as D'Arcy, Hovav, and Galletta (2009) found that users' awareness of countermeasures impact perceptions of sanctions, which in turn deters users' IS misuse intention and Bulgurcu, Cavusoglu, and Benbasat (2009) found that general security awareness influenced users' attitude toward IS policy (ISP) compliance, which in turn influenced their ISP compliance intention. More specifically, Donalds (2015) found that cybersecurity awareness directly influenced cybersecurity compliance behaviour. We therefore argue that general security awareness will directly influence individual's general security compliance behaviour. Thus, the following hypotheses:

H6. General security awareness directly influences general security compliance behaviour.

Mamonov and Benbunan-Fich (2018) conducted an empirical study to evaluate the effects of an exposure to general information security threats on the strength of passwords; they found statistically significant support for the positive effects of awareness of information security threats on the strength of newly chosen passwords. In fact, Mamonov and Benbunan-Fich (2018) reported that the treatment group exposed to the security breach news used much stronger (500x) passwords. Likewise, Stanton et al. (2005) found that security awareness had a direct relationship with individuals changing their passwords more frequently as well as using stronger passwords. We therefore argue that general security awareness will directly influence individual's password compliance security behaviour. Thus, the following hypothesis is proposed:

H7. General security awareness directly influences password security compliance behaviour.

6.5.5 Security Self-Efficacy

Self-efficacy has its roots in social cognitive theory and refers to an individual's ability or judgment of his or her ability to perform an action (Bandura, 1977). Self-efficacy has been shown to have a significant impact on an individual's ability to accomplish or perform a task. For instance, Compeau and Higgins (1995) found that self-efficacy exerts a strong influence on individual's performance with computer use. That is, Compeau and Higgins (1995) found that individuals with higher self-efficacy regarding IS use are more likely to employ such systems in their work than individuals with lower self-efficacy. Self-efficacy has also been found to influence various information security-related behaviours such as IS policy compliance intention (Bulgurcu et al., 2010; Herath & Rao, 2009b), computer security related behaviours (D'Arcy & Lowry, 2019; Ng et al., 2009), users' intention to use anti-spyware software (Johnston & Warkentin, 2010), among others. An individual who perceives him/herself in having the ability to undertake general cybersecurity security recommended behaviours is more likely to comply with those behaviours and best practices. Thus, we hypothesize:

H8. Security self-efficacy directly influences general security compliance behaviour.

The study of Jayanti and Burns (1998) showed that self-efficacy has a statistically significant impact on preventive health care behaviour. Given that password compliance behaviour can be considered to be a preventive behaviour, then this result from Jayanti and Burns (1998) suggests that security self-efficacy would influence password compliance behaviour. Further, self-efficacy has been found to influence password guidelines compliance intention (Mwagwabi, McGill, & Dixon, 2014). An individual that perceives him/herself in having the ability to undertake password best practices is more likely to comply with those behaviours and best practices. Thus, we hypothesize:

> **H9**. Security self-efficacy directly influences password security compliance behaviour.

6.6 Methodology

Our methodology for investigating the Donalds and Osei-Bryson model can be described as a four-step process: 1) adoption and validation of an instrument for collecting data about the constructs defined in the model; 2) collection of survey data; 3) conducting measurement model tests to determine whether the cybersecurity constructs' measures in this study are consistent with Donalds and Osei-Bryson' understanding of the nature of the factors; and 4) use of regression analysis to evaluate and describe the causal links existing between the constructs in the model.

Steps 1 & 2: Measurement scale and data collection

Recall, Donalds and Osei-Bryson (2017) in applying the steps of the Peircian abduction framework first used existing theory to identify potential predictor and determinant individual cybersecurity compliance behaviour variables, then collected DSI and cybersecurity-related data, followed by EFA of the cybersecurity-related variables to explain the structure of the data and finally, conducted DT induction of both cybersecurity and DSI data, to identify hypotheses for future testing. Thus, in this study our measurement scale consisted of items relating to DSI and individual cybersecurity compliance behaviour. We therefore adopted the 20 item DSI measures as proposed by Rowe and Mason (1987) as well as the measurement items for all the cybersecurity constructs in the Donalds and Osei-Bryson model from the Donalds and Osei-Bryson (2017) study since all the constructs have related measurement items developed and validated by previous studies (see Appendix A). Each cybersecurity construct (i.e. *password compliance behaviour, general security compliance behaviour, general security awareness, general security orientation* and *security self-efficacy*) was measured reflectively with multiple items, based on a 5-point Likert-like scale, rated from 1= 'Strongly disagree' to 5 = 'Strongly agree'.

It should be noted that although the 5-point Likert scale has been criticized by some researchers, it has also been successfully applied in various research projects (Dwivedi, Kapoor, Williams, & Williams, 2013; Shareef, Kumar, Dwivedi, &

Kumar, 2016; Triantoro, Gopal, Benbunan-Fich, & Lang, 2019). It should also be noted that Dawes (2008, p. 1) in discussing the results of his study that addressed:

> how using Likert-type scales with either 5-point, 7-point or 10-point format affects the resultant data in terms of mean scores, and measures of dispersion and shape. … The 5- and 7-point scales were rescaled to a comparable mean score out of ten,

noted that this study:

> found that the 5- and 7-point scales produced the same mean score as each other, once they were rescaled. However, the 10-point format tended to produce slightly lower relative means … In terms of the other data characteristics, there was very little difference among the scale formats in terms of variation about the mean, skewness or kurtosis. This study is "good news" for research departments or agencies … 5- and 7-point scales can easily be rescaled with the resultant data being quite comparable.
>
> (Dawes, 2008, p. 1)

We collected data via a web-based survey from individuals employed in Jamaican companies as well as faculty members, graduate and some undergraduate students with working experience that are affiliated with an institution of higher learning. This type of mixed group sampling is commonly used in IS research. In their study that presents a systematic review of empirical research on cybersecurity issues, Lu (2018) notes that papers reviewed treated individuals as administrative personnel, clients, computer users, consumers, internet users and students. To elicit participation, the survey was advertised in several undergraduate and graduate classes, sent to faculty members of the Business School in which one of the researcher is affiliated and sent to individuals in other Jamaican institutions. Overall, the survey link was sent/advertised to approximately 510 individuals. We received 248 responses, yielding a 48.6% response rate. Table 6.5 summarizes the socio-demographic information of the respondents. Respondents were employed in varying industries. Among the respondents, approximately 68% were females and approximately 71% were between the age range 18 and 35.

Step 3: Measurement validation assessment

In this step, our focus was assessing the measurement model for the cybersecurity variables only. More specifically, to verify whether this study's cybersecurity-related factor structure of the observed variables align with those in the Donalds and Osei-Bryson model, we conducted several tests of reliability and validity. We note that only the cybersecurity variables (i.e. *general security awareness, general security*

Table 6.5 Socio-demographic Characteristics

Gender	Frequency	Percent
Male	80	32.3
Female	168	67.7
Organization category		
Banking & Financial Services	54	21.8
Telecommunications/Information Technology	25	10.1
Travel/Hotel Industry	11	4.4
Education	94	37.9
Law/Legal Services	6	2.4
Real Estate	11	4.4
Government: Security Services (e.g. Police, Army)	3	1.2
Government: Other	10	4.0
Health Care/Medical	3	1.2
Manufacturing	9	3.6
Power/Energy	2	0.8
Other	20	8.1
Age range		
18–21	103	41.5
22–35	74	29.8
36–45	44	17.7
46–55	27	10.9

orientation, security self-efficacy, general security compliance behaviour, and *password compliance behaviour*) are used in these tests since *DominantOrientation* and *DominantDecisionStyle* are binary and multi-value categorical variables, respectively, and these reliability and validity tests are not applicable to categorical variables.

To ensure the individual item reliability, we examined factor loadings of individual measures on their respective underlying constructs. All of the measurement item loadings on their respective constructs were above the recommended minimum value of 0.708 (Hair, Hult, Ringle, & Sarstedt, 2014) (see Table 6.6). Moreover,

Table 6.6 Outer Model Results Summary

Construct	Item	Loading	Indicator Reliability	CR	AVE	Cronbach α	Discriminant Validity?
Password Compliance Behaviour (PWCB)	PWCB1	0.937	0.878	0.876	0.780	0.732	Yes
	PWCB2	0.826	0.682				
General Security Compliance Behaviour (GSCB)	GSCB5	0.921	0.848	0.956	0.877	0.930	Yes
	GSCB6	0.954	0.910				
	GSCB7	0.934	0.872				
General Security Awareness (GSAW)	GSAW1	0.956	0.914	0.962	0.895	0.941	Yes
	GSAW2	0.954	0.910				
	GSAW3	0.928	0.861				
Security Self-Efficacy (SLEF)	SLEF2	0.806	0.650	0.918	0.691	0.887	Yes
	SLEF3	0.750	0.563				
	SLEF4	0.789	0.623				
	SLEF5	0.897	0.805				
	SLEF6	0.903	0.815				
General Security Orientation (GSOR)	GSOR1	0.791	0.626	0.885	0.720	0.804	Yes
	GSOR2	0.893	0.797				
	GSOR3	0.859	0.738				

since all the measurement item loadings are greater than the minimum recommended value, the result also confirms the measurement theory of the Donalds and Osei-Bryson model.

To assess the latent variable internal consistency reliability, we calculated Cronbach's alpha and composite reliability. A Cronbach's alpha value and composite reliability value of 0.7 or greater is considered acceptable (Gefen, Straub, & Boudreau, 2000; Nunnally & Bernstein, 1994). As shown in Table 6.6, all Cronbach's alpha values are greater than 0.7 and the composite reliability values are greater than 0.8, an indication that all constructs had adequate reliability scores.

To evaluate convergent validity, individual indicator reliability (Hair et al., 2014) and the average variance extracted (AVE) (Chin, 1998; Fornell & Larcker, 1981) are assessed. Indicator reliability is the square of a standardized indicator's loading and should have a minimum value of 0.5; representing how much of the variation in an item is explained by the construct (Hair et al., 2014). As displayed in Table 6.6, all indicator reliability is above the minimum 0.5 threshold value. Fornell and Larcker (1981) propose a cut-off value of 0.5 for AVE; this indicates that, on average, the construct accounts for at least 50% of the variance of its indicators. As seen in Table 6.6, the AVE of each cybersecurity construct exceeds the minimum cut-off value.

The cross-loadings and the Fornell–Larcker criterion allow for the checking of discriminant validity. When an indicator's loading on a construct is higher than all of its cross-loadings with other constructs, discriminant validity is established. As can be seen from the inspection of Appendix B, each indicator loading is much higher on its assigned construct than on the other constructs. According to the Fornell–Larcker criterion (Fornell & Larcker, 1981), the square root of the AVE of each construct should be higher than its correlation with other constructs. Table 6.7

Table 6.7 Latent Variable Correlations

	GSAW	GSCB	GSOR	PWCB	SLEF
General Security Awareness (GSAW)	**0.9461**				
General Security Compliance Behaviour (GSCB)	0.3014	**0.9367**			
General Security Orientation (GSOR)	0.2866	0.4048	**0.8484**		
Password Compliance Behaviour (PWCB)	0.3102	0.3109	0.2923	**0.8834**	
Security Self-Efficacy (SLEF)	0.3194	0.3367	0.1922	0.3148	**0.8315**

Note: The square root of the AVE is shown on the diagonal.

shows that the square root of the AVE (along the diagonal) for each construct exceeds the inter-correlations of the construct with other constructs, supporting discriminant validity.

While several statistical remedies have been proposed to address common method variance (CMV), there is no consensus in the literature about how to detect and control for it. According to Chin, Thatcher, Wright, and Steel (2013, pp. 1), 'to date, methodologists have yet to agree upon a best practice for detecting and controlling for CMV'. Nonetheless, to test for the potential of CMV in this study, we followed the approach used by Liu, Chan, Yang, and Niu (2018), who: (1) inspected the correlation matrix among the latent variables; and (2) conducted Harman's single factor test. As shown in Table 6.7, the largest correlation is 0.4048 (the correlation of GSOR and GSCB), which is well below the suggested extremely high correlation of 0.90, which indicates CMV. Since low correlations exist among the latent variables, CMV influence is minimal. The results from our Harman's single factor test showed that a single factor explained 20.24% of the total variance extracted, which is far less than 50%, indicating that CMV is not an issue in our study.

Step 4: Regression analysis

In this step, we use multiple linear regressions to conduct our statistical analysis of the validity of the causal links, i.e. the hypotheses, specified in Donalds and Osei-Bryson model. This approach is appropriate for our study as it is well suited for assessing relationships between several predictor and target variables as well as for assessing models containing categorical and interval variables. The reader should note that all the variables in this model are on an interval scale with the exception of two categorical variables, i.e. *DominantOrientation* (*DomOR*) and *DominantDecisionStyle* (*DomDS*). The binary categorical variable *DomOr* (*Idea vs. Action*) can be directly represented in regression analysis. In accordance with traditional practice for dealing with non-binary categorical variables in regression analysis, these are indirectly represented by multiple binary numeric dummy variables, where a given potential predictor variable is considered to have a statistically significant impact on a given target variable if any of its associated dummy variables has a statistically significant impact on the given target variable. Recall, the decision style of an individual is either *analytic, conceptual, behavioural* or *directive* (see Figure 6.1). Therefore, if an individual's dominant decision style is identified as *analytic*, in our regression analysis that variable is assigned 1 while 0 is assigned to all the other decision-style variables (i.e. *conceptual, behavioural* and *directive*). Table 6.8 displays dummy variables for all possible combinations of value of the *DomDS* variable. However, it should be noted that for a given regression equation, only three of the four binary decision-style variables could be used in the regression analysis, and this is what we actually did. Table 6.8 is not meant to imply that all four binary variables are required; rather Table 6.8 offers a means for interpreting the results of the regression analyses as it provides information on the meaning of each value of each of the binary decision-style variable.

Table 6.8 Dummy Variables Representing Dominant Decision Style

Dummy Variable	Level	Dominant Decision Style
DomDS_A	1	Analytical
	0	Conceptual or Behavioural or Directive
DomDS_B	1	Behavioural
	0	Analytical or Conceptual or Directive
DomDS_C	1	Conceptual
	0	Analytical or Behavioural or Directive
DomDS_D	1	Directive
	0	Analytical or Conceptual or Behavioural

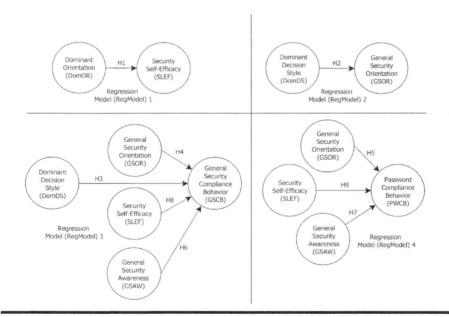

Figure 6.4   Multiple-regression models

The Donalds and Osei-Bryson model includes four variables (i.e. *SecuritySelf-Efficacy*(*SLEF*), *GeneralSecurityOrientation*(*GSOR*), *GeneralSecurityComplianceBehaviour* (*GSCB*), *PasswordSecurityComplianceBehaviour* (*PWCB*)), each of which is the target variable for one or more causal links. For each of these target variables, we used a separate regression model to determine whether the existence of the relevant causal link(s) is/are supported by statistical analysis. Figure 6.4 shows the various regression models assessed.

We used SAS Enterprise Miner software to conduct our statistical analysis. Table 6.9 displays the results of our statistical analysis for the causal links, whose existence are supported at the 5% level of significance. Of note, the Level column in Table 6.9 applies only to the categorical (binary and multi-value) variables (*DomOR* & *DomDS*) and to those causal links for which the antecedent is a categorical variable; N/A is displayed otherwise.

Specifically, the results show that the path from *DominantOrientation (DomOR)* to *SecuritySelf-Efficacy (SLEF)* (i.e. RegModel 1) is statistically significant. The result of RegModel 1 suggests that assuming that the only difference between two individuals is their dominant orientation then the individual with an *Idea* orientation will have a higher level of *SecuritySelf-Efficacy* than the individual with an *Action* orientation. This follows because the coefficient for *DominantOrientation* is negative (i.e. -0.17148) when *DominantOrientation* is *Action* and 0 when *DominantOrientation* is *Idea*.

The reader may observe that for each of the regression models that involve a *DominantDecisionStyle (DomDS)* as a potential predictor (i.e. RegModels 2 & 3), that at least one of the associated binary dummy variables is a statistically significant predictor of the relevant target variable, and so *DominantDecisionStyle* can be considered to be a statistically significant predictor of the relevant target variables.

More specifically, the results for Model 2 suggest that assuming that the only difference between two individuals is their dominant decision style, then the individual with a *Directive* dominant decision style will have a higher level of *GeneralSecurityOrientation (GSOR)* than the individual with another dominant decision style. This follows because the coefficient for *DominantDecisionStyle_Directive* is negative when *DominantDecisionStyle_Directive* is 0.

Likewise, the results for Model 3 suggest that assuming that the only difference between two individuals is their dominant decision style then the individual with a *Behavioural* dominant decision style will have a higher level of *GeneralSecurityComplianceBehaviour (GSCB)* than the individual with another dominant decision style. This is because the coefficient for *DominantDecisionStyle_Behavioural* is negative when *DominantDecisionStyle_Behavioural* is 0.

The results also show that the paths from *GeneralSecurityAwareness (GSAW)*, *GeneralSecurityOrientation* and *SecuritySelf-Efficacy* to *PasswordComplianceBehaviour (PWCB)* (i.e. RegModel 4) are all statistically significant.

In summary, the tests of the regression models show that dominant decision style, general security orientation, general security awareness and security self-efficacy are important factors of individual's general security compliance behaviour. Further, our results show that security orientation, general security awareness and security self-efficacy exert significant influence on individual's password compliance behaviour. Dominant orientation has indirect effect, through security self-efficacy, on password security compliance behaviour. The results, therefore, indicate that the existence of each causal link of the Donalds and Osei-Bryson model is supported at the 5% level of significance.

Table 6.9 Results of the Hypotheses Tests

RegModel	Label	Path			Level	Coefficient	p-value	Result
1	H1	DomOR	↑	SLEF	Action	-0.17148	0.021661*	Supported
2	H2	DomDS_D	↑	GSOR	0	-0.23644	0.0004256*	Supported
3	H3	DomDS_B	↑	GSCB	0	-0.28071	0.034210*	Supported
	H4	GSOR	↑	GSCB	N/A	0.38907	0.000000*	Supported
	H6	GSAW	↑	GSCB	N/A	0.14446	0.012527*	Supported
	H8	SLEF	↑	GSCB	N/A	0.266947	0.000153*	Supported
4	H5	GSOR	↑	PWCB	N/A	0.20225	0.00398244*	Supported
	H7	GSAW	↑	PWCB	N/A	0.16623	0.00410887*	Supported
	H9	SLEF	↑	PWCB	N/A	0.23847	0.00073900*	Supported

$* \rho < 0.05$

6.7 Discussion, Implications, Limitations and Future Research

6.7.1 Discussion of Findings

In this study, we examined the individual cybersecurity compliance behaviour model proposed by Donalds and Osei-Bryson. This model identifies several antecedents to individual cybersecurity compliance behaviour, including decision style and dominant (Idea/Action) orientation, to provide theoretical explanations for individuals' actual cybersecurity compliance behaviour. Overall, we found strong empirical support for the hypotheses of the Donalds and Osei-Bryson model. Specifically, our results provide empirical support for the claim that an individual's *dominant decision style* influences his/her cybersecurity compliance behaviour and other antecedents of such behaviour as the relationship between *dominant decision style* and *general security compliance behaviour* as well as *dominant decision style* and *general security orientation* are statistically significant. Moreover, *dominant (Idea/Action) orientation* is a key influencer of *security self-efficacy*, indirectly influencing security compliance behaviour. *General security orientation* also significantly influences *general security compliance behaviour* as well as *password security compliance behaviour*. These results are consistent with the result of Daskalakis, Katharaki, Liaskos, and Mantas (2010) study which found that nursing students in applying security concepts and practices were significantly influenced by their general security orientation. The relationship between *security self-efficacy* and *general security compliance behaviour* as well as *security self-efficacy* and *password security compliance behaviour* are also statistically significant. These findings too are consistent with that of Rhee, Kim, and Ryu (2009) which found that self-efficacy in information security influenced the use of security software as well as the security care behaviour related to computer/Internet usage. Similarly, Li et al. (2019) provide empirical evidence for the link between employees' self-efficacy and their information security protection behaviour. Moreover, others found self-efficacy to have a significant influence on user's intention to comply with information security policies (e.g. Bulgurcu et al., 2010; Herath & Rao, 2009b; Siponen et al., 2007). Another key influencer of *general security compliance behaviour* and *password security compliance behaviour* is *general security awareness*. Other studies also found the relationship between security awareness and security behaviour statistically significant. For instance, Siponen and Vance (2014) found that information security awareness has a statistically significant impact on employees' compliance with information security policy; Bulgurcu et al. (2010) found that security awareness exerts statistically significant influence on an employee's attitude toward compliance; Stanton et al. (2005) report statistically significant relationships between password behaviours and security awareness; and Donalds (2015) found that cybersecurity awareness significantly influences employees cybersecurity compliance behaviour with established cybersecurity policies.

6.7.2 Contribution to Theory

For IS security research and theory, we have heeded the call by others to incorporate 'new methodological approaches' to augment our understanding of individuals' security motivations (Warkentin & Willison, 2009, p. 102). Further, according to others (e.g. Warkentin & Willison, 2009), IS researchers should expand their horizons and incorporate new theoretical foundations to learn from other cognitive behavioural sciences. In this study, we have empirically validated the causal links of a new individual cybersecurity compliance behaviour model proposed by Donalds and Osei-Bryson (2017). This model differs significantly from most previously proposed security models in that it focuses on individuals' actual security behaviour and not their security intention behaviour. Moreover, the Donalds and Osei-Bryson model incorporates a new theoretical lens, decision-style theory, to investigate the cybersecurity phenomenon. Our study is, to our best knowledge, the first to empirically test the influence of individual's decision style on their cybersecurity compliance behaviour. Our study shows that an individual's dominant decision style exerts a significant influence on their general security compliance behaviour as well as his/her corresponding general security orientation. Further, our findings show that a trait-based characteristic, specifically, an individual's dominant orientation, exerts significant influence on their security self-efficacy. These results suggest that it could be valuable for cybersecurity research to expand the set of intrinsic variables that should be explored as antecedents of security compliance behaviour.

Relatedly, we have demonstrated how the hybrid Peircian knowledge discovery abduction framework proposed by Osei-Bryson and Ngwenyama (2011) and Kositanurit et al. (2011) can be used for empirically based theory development. Interestingly, apart from the hypotheses that were abducted in the study of Donalds and Osei-Bryson (2017), another important result is that the data analysis indicates that security compliance behaviour, which was initially conceptualized as a single construct, should be represented by two constructs (i.e. *General Security Compliance Behaviour (GSCB)*, *Password Compliance Behaviour (PWCB)*).

6.7.3 Contribution to Practice

As noted earlier, individual security compliance behaviour has been a challenge for public and private organizations. Given the high costs of remediating internal individuals' security incidents, an explanatory model that offers guidance to decision-makers on improving security compliance behaviour could be valuable. The results of our study show that not only extrinsic factors (i.e. *general security awareness* and *security self-efficacy*), which are generally the focus of organizations, but intrinsic factors (i.e. *general security orientation*, *dominant decision style* and *dominant orientation*) also influence individuals' cybersecurity compliance behaviour. Extrinsic motivation is influenced by external sources to the individual and could include cybersecurity training and awareness campaigns. Intrinsic motivation, on the other hand, is derived from an individual's innate interest or satisfaction in performing an action or behaviour, and which is not based on external stimuli. According to decision-style theory, individuals have different decision styles, which elicits specific preferences, such as having a strong need for structure or having a high tolerance for ambiguity, or prefer acting to thinking, written reports over meetings or vice versa, and still others may use rather considerable information in decision-making, yet others use primarily intuition. These kinds of preferences can shed light on how individuals think about security compliance and ultimately, influence their cybersecurity compliance behaviour. Thus, with this knowledge organizations can adopt appropriate management practices that support the decision styles of individuals in organizations.

With respect to the extrinsic variables (i.e. *general security awareness* (*GSAW*) and *security self-efficacy* (*SLEF*)), the decision-maker could develop training and other appropriate programmes to improve the given employee scores for these extrinsic variables (e.g. *SLEF*, *GSAW*). Further the *dominant orientation* (*DomOR*) → *SLEF* link suggests that with respect to the designing of programmes to improve *SLEF*, the *DomOR* (i.e. Idea/Action orientation) of the employees should be taken into consideration.

With respect to the intrinsic variables (i.e. *general security orientation* (*GSOR*), *dominant decision style* (*DomDS*), *DomOR*), although each of these variables has either a direct impact (e.g. *DomDS* → *GSCB*; *GSOR* → *GSCB*) or indirect impact (e.g. *DomDS* → *GSCB*; *DomDS* → *PWCB*; *DomOR* → *PWCB*) on security compliance behaviour (*GSCB* and/or *PWCB*), the decision-maker is not able to change the value of these intrinsic variables. However, the decision-maker could be able to determine which employee is/are assigned to situations that are highly sensitive to individual security compliance behaviour. Our explanatory model could be used to provide assistance to decision-makers via the relevant values of these intrinsic variables.

6.7.4 Limitations and Future Research

There are some limitations in this study that create opportunities for further research. First, similar to many studies we do not claim that all relevant antecedents of cybersecurity compliance behaviour were included in the Donalds and Osei-Bryson model. For instance, information security policy formulation and effective implementation (Doherty, Anastasakis, & Fulford, 2009; Singh, Picot, Kranz, Gupta, & Ojha, 2013), as well as information security policy awareness and training (Whitman, 2004), are factors that contribute to security effectiveness; yet, the effect of these factors on individual cybersecurity compliance behaviour were not considered in the Donalds and Osei-Bryson model. Future studies then could explore the influences of other relevant extrinsic antecedents of security compliance behaviour along with those in the Donalds and Osei-Bryson model. Further, other relevant antecedent intrinsic variables, particularly those such as individual decision styles that have not been previously explored in cybersecurity research, could also be explored in future studies.

Our study investigates the influence of decision styles on individual cybersecurity compliance and other antecedents of such behaviour. Since the study by Donalds and Osei-Bryson (2017) is the only study that incorporates decision-style theory to investigate the cybersecurity compliance phenomenon, one possible direction for future research is for others to investigate the role that decision-style theory may play in influencing individuals' cybersecurity or other computer security compliance behaviour. For instance, future research can use the DSI measures proposed by Rowe and Mason (1987) with other models situated in different computer security contexts such as Theory of Planned Behaviour (Ajzen, 1991; Fishbein & Ajzen, 1975).

Similar to most empirical studies, our survey participants were located in a specific geographic and cultural context. However, as noted by Davison and Martinsons (2016) context is an important issue when considering the scope for which a theory is valid. Thus, there is a need for future research that would involve the empirical evaluation of the Donalds and Osei-Bryson model in different geographic, cultural and other contexts to determine its boundaries and identify situations wherein its components fail to explain the phenomenon. The reader may note that this need is not limited to our study, but as suggested Davison and Martinsons (2016) apply to a large volume of empirical studies.

6.8 Conclusion

Individual security/cybersecurity compliance behaviour remains a challenge for entities. Empirical evidence indicates that the top cause for security incidents is largely due to individuals failing to comply with security best practices. In response, IS scholars have proposed several models based on a variety of theories, to explain what influences individual security compliance behaviour. However, individual cybersecurity compliance behaviour remains a challenge for organizations. In this study, we seek to augment and diversify research on individual security/cybersecurity compliance behaviour by examining a new cybersecurity model proposed by Donalds and Osei-Bryson (2017). Specifically, we seek to examine the influence of decision styles on individual cybersecurity compliance behaviour and other antecedents of such behaviour, as specified in the Donalds and Osei-Bryson model. For IS security researchers, this study makes important contributions towards understanding individual cybersecurity compliance behaviour by interrogating a new individual cybersecurity compliance behaviour model that incorporates new theoretical lens as well as utilizing a new methodological approach for empirically based theory development. By testing the relationships between individual's dominant decision style, dominant orientation, general security orientation, general security awareness and security self-efficacy on their cybersecurity compliance behaviour, this study assesses the effectiveness of these motivators and offers suggestions regarding management practices that can improve individual cybersecurity compliance behaviour as well as appeal to the different decision styles of individuals in organizations. Our results suggest that (a) dominant orientation influences individual's security self-efficacy; (b) dominant decision style influences individual's general security orientation; (c) general security orientation, security self-efficacy, general security awareness and dominant decision-style influence individual general security compliance behaviour; and (d) general security awareness, general security orientation and security self-efficacy influence individual's password compliance behaviour. Thus, our findings suggest that individual's cybersecurity compliance behaviour is influenced by intrinsic factors, such as decision style and security orientation, as well as extrinsic factors.

Appendix A – Description of the Constructs

Table A1   Constructs, Items & Sources

Construct	Code	Item	Source
Password Compliance Behaviour (PWCB)	PWCB1	I use different passwords for my different online accounts (e.g. online banking/shopping, Facebook, email)	Anwar et al. (2017); Donalds and Osei-Bryson (2017); Special Eurobarometer 390 (2012)
	PWCB2	I have changed the passwords to access my different online accounts (e.g. online banking/ shopping, Facebook, email) during the past 12 months	
General Security Compliance Behaviour (GSCB)	GSCB5	I never usually send sensitive information (such as account numbers, passwords, and ID numbers via email or using social media	Anwar et al. (2017); Donalds and Osei-Bryson (2017); Special Eurobarometer 390 (2012)
	GSCB6	Concerns about security issues made me visit only websites I know/trust or click on URLs if I know where the URLs will really take me	
	GSCB7	Concerns about security issues made me not open emails from people I don't know and/or only use my own computer	

(Continued)

Table A1 (Continued)

Construct	Code	Item	Source
General Security Awareness (GSAW)	GSAW1	Overall, I am aware of potential information/cybersecurity threats and their negative consequences	Bulgurcu et al. (2010); Donalds and Osei-Bryson (2017)
	GSAW2	I understand the concerns regarding information/cybersecurity threats and the risks they pose in general	
	GSAW3	I have sufficient knowledge about the cost of potential information/cybersecurity threats	
General Security Orientation (GSOR)	GSOR1	I read information/cybersecurity bulletins or newsletters	Donalds and Osei-Bryson (2017); Ng et al. (2009)
	GSOR2	I am concerned about information/cybersecurity incidents and try to take actions to prevent them	
	GSOR3	I am usually mindful about computer security	
Security Self-Efficacy (SLEF)	SLEF2	I feel confident updating security patches to the operating system	Anwar et al. (2017); Donalds and Osei-Bryson (2017); Rhee et al. (2009)
	SLEF3	I feel confident setting the Web browser to different security levels	
	SLEF4	I feel confident using different programmes to protect my information and information system	
	SLEF5	I feel confident handling virus-infected files and/or getting rid of malware/spyware	
	SLEF6	I feel confident learning the method to protect my information and information system	

Note: Scale measurement used for all items: 1 = Strongly disagree ...... 5 = Strongly agree

Appendix B – Loadings & Cross Loadings

Table B1   Item Loading and Cross Loadings

	GSAW	*GSCB*	*GSOR*	*PWCB*	*SLEF*
PWCB1	0.311678	0.325807	0.324999	**0.936888**	0.323022
PWCB2	0.222401	0.201305	0.159206	**0.826451**	0.214902
GSCB5	0.280805	**0.921371**	0.341546	0.227537	0.336586
GSCB6	0.290915	**0.954296**	0.382127	0.300090	0.299894
GSCB7	0.275416	**0.934190**	0.411429	0.342224	0.310488
GSAW1	**0.956370**	0.309997	0.249183	0.293273	0.310092
GSAW2	**0.953579**	0.301899	0.301960	0.274496	0.321252
GSAW3	**0.928110**	0.241011	0.263461	0.313592	0.274009
GSOR1	0.140600	0.344856	**0.790750**	0.246347	0.167791
GSOR2	0.352849	0.372722	**0.892762**	0.281687	0.137608
GSOR3	0.222179	0.304520	**0.858519**	0.207125	0.189983
SLEF2	0.285307	0.324436	0.198178	0.244019	**0.806400**
SLEF3	0.230124	0.257184	0.159861	0.289160	**0.750160**
SLEF4	0.257575	0.253741	0.116172	0.229571	**0.789027**
SLEF5	0.271393	0.284294	0.163861	0.262508	**0.897410**
SLEF6	0.279283	0.273091	0.153195	0.278492	**0.903440**

Note: GSAW = General Security Awareness; GSCB = General Security Compliance Behaviour; GSOR = General Security Orientation; PWCB = Password Compliance Behaviour; SLEF = Security Self-efficacy

Appendix C – Methodology Followed to Generate the Donalds and Osei-Bryson Model

The Donalds and Osei-Bryson Model was generated by applying the steps from the methodology presented by Osei-Bryson and Ngwenyama (2011) as well as executing an additional step, 'Exploratory Factor Analysis'. In general, the methodology incorporates data mining techniques, such as decision tree induction, to generate hypotheses which can then be tested in future. Table C1 details the process undertaken in generating the Donalds and Osei-Bryson Model.

Table C1   Steps Applied in Generating the Donalds and Osei-Bryson Model

Step	Description	Detail of what was done
1	Use existing theory to select potential direct and indirect predictor variables for security compliance behaviour.	Identified some potential direct and indirect variables of cybersecurity compliance behaviour, which are: security compliance behaviour, security awareness, general security orientation, security self-efficacy and decision styles.
2	Collect relevant data.	*2.1 Develop appropriate data collection instruments.* a) *Non-DSI based Variables*: Items were adapted from prior studies to measure security compliance behaviour, security awareness, general security orientation and security self-efficacy. These constructs were measured reflectively, based on a 5-point Likert-like scale anchored 1 = 'Strongly disagree' and 5 = 'Strongly agree'. b) *DSI based Variables*: The 20 item standard Decision Style Inventory (DSI) questionnaire proposed by Rowe and Mason (1987) was adopted and used to measure individual's decision-making styles. *2.2 Data Collection* Data were collected from 105 participants via a web-based survey.
3	Conduct exploratory factor analysis.	Exploratory factor analysis was conducted only on the reflectively measured potential predictor variables. Of the four cybersecurity related potential predictor variables (i.e. security compliance behaviour, security awareness, general security orientation and security self-efficacy), five factors emerged to explain the maximum portion of the variance in the original variables, i.e. *password compliance behaviour, general security compliance behaviour, general security awareness, general security orientation* and *security self-efficacy*.

(Continued)

Table C1 (Continued)

Step	Description	Detail of what was done
4	Use decision tree induction technology to do recursive partitioning of the given dataset resulting in rulesets. Abduct hypotheses from the results of the decision tree induction. Sibling rules hypotheses will be generated using the approach presented in Osei-Bryson & Ngwenyama (2011).	*4.1 Each Dependent Variable as Target:* a) For each dependent variable (i.e. *PWCB, GSCB*), decision tree induction (DTI) was conducted in which with the given dependent variable is the target variable, and all the other non-dependent variables (i.e. *SLEF, GSOR, GSAW, DomDS, DomOR*) are included as the potential predictor variables. b) Based on the resulting DT, Sibling Rules Hypotheses were generated & statistically evaluated. c) A tentative Causal Link was generated for each Sibling Rules Hypothesis that was supported by the statistical analysis. d) For only those tentative Causal Links for which a logical justifying explanation is provided, a corresponding hypothesis was abducted for inclusion in the model. *4.2 Each Potential Mediator Variable as Target:* a) Each non-decision style potential predictor variable (i.e. *SLEF, GSOR, GSAW*) that is not a dependent variable is considered to be a tentative mediator variable. DTI was conducted in which each tentative mediator variable was the target variable (i.e. DomDS, DomOR), and the decision styles based variables are included as the potential predictor variables. b) Based on the resulting DT, Sibling Rules Hypotheses were generated & statistically evaluated. c) A tentative Causal Link was generated for each Sibling Rules Hypothesis that was supported by the statistical analysis. d) For only those tentative Causal Links for which a logical justifying explanation is provided, a corresponding hypothesis was abducted for inclusion in the model.
5	Include Previously Proposed Hypotheses	a) Use existing theory to identify relevant hypotheses and corresponding causal links where in each case the antecedents & consequents is either a non-decision-style potential predictor variable (i.e. *SLEF, GSOR, GSAW*) or a dependent variable. b) Include each such hypothesis in the model.

(Continued)

Acknowledgement

The material in this chapter previously appeared in Donalds and Osei-Bryson (2020). Cybersecurity compliance behaviour: Exploring the influences of individual decision style and other antecedents. *International Journal of Information Management, 51*. doi: https://doi.org/10.1016/j.ijinfomgt.2019.102056

Note

1 In this paper, 'individual security compliance behavior' refers to individuals' compliance with established security best practices/policies, such as using strong/difficult to guess passwords and using different passwords for different applications/sites.

References

Ajzen, I. (1991). The theory of planned behaviour. *Organizational Behaviour and Human Decision Processes, 50*(2), 179–211.

Ali, A. J. (1993). Decision-making style, individualism, and attitudes toward risk of Arab executives. *International Studies of Management & Organization, 23*(3), 53–73.

Andoh-Baidoo, F. K., Osei-Bryson, K. M., & Amoako-Gyampah, K. (2013). A hybrid decision tree based methodology for event studies and its application to e-commerce initiative announcements. *ACM SIGMIS Databases: The DATA BASE for Advances in Information System, 44*(1), 78–101.

Anwar, M., He, W., Ash, I., Yuan, X., Li, L., & Xu, L. (2017). Gender difference and employees' cybersecurity behaviours. *Computers in Human Behaviour, 69*(C), 437–443.

Baiocco, R., Laghi, F., & D'Alessio, M. (2009). Decision-making style among adolescents: Relationship with sensation seeking and locus of control. *Journal of Adolescence, 32*(4), 963–976.

Bandura, A. (1977). Self-efficacy: Toward a unifying theory of behaviour change. *Psychological Review, 84*(2), 191–215.

Barlow, J. B., Warkentin, M., Ormond, D., & Dennis, A. R. (2013). Don't make excuses! Discouraging neutralization to reduce IT policy violation. *Computers & Security, 39*, 145–159.

Bavol'ár, J., & Orosová, O. g. (2015). Decision-making styles and their associations with decision-making competencies and mental health. *Judgment and Decision-making, 10*(1), 115–122.

Boss, S. R., Kirsch, L. J., Angermeier, I., Shingler, R. A., & Boss, R. W. (2009). If someone is watching, I'll do what I'm asked: Mandatoriness, control, and information security. *European Journal of Information Systems, 18*, 151–164.

Bruine de Bruin, W., Del Missier, F., & Levin, I. P. (2012). Individual differences in decision-making competency. *Journal of Behavioural Decision-making, 25*(4), 329–330.

Bulgurcu, B., Cavusoglu, H., & Benbasat, I. (2009, August 6-9). Roles of Information Security Awareness and Perceived Fairness in Information Security Policy Compliance. *Paper presented at the 15th Americas Conference on Information Systems*, San Francisco, California.

Bulgurcu, B., Cavusoglu, H., & Benbasat, I. (2010). Information security policy compliance: An empirical study of rationality-based beliefs and information security awareness. *MIS Quarterly, 34*(3), 523–548.

Cardona, O. D. (2004). The need for rethinking the concepts of vulnerability and risk from a holistic perspective: A necessary review and criticism for effective risk management. In G. Bankoff, G. Frerks, & D. Hilhorst (Eds.), *Mapping Vulnerability: Disasters, Development and People* (pp. 37–51). London: Earthscan.

Chan, M., Woon, I., & Kankanhalli, A. (2005). Perceptions of information security in the workplace: Linking information security climate to compliant behaviour. *Journal of Information Privacy & Security, 1*(3), 18–41.

Chen, Y., Ramamurthy, K., & Wen, K.-W. (2012). Organizations' information security policy compliance: Stick or carrot approach? *Journal of Management Information Systems, 29*(3), 157–188. doi: 10.2753/MIS0742-1222290305

Chin, W. W. (1998). Issues and opinion on structural equation modeling. *MISQ, 22*(1), 7–16.

Chin, W. W., Thatcher, J. B., Wright, R. T., & Steel, D. (2013). Controlling for Common Method Variance in PLS Analysis: The Measured Latent Marker Variable Approach. New Perspectives in Partial Least Squares and Related Methods. Springer Proceedings in Mathematics & Statistics. In A. Herve, W. W. Chin, E. V. Vincenzo, R. Giorgio, & T. Laura (Eds.), *New Perspectives in Partial Least Squares and Related Methods* (Vol. 56, pp. 231–239). New York, NY: Springer.

Compeau, D. R., & Higgins, C. A. (1995). Computer self-efficacy: Development of a measure and initial test. *MIS Quarterly, 19*(2), 189–211.

Crossler, R. E., & Bélanger, F. (2014). An extended perspective on individual security behaviours: Protection motivation theory and a unified security practices (USP) instrument. *DATA BASE for Advances in Information Systems, 45*(4), 51–71.

Crossley, C., & Highhouse, S. (2005). Relation of job search and choice process with subsequent satisfaction. *Journal of Economic Psychology, 26*(2), 255–268.

Cybersecurity Insiders. (2018). Insider Threat 2018 Report. Retrieved from https://crowdresearchpartners.com/portfolio/insider-threat-report/

D'Arcy, J., & Lowry, P. B. (2019). Cognitive-affective drivers of employees' daily compliance with information security policies: A multilevel, longitudinal study. *Information Systems Journal, 29*(1), 43–69.

D'Arcy, J., Hovav, A., & Galletta, D. (2009). User awareness of security countermeasures and its impact on information systems misuse: A deterrence approach. *Information Systems Research, 20*(1), 79–98.

Daskalakis, S., Katharaki, M., Liaskos, J., & Mantas, J. (2010). Behavioural Security: Investigating the Attitude of Nursing Students Towards Security Concepts and Practices. In A. Chryssanthou, I. Apostolakis, & I. Varlamis (Eds.), *Certification and Security in Health-Related Web Applications: Concepts and Solutions* (1st ed., p. 352). Hershey, PA: IGI Global.

Davison, R. M., & Martinsons, M. G. (2016). Context is king! Considering particularism in research design and reporting. *Journal of Information Technology, 31*(3), 241–249.

Dawes, J. (2008). Do data characteristics change according to the number of scale points used? An experiment using 5-point, 7-point and 10-point scales. *International Journal of Market Research, 50*(1), 61–104.

Deci, E. L., & Ryan, R. M. (1985). *Intrinsic Motivation and Self-Determination in Human Behaviour*. New York: Plenum.

Doherty, N. F., Anastasakis, L., & Fulford, H. (2009). The information security policy unpacked: A critical study of the content of university policies. *International Journal of Information Management, 29*(6), 449–457.

Donalds, C. (2015). Cybersecurity Policy Compliance: An Empirical Study of Jamaican Government Agencies. *Paper Presented at the SIG GlobDev Pre-ECIS Workshop*, Munster, Germany.

Donalds, C., & Barclay, C. (2021). Beyond technical measures: a value-focused thinking appraisal of strategic drivers in improving information security policy compliance. *European Journal of Information Systems*, 1–16. doi:10.1080/0960085X.2021.1978344.

Donalds, C., & Osei-Bryson, K.-M. (2017). Exploring the Impacts of Individual Styles on Security Compliance Behaviour: A Preliminary Analysis. *Paper Presented at the SIG ICT in Global Development, 10th Annual Pre-ICIS Workshop*, Seoul, Korea.

Driver, M. J. (1979). Individual Decision-making and Creativity. In S. Kerr (Ed.), *Organizational Behaviour* (pp. 59–91). Columbus, OH: Grid Publishing.

Dwivedi, Y. K., Kapoor, K., Williams, M. D., & Williams, J. (2013). RFID systems in libraries: An empirical examination of factors affecting system use and user satisfaction. *International Journal of Information Management, 33*(2), 367–377. doi: 10.1016/j.ijinfomgt.2012.10.008

Fishbein, M., & Ajzen, I. (1975). *Belief, Attitude, Intention and Behaviour: An Introduction to Theory and Research*. Reading, MA: Addison-Wesley.

Fornell, C., & Larcker, D. F. (1981). Evaluating structural equation models with unobservable variables and measurement error. *Journal of Marketing Research, 18*(1), 39–50.

Fox, T. L., & Spence, J. W. (2005). The effect of decision style on the use of a project management tool: An empirical laboratory study. *The DATA BASE for Advances in Information Systems, 36*(2), 28–41.

French, D. J., West, R. J., Elander, J., & Wildin, J. M. (1993). Decision-making style, driving style, and self-reported involvement in road traffic accidents. *Ergonomics, 36*(6), 627–644.

Furnell, S., & Clarke, N. L. (2012). Power to the people? The evolving recognition of human aspects of security. *Computers & Security, 31*(8), 983–988. doi: 10.1016/j.cose.2012.08.004

Gefen, D., Straub, D. W., & Boudreau, M.-C. (2000). Structural equation modeling and regression: Guidelines for research practice. *Communications of the Association for Information System, 4*(7), 2–76.

Hafni, R. N., & Nurlaelah, E. (2018). Analyzing students' decision-making style in prior knowledge of mathematical critical thinking skill. *Pancaran Pendidikan, 7*(1), 178–185.

Hair, J. F., Hult, G. T. M., Ringle, C. M., & Sarstedt, M. (2014). *A Primer on Partial Least Squares Structural Equation Modeling (PLS-SEM)*. Thousand Oaks: Sage.

Hansche, S. (2001). Designing a security awareness program: Part 1. *Information Systems Security, 9*(6), 14–22.

Harren, V. A. (1979). A model of career decision-making for college students. *Journal of Vocational Behaviour, 14*(2), 119–133. doi: 10.1016/0001-8791(79)90065-4

Haystax Technology. (2017). *Insider Attacks - 2017 Insider Threat Study*. Retrieved from https://haystax.com/blog/whitepapers/insider-attacks-industry-survey/

Henderson, J. C., & Nutt, P. C. (1980). The influence of decision style on decision-making behaviour. *Management Science, 26*(4), 371–386.

Herath, T., & Rao, H. R. (2009a). Encouraging information security behaviours: Role of penalties, pressures and perceived effectiveness. *Decision Support Systems, 47*(2), 154–165.

Herath, T., & Rao, H. R. (2009b). Protection motivation and deterrence: A framework for security policy compliance in organisations. *European Journal of Information Systems, 18*(2), 106–125. doi: 10.1057/ejis.2009.6

Hu, Q., Xu, Z., Dinev, T., & Ling, H. (2011). Does deterrence work in reducing information security policy abuse by employees? *Communications of the ACM, 54*(6), 54–60.

Ifinedo, P. (2014). Information systems security policy compliance: An empirical study of the effects of socialisation, influence, and cognition. *Information & Management, 51*(1), 69–79.

Jayanti, R. K., & Burns, A. C. (1998). The antecedents of preventive health care behaviour: An empirical study. *Academy of Marketing Science Journal, 26*(1), 6–15.

Johnston, A. C., & Warkentin, M. (2010). Fear appeals and information security behaviours: An empirical study. *MIS Quarterly, 34*(3), 549–566.

Kankanhalli, A., Teo, H.-H., Tan, B. C. Y., & Wei, K.-K. (2003). An integrative study of information systems security effectiveness. *International Journal of Information Management, 23*(2), 139–154.

Kositanurit, B., Osei-Bryson, K.-M., & Ngwenyama, O. (2011). Re-examining information systems user performance. *Expert Systems with Applications, 38*(6), 7041–7050. doi: 10.1016/j.eswa.2010.12.011

Larson, J. R. J., Foster-Fishman, P. G., & Franz, T. M. (1998). Leadership style and the discussion of shared and unshared information in decision-making groups. *Personality and Social Psychology Bulletin, 24*(5), 482–495.

Li, L., He, W., Xu, L., Ash, I., Anwar, M., & Yuan, X. (2019). Investigating the impact of cybersecurity policy awareness on employees' cybersecurity behaviour. *International Journal of Information Management, 45*, 13–24. doi: 10.1016/j.ijinfomgt.2018.10.017

Liu, S., Chan, F. T. S., Yang, J., & Niu, B. (2018). Understanding the effect of cloud computing on organizational agility: An empirical examination. *International Journal of Information Management, 43*, 98–111.

Lu, Y. (2018). Cybersecurity research: A review of current research topics. *Journal of Industrial Integration and Management, 3*(4). doi:10.1142/S2424862218500148

Mamonov, S., & Benbunan-Fich, R. (2018). The impact of information security threat awareness on privacy-protective behaviours. *Computers in Human Behaviour, 83*, 32–44. doi: 10.1016/j.chb.2018.01.028

Martinsons, M. G., & Davison, R. M. (2007). Strategic decision-making and support systems: Comparing american, japanese and chinese management. *Decision Support Systems, 43*(1), 284–300.

Mech, T. F. (1993). The managerial decision styles of acadetnic library directors. *College & Research Libraries, 54*(5), 375–386.

Moody, G. D., Siponen, M. T., & Pahnila, S. (2018). Toward a unified model of information security policy compliance. *MIS Quarterly, 42*(1), 285–311.

Mwagwabi, F., McGill, T., & Dixon, M. (2014, January 6–9). Improving Compliance with Password Guidelines: How User Perceptions of Passwords and Security Threats Affect Compliance with Guidelines. *Paper Presented at the 47th Hawaii International Conference on System Sciences*, Waikoloa, Hawaii.

Ng, B.-Y., Kankanhalli, A., & Xu, Y. C. (2009). Studying users' computer security behaviour: A health belief perspective. *Decision Support Systems, 46*(4), 815–825.

Nunnally, J. C., & Bernstein, I. H. (1994). *Psychometric Theory* (3rd ed.). New York: McGraw-Hill.

Nutt, P. C. (1990). Strategic decision made by top executive and middle managers with data and process dominant styles. *Journal of Management Studies, 27*(2), 172–194.

Osei-Bryson, K.-M., & Ngwenyama, O. K. (2011). Using decision tree modeling to support piercian abduction in is research: A systematic approach for generating and evaluating hypotheses for systematic theory development. *Information Systems Journal, 21*(5), 407–440.

Pahnila, S., Siponen, M. T., & Mahomood, A. (2007, January 3–6). Employees' behaviour towards IS security policy compliance. *Paper Presented at the 40th Hawaii International Conference on System Sciences*, Waikoloa, Big Island, Hawaii.

Pedram, S., & Garkaz, M. (2016). Studying the relationship between voluntary disclosure, decision-making styles, and information asymmetry in tehran stock exchange. *Journal of Financial and Actuarial Mathematics and Management, 26*(4), 1–6.

Ponemon Institute. (2016). *2016 Cost of Insider Threats Benchmark - Study of Organizations in the United States*. Retrieved from https://learn.dtexsystems.com/rs/173-QMH-211/images/2016%20Cost%20of%20Insider%20Threats.pdf

Rhee, H.-S., Kim, C., & Ryu, Y. U. (2009). Self-efficacy in information security: Its influence on end users' information security practice behaviour. *Computers & Security, 28*(8), 816–826.

Rowe, A. J., & Boulgarides, J. D. (1983). Decision styles—A perspective. *Leadership & Organization Development Journal, 4*(4), 3–9.

Rowe, A. J., & Boulgarides, J. D. (1992). *Managerial Decision-making: A Guide to Successful Business Decisions*. New York, USA: McMillan.

Rowe, A. J., & Mason, R. O. (1987). *Managing with Style: A Guide to Understanding Assessing, and Improving Decision-making*. San Francisco, CA: Jossey-Bass.

Ryan, R. M., & Deci, E. L. (2000). Self-determination theory and the facilitation of intrinsic motivation, social development, and well-being. *American Psychologist, 55*(1), 68–78.

Safa, N. S., Sookhak, M., Von Solms, R., Furnell, S., Ghani, N. A., & Herawan, T. (2015). Information security conscious care behaviour formation in organizations. *Computers & Security, 53*, 65–78. doi: 10.1016/j.cose.2015.05.012

Scott, S. G., & Bruce, R. A. (1995). Decision-making style: the development and assessment of a new measure. *Educational and Psychological Measurement, 55*(5), 818–831.

Shareef, M. A., Kumar, V., Dwivedi, Y. K., & Kumar, U. (2016). Service delivery through mobile-government (mGov): Driving factors and cultural impacts. *Information Systems Frontiers, 18*(2), 315–332.

Singh, A. N., Picot, A., Kranz, J., Gupta, M. P., & Ojha, A. (2013). Information security management (ISM) practices: Lessons from select cases from india and germany. *Global Journal of Flexible Systems Management, 14* (4), 225–239.

Singh, J. V. (1986). Performance, slack, and risk taking in organizational decision-making. *Academy of management Journal, 29*(3), 562–585.

Singh, R., & Greenhaus, J. (2004). The relation between career decision-making strategies and person-job fit: A study of job changers. *Journal of Vocational Behaviour, 64*(1), 198–221.

Siponen, M. T. (2000). A conceptual foundation for organizational information security awareness. *Information Management & Computer Security Journal, 8*(1), 31–41.

Siponen, M. T., Pahnila, S., & Mahmood, A. (2007). Employees' Adherence to Information Security Policies: An Empirical Study. In H. Venter, M. Eloff, L. Labuschagne, J. Eloff, & R. von Solms (Eds.), *SEC 2007. New Approaches for Security, Privacy and Trust in Complex Environments* (Vol. 232, pp. 133–144). Boston, MA: Springer.

Siponen, M. T., & Vance, A. (2010). Neutralization: New insights into the problem of employee information systems security policy violations. *MIS Quarterly, 34*(3), 487–502.

Siponen, M. T., & Vance, A. (2014). Guidelines for improving the contextual relevance of field surveys: The case of information security policy violations. *European Journal of Information Systems, 23*(3), 289–305.

Special Eurobarometer 390. (2012). *Cyber Security* (S1058_77_2_EBS390). Retrieved from http://ec.europa.eu/commfrontoffice/publicopinion/archives/eb_special_399_380_en.htm#390

Stanton, J. M., Stam, K. R., Mastrangelo, P., & Jolton, J. (2005). Analysis of end user security behaviours. *Computers & Security, 24*(2), 124–133.

Sternberg, R. J., & Zhang, L.-F. (Eds.). (2001). *Perspectives on Thinking, Learning, and Cognitive Styles* (1st ed.). New York, NY: Routledge.

Thunholm, P. (2004). Decision-making style: Habit, style or both? *Personality and Individual Differences, 36*(4), 931–944. doi: 10.1016/S0191-8869(03)00162-4

Triantoro, T., Gopal, R. D., Benbunan-Fich, R., & Lang, G. (2019). Would you like to play? A comparison of a gamified survey with a traditional online survey method. *International Journal of Information Management, 49*, 242–252.

Vance, A., & Siponen, M. T. (2012). IS security policy violations: A rational choice perspective. *Journal of Organizational and End User Computing, 24*(1), 21–41.

Vance, A., Siponen, M. T., & Pahnila, S. (2012). Motivating IS security compliance: Insights from habit and protection motivation theory. *Information & Management, 49*(3–4), 190–198.

Vroom, C., & von Solms, R. (2004). Towards information security behavioural compliance. *Computers & Security, 23*(3), 191–198.

Wall, J. D., Palvia, P., & Lowry, P. B. (2013). Control-related motivations and information security policy compliance: The role of autonomy and efficacy. *Journal of Information Privacy and Security, 9*(4), 52–79. doi: 10.1080/15536548.2013.10845690

Warkentin, M., & Willison, R. (2009). Behavioural and policy Issues in information systems security: The insider threat. *European Journal of Information Systems, 18*(2), 101–105.

Whitman, M. E. (2004). In defense of the realm: Understanding the threats to information security. *International Journal of Information Management, 24*(1), 43–57.

Yeniman, Y., Ebru Akalp, G., Aytac, S., & Bayram, N. (2011). Factors influencing information security management in small-and medium-sized enterprises: A case study from turkey. *International Journal of Information Management, 31*(4), 360–365.

Yeo, B., & Grant, D. (2018). Predicting service industry performance using decision tree analysis. *International Journal of Information Management, 38*(1), 288–300.

Chapter 7

Individual Decision-Making Styles and Employees' Security Compliance Behaviour: Reflections using an Alternate Lens

7.1 Introduction

The current era is dominated by the use of information and communication technologies (ICTs) in the lives and activities of individuals, organizations and governments. However, increased adoption of ICTs is positively correlated with increased technological threats and economic loss. For instance, the WannaCry ransomware attack in May 2017 affected more than 200,000 victims in 150 countries (McAfee Labs, 2017). To cope with these technological or cybersecurity threats, security stakeholders have implemented technology-based protection solutions and conducted cybersecurity awareness activities for users. Users are recognized as key threats to achieving security because they often fail to adhere to cybersecurity best practices. According to researchers, users are often considered the 'weakest link in the chain' of system security (Warkentin and Willison, 2009).

DOI: 10.1201/9781003028710-9

Rowe and Boulgarides (1983) noted that cognitive theorists have long argued that individual decision-making style (DMS) is an important determinant of behaviour. Rowe and Boulgarides (1992) argued that once the DMS of an individual is known, then one is more likely to be able to predict outcomes in terms of the individual's decision behaviour. Recent results from Donalds and Osei-Bryson (2020) suggest that an individual's dominant DMS impacts his/her *cybersecurity compliance* behaviour.

7.2 Description of the Research Problem

The objective of this research is to continue the exploration of the relationship (s) between the employee's individual DMS and the corresponding cybersecurity compliance behaviour. In an earlier paper of Donalds and Osei-Bryson (2020), individual DMS was modelled using the decision-style inventory (DSI) framework (Rowe, 1981; Rowe & Boulgarides, 1983; Rowe & Mason, 1987). Given that there are other ways of modeling DMS (e.g. Scott & Bruce, 1995; Harren, 1979), in this study we explore the relationship using such a DMS model. Further, while Donalds and Osei-Bryson (2020) only considered linear relationships, in this chapter we will also consider nonlinear relationships in a manner that will allow us to explore conditions under which DMS has a positive or negative impact on cybersecurity compliance behaviour.

7.3 Importance of the Research Problem

Minimizing the occurrence of breaches in its security is obviously in the best interest of every organization. This is especially relevant in today's fast-paced environment where organizations are dependent on the ICT for economic and competitive sustainability. If the Individual's decision style is an important, though often unconsidered, attribute that could be used to develop programmes that improve the likelihood that employees engage in appropriate cybersecurity behaviour then a better understanding of the relationships could be beneficial to organizations. It should also be noted that apart from the studies of Donalds and Osei-Bryson (2017, 2020) there is no known study that examines the relationship between the employee's DMS and the corresponding cybersecurity compliance behaviour.

7.4 Overview on Individual Decision-Making Style (DMS)

7.4.1 Decision-Making Style and Behaviour

Individuals in organizations are required to make decisions daily. While these decisions vary vastly, such as how to predict consumer reaction to a new marketing promotion or whether to comply with established security best practices, experts argue that individuals have 'habitual response patterns' in approaching various decision situations in consistent similar ways over time (Scott & Bruce, 1995; Thunholm, 2004). Others argue that talent, skill, experience and a 'hidden factor' typically influence individuals' decisions (Rowe & Mason, 1987). According to Rowe and Mason (1987), we tend to ignore this 'hidden factor' yet it is such an important part of how humans think and act; it forms a fundamental base that accounts for everything that a person does. These 'habitual response patterns' or 'hidden factor' applied in decision-making are commonly referred to as DMSs (Rowe & Mason, 1987; Scott & Bruce, 1995; Thunholm, 2004).

Driver (1979) defines DMS as a habitual pattern individuals use in decision-making, while Harren (1979) defines it as an individual characteristic for perceiving and responding to decision-making tasks. Rowe and Boulgarides (1992) define DMS as the way an individual visualizes and thinks about situations. Further, it is the way an individual perceives and comprehends stimuli and how s/he chooses to respond. Scott and Bruce (1995) define it as the habit-based propensity exhibited by an individual to react in a certain way in a specific decision context. They explained further that DMSs are individuals' characteristic mode of perceiving and responding to decision-making tasks. Sternberg and Zhang (2001) propose a working definition of DMS as a habitual pattern or preferred way of doing something that is consistent over time and across activities. Although these definitions vary, implicit in these definitions is that an individual's decision-making behaviour approach is (1) intrinsic to the individual; (2) considered fairly stable over time; (3) that individuals have different DMSs based on the most dominant individual characteristic of their approach to the decision situation and (4) that DMS influences the individual's action/behaviour.

DMS is also described as a cognitive process which represents the way an individual approaches a problem (Rowe & Mason, 1987). That is, an individual's DMS reflects the way s/he visualizes, thinks and interprets situations. According to Rowe and Mason (1987), different individuals will make different decisions because they use different methods to perceive and evaluate information. For instance, some individuals prefer acting to thinking, others think quickly while others slowly, others are concerned with the rules whereas others are concerned with people's feelings. Still, others are innovative, take risks, are creative, depend more on intuition than on fact (Mech, 1993). According to Nutt (1990), DMS offers a way to understand why managers, faced with seemingly identical situations, use such different decision processes. DMS then can help us identify the different types of individual decision-makers and could help us understand how the individual thinks about situations and ultimately, their decision behaviour. Nutt (1990) also found that decision style depicts an individual's belief system, including classification categories and sorted data that are taken for granted and unconsciously applied in decision-making. Rowe and Boulgarides (1992) suggest that once we know an individual's DMS we will be able to predict outcomes in terms of decision behaviour. This type of knowledge could prove useful to the IS community in understanding why individuals make certain security/cybersecurity compliance or non-compliance decisions as well as be able to predict individuals' security/cybersecurity compliance behaviour.

Prior research has investigated the relationship between DMS and the behaviour of individuals. For instance, Henderson and Nutt (1980) found DMS to be a significant factor in explaining individuals' decision behaviour of project adoption as well as perception of risk. Bavol'ár and Orosová (2015) found statistically significant relationships between DMSs and higher and lower decision-making competencies as well as between DMSs and mental health indicators such as stress and well-being, stress and depression and well-being and depression. Pedram and Garkaz (2016) also found that different DMSs explain significant differences in how individuals' process information, in terms of volume and processing time. Fox and Spence (2005) too, found that DMS significantly influenced project managers' behaviour in regards to the use of a project management tool, specifically, the time required to complete an initial project plan as well as the accuracy of the plan. Another study investigated education leaders' DMS behaviour and found that some leaders are more likely to repeat information while others are more likely to discuss information (Larson, Foster-Fishman, & Franz, 1998). Mech (1993) found that library directors with less administrative experience were more likely to have a people-oriented DMS than directors with more administrative experience. DMS has also been found to influence academic achievement (Baiocco, Laghi, & D'Alessio, 2009; Hafni & Nurlaelah, 2018), decision-making competences (Bruine de Bruin, Del Missier, & Levin, 2012) and various other performance criteria including job satisfaction (Crossley & Highhouse, 2005) and person-job fit (Crossley & Highhouse, 2005; R. Singh & Greenhaus, 2004). The results of these studies support the claim that DMS is an important determinant of behaviour.

Martinsons and Davison (2007) observed that in different cultures, different individual decision styles are dominant, and that these differences determine the types of decision support system that are most appropriate. For example, they noted that in several non-Western societies, decision-makers 'focus on collective interests, emphasize relationships and intuition (at the expense of factual analysis), and discourage conflicting views that would threaten group harmony or the face of the individual', with some having 'greater acceptance of tacit knowledge management'. To paraphrase Martinsons & Davison (2007), for such non-Western societies, knowledge management systems (KMSs) that support interpersonal communications and encourage tacit knowledge sharing and individual discretion would be more helpful than KMSs that mainly involve codified knowledge.

7.4.2 Decision-Style Inventory (DSI)

The DSI devised by Rowe (1981) and further elaborated by Rowe & Boulgarides (1983) and Rowe & Mason (1987) is a cognitive management tool to understand the type of decisions an individual is likely to make under certain situations. Each individual has a characteristic method or approach for making decisions, which will have its own strengths and weaknesses (DSI, 2013). Understanding more about one's likely behaviour or decisions can help not only the individuals but also the organizations in more strategic decision-making.

Within the context of the decision-style model, there are four decision styles: *Directive, Analytical, Conceptual* and *Behavioural*. Each of these styles has its own characteristics with regards to level of tolerance for ambiguity, need for structure, people or task orientation and so on (Table 7.1). The decision style captures three varying factors as concepts (Rowe & Mason, 1987).

The DSI has been applied in multiple contexts. (Nutt, 1993) applied the method to measure attitude toward ambiguity and uncertainty and to determine the style of the participating top executives. The participants were asked to evaluate eight capital expansion projects in terms of adoptability and risk. Inferences about decision-making were drawn from these evaluations. The tolerance for ambiguity and uncertainty scores and the adoptability and risk ratings were associated with the participant's style. Top executives with a flexible style who have access to each of the modes of understanding were found to be aggressive decision-makers with a high tolerance for ambiguity and uncertainty. Fox and Spence (1999) surveyed a group of over 200 project managers from across the United States, attempting to measure their DMSs, especially as they relate to project management activity. The survey not only identifies a person's propensity towards a particular style of decision-making, but also his or her propensity towards brain dominance, an idea or action

Table 7.1 DSI Framework – DMS Categories and Characteristics (Rowe & Boulgarides, 1994)

Style	Description
Analytical	Achievement-oriented without the need for external rewards; make decisions slowly because of orientation to examine the situation thoroughly and consider many alternatives systematically
Behavioural	Strong people orientation, driven primarily by a need for affiliation; typically receptive to suggestions, willing to compromise, and prefer loose controls
Conceptual	Achievement and people oriented with the need for external rewards; make decisions slowly because orientation to examine the situation thoroughly and consider many alternatives systematically
Directive	Results and power oriented but have a low tolerance for ambiguity & cognitive complexity. They prefer to consider a small number of alternatives based on limited information.

orientation, and a preferred management level of decision-making. Durkin (2004) reports on a study into Internet banking that focuses on the extent to which 480 retail-bank customers can be clustered according to an adapted decision-making framework. How such clusters can help influence the adoption of the Internet-banking interface is explored. Findings show an encouraging match between the four sample clusters identified from the case bank and the a priori classification of decision styles. Martinsons and Davison (2007) examined the IS issues that arise from the discovery of the distinctively American, Japanese and Chinese styles of strategic decision-making. The existence of international differences in analysing and conceptualizing strategic decisions raises doubts about the global applicability of Information Systems such as decision support systems and executive information systems.

7.4.3 DMS Framework of Scott and Bruce

Scott and Bruce (1995) presented and empirically evaluated a DMS framework in which individual DMS is represented using five factors: *Avoidant, Dependent, Intuitive, Spontaneous* and *Rational* (see Table 7.2). From their empirical evaluation of the 5-factor framework, Scott and Bruce (1995) concluded that these factors could be considered to be independent but also overlapping, and that the DMS of a given individual could be appropriately represented by a combination of these 5 factors. It should be noted that this framework is an extension of that presented by Harren (1979), which included only the *Dependent, Intuitive* and *Rational* factors. Harren's framework has been further explored by other researchers (e.g. Phillips, Pazienza, & Ferrin, 1984).

Table 7.2   DSI Framework – DMS Factors and Descriptions

Factor	Characteristics
Avoidant (AVOD)	Attempts to avoid decision-making whenever possible
Dependent (DPND)	Searches for advice and direction from others
Intuitive (INTD)	Relies on hunches and feelings, 'attention to details in the flow of information rather than systematic search for and processing of information and a tendency to rely on premonitions and feelings'
Spontaneous (SPND)	'a feeling of immediacy and a desire to come through the decision-making process as quickly as possible'
Rational (RATD)	Does a thorough search for and logical evaluation of alternatives

7.5 DMS and Cybersecurity Compliance

Despite prior works investigating the influence of DMS on behaviour and other outcomes in various domains (Henderson and Nutt, 1980; Bavol'ár and Orosová, 2015; Fox and Spence, 2005; Baiocco, Laghi, & D'Alessio, 2009; Hafni & Nurlaelah, 2018; Bruine de Bruin, Del Missier, & Levin, 2012; Crossley & Highhouse, 2005; Crossley & Highhouse, 2005; Singh & Greenhaus, 2004), the question of how DMS influences cybersecurity compliance behaviour and other antecedents of such behaviour remains largely unexplored. The Donalds and Osei-Bryson model (see Figure 7.1 & Table 7.3), to the researchers' best knowledge, is the only model that has incorporated decision-style theory to address the phenomenon of individuals' cybersecurity compliance behaviour.

The reader may have observed that in Figure 7.1, cybersecurity compliance behaviour is represented by the two dependent variables: *Password Compliance Behaviour* and *General Security Compliance Behaviour*. In this study, our dependent variable will be *Cyber-Security Policy Compliance Intention* (SINT). Further, given the DMS framework that we will be using the *Dominant Orientation* variable is not relevant (Table 7.4).

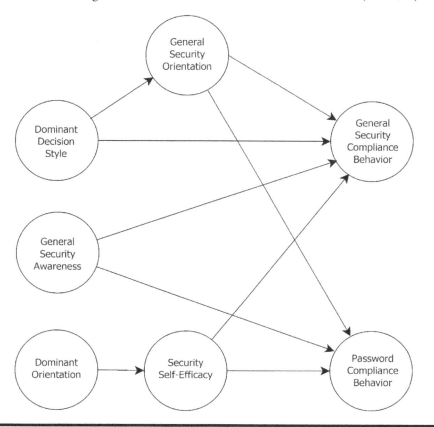

Figure 7.1 Donalds and Osei-Bryson's model (Donalds & Osei-Bryson, 2020)

Table 7.3   Description of Constructs of the Donalds and Osei-Bryson's (2020) Model

Construct	Description/Definition
General Security Orientation (GSOR)	An individual's predisposition and interest concerning practicing cybersecurity actions Donalds and Osei-Bryson (2017); Ng, Kankanhalli and Xu (2009).
General Security Awareness (GSAW)	An individual's overall awareness/mindfulness and understanding of potential issues related to cybersecurity and their ramifications Bulgurcu et al. (2010); Donalds and Osei-Bryson (2017).
Security Self-Efficacy (SELF)	An individual's ability or judgment of his or her ability to perform cybersecurity actions in such a manner that minimizes the risk of security breaches/incidents Bandura (1977); Donalds and Osei-Bryson (2017).
General Security Compliance Behaviour	An individual's compliance with established security best practices/policies.
Password Compliance Behaviour	An individual's compliance with established password security best practices/policies.
Dominant Decision Style	Indicates that an individual frequently uses a particular decision-making style over other decision-making styles Rowe and Boulgarides (1992).
Dominant Orientation	Indicates an individual's preference for acting (action-oriented) or thinking (idea-oriented) Rowe and Mason (1987).

Table 7.4   Factor Representing Cybersecurity Compliance

Factor	Description/Definition
IS Policy Compliance Intention (SINT)	An employee's intention is to protect the information and technology resources of the organization from potential security breaches by complying with the requirements of the ISP Bulgurcu et al. (2010).

Our study will thus involve an exploration of the function:

$$\text{SINT} = f\left(\text{GSOR,GSAW,SELF,subset of DMS factors}\right)$$

where f(GSOR, GSAW, SELF, subset of DMS factors) is a polynomial of order 2, thus allowing for exploration of interactions between the independent variables.

7.6 Research Methodology

Our research methodology can be considered to be based on the hybrid Peircian abduction framework proposed by Osei-Bryson and Ngwenyama (2011) and the hybrid process for empirically-based theory development by Kositanurit, Osei-Bryson, and Ngwenyama (2011), where the latter parallels the traditional ideal model of scientific inquiry. In Table 7.5, we have divided hybrid process of Kositanurit, Osei-Bryson and Ngwenyama (2011) into two main phases, with what is being done in this chapter being almost equivalent to Phase 1.

Table 7.5   Hybrid Process for Empirically Bases Theory Development

Phase	*Step*	*Description*
1	1	■ 1a: Use existing theory to identify variables that are likely to be relevant to the phenomena of interest. ■ 1b: Based on Substep 1a, gather data related to the phenomena of interest.
	2	■ 2a: Use data mining approach to do automatic generation and preliminary testing of hypotheses. ■ 2b: Based on the results of Substep 2a, generate a preliminary model that appears to explain the phenomena of interest. ■ 2c: The researcher examines, and if necessary, revises the preliminary model that was generated in Substep 2b. This revision may be based on the researcher's knowledge of existing theory.
2	3	■ Design an experiment to test the logical consequences of the hypotheses. Conventional data analysis approaches may be included in the experimental design.
	4	■ 4a: Collect observations about the phenomena. ■ 4b: Conduct measurement validity. ■ 4c: Determine if hypotheses of the current model are supported based on data analysis of the given dataset.

More specifically, the research methodology involved the following activities:

1a – Use Existing Theory to Identify Relevant Variables
1b – Instrument Development and Data Collection
2a.1 – Factor Analysis
2a.2 – Data Mining using Regression Analysis
2b – Interpretation of the Results

7.7 Results

7.7.1 Use Existing Theory to Identify Relevant Variables

As noted previously, the model described in Figure 7.1 will provide the basis for our exploration, though with a different representation for individual DMS (see Table 7.2) than was used in Donalds and Osei-Bryson (2020). Our study will thus involve an exploration of the function:

$$SINT = f\left(GSOR, GSAW, SELF, \text{subset of DMS factors}\right).$$

7.7.2 Instrument Development and Data Collection

The measurement scale for each construct was adapted/adopted from previously validated scales. We pretested the survey instrument using an expert panel of eight IT professionals and academics, who provided feedback to improve wording and validity. After making changes regarding wording, the panel experts agreed that the items were clearly written, realistic and relevant, confirming face and content validity. All constructs were measured reflectively with multiple items, based mainly on a 5-point Likert-like scale, rated from 1 = 'Strongly disagree' to 5 = 'Strongly agree'.

Data were collected from employees in a large financial institution in Jamaica during the last quarter of 2019. The survey was installed on the institution's Intranet and an email was sent to all employees soliciting their participation. Of the 600 employees, 155 responses were received, yielding a response rate of 25.8%. Of the respondents, 60.6% are females; 55% are between the age range 20 and 39; over 54% have served in the organization between 0 and 10 years; and 86.5% hold undergraduate and graduate degrees.

7.7.3 Factor Analysis

The variables that are used in this chapter are a subset of the data that were collected. Factor analysis was conducted based on established protocols. This allowed for the identification of the items that could be appropriately assigned to each factor, and thus for the calculation of the factor scores for the factors used in this study.

7.7.4 Regression Analysis

7.7.4.1 Model 1 – Results and Interpretation

As noted earlier, our regression analysis would be based on a polynomial of degree 2 that allowed for interactions between the input variables including allowing a variable to interact with itself. For our first model (i.e. Model 1) the candidate predictors are *GSAW, GSOR, SELF,* and all five DMS variables (i.e. *AVOD, DPND, ITND, SPND,* and *RATD*).

Table 7.5 provides results from this regression analysis in the form of the main effects and interaction effects that are statistically significant at the 0.05 level, along with the corresponding coefficients. The associated R-squared value is 0.537, while the associated R-squared value for the main effects-only model is 0.449.

The results displayed in Figure 7.2 suggest the following:

$$SINT = -0.1183$$
$$+ 0.809399 * RATD - 0.18951 * RATD * SELF$$
$$- 0.16798 * SPND * SPND + 0.15137 * SPND * GSOR$$
$$+ 0.120845 * AVOD * GSAW - 0.10737 * AVOD * SELF$$

An interesting but possibly surprising observation is that this regression equation suggests that the impact of *Security Self-Efficacy* (*SELF*) on *SINT* is negative. Unsurprisingly it suggests that the impacts of *General Security Awareness* (*GSAW*) and *General Security Orientation* (*GSOR*) are positive. Concerning the impact of *SELF* on *SINT* this could be because when the individual believes him/herself to be highly competent, he/she places less attention/focus on compliance and security messages/warnings.

We will now explore the conditions in which the identified DMS factors (i.e. *RATD, SPND, AVOD*) and the other predictors have positive or negative statistical

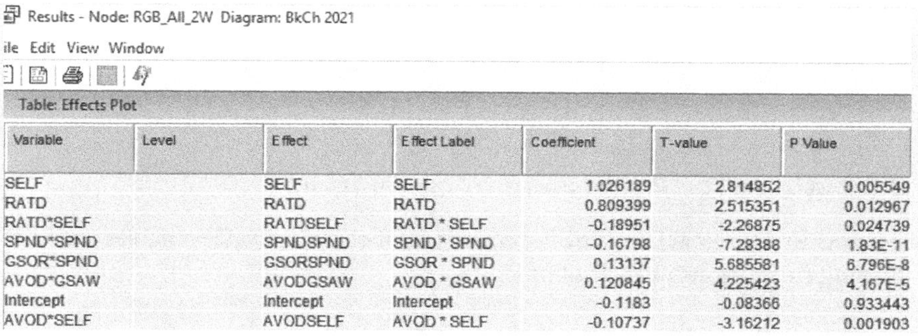

Results - Node: RGB_All_2W Diagram: BkCh 2021

ile Edit View Window

Table: Effects Plot

Variable	Level	Effect	Effect Label	Coefficient	T-value	P Value
SELF		SELF	SELF	1.026189	2.814852	0.005549
RATD		RATD	RATD	0.809399	2.515351	0.012967
RATD*SELF		RATDSELF	RATD * SELF	-0.18951	-2.26875	0.024739
SPND*SPND		SPNDSPND	SPND * SPND	-0.16798	-7.28388	1.83E-11
GSOR*SPND		GSORSPND	GSOR * SPND	0.13137	5.685581	6.796E-8
AVOD*GSAW		AVODGSAW	AVOD * GSAW	0.120845	4.225423	4.167E-5
Intercept		Intercept	Intercept	-0.1183	-0.08366	0.933443
AVOD*SELF		AVODSELF	AVOD * SELF	-0.10737	-3.16212	0.001903

Figure 7.2 Model 1 – Results of Regression Analysis

Table 7.6 Model 1 – Conditions for Which DMS Factors Positively or Negatively Impact SINT

Factor	Regression Eq. Extract	Derivative	Direction of Impact
RATD	0.809399*RATD − 0.18951*RATD*SELF	0.809399 − 0.18951*SELF	■ Positive if SELF < 4.27; ■ Negative otherwise
SPND	− 0.16798*SPND*SPND + 0.15137*SPND*GSOR	− 2*0.16798*SPND + 0.15137*GSOR	■ Negative if SPND > 0.451*GSOR
AVOD	+ 0.120845*AVOD*GSAW − 0.10737*AVOD*SELF	0.120845*GSAW − 0.10737*SELF	■ Negative if GSAW < 0.89*SELF

impacts on *SINT*. To do so we use the parts of our regression equation that includes the given DMS factor (i.e. 'Regression Eq. Extract' column of Table 7.6) then obtain its derivative (i.e. 'Derivative' column of Figure 7.2) since a positive value for the derivative indicates the conditions under which the factor has a positive impact, while the negative value for the derivative indicates the conditions under which the factor has a negative impact.

These results suggest that the relationship between the DMS and intended cybersecurity compliance is very complex, and is impacted by the values of the other predictor variables:

- Being more rational (*RATD*) will result in a higher level of cybersecurity compliance depending on whether the level of perceived cybersecurity self-efficacy (*SELF*) is below a threshold (i.e. SELF < 4.27);
- Whether a high SPND score will result in a lower level of cybersecurity compliance depends on the corresponding relationship between SPND & GSOR is impactful (i.e. SPND > 0.451*GSOR).
- Whether a high AVOD score will result in a lower level of cybersecurity compliance depends on the corresponding relationship between GSAW & SELF is impactful (i.e. GSAW < 0.89*SELF).

7.7.4.2 Model 2 – Results and Interpretation

Scott and Bruce (1995) empirical evaluations of the five DMS variables noted the following correlations in their samples:

- Negative correlations: (*RATD* & *AVOD*); (*RATD* & *SPND*); (*RATD* & *INTD*);
- Positive correlations: (*SPND* & *INTD*); (*DPND* & *AVOD*)

Results - Node: RGB_DX2_2W Diagram: BkCh 2021

File Edit View Window

Table: Effects Plot

Variable	Level	Effect	Effect Label	Coefficient	T-value	P Value
GSOR		GSOR	GSOR	1.393483	6.059395	1.068E-8
Intercept		Intercept	Intercept	0.753586	1.698987	0.091409
GSAW*GSOR		GSAWGSOR	GSAW * GSOR	-0.27937	-5.02675	1.412E-6
RATD*SELF		RATDSELF	RATD * SELF	-0.19197	-5.72932	5.399E-8
GSAW*SELF		GSAWSELF	GSAW * SELF	0.183525	5.6177	9.226E-8
GSAW*RATD		GSAWRATD	GSAW * RATD	0.178461	6.433577	1.603E-9

Figure 7.3 Model 1 – Results of Regression Analysis

For our Model 2, we will use the following candidate predictor variables: *GSAW*, *GSOR*, *SELF*, *RATD* and *DNPD*. Here rather than including all five DMS variables, we only include the two that are not correlated.

Figure 7.3 provides results from this regression analysis in the form of the main effects and interaction effects that are statistically significant at the 0.05 level, along with the corresponding coefficients. The associated R-squared value is 0.475

The results displayed in Table 7.6 suggest the following:–

$$\begin{aligned} \text{SINT} = {} & 0.753586 \\ & + 1.393483 * \text{GSOR} - 0.27937 * \text{GSAW} * \text{GSOR} + 0.183525 * \text{GSAW} * \text{SELF} \\ & - 0.19197 * \text{RATD} * \text{SELF} + 0.178461 * \text{GSAW} * \text{RATD} \end{aligned}$$

We will now explore the conditions in which the identified DMS variable (i.e. *RATD*) and the other predictors have positive or negative statistical impacts on *SINT*. Table 7.7 presents these results.

These results suggest that the relationship between the DMS and intended cybersecurity compliance is very complex, and is impacted by the values of the other predictor variables:

- Whether being more rational will result in a higher level of cybersecurity compliance depends on the relationship between *General Security Awareness* and perceived *Self-Efficacy* (i.e. GSAW > 1.08*SELF);
- Whether a higher level of *General Security Orientation* will result in a higher level of cybersecurity compliance depends on the corresponding level of *General Security Awareness* (i.e. GSAW < 4.8);
- Whether a higher level of *General Security Awareness* will result in a higher level of cybersecurity compliance depends on the relationship between *General Security Orientation*, perceived *Self-Efficacy*, and the level of rationality (i.e. GSOR < .0.66*SELF + 0.64*RATD);

Table 7.7 Model 2 – Conditions for Which DMS Factors Positively or Negatively Impact SINT

Factor	Regression Eq. Extract	Derivative	Direction of Impact
RATD	$-0.19197{*}RATD{*}SELF +$ $0.178461{*}GSAW{*}RATD$	$-0.19197{*}SELF +$ $0.178461{*}GSAW$	■ Positive only if $GSAW > 1.08{*}SELF$
GSOR	$1.393483{*}GSOR$ $-0.27937{*}GSAW{*}GSOR$	1.393483 $-0.27937{*}GSAW$	■ Positive only if $GSAW < 4.8$
GSAW	$-0.27937{*}GSAW{*}GSOR$ $+0.183525{*}GSAW{*}SELF$ $+0.178461{*}GSAW{*}RATD$	$-0.27937{*}GSOR$ $+0.183525{*}SELF$ $+0.178461{*}RATD$	■ Positive only if $GSOR < .0.66{*}SELF$ $+0.64{*}RATD$
SELF	$0.183525{*}GSAW{*}SELF$ $-0.19197{*}RATD{*}SELF$	$0.183525{*}GSAW$ $-0.19197{*}RATD$	■ Positive only if $GSAW >$ $1.05{*}RATD$

■ Whether a higher level of perceived *Self-Efficacy* will result in a higher level of cybersecurity compliance depends on the relationship between *General Security Awareness* and the level of rationality (i.e. $GSAW > 1.05{*}RATD$).

7.8 Conclusion

In this chapter, we conducted an exploration of the relationships between individual DMS and cybersecurity compliance using different DMS variables than were used in previous research. The results of this research have implications for both theory and practice.

With regard to practice, we expect that organizations would be interested in knowing the impacts of both discretionary (e.g. *GSAW*) variables and non-discretionary variables (e.g. *GSOR, RATD*) on the level of *Security Compliance* since this could help them in several ways. For example, with respect to discretionary variables it could identify the employees in which they can invest less while achieving the same or higher level of security compliance. This would be of particular importance to organizations with budget and other type's resource constraints including small and medium enterprises (SMEs) and other types of enterprises in developing countries. For example, for projects which require a high level of security compliance, at the point of assignment of employees to such projects, the non-discretionary variables (e.g. *GSOR, RATD*) could be used to identify employees who would be a good fit.

With regard to theory, our approach offers the opportunity to abduct new hypotheses that relate to antecedents of cybersecurity compliance behaviour. At a minimum, this is another study along with those of Donalds and Osei-Bryson (2017, 2020) whose results suggest that individual DMS has statistically significant impacts on cybersecurity compliance behaviour. Our results suggest that some of such hypotheses could involve DMS variables as moderators.

We consider these results to be preliminary because it is not certain that our sample is sufficiently representative of the various organizational and cultural contexts that exist, and so these results should be subjected to future empirical analysis. However, there seems to be a good reason to expect that inclusion of DMS variables in causal models that explain and/or predict security compliance will be shown to be warranted.

References

Ali, A. (1989). Decision styles and work satisfaction of Arab executives: A cross- national study. *International Studies of Management and Organization, 19*(2), 22–37.

Atkinson, R., Crawford, L., & Ward, S. (2006). Fundamental uncertainties in projects and the scope of project management. *International Journal of Project Management, 24,* 687–698.

Baiocco, R., Laghi, F., & D'Alessio, M. (2009). Decision-making style among adolescents: Relationship with sensation seeking and locus of control. *Journal of Adolescence, 32*(4), 963–976.

Bandura, A. (1977). Self-efficacy: Toward a unifying theory of behaviour change. *Psychological Review, 84*(2), 191–215.

Barclay, C. (2008). Towards an integrated measurement of is project performance: The project performance scorecard. *Information Systems Frontiers, 10,* 331–345.

Bavol'ár, J., & Orosová, O. (2015). Decision-making styles and their associations with decision-making competencies and mental health. *Judgment and Decision Making,* 10(1), 115–122.

Bazerman, M., & Moore, D. A. (2012). *Judgment in Managerial Decision Making.* 7th Edition. Hoboken, NJ: John Wiley & Sons.

Benbasat, I., Goldstein, D. K., & Mead, M. (1987). The case research strategy in studies of information systems. *MIS Quarterly, 11*(3), 368.

Boulgarides, J. D., & Oh, M. D. (1985). A comparison of Japanese, Korean and American managerial decision styles: An exploratory study. *Leadership & Organization Development Journal; Leadership & Organization Development Journal.* 6 (8), 9–11.

Bresnen, M., Edelman, L., Newell, S., Scarbrough, H., & Swan, J. (2003). Social practices and the management of knowledge in project environments. *International Journal of Project Management, 21*(3), 157–166.

Bulgurcu, B., Cavusoglu, H., & Benbasat, I. (2010). Information security policy compliance: An empirical study of rationality-based beliefs and information security awareness. *MIS Quarterly, 34*(3), 523–548.

Chan, R., & Rosemann, M. (2001). Managing knowledge temporary organization. *Journal of Systems and Information Technology, 5*(2), 37–53.

Conroy, G., & H. Soltan, (1998). ConSERV, as a continual audit concept to provide traceability and accountability over the project life cycle. *International Journal of Project Management, 16*(3), 185–197.

Crawford, L., Morris, P., Thomas, J., & Winter, M., (2006). Practitioner development: From trained technicians to reflective practitioners, *International Journal of Project Management, 24,* 722–733.

152 ■ *Cybercrime and Cybersecurity in the Global South*

Creswell, M., & Miller, D. (2008). Determining the validity in qualitative inquiry. *Theory in Practice, 39*(3), 124–130.

Crossley, C., & Highhouse, S. (2005). Relation of job search and choice process with subsequent satisfaction. *Journal of Economic Psychology, 26*(2), 255–268.

Darke, P., Shanks, G., & Broadbent, M. (1998). Successfully completing case study research: Combining rigor, relevance and pragmatism. *Information Systems Journal, 8*, 273–289.

Decision Style Inventory. 2013 Retrieved on September 3, 2013 at http://www.dsitest.com/

Dillman, D. A. (2000). *Mail and Internet Surveys: The Tailored Design Method.* (Vol. 2). New York: Wiley.

Disterer, G. (2002). Management of project knowledge and experiences. *Journal of Knowledge Management, 6*(5), 512–520.

Donalds, C., & Osei-Bryson, K. M. (2017). Exploring the impacts of individual styles on security compliance behavior: A preliminary analysis. In *SIG ICT in Global Development, 10th Annual Pre-ICIS Workshop*, Seoul, Korea.

Donalds, C., & Osei-Bryson, K. M. (2020). Cybersecurity compliance behavior: Exploring the influences of individual decision style and other antecedents. *International Journal of Information Management, 51*, 102056.

Drucker, P. F. (1993). *Post-Capitalist Society.* New York: Butterworth Heineman.

Durkin, M. (2004). In search of the internet-banking customer: Exploring the use of decision styles. *International Journal of Bank Marketing, 22*(7), 484–503.

Fox, T. L., & Spence, J. W. (1999). An examination of the decision styles of project managers: Evidence of significant diversity. *Information & Management, 36*(6), 313–320.

Fox, T. L., & Wayne Spence, J. (2005). The effect of decision style on the use of a project management tool: An empirical laboratory study. *ACM SIGMIS Database, 36*(2), 28–42

Gibbert, M., Guigrok, W., & Wicki, B. (2008). What passes as a rigorous case study. *Strategic Management Journal, 29*, 1465–1475.

Grover, V. & Davenport, T. H. (2001). General perspectives on knowledge management: Fostering a research agenda. *Journal of Management Information Systems, 18*(1), 5–21.

Gurteen, D. (1998). Knowledge, creativity and innovation. *Journal of Knowledge Management, 2*(1), 5–13.

Hafni, R. N., & Nurlaelah, E. (2018). Analyzing Students' Decision-Making Style in Prior Knowledge of Mathematical Critical Thinking Skill. *Pancaran Pendidikan, 7*(1), 178–185.

Hansen, M.T., Nohria, N., & Tierney, T. (1999). What's your strategy for managing knowledge? *Harvard Business Review, 77*(2), 106–116.

Harren, V. A. (1979). A model of career decision making for college students. *Journal of Vocational Behavior, 14*(2), 119–133.

Henderson, J. C., & Nutt, P. C. (1980). The Influence of Decision Style on Decision Making Behavior. *Management Science, 26*(4), 371–386.

Kankanhalli, A., Teo, H.-H., Tan, B. C. Y., & Wei, K.-K. (2003). An integrative study of information systems security effectiveness. *International Journal of Information Management, 23*(2), 139–154.

Kasvi, J.J.J., Vartiainen, M., & Hailikari, M. (2003). Managing knowledge and knowledge competences in projects and project organisations. *International Journal of Project Management, 21*(8), 571–582.

Kock, N., & McQueen, R. (1998). Knowledge and information communication in organizations: An analysis of core, support and improvement processes. *Knowledge and Process Management, 5*(1), 29–40.

Kositanurit, B., Osei-Bryson, K.-M., & Ngwenyama, O. (2011). Re-examining information systems user performance. *Expert Systems with Applications, 38*(6), 7041–7050. doi: 10.1016/j.eswa.2010.12.011

Larson, J. R. J., Foster-Fishman, P. G., & Franz, T. M. (1998). Leadership style and the discussion of shared and unshared information in decision-making groups. *Personality and Social Psychology Bulletin, 24*(5), 482–495.

Leonard-Barton, D. (1990). A dual methodology for case studies: Synergistic use of a longitudinal single site with replicated multiple sites. *Organization Science, 1*(3), 248–266.

Love, P. E. D. (2005). *Management of Knowledge in Project Environments*. Amsterdam: Elsevier.

Martinsons, M. G., & Davison, R. M. (2007). Strategic decision making and support systems: Comparing American, Japanese and Chinese management. *Decision Support Systems, 43*(1), 284–300.

Mech, T. F. (1993). The Managerial Decision Styles of Acadetnic Library Directors. *College & Research Libraries, 54*(5), 375–386.

Morris, P.W.G., Crawford, L. Hodgson, D., Shepherd, M.M., & Thomas, J. (2006) Exploring the role of formal bodies of knowledge in defining a profession – The case of project management. *International Journal of Project Management, 24*, 710–721.

Newell, S., Scarbrough, H., Swan, J., Robertson, M., & Galliers, R.D., (2002). The importance of process knowledge for cross project learning: evidence from a UK hospital. *Proceedings of the 35th Annual Hawaii International Conference on System Sciences*, Hawaii.

Ng, B.-Y., Kankanhalli, A., & Xu, Y. C. (2009). Studying users' computer security behavior: A health belief perspective. *Decision Support Systems, 46*(4), 815–825.

Nonaka, I. (1994). A Dynamic theory of organizational knowledge creation. *Organization Science, 5*(1), 4–37.

Nonaka, I., & Takeuchi, H. (1995). *The Knowledge-Creating Company: How Japanese Companies Create the Dynamics of Innovation*. USA: Oxford University Press.

Nutt, P. C. (1990). Strategic decision made by top executive and middle managers with data and process dominant styles. *Journal of Management Studies, 27*(2), 172–194.

Nutt, P. C. (1993). Flexible decision styles and the choices of top executives. *Journal of Management Studies, 30*(5), 695–721.

Osei-Bryson, K.-M., & Ngwenyama, O. K. (2011). Using decision tree modeling to support Piercian abduction in IS research: A systematic approach for generating and evaluating hypotheses for systematic theory development. *Information Systems Journal, 21*(5), 407–440.

Osei-Bryson, K.-M., & Ngwenyama, O. K. (2014). *Advances in Research Methods for Information Systems Research: Data Mining, Data Envelopment Analysis, Value Focused Thinking*. New York: Springer.

Phillips, S. D., Pazienza, N. J., & Ferrin, H. H. (1984). Decision-making styles and problem-solving appraisal. *Journal of Counseling Psychology, 31*(4), 497.

Pinsonneault, A., & Kraemer, K. L. (1993). Survey research methodology in management information systems: an assessment. *Journal of management information systems, 10*(2), 75–105.

Project Management Institute PMI. (2008). *A Guide to the Project Management Body of Knowledge (PMBOK® Guide)*. 4th ed. Newtown Square, PA: Project Management Institute.

Reich, B. H. (2007). Managing knowledge and learning in IT projects: A conceptual framework and guidelines for practice. *Project Management Journal, 38*(2), 5–17.

Rowe, A. (1981). *The Decision Style Inventory. Los Angeles: University of Southern California.*

Rowe, A. J., & Boulgarides, J. D. (1983). Decision styles—A perspective. *Leadership & Organization Development Journal, 4*(4), 3–9.

Rowe, A. J., & Boulgarides, J. D. (1992). *Managerial Decision Making: A guide to Successful Business Decisions.* New York, USA: McMillan.

Rowe, A. J., & Boulgarides, J. D. (1994). *Managerial Decision Making.* Prentice-Hall, Englewood Cliffs, NJ.

Rowe, A., & Mason, R.O. (1987). *Managing with Style: A Guide to Understanding, Assessing, and Improving Decision Making.* San Francisco: Jossey-Bass.

Scarbrough, H., Bresnen, M., Edelman, L. F., & Laurent, S. (2004). The processes of project-based learning: An exploratory study. *Management Learning, 35*, 491–506.

Scheepers, R., K. Venkitachalam, & M.R. Gibbs, (2004) Knowledge strategy in organizations: Refining the model of Hansen, Nohria and Tierney. *Journal of Strategic Information Systems 13(3)*, 201–222.

Scott, S. G., & Bruce, R. A. (1995). Decision-making style: The development and assessment of a new measure. *Educational and psychological measurement, 55*(5), 818–831.

Shenhar, A.J., Dvir, D., Levy, O., & Maltz, A. C. (2001). Project success: A multidimensional strategic concept. *Long Range Planning, 34*, 699–725.

Singh, R., & Greenhaus, J. (2004). The relation between career decision-making strategies and person-job fit: A study of job changers. *Journal of Vocational Behavior, 64*(1), 198–221.

Stanleigh, M. (2006). From crisis to control: New standards for project management. *Ivey Business Journal, 70*(4), 1–4.

Statistical Institute of Jamaica (Statin), Jamaica Industrial Classification. (n.d.) retrieved July 12, 2014, from http://statinja.gov.jm/Jamaica%20Industrial%20Classification%20 Structure%20Revised%20-%202005.pdf

Sternberg, R. J., & Zhang, L.-F. (Eds.). (2001). *Perspectives on Thinking, Learning, and Cognitive Styles* (1st ed.). New York, NY: Routledge.

Straub, D.W. (1989). Validating instruments in MIS research. *Management Information Systems Quarterly, 13*(2), 147–169.

Tanur, J.M. (1982). Advances in methods for large-scale surveys and experiments. In R. McAdams, N.J. Smelser, & D.J. Treiman (Eds.), *Behavioral and Social Science Research: A National Resource, Part II*, 589–619. Washington, D.C.: National Academy Press.

The Standish Group. (2007). CHAOS 2007 REX: A Standish Group Research Exchange.

Thunholm, P. (2004). Decision-making style: Habit, style or both? *Personality and Individual Differences, 36*(4), 931–944.

Turner, J. R., & Müller, R. (2005, June). The project manager's leadership style as a success factor on projects: A literature review. *Project Management Institute, 36*(1), 59–61.

Warkentin, M., & Willison, R. (2009). Behavioral and policy issues in information systems security: The insider threat. *European Journal of Information Systems, 18*(2), 101–105.

Weiser, M. and J. Morrison, (1998) Project memory: Information management for project teams. *Journal of Management Information Systems, 14*(4), 149–166.

Yousef, D. A. (1998). Predictors of decision-making styles in a non-western country. *Leadership and Organization Development Journal, 19*(7), 366–373.

Zmud, R. W. (1979). Individual differences and MIS success: A review of the empirical literature. *Management Science, 25*(10), 966–979.

DEVELOPING SOLUTIONS FOR MANAGING CYBERSECURITY RISKS

III

Chapter 8

Designing an Effective Cybersecurity Programme in the Organization for Improved Resilience

8.1 Introduction

The cybersecurity landscape continues to show a rapid evolution of threats and vulnerabilities. The evidence shows that this form of risk, i.e. the threats and vulnerabilities, is of significant concern to organizations as malicious actors continue to find innovative methods to breach organizational defences. This means that many businesses and government agencies are being exposed or unprotected as they struggle to manage the demands of cybersecurity with limited resources or know-how to effectively mitigate the risks. According to the FBI Internet Crime Report (FBI, 2020), the number of reported security incidents and losses associated with them continues to increase annually. Security breaches such as business email compromise (BEC), ransomware, data breach and other common compromises account for billions of dollars in losses (FBI, 2020). Further, victims of security incidents also suffer significant hidden economic costs such as system downtime, reduced efficiency, incidence response costs, brand damage among others (Smith & Lostri, 2020).

DOI: 10.1201/9781003028710-11

Despite the escalating risks many businesses and government agencies still suffer from governance lapses and are without current or well-defined programmes to help inform stakeholders on approaches to maintain security and enterprise continuity. In Jamaica and other countries in the Caribbean, many businesses and areas of government do not have a formal security programme. In some cases, such as the smaller organizations, the situation is even more alarming, as cybersecurity is not even on the radar or prioritized. This may be due to several reasons, including the recurring issues of resource constraints. However, it is argued that in today's hyper-connected environment, businesses and government agencies are putting themselves at risk, both in terms of risk of security breaches and risk of financial losses.

According to Barclay (2014a), to effectively manage cybersecurity risks, organizations must attain security advantage. This necessitates having a capability-centric approach to identifying and responding to cybersecurity risks, including threats and vulnerabilities. This involves understanding how cybercriminals and insiders may act, addressing the weaknesses and vulnerabilities in the critical information assets and people, and improving the necessary resources and capabilities (know-how) needed to achieve a more secure cyber and information environment. The objective of this chapter is therefore to introduce a parsimonious model in relation to a cybersecurity programme and outline the critical success factors to operationalize this programme in any organization. Within this context, a cybersecurity programme is a set of coordination actions and measures undertaken by an organization to reduce its cybersecurity risk and to achieve security advantage. A cybersecurity programme provides benefits to the organization by focusing on the priorities and roadmap required to bolster the security and resilience of the organization's systems, networks and other information assets. It provides a holistic view of the actions needed to achieve sound cybersecurity management across the enterprise. It defines not only technical but operational, management and legal and regulatory baseline measures. A design science (DS) approach is adopted in the study to communicate the constituents of the framework, its utility and value in helping to manage cybersecurity risks in the organization.

8.2 Background

8.2.1 The Cost of Security Breaches

The 2021 Cost of Data Breach Report (Ponemon Institute, 2021) reinforces that government agencies and businesses in diverse sectors continue to be at risk of a security event and grapple with finding methods to effectively mitigate. According to the report, the economic cost of a breach is on the rise, accounting for a 10% increase over 2020. The report (Ponemon Institute, 2021) observes that costs were significantly lower for some organizations with a more mature security posture, and higher for organizations that lagged in the adoption of security technologies such as security AI and automation, zero-trust and cloud security. Further, the average time to identify and contain a breach is dependent on serval factors such as the type of data breach, attack vector, factors such as the use of security AI and automation and cloud modernization stage.

The most frequent initial attack vectors were compromised credentials, phishing, cloud misconfiguration with other attack vectors being malicious insiders, vulnerabilities in third-party software, system error, social engineering and BEC (Ponemon Institute, 2021). Personal data continue to be an attractive target for malicious actors, as according to the report (Ponemon Institute, 2021), customer personal data was involved in 44% of all breaches. Other types of compromised records include anonymized customer data breaches, employee personal data, intellectual property and other sensitive data.

Smith and Lostri (2020) note that ransomware remains the fastest-growing part of cybercrime. Ransomware attacks are found to be more expensive than the average data breach, where the cost does not include the cost of the ransom (Ponemon Institute, 2021). In responding to these attacks, organizations experience costs in terms of escalation, notification, lost business and response costs (Ponemon Institute, 2021). Lost business, for example, accounts for 38% of the average total cost associated with a data breach which includes business disruption and revenue losses from system downtime, cost of lost customers and acquiring new customers, reputation losses and diminished goodwill. Other cost factors are detection and escalation costs and notification and post data breach response (Ponemon Institute, 2021). The elements are consistent with Smith and Lostri (2020) who report that organizations suffer significant hidden economic costs associated with security events such as system downtime, reduced efficiency, incidence response costs, brand damage.

8.2.2 Managing Cybersecurity Risks

With the escalating security breaches and cost impact on organizations, managing cybersecurity risks must be an essential part of business operations. Cybersecurity risk can be described as the likelihood of a security breach event experienced by the organization. Given the threat landscape, this likelihood increases, particularly where there is less cybersecurity risk maturity in the organization, or the cybersecurity posture is low. Cybersecurity risk management therefore is concerned with the process of managing cybersecurity risk with the utilization of technical and organizational actions to include policies, security tools and other measures.

Two frameworks or models that are applicable in managing cybersecurity risks are discussed. These are NIST framework (NIST, 2014) and the Cybersecurity Capability Maturity Model (CCMM) (Barclay, 2014a).

8.2.2.1 NIST Framework

The NIST framework for improving critical infrastructure cybersecurity serves to improve cybersecurity risk management in critical infrastructure (NIST, 2014). According to Stine et al. (2014), the Cybersecurity Framework

> provides a prioritized, flexible, repeatable, and cost-effective approach, including information security measures and controls to help owners and operators of critical infrastructure and other interested entities to identify, assess, and manage cybersecurity-related risk while protecting business confidentiality, individual privacy and civil liberties.
>
> (p.1)

The Framework comprises of three components, namely the Framework Core, the Implementation Tiers and the Framework Profiles. The Core consists of a set of cybersecurity activities that are intended to result in specific cybersecurity outcomes. These are represented as the functions, which are identify, protect, detect, respond and recover (Figure 8.1). Identify function serves to develop an organizational understanding to manage cybersecurity risk to systems, people, assets, data and capabilities. This includes an appreciation of the business context, the resources that support critical functions and the related cybersecurity risks that enable an organization to focus and prioritize its efforts, consistent with its risk management strategy and business needs. Protect function serves to develop and implement appropriate safeguards to ensure delivery of critical services. This involves supporting the ability to limit or contain the impact of a potential cybersecurity event. Detect function serves to develop and implement appropriate activities to identify the occurrence of a cybersecurity event. The timely discovery of cybersecurity events is an important requirement of this step. Respond function serves to develop and implement appropriate activities to take action regarding a detected cybersecurity incident. This includes the ability to contain the impact of a potential cybersecurity incident. Recover function serves to develop and implement appropriate activities

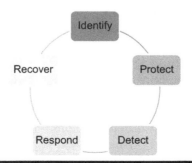

Figure 8.1   NIST framework

to maintain plans for resilience and to restore any capabilities or services that were impaired due to a cybersecurity incident. This includes timely recovery to normal operations to minimize the impact of a cybersecurity incident.

8.2.2.2 Cybersecurity Capability Maturity Model

The Cybersecurity Capability Maturity Model (CCMM) provides guidance on the necessary considerations and requirements to achieve and maintain security advantage. It is therefore a useful tool for organizations in their planning of a cybersecurity programme. The CCMM consists of five dimensions, namely the cyber environment, operations, legal and regulatory, technologies and capabilities (Barclay, 2014b). It is argued that these dimensions can serve as a platform for the areas of considerations in planning a holistic programme to reduce cybersecurity risks.

The dimensions are discussed (see Figure 8.2). The 'Environment' dimension represents the dynamic cyberspace and operational ecosystem. It takes into account the good and bad actors in the ecosystem and the evolution or adaptation that takes place as a result of the varying and sometimes contending forces. The 'Capabilities' dimension addresses developing the requisite know-how to build capabilities in cybersecurity. This involves education, training and development on subjects that span the dimensions of CCMM. It is argued that enhancement in capabilities will promote investment in capacities relating to people, processes and information systems artefacts. The 'Technologies' dimension considers the current and emerging ICTs and emphasizes that these occurrences can both enhance and impede

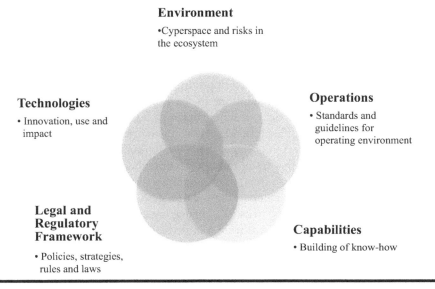

Figure 8.2   Dimensions of CCMM

cybersecurity management since both good and bad actors will seek to leverage the development of technologies. The 'Operations' dimension represents the standards, good practices, cultural norms that assist the specific operating environment in achieving security advantage. The 'Operations' dimension therefore contemplates the resources necessary to obtain the outcomes from the other dimensions. The 'Legal and regulatory' dimension represents the rules-based structure that informs the strategic implementation enforcement and monitoring of the ecosystem. This includes the holistic process implications of legislative development, implementation and enforcement (e.g. Barclay, 2014b) and the policy or strategy development life cycle.

8.3 Design Science Methodology

Design is a common feature of the world we live in. Design representations are seen in art, engineering and other fields. DS research seeks to represent the stages of design that extends beyond routine in a manner to allow for structured adaptation. According to Hevner et al. (2004), DS research methodology involves the creation and evaluation of artefacts that can be used to solve identified problems in specific contexts. The output of a DS research can be a construct, model, method, framework or other form of artefacts. Thus, an artefact may include any designed solution or object that solves a problem within a certain context (Gregor & Hevner, 2011; Peffers et al., 2007), thereby providing a link between research and practice (Peffers et al., 2007). This research thereby seeks to design a framework, a cybersecurity programme that aims to serve as a guide for organizations in the management of their cybersecurity risks in a holistic manner that represents the cycle of planning, identifying, resolving risks and learning from the experiences. The originality of the framework is in the structure and processes.

DS research contribution comprises an invention, improvement, or exaptation (Gregor & Hevner, 2013). An invention produces new solutions to new problems. An improvement creates better solutions in the form of more efficient and effective products, processes, services, technologies, or ideas by developing new solutions for known problems. Exaptation extends known design knowledge into a new field which is non-trivial and interesting, thereby extending known solutions to new problems. In that regard, this study offers a scientific contribution in the form of an improvement. The cybersecurity programme framework consists of known solutions relating to processes and models to provide a guidance model in the cyber and information security domain(s) to assist in managing cybersecurity risks. The stages of the cybersecurity programme provide a more realistic roadmap or at minimum an alternative roadmap that managers can contemplate in managing risks relating to cybersecurity and its ecosystem.

The DS approach encapsulates the design outcome of this study and serves as a link between research and practice and adds to the research dialogue on suitable frameworks for managing cybersecurity risks in organizations, from both a technical and non-technical standpoint. The study also follows the tradition of similar studies that have adopted the DS methodology in their diverse research contexts. For instance, the development of a framework for measuring the performance of programmes of projects (Barclay & Osei-Bryson, 2009), the development of a cybersecurity capability maturity model (Barclay, 2014a) and the development of a framework for building national cybersecurity strategy (Dennis, et al., 2014).

Table 8.1 outlines the steps in applying the DS methodology, according to the seminal proposal of Peffers et al. (2007).

Table 8.1   DS Approach and Application to Research

DS Steps	Application
Step 1: Problem identification and motivation.	The research problem and justification of the value of a solution are identified at this stage. The need to find measures to mitigate the growing cybersecurity risks experienced by organizations is the motivation behind this study. Previous sections highlight the escalating threats and security breaches being identified within the landscape. In addition, security research (e.g. Ponemon, 2021) is consistent with the experience that highlights that mature processes and information systems tools are necessary for mitigating the various forms of cybersecurity risks.
Step 2: Objectives of a solution.	Based on the identified problem and motivation, the objectives of the solution are identified. The objective of the study is therefore to introduce a framework that represents practical steps organizations can adopt to minimize cybersecurity risks, protect their ecosystems, respond to breaches and build capabilities over time.
Step 3: Design and development.	This step involves the solution or artefact being created to address the outcome of the previous steps. The cybersecurity programme is strongly influenced by practical experience and insights into basic elements that organizations can contemplate as they develop their cybersecurity posture. The steps are also consistent with standard risk management and project management frameworks. The dimensions of CCMM also influence the main considerations. As with the framework steps, continuous refinement will embody the development of the framework as it is operationalized and tested.

(Continued)

Table 8.1 (Continued)

DS Steps	Application
Step 4: Demonstration.	Explication of how the artefact fulfils its objectives or solves the stated problem(s) is done. At this stage of the research, a proof of concept of the artefact is demonstrated through the use of informed arguments to illustrate the solution's utility and relevance. This demonstration strategy is appropriate based on the suggestions of Gregor and Hevner (2013) and Hevner et al. (2004).
Step 5: Evaluation.	The evaluation step observes and measures how well the artefact supports a solution to the problem. It involves comparing the objectives of a solution to actual observed results from the use of the artefact in the demonstration. Hevner et al. (2004) proposed five types of evaluation approaches that have been used extensively in DS studies. A descriptive evaluation method that includes the use of informed arguments is used here. Future efforts will include the application of other types of evaluation techniques.
Step 6: Communication.	This step involves communicating the artefact's development. The problem and its importance, the artefact, its utility and novelty, the rigour of its design, and its effectiveness to researchers and other relevant audiences are shared. This step is applied through the reporting of the artefact's background and characteristics in this paper.

8.4 Cybersecurity Programme Framework

A well-developed and enforced cybersecurity programme involves defined strategies, procedures and controls that can provide a strong guide or standard of practice in responding to cybersecurity risks. The cybersecurity programme framework, Figure 8.3, places the programme activities in context. The framework establishes a coherent set of processes that are required in helping to develop a sound and comprehensive security programme. This in turn will establish and maintain baseline standard of practice and competency for the organization. It is important to note that stages are non-linear as in practice iteration and refinements are necessary as part of a living process or programme. Table 8.2 provides a summary of the steps.

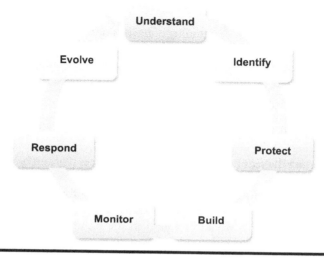

Figure 8.3   Cybersecurity programme framework

Table 8.2   Cybersecurity programme framework

Process	Description
Understand	Builds an understanding of the business and cybersecurity environment and their potential impact on the organization.
Identify	Determines the set of security risks in the operating environment. This includes detecting threats and vulnerabilities in critical infrastructure systems, processes and people.
Protect	Determines and adopts the appropriate measures necessary to bolster the security of the operating environment, including critical information assets and infrastructure.
Build	Designs measures to build capacity in people and the operating environment.
Monitor	Scrutinizes the measures and operating environment and apply remedial measures.
Respond	Creates an environment that can respond to and recover from security events and breaches, and apply enforcement mechanisms where appropriate.
Evolve	Tests the environment to validate that learning is taking place.

8.4.1 Step 1: Understand the Environment

This step serves to build an understanding of the business and cybersecurity environment and their potential impact on the organization. Activities involve outlining the set of activities to create the cybersecurity programme. A determination of the essential elements required to attain compliance or successful cybersecurity resilience is undertaken at this stage. Understanding the ecosystem entails:

1. Understanding the desired state of security maturity, baseline and cybersecurity readiness of the organization.
2. Appreciating the set of standards and good practices that can be relied on during the exercise.
3. Being able to identify the organization's critical information infrastructure, assets and processes. The detail may differ among organizations, however, some common forms would be found in the technology to support critical areas of the business, the network infrastructure, specific information systems that use critical processes and activities.
4. Being able to identify the key human resources for technical, operational, management and legal skills, roles and responsibilities required to achieve the planned outcomes.

8.4.2 Step 2: Identify the Security Risks

This step serves to determine the set of security risks in the operating environment. This includes detecting threats and vulnerabilities in critical infrastructure systems, processes and people. This step also serves to determine the extent of the potential scale and impact of the risks to the organization. It is acknowledged that organizations' operating environments may differ and thereby they may be faced with different types of risks due to their context, or level of experience and maturity in dealing with specific types of cyber risks or they have more resources such as technology-enabled cybersecurity solutions. In addition, the environment may change due to external and internal factors. Arguably, ransomware and certain types of scams were not prevalent a few years ago. Therefore, an organization must continuously understand and assess the threat landscape and the level of risks these cybersecurity risks have on their infrastructure and ecosystem. Measures such as security audits and risk assessments are recommended at this stage. To identify the risks, some activities include:

1. Assessing the critical information infrastructure and assets.
2. Assessing risks at points in the ecosystem such as the supply chain and managed service providers.
3. Identifying key points of vulnerabilities and attack vectors.
4. Identifying key areas of strengths in the ecosystem.
5. Determining access and availability of budget and manpower to support.

8.4.3 Step 3: Protect the Environment

This step serves to determine and adopt the appropriate measures necessary to bolster the security of the operating environment, including critical information assets and infrastructure. This includes the appropriate technical and organizational measures to bolster the environment, such as to:

1. Implement organizational measures to strengthen processes and know-how to support the development of plans, strategies and technical guidance.
2. Implement technologies to harden the network, provide early warnings and secure the infrastructure across the ecosystem.

8.4.4 Step 4: Build Capabilities

This serves to design measures to build capacity from the perspective of the human, physical and computing environment. This requires investment in training and awareness, procurement of appropriate security physical infrastructure and information systems. In turn, an expected outcome is improved capabilities in specific areas that can allow the organization to stem risks and obtain security advantage (Barclay, 2014). This includes:

1. Confirming capacity needs (current and future).
2. Developing training and education.
3. Investing in and developing the infrastructural capacity to improve security posture.
4. Deploying appropriate solutions.

8.4.5 Step 5: Monitor Performance

This step serves to scrutinize the implemented measures and operating environment and apply remedial measures. The key question is whether the measures are working, and where they are not ensuring that the appropriate corrective actions are taken. Also implicit at this stage is the continuous surveillance of the ecosystem and landscape to identify new threats, vulnerabilities or even countermeasures that may not have been present when the measures were adopted.

8.4.6 Step 7: Respond to Breaches

This serves to enable the organization to respond to and recover from security events and breaches and apply enforcement mechanisms where appropriate. With knowledge of what is happening in the internal and external environment, suitable response strategies can be devised and put into action. Business continuity in the face of a security event is critical and therefore the organization must be able to stress-test its systems and processes to get a sense of its ability to be resilient.

In addition, adopting enforcement mechanisms in the event of breaches and non-adherences is also recommended.

8.4.7 Step 8: Evolve in a Dynamic Environment

This step serves to essentially tests the environment to validate that learning is taking place. The ability to adapt and evolve based on changing needs, demands and events are necessary with any organizational framework, document. With the characteristics of cybersecurity and the rapidly changing landscape, it is essential that the organization can adapt and be responsive to evolving needs. The revisions of plans and strategies, evaluation of good cybersecurity practices and continuous assessment and learning are contemplated at this stage.

8.5 Operationalizing the Cybersecurity Framework

An important outcome of the process is the development of a comprehensive set of documents, including the strategy and suite of policies to be implemented and enforced, and the deployment of technology-enabled tools required to meet the strategic cybersecurity intent. Thus, to operationalize the framework, the interaction of strategy, technology, people and process are necessary to manage the cybersecurity risks in the ecosystem. The strategy details the roadmap in optimizing security. It is the plan of action developed to inform the organizational security policy, and activities to maintain or improve the security levels of the organization, its people, processes and critical infrastructure. It informs the contents of the policy documents such as data security, incident management, network security and personnel security to name a few. These policies facilitate organizational control by informing the desired state and specific outcomes must be assured. From this, a detailed set of operational plans and procedures are developed. In addition, information systems security solutions, e.g. endpoint protection, security AI and automation, and firewalls are implemented. All these components are closely related (Figure 8.4) and guide the full cybersecurity and incident management life cycles.

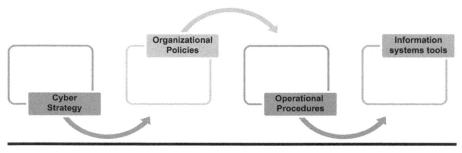

Figure 8.4   Stages of operationalization of the cybersecurity programme

8.6 Critical Success Factors

No matter how well a strategy is prepared, it is leadership, commitment and team that determines how effective the cybersecurity strategy will become. Critical success factors relate to the elements that help to advance the successful deployment of the activity or influence the outcome that achieves stated objectives and expectations of the stakeholders. Multiple critical success factors can impact the effective execution or operations of the cybersecurity programme (Figure 8.5). Based on professional experience in the field, several are identified, which are consistent with scientific knowledge.

8.6.1 Business Alignment

Alignment of business and IT functions is a good practice for organizations, yet according to scholars, this important step remains a significant challenge (e.g. Luftman, et al., 2017). The cybersecurity-business alignment challenge is likely even more daunting. Alignment of the business strategy and cybersecurity programme objectives is necessary to achieve cohesiveness and success. Therefore, integrating cybersecurity into the organization's mandates and strategic outlook is important, in that way, there is an increased likelihood that the cybersecurity framework matches the direction, goals and business priorities of the organization.

8.6.2 Good Governance Practices

Governance is the bedrock of standards and maturity. Equipping the organization with clear measures regarding transparency, accountability, confidentiality, integrity

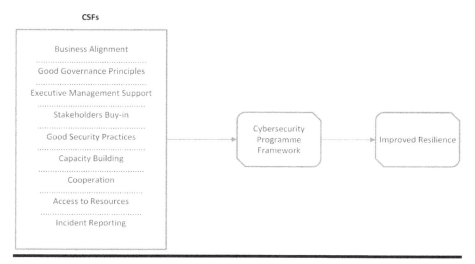

Figure 8.5   CSFs of cybersecurity programme

will have a positive impact on the effective management of the cybersecurity programme. Enforcement of the measures within the cybersecurity programmes is also an important part of accountability and governance. This shows employees and other stakeholders that actions or lack thereof have consequences.

8.6.3 Executive Management Support

Executive or top management support is a critical determinant of the success of organizational activities (e.g. Young & Jordan, 2008). The level of awareness and interest of executive management in securing the critical infrastructure within the ecosystem establishes commitment and drive to enhancing the organizational cybersecurity maturity and resilience. It is therefore recommended that support is obtained and managed throughout the life of the cybersecurity programme, ideally with clear evidence that they are driving this process.

8.6.4 Stakeholder Buy-in

Similar to top management support, the level of support and commitment of the key stakeholders can determine the success or failure of the cybersecurity programme. Employees or contractors' attitudes towards cybersecurity can help or hinder the efforts of the organization. Strategies such as involving the stakeholders in the process, creating awareness campaigns on the importance of the initiative and its impact on the stakeholders if efforts fail are useful tactics to improve levels of buy-in.

8.6.5 Good Security Practices

An assessment of the cybersecurity landscape reinforces the importance of good security standards and their adoption. For example, Chapter 11 (Values of Optimising Cyber Hygiene Practices in MSMEs) discusses the impact of cyber-hygiene practices on the cybersecurity posture of MSMEs where it is shown that good hygiene practices result in good cybersecurity health. In addition, organizations must carefully assess the applicability of respective standards and choose the best fit. This can be based on the size of the organization and the cost to implement. The key takeaway however is that there must be sound baseline cybersecurity standards to adhere to in order to improve resilience.

8.6.6 Capacity Building

Capability building is typically considered solely within the people context in the discourse of cybersecurity (e.g. ITU, 2020). However, this study views capacity as spanning the dimensions of people, infrastructure, processes, and systems. Therefore, building capacity to manage cybersecurity risks can take any of those forms. However, for the optimum effect, it is best to consider capacity building holistically and identify measures to increase cybersecurity knowledge among employees, improve the organizational processes to support cybersecurity and invest and develop information systems tools to improve organizational resilience.

8.6.7 Cooperation and Partnerships

For some stakeholders, this may appear unrealistic, especially among competing governmental agencies or private bodies. However, it has become good security practice to engage in cooperation at the national and organizational levels. Notably, cybersecurity models rely on cooperation as a key indicator of the level of maturity of a country (e.g. Barclay, 2014a; ITU, 2020). Therefore, extending cooperation to the organizational level is sound practice. This is further supported by the research conducted in the cybersecurity hygiene practices in MSMEs where cooperation and partnerships/alliances were identified as important values and objectives identified in helping to enhance cybersecurity practices. This emphasizes that cybersecurity is a shared responsibility and thus more engaged organizations that are committed to sharing experiences and ideas are those that will experience greater success in managing cybersecurity risks.

8.6.8 Access to Resources

The findings from the research on cybersecurity hygiene practices in MSMEs, i.e. Chapter 11 (Values of Optimising Cyber Hygiene Practices in MSMEs) endorse the importance of organizations having access to resources to be able to effectively execute the cybersecurity programmes. Smaller organizations and entities in developing countries are mindful of the impact limited resources such as finance and manpower have on their effectiveness. It is therefore key that organizations carefully plan, budget and prioritize to ensure that they obtain the best results.

8.6.9 Incident Reporting

Organizations typically underreport cybersecurity breaches. This situation is supported by regional CIRTs, such as those in the Caribbean, that have admitted the difficulty in organizations reporting incidents when they occur. This is largely attributed to factors such as the risk of damage to reputation or image or loss of business (see Ponemon Institute, 2021). However, we argue that reporting improves an understanding of the cybersecurity environment and aid incident management and law enforcement practices. These outcomes will in turn improve the cybersecurity posture and maturity levels of organizations.

8.7 Conclusion

Resilience is synonymous with strength and is viewed as the ability to quickly recover from challenges or obstacles. Within, the cybersecurity context, we see resilience as the ability to mitigate against cybersecurity risks and efficiently recover in the event of a breach and learn from the experience and from that of others. Given the growing risks present in the cybersecurity landscape, this is an important characteristic of an organization. This study introduces a cybersecurity framework to aid an organization in achieving this characteristic. Through the application of technical and organizational measures to understand, identify, protect, build, monitor, respond to cybersecurity risks and learning from experience, it is argued that the organization can enhance its cybersecurity posture and maturity. The study also identifies CSFs associated with organizational activities to minimize cybersecurity risks to the organizations. Some CSFs include access to resources, good security practices, incident reporting cooperation, good governance practices and executive management support.

The cybersecurity framework is in its formative stages. Future research will entail further refinements and evaluation to improve its utility to managers, examining CSFs in managing cybersecurity risks and assessing the CSF conceptual relationships. The study also has implications for policymakers in highlighting key elements of consideration in designing cybersecurity risk strategies and policies and the factors that aid in successful operationalization and adoption.

Acknowledgement

This chapter includes material that was previously presented by C. Barclay at a local conference and printed in the Jamaica Computer Society's magazine in October 2013.

References

Barclay, C. (2014a). Sustainable Security Advantage in a Changing Environment: The Cybersecurity Capability Maturity Model (CM2). In *Proceedings of the 2014 ITU Kaleidoscope Academic Conference: Living in a Converged World-Impossible Without Standards?* (pp. 275–282). IEEE, St. Petersburg, Russia.

Barclay, C. (2014b). Using frugal innovations to support cybercrime legislations in small developing states: Introducing the cyber-legislation development and implementation process model (CyberLeg-DPM). *Information Technology for Development, 20*(2), 165–195.

Barclay, C., & Osei-Bryson, K. M. (2009). Toward a more practical approach to evaluating programs: The multi-objective realization approach. *Project Management Journal, 40*(4), 74–93.

Dennis, A., Jones, R., Kildare, D., & Barclay, C. (2014). Design Science Approach to Developing and Evaluating a National Cybersecurity Framework for Jamaica. *The Electronic Journal of Information Systems in Developing Countries, 62*(1), 1–18.

FBI. (2020). *2020 Internet Crime Report*. Retrieved from https://www.ic3.gov/Media/PDF/AnnualReport/2020_IC3Report.pdf

Gregor, S., & Hevner, A. R. (2011). Introduction to the special issue on design science. *Information Systems and e-Business Management, 9*(1), 1–9.

Gregor, S., & Hevner, A. R. (2013). Positioning and presenting design science research for maximum impact. *MIS Quarterly, 37*(2), 337–355.

Hevner, A. R., March, S. T., Park, J., & Ram, S. (2004). Design science in information systems research. *MIS Quarterly, 28*(1), 75–105.

ITU. (2020). *Global Cybersecurity Index 2020 Measuring commitment to cybersecurity*. Retrieved from https://www.itu.int/en/myitu/Publications/2021/06/28/13/22/Global-Cybersecurity-Index-2020

Luftman, J., Lyytinen, K., & Zvi, T. B. (2017). Enhancing the measurement of information technology (IT) business alignment and its influence on company performance. *Journal of Information Technology, 32*(1), 26–46.

National Institute for Standards and Technology (NIST). (2014). *Framework for Improving the Critical Infrastructure Cybersecurity: Version 1.0*, 12 February 2014. https://www.nist.gov/system/files/documents/cyberframework/cybersecurity-framework-021214.pdf

Peffers, K., Tuunanen, T., Rothenberger, M. A., & Chatterjee, S. (2007). A design science research methodology for information systems research. *Journal of Management Information Systems, 24*(3), 45–77.

Ponemon Institute/IBM Security Intelligence. 2021 Cost of Data Breach Report. Retrieved from https://www.ibm.com/security/data-breach

Smith, Z.M., & Lostri, E. (2020). *The Hidden Costs of Cybercrime*. Retrieved from https://www.mcafee.com/enterprise/en-us/assets/reports/rp-hidden-costs-of-cybercrime.pdf

Stine, K. , Quill, K., & Witte, G. (2014), *Framework for Improving Critical Infrastructure Cybersecurity*. Gaithersburg, MD: ITL Bulletin, National Institute of Standards and Technology, [online], https://tsapps.nist.gov/publication/get_pdf.cfm?pub_id=915476 (Accessed July 29, 2021)

Young, R., & Jordan, E. (2008). Top management support: Mantra or necessity?. *International Journal of Project Management, 26*(7), 713–725.

Chapter 9

The Cybersecurity Capability Maturity Model for Sustainable Security Advantage

9.1 Introduction

Privacy and security are principal concerns in today's highly connected world. Cybercrime and security breaches are known to have a negative impact on the growth, development and security of organizations and economies. According to the latest estimates, the global cost of cybercrime is close to US$1 trillion (Smith & Lostri, 2020). Therefore, the security challenge is to defend against the 'unknown, the uncertain, the unseen and the unexpected' (Rumsfeld, 2002), and as such, the focus should be less on the threats and more on how one may be threatened and what is needed to deter and defend against such threats (Rumsfeld, 2002). While these directives were given within the context of military transformation, they also resonate within the information and cybersecurity domain(s). Studies continue to show that the fight against cybercrimes requires both offensive and defensive measures. This is necessary in order to gain a firm and sustainable security advantage. Security advantage is therefore defined as the ability to effectively identify, assess, plan, manage, and respond to risks, including threats and vulnerabilities through a capability-based approach. In other words, the focus is to:

1. critically examine how cybercriminals and insiders may act;
2. address any weaknesses and vulnerabilities in the critical information assets and people; and
3. improve the necessary resources and capabilities (know-how) needed to achieve a more secure cyber and information environment.

For many countries achieving security advantage is a challenging task. The developing regions, which account for a significant portion of the online users, are especially at risk since they tend to be burdened with the relatively high vulnerability of cyberattacks and low resource capabilities. Therefore, the study is motivated by the search to understand whether countries know what to do to minimize threats and vulnerabilities to achieve security advantage or to identify a general security toolkit that can aid in achieving a minimum level of security assurance. It is reasoned that to move forward, an understanding of the level of readiness, requirements and capabilities needed to achieve security advantage is necessary. However, an analysis of academic discourse on cybercrime and security shows that a standardized mechanism to help guide the attainment of security advantage is largely missing, except for a few exceptions. Two of these exceptions are the National Initiative for Cybersecurity Education's NICE Cybersecurity Capability Maturity Model (NIST, 2020) and The Community Cyber Security Maturity Model (CCSMM) (White, 2011). The NICE framework is described as a reference for describing and sharing information about cybersecurity work levels and is centred on the skilled practitioners, integrated governance, and process and analytics for workforce planning in the organization. CCSMM may be considered threat-centred where each level is indicative of the types of threats and the associated activities at each level.

The current state of the art suggests that additional discourse on cybersecurity maturity models should have certain requirements, i.e. they should possess proactive and offensive strategies; grounded in science, and aligned to the dynamism of the cyber environment. Additionally, the continued development of threat-based and/or capability-based solutions and their impact needs to be evaluated from an academic standpoint to propel innovation in this important area. This research delves into this arena by coupling a mature area i.e. maturity models with the evolving area of cybersecurity to offer a capability-centred solution to improving competencies that are targeted at deriving effective responses to cybersecurity threats and vulnerabilities.

This research presents the CCMM, which was first presented in Barclay (2014a). CCMM is a model that illustrates the stages of readiness or preparedness to respond to threats, vulnerabilities and technological advancement that exists within the continuously evolving environment. The model is refined to explain the five dimensions of CCMM, which are the cyber environment, operations, legal and regulatory, technologies and capabilities. CCMM includes six steps centred on 'capability-constituents' of society, operational, education, innovation and development, technical, business and legal and regulatory measures. The spectrum of maturity and capability include undefined, initial, basic, defined, dynamic and optimizing stages.

The Design Science (DS) methodology is applied in the development of CCMM artefacts. This approach is chosen because it involves the analysis of the designed artefacts to help understand, explain and improve on the behaviour of the social systems that the artefact becomes a part of (Gregor & Hevner, 2013). Within this context, many countries are without formal measures or know-how to achieve security advantage or are using rudimentary tools that put them at a disadvantage and impede the development of sound cyber/information infrastructure. Therefore, this study hopes to extend the discourse on cybersecurity and contribute to practice by providing an artefact that offers utility in improving security routines and practices, which it is hoped will lead to a safer networked environment. It also offers significance to standard development since the identification of commonly agreed capabilities can be used as indicators of a country's level of preparedness.

9.2 Research Background

9.2.1 Cybercrime, Security and Strategy

Routine Activity Theory (e.g. Cohen & Felson, 1979) is one seminal theory that can be used to explain how crime risks increase in the current technological landscape. It suggests that crime risks increase on the convergence of a motivated offender, a suitable target and the absence of a capable guardian. Based on the nature of the Internet, the proliferation of social networking sites and other applications and limited awareness of users, the rate of cybercrimes is likely to continue to increase. Therefore, capable guardianship is imperative.

There are multiple definitions of cybercrime. Cybercrime refers to actions that are illegal under cybercrime or other enactments. A review of the definition shows the general inclusion of traditional illegal behaviours and new forms of criminal acts done electronically or with a computer device. According to Barclay (2017), cybercrime or computer crime relates to any criminal act that affects the confidentiality, integrity and availability of a computer or network, or the privacy and security of a person online. A useful classification of cybercrime distinguishes between four different types of offences: offences against the confidentiality, integrity and availability of computer data and systems; computer-related offences; content-related offences; and copyright-related offences (COE, 2001).

Cybersecurity also has varied definitions. Cybersecurity is generally contextualized as the protection of the tangible components of the information systems, i.e. computers, networks, programmes and data from unintended or unauthorized access change or destruction. However, the scope can be extended to include the protection of critical assets, including information assets or infrastructure, people and even processes. For instance, the US in a 2013 Cybersecurity Executive Order identified its national critical infrastructure to be its natural gas and oil pipelines, storage sites and refineries as well as electric generation, transmission and distribution facilities. Since that time, many countries have recognized their critical infrastructure as a key part of their cybersecurity posture and strategy. Generally, countries will likely have context-specific assets that are due priority attention and protection from cyber threats. The ITU (n.d.) provides a comprehensive definition that includes in part

> the collection of tools, policies, security concepts, security safeguards, guidelines, risk management approaches, actions, training, best practices, assurance and technologies that can be used to protect the cyber environment and organization and user's assets

The definition underlines the necessity for improvements in skills and knowledge to produce the necessary safeguards and guidance that can be followed to provide assurance.

An understanding of cybercrime and security is a necessary step in the provision of offensive and defensive measures for a more secure environment. This is articulated in a national or organizational cybersecurity strategy. The strategy defines how these measures are operationalized and therefore form an important step in developing an effective security posture at the organizational or national level. A UN Report (2013) reveals that only 30% of responding countries indicated the existence of a national cybercrime strategy. Countries in Africa, Asia and Oceania reported the lowest levels of cybersecurity or cybercrime strategies with approximately 50% of these countries indicating that such an instrument did not exist. Since then, there has been improvement; however, there are still a number of countries that are without a strategy. This dilemma underlines the challenges in many countries to identify or harness the capabilities to successfully integrate security knowledge and promote national security.

9.2.2 Capabilities and Competitive Advantage

According to Grant (1996), organizational capabilities constitute the fundamental source of sustained competitive advantage. This is also applicable at the national level and in the determination of a strategy for cybersecurity. Capabilities are alternatively referred to as knowledge, competencies, routines or innovations within the organization. The dynamic capabilities theory is one of the principal theories on developing organizational capabilities (Teece & Pisano, 1994). Teece and Pisano (1994) describe dynamic capabilities as the 'ability to integrate, build and reconfigure internal and external competences to address rapidly changing environments'. This viewpoint underlines the need to be flexible and dynamic in addressing resource demands based on the changing environment. This is especially relevant in today's hyperconnected environment.

Barney (1991) describes competitive advantage as the ability to implement a value-creating strategy that is not simultaneously being implemented by any current or potential competitor. Similarly sustained competitive advantage is competitive advantage combined with other firm's inability to duplicate the benefits of the value-creating strategy. Placing perspective within the context of the security environment, an advantage is sought over the criminals; therefore, it can be constituted as rivalry with cybercriminals where the country's ability to implement an effective security strategy that cannot be (easily) penetrated by criminal insiders and outsiders would be considered a security advantage. Sustained security advantage therefore is the achievement of security advantage and criminals' inability to exploit vulnerabilities due to the country's ability to keep pace with criminals, harness technological advancement and support continuous capacity building and development.

Multiple sources of competitive advantage are proffered by experts which provide a platform for understanding security advantage. For instance, various scholars suggest that knowledge (e.g. Argote & Ingram, 2000), ICT (e.g. Powell & Dent-Micallef, 1997), human resources (e.g. Barney & Wright, 1997) and customer value (e.g. Woodruff, 1997) can have a considerable impact on an organization's performance or competitive advantage. Porter (2008) also identifies five forces that shape competitiveness as the bargaining power of suppliers and buyers, threats of new entrants and substitute products or services and rivalry among competitors. Porter (2011) further suggests that a nation's competitiveness depends on its capacity to innovate and upgrade and offers four determinants of national competitive advantage: factor conditions, demand conditions, related and supporting industries and strategy, structure and rivalry. Factor conditions refer to the nation's position in factors of production such as skilled labour or infrastructure. Demand conditions refer to the nature of home-market demand for products and services. Related and supporting industries refer to the presence or absence of supplier industries and other related industries. Strategy, structure and rivalry refer to conditions governing how companies are created, organized and managed along with the nature of the domestic rivalry. Drawing a parallel to the security environment these sources of competitiveness may relate to the capacity of the citizens or actors in the environment, the nature of security development in the country and demand for privacy and security, the network of products and services to support the security demand conditions and the nature of the dynamism in the environment, rivalry with criminals and how security strategies are created, organized and managed.

9.2.3 Capability Maturity Model

The Capability Maturity Models (CMMs) including CMM Integration (CMMI) (CMMI, 2002) were developed to provide process improvement in organization processes including software development and management cycle. CMMs contain the essential elements of effective processes for one or more bodies of knowledge. The key differences between CMM and CMMI are that CMM was designed for the software industry specifically and has 18 process areas while CMMI has applicability to other industries and has 25 process areas. The purpose of CMMI is to provide guidance for improving the organization's processes and ability to manage the development, acquisition, and maintenance of products or services. The CMMI is noted to aid in improving product quality, reducing cycle time and cost and improving the ability to meet project targets. There are six capability levels, designated by the numbers 0 through 5:

0. Incomplete
1. Performed
2. Managed
3. Defined
4. Quantitatively Managed
5. Optimizing.

An incomplete process as the name suggests is a process that is either not performed or partially performed. This may occur where one or more of the specific goals of the process area are not satisfied. Capability Level 1 process is characterized as a performed process that is characterized by unpredictability and is primarily reactive in nature. Level 2 is characterized by processes that are repeatable. It also uses basic project management to track cost and schedule and is reactive in nature. Level 3 is a proactive process level and is characterized by defined processes that are well understood by the organization. Standards, procedures, tools and methods are developed to aid the completion of tasks. Level 4 is characterized by measurement where quality and process performance are established and used as criteria in managing the process. The quality and process performance are understood in statistical terms and are managed throughout the life of the process. Level 5 is characterized as an optimizing process that is changed and adapted to meet relevant current and projected business objectives. The level focuses on continually improving the process performance through both incremental and innovative technological improvements.

9.3 DS Research Approach

DS research methodology involves the creation and evaluation of artefacts that can be used to solve identified problems in the environment (Hevner et al., 2004). An artefact can be described as an entity or thing that has or can be transformed into, material existence as an artificially made object (e.g. model and instantiation) or process (e.g. method and software) (Hevner et al., 2004). In short, the artefact may include any designed solution or object that solves a problem within a certain context (Gregor & Hevner, 2011; Peffers et al., 2007), thereby providing a link between research and practice (Peffers et al., 2007). This research thereby seeks to develop a standardized model to aid in the determination of a country or organization's readiness and preparedness to effectively counter cybercrimes and manage cybersecurity processes. The CCMM is the artefact, a formal CMM, where the model is a simplified depiction of the world, specifically the cyber environment. Its originality is in the structure, dimensions and characteristics of the maturity levels.

DS research contribution can be categorized into an invention, improvement, or exaptation (Gregor & Hevner, 2013). An invention presents new solutions to new problems. It is a radical breakthrough that is a clear departure from the accepted ways of thinking and doing. An improvement creates better solutions in the form of more efficient and effective products, processes, services, technologies, or ideas by developing new solutions for known problems. Exaptation involves an extension of known design knowledge into a new field which is non-trivial and interesting, that is, extending known solutions to new problems. This study therefore offers contribution in the form of an improvement where known solutions of maturity models are used to apply in the cyber and information security domain(s) to outline the stages of progressive development an entity can take as it improves its maturity and capability in the management of cybersecurity. This contribution is a departure from existing models such as CMM and CMMI in terms of both form and substance. The six stages of capabilities provide a more realistic roadmap or at minimum an alternative roadmap and focus not on the risks or threats, but the capabilities needed to achieve security advantage. The five dimensions also seek to reflect the practical elements of managing cybersecurity.

This approach is suitable for this research since it serves to provide a link between research and practice in the development of CCMM, thus providing a contribution in the form of an improvement to the current knowledge base. Further, the DS methodology has been applied successfully in multiple contexts which have some parallel to this study, for example, in project management (Barclay & Osei-Bryson, 2009), cybersecurity strategy development (Dennis, et al., 2014) and engineering method (Rosenkranz & Holten, 2011).

Peffers et al. (2007) provide a clear outline of the steps necessary to help assure the successful application of the DS methodology. The approach and its application to the research is described in Table 9.1.

Table 9.1   DS Approach and Application to Research

DS Steps	Application
Step 1: Problem identification and motivation.	The research problem and justification of the value of a solution are identified at this stage. It is noted that cybercrimes continue to evolve, new vulnerabilities and threats are detected daily including malware, ransomware software and systems vulnerabilities. Two key issues are underlined, the resources needed to effectively defend a group's critical information asset and people are mounting and there are divergent approaches or measures to help determine how one is performing or what requirements are necessary to effectively manage. Therefore, there is the motivation to offer a simplified tool that can aid in this objective.
Step 2: Objectives of a solution.	Based on the identified problem and motivation, the objectives of the solution are identified. The objective of the study is to offer a model that can be used as a basis for the assessment of readiness to effectively manage cybersecurity considerations and identify the capabilities required to do so.
Step 3: Design and development.	This involves the solution or artefact being created to address the outcome of the previous steps. CCMM is influenced by several considerations, creation of the solution or artefact. The model is informed by maturity models, current cybersecurity practice, management and strategy literature. Six steps of progressive maturity and five dimensions of considerations to tackle cybersecurity issues are offered. This is explained in detail in the subsequent section. It is anticipated that the development and refinement will be an iterative process to enhance the features and operationalization of the artefact. The first iteration was produced by Barclay (2014a, b).
Step 4: Demonstration.	Explication of how the artefact fulfils its objectives or solves the stated problem(s) is done. At this stage of the research, a proof of concept of the artefact is demonstrated through the use of informed arguments to illustrate the solution's utility and relevance. This demonstration strategy is appropriate based on the suggestions of Gregor and Hevner (2013) and Hevner et al. (2004).

(Continued)

Table 9.1 (Continued)

DS Steps	Application
Step 5: Evaluation.	The evaluation step observes and measures how well the artefact supports a solution to the problem. It involves comparing the objectives of a solution to actual observed results from the use of the artefact in the demonstration. Hevner et al. (2004) proposed five types of evaluation approaches that have been used extensively in DS studies. A descriptive evaluation method that includes the use of informed arguments is used here. Future efforts will include the application of other types of evaluation techniques.
Step 6: Communication.	This step involves communicating the artefact's development. The problem and its importance, the artefact, its utility and novelty, the rigour of its design, and its effectiveness to researchers and other relevant audiences are shared. This step is applied through the reporting of the artefact's background and characteristics in this paper.

9.4 Cybersecurity Capability Maturity Model (CCMM)

CCMM is intended to provide guidance on the necessary considerations and requirements to achieve and maintain security advantage. The principal underlying pillars comprise society, technical, operations and business, legal and regulatory, education and capability building measures. These pillars further inform the five dimensions of CCMM consisting of the *cyber environment, operations, legal and regulatory, technologies and capabilities*.

9.4.1 Security Advantage and Building Capabilities

To promote security advantage through advancement in capabilities, a five-factor model is proposed. This five-factor model in turn influences the dimensions and stages of CCMM as the basis for capability development in cybersecurity. It is proposed that to achieve sustainable security advantage countries need to dynamically build their capabilities to manage risks, counter threats, vulnerabilities and leverage advances in technology (Figure 9.1). Some of the commonly expected outcomes enhancing security advantage include strategy and policy design and implementation, secured infrastructure and plans, laws and regulations, curriculum design and implementation, partnerships and information sharing and formal assessments of the environment including risks and technological opportunities and actors. These outcomes span the dimensions of CCMM.

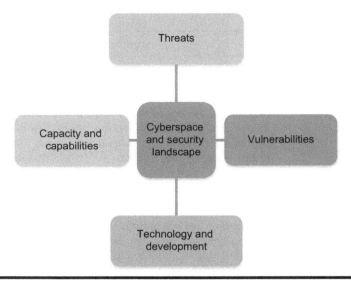

Figure 9.1   Five-factor model of the cyberenvironment

Technological development serves as an enabler to further advancement and a platform for new threats and vulnerabilities. The environment consists of rivalry and dynamism due to events such as technological development, changes in social norms and other factors. Threats from criminal insiders and outsiders, vulnerabilities in critical assets and capabilities of members of the society interact where the more advanced the capabilities the better able the society is to counter any changes or shock from the other factors.

Threats and vulnerabilities are key risks to the cyberenvironment. Vulnerabilities are inherent exposures in systems and people while threats are outward facing, i.e. the likelihood of attacks, breaches and crimes based on the actors involved and level of exposure, motivation and other factors that may impact a country or organization's ability to effectively manage these risks.

Capabilities span the dimensions and pillars and ought to be responsive to the dynamism of the environment. Therefore, at the national level focus can be on the development of capabilities in different areas, pillars or dimensions (legal and regulatory or operations) to enhance security advantage. Development of capabilities is the central theme in advancing maturity towards managing cybersecurity. Analysis of the environment and literature has shown that competencies that extend beyond technical measures are imperative to combating cybercrimes (e.g. Barclay, 2013). Progressive development of routines and competencies in the different areas are envisioned as different stages of maturity are achieved. Further, it is expected that an optimal mix of capabilities necessary to maintain security advantage will evolve with changes in the environment. The levels of integration of knowledge impact the maturity

Environment

•Cyperspace and risks in the ecosystem

Technologies

• Innovation, use and impact

Operations

• Standards and guidelines for operating environment

Legal and Regulatory Framework

• Policies, strategies, rules and laws

Capabilities

• Building of know-how

Figure 9.2   Dimensions of CCMM

levels illustrated in CCMM. Teece et al. (1997) identify three characteristics of knowledge integration that are applicable here: *efficiency, extent and flexibility*. In other words, the depth and breadth of integration of capabilities, combined with the ability to dynamically respond to environmental changes across sectors can be sound indicators of innovation, know-how and advancement.

As indicated, the five-factor model informs the dimensions of CCMM and the model is applicable to the national and organizational levels. The five dimensions of CCMM are the cyber environment, operations, legal and regulatory, technologies and capabilities (Figure 9.2).

The Environment represents the dynamic cyberspace and operational ecosystem. The emerging risks inherent in the environment include threats, breaches and risks inherent in the people, systems and technologies. It involves the good and bad actors in the ecosystem and the evolution or adaptation that takes place as a result of the varying and sometimes contending forces.

The Capabilities dimension represents developing the know-how to build capabilities in cybersecurity. This involves education, training and development on subjects that span the dimensions of CCMM. For example, in terms of education, areas of technical competency aligned to the security bodies of knowledge, laws, standards and regulations, psychology could be part of the core focus, for example, and will impact the other areas. The promotion of formal education from primary to tertiary levels, research and awareness across all sectors of society are anticipated. Building capabilities across the cybersecurity body of knowledge is also contemplated, where a country may prioritize one or more specific areas based on capacity.

The Technologies dimension represents the current and emerging ICTs. These can impact the demand and supply side of the risks i.e. technologies that aid cybersecurity and technologies that impede cybersecurity.

The Operations dimension represents the standards, good practices, cultural norms that assist the specific operating environment in achieving security advantage. It therefore contemplates the resources necessary to obtain the outcomes from the other dimensions.

The Legal and regulatory dimension represents the rule-based structure that informs the strategic implementation enforcement and monitoring of the ecosystem. This contemplates full process implications of legislative development, implementation and enforcement (e.g. Barclay, 2014b) and the policy or strategy development life cycle. Therefore, it considers activities beyond the development of appropriate laws to the supporting processes to ensure that the laws are effective and are being effectively enforced.

9.4.2 Levels of CCMM

There are six capability and maturity levels for improving security advantage and cybersecurity capabilities which are indicated by Levels 0 to 5 (Table 9.1). The stages of human development are used to define the transition since a corollary can be seen, in that, through advancement in age and experience maturity is generally achieved. Also, it helps to clearly describe the level of capabilities or competencies in cybersecurity achieved at each stage:

1. Undefined or Prenatal;
2. Initial or Infant;
3. Basic or Child;
4. Defined or Adolescent;
5. Dynamic or Adult;
6. Optimizing or Sage.

Level 0 stage is characterized by an undefined process which is the lowest possible level of capabilities. At this stage, there is a lack of coordinated cybercrime strategy, policy or existing laws. In other words, efforts are largely non-existent. Some reports (e.g., UNODC, 2013) may indicate that there may be developing economies that are still at this stage.

Level 1 stage is characterized by an initial process that is at an infancy level and efforts are predominantly fractured and disconnected. Generally, only one area of capability is the centre of focus, for example, a technical measure such as the development of an emergency response team (CERT). Also, the approach is largely reactive and threat-based. Therefore, a focus on the implementation of specialized teams e.g. a CERT without coordinated solutions in areas of legislation, capacity building and general awareness would indicate a country's first step in preparedness.

Level 2 stage is characterized by a basic stage that improves on the initial stage. There is still a reactive and threat-based approach, and at minimum, one additional capability is considered, such as an implementation of a CERT programme accompanied by ad-hoc legislative development. Here the focus is still on threats; therefore, any devised strategies will only be in response to perceived threats or vulnerabilities that are considered high priority.

Level 3 stage is characterized by a defined process that improves on the basic stage. The approach is more coordinated and likely to be government or agency-led. A majority but not all of the capabilities are the focus of the cybersecurity approach at the national level. Therefore, considerations across the spectrum of capacity development, legal requirements, technical and operational considerations, etc., would likely be represented in a formal strategy or policy. There is also a good level of knowledge integration with a shift to proactive offensive measures such as monitoring and detection capabilities, and legislative development and enforcement.

Level 4 stage is characterized by a dynamic process that improves on the defined stage. A capability-centred approach to cybersecurity management is undertaken with strong coordinated and proactive measures. All the capabilities are undertaken with a strong emphasis on education and training for example. Therefore, critical assessment is made of the environment with the prediction of trends, and strategies or countermeasures are developed to respond. In other words, the areas of technical measures, business, legislative and regulatory measures and capacity building are considered individually and holistically to improve security advantage.

Level 5 stage is characterized by an optimizing process that improves Level 4 or the fifth stage of maturity. A capability-centred -approach to cybersecurity management is also undertaken with coordinated proactive measures. All the pillars of capabilities are harnessed with a strong emphasis on innovation and research with advanced prevention and detection measures available across key sectors of society. Innovative approaches are continuously examined and developed to improve and maintain a secure environment.

It is worth noting that while the study is influenced by CMMs, it does not seek to be a replica and offers its own unique contributions. The CCMM distinguishes itself through distinct indicators and areas of cybersecurity capabilities. The levels of knowledge integration of the pillars of capabilities (i.e. society, education, operational, technical, business, and legal) are used as the basis to indicate the levels of maturity in CCMM. CCMM is distinct from CMMI in the following ways: it is not relating to software or industry but rather the environment since a holistic view is necessary to respond to cybersecurity concerns; the stages of maturity are determined by multidimensional capabilities, and it is not focused on measurement or to be quantitatively management but rather on a comprehensive multi-perspective strategy to creating and maintaining security advantage. It also distinguishes itself from existing cybersecurity models in its approach by adopting a capability-centred approach and using different indicators for maturity.

The CCMM can provide utility to countries interested in developing capabilities to enhance their cybersecurity efforts. Although it is at preliminary stages, the dimensions or pillars of capabilities identify possible areas of focus that ought to be considered in a holistic and coordinated cybersecurity strategy.

9.5 Conclusion

The research underlines the importance of achieving and maintaining security advantage in today's society. Two contributions are presented: the development of the five-factor model capability perspective and the development of CCMM which consists of the cyber environment, operations, legal and regulatory, technologies and capabilities dimensions. The five-factor model serves as a basis for the key considerations for developing and maintaining security advantage where there is a paradigm shift from a threat-based perspective and towards a capability-based perspective. Thus, the focus is on the development of capabilities encompassing the development of key human resources and attention to innovation to keep pace with technological development, threats and vulnerabilities within the dynamic environment. CCMM is introduced as a basis to help guide nations in the development of competencies and skills necessary to proactively manage the dynamism and rivalries in the cyber environment. Six stages of maturity are proposed from Level 0 to Level 5 where the efficiency, extent and dynamism of the capabilities are used as the basis to determine advancement.

The study contributes to both research and practice. It is now accepted that discourse on cybersecurity must extend beyond technical solutions; therefore, this study extends the discourse to include considerations that hitherto reside in management and strategy domains. Government and policy-makers can find value and utility in the CCMM artefact. Development of policies can be guided by attention to specific dimensions and pillars of capabilities to gradually enhance citizens' skills and competencies in cybersecurity and develop maturity over time, for example. Future works will involve the continued review and refinement of CCMM and the further evaluation of the artefact in order to examine its application and utility.

Acknowledgement

This chapter includes material that previously appeared in Barclay, C. (2014). Sustainable security advantage in a changing environment: The Cybersecurity Capability Maturity Model (CM²). In *Proceedings of the 2014 ITU Kaleidoscope academic conference: Living in a converged world-Impossible without standards?* (pp. 275–282). IEEE.

References

Argote, L., & Ingram, P. (2000). Knowledge transfer: A basis for competitive advantage in firms. *Organizational Behavior and Human Decision Processes, 82*(1), 150–169.

Barclay, C. (2014a). Sustainable security advantage in a changing environment: The Cybersecurity Capability Maturity Model (CM2). In *Proceedings of the 2014 ITU kaleidoscope academic conference: Living in a converged world-Impossible without standards?* (pp. 275–282). IEEE.

Barclay, C. (2014b). Using frugal innovations to support cybercrime legislations in small developing states: Introducing the cyber-legislation development and implementation process model (CyberLeg-DPM). *Information Technology for Development, 20*(2), 165–195.

Barclay, C. (2017). Cybercrime and legislation: a critical reflection on the Cybercrimes Act, 2015 of Jamaica. *Commonwealth Law Bulletin, 43*(1), 77–107.

Barclay, C., & Osei-Bryson, K. M. (2009). Toward a more practical approach to evaluating programs: The Multi-Objective Realization approach. *Project Management Journal, 40*(4), 74–93.

Barney, J. (1991). Firm resources and sustained competitive advantage. J*ournal of Management, 17*(1), 99–120.

Barney, J. B., & Wright, P. M. (1997). On becoming a strategic partner: The role of human resources in gaining competitive advantage. *Human Resource Management: Published in Cooperation with the School of Business Administration, The University of Michigan and in alliance with the Society of Human Resources Management, 37*(1), 31–46.

CMMI, Team, C. P. (2002). *Capability Maturity Model® Integration (CMMI SM), Version 1.1.* Pittsburgh, PA: Software Engineering Institute, Carnegie Mellon University/ SEI-2002-TR-012.

COE. (2001). *Council of Europe Convention on Cybercrime (CETS No. 185)*, available at: https://www.coe.int/en/web/conventions/

Cohen, L. E., & Felson, M. (1979). Social change and crime rate trends: A routine activity approach. *American Sociological Review*, 588–608.

Dennis, A., Jones, R., Kildare, D., & Barclay, C. (2014). Design Science Approach to Developing and Evaluating a National Cybersecurity Framework for Jamaica. *The Electronic Journal of Information Systems in Developing Countries, 62*(1), 1–18.

Grant, R. M. (1996). Prospering in dynamically-competitive environments: Organizational capability as knowledge integration. *Organization Science, 7*(4), 375–387.

Gregor, S., & Hevner, A. R. (2011). Introduction to the special issue on design science. *Information Systems and e-Business Management, 9*(1), 1–9.

Gregor, S., & Hevner, A. R. (2013). Positioning and presenting design science research for maximum impact. *MIS Quarterly, 37*(2), 337–355.

Hevner, A. R., March, S. T., Park, J., & Ram, S. (2004). Design science in information systems research. *MIS Quarterly, 28*(1), 75–105.

ITU (n.d.). *Overview of Cybersecurity*, Retrieved from http://www.itu.int/en/ITU-T/study-groups/com17/Pages/cybersecurity.aspx

NIST. (2020). *National Institute of Standards and Technology Special Publication 800-181 Natl. Inst. Stand. Technol. Spec. Publ. 800-181* Rev. 1, 27 (November 2020) doi:10.6028/ NIST.SP.800-181r1

Peffers, K., Tuunanen, T., Rothenberger, M. A., & Chatterjee, S. (2007). A design science research methodology for information systems research. *Journal Of Management Information Systems, 24*(3), 45–77.

Porter, M. E. (2008). The five competitive forces that shape strategy. *Harvard Business Review, 86*(1), 78.

Porter, M. E. (2011). *Competitive advantage of nations: creating and sustaining superior performance*. New York: Simon and Schuster.

Powell, T. C., & Dent-Micallef, A. (1997). Information technology as competitive advantage: The role of human, business, and technology resources. *Strategic Management Journal, 18*(5), 375–405.

Rosenkranz, C., & Holten, R. (2011). The variety engineering method: Analyzing and designing information flows in organizations. *Information Systems and e-Business Management, 9*(1), 11–49.

Rumsfeld, D. H. (2002). Transforming the military. *Foreign Affairs, 81*, 20.

Smith, Z.M., & Lostri, E. (2020). *The Hidden Costs of Cybercrime*. Retrieved from https://www.mcafee.com/enterprise/en-us/assets/reports/rp-hidden-costs-of-cybercrime.pdf

Teece, D., & Pisano, G. (1994). The dynamic capabilities of firms: An introduction. *Industrial And Corporate Change, 3*(3), 537–556.

Teece, D. J., Pisano, G., & Shuen, A. (1997). Dynamic capabilities and strategic management. *Strategic Management Journal, 18*(7), 509–533.

UNODC. (2013). Comprehensive Study on Cybercrime. Retrieved from http://www.unodc.org/documents/organizedcrime/UNODC_CCPCJ_EG.4_2013/CYBERCRIME_STUD Y_210213.pdf

White, G. B. (2011, November). The Community Cyber Security Maturity Model. In *Technologies for Homeland Security (HST), 2011 IEEE International Conference on* (pp. 173–178). IEEE, Waltham, MA, USA.

Woodruff, R. B. (1997). Customer value: The next source for competitive advantage. *Journal of the Academy of Marketing Science, 25*(2), 139–153.

Chapter 10

An Enhanced Value-Focused Thinking Methodology for Addressing Cybersecurity Concerns

10.1 Introduction

The Value Focused Thinking (VFT) methodology as the name suggests is value-centric where the values are the core set of considerations that is of concern within a specific decision context. Therefore, it focuses on the fundamental objectives (i.e. *What it is I want from the situation?*) and the means objectives (i.e. *How I am going to achieve it?*). Within the context of the VFT methodology, a means-objective (MO) is an objective that is required in order to directly achieve a parent fundamental-objective (FO) or another MO. The VFT paradigm can be contrasted with the more conventional alternative focused thinking (AFT) approach in three ways: (1) the effort in making the values explicit, this important step is done before other activities and these values are used to (2) identify decision opportunities and (3) create alternatives. The AFT approach instead focuses on identifying alternatives and then the objectives or the values of the tasks follow (Keeney, 1996). Keeney contends that this traditional approach is a reactive approach and is a limited way to think through decision situations.

Benefits of the VFT approach (Keeney, 1992, p. 24–27) include

1. *Uncovering hidden objectives.* Hard thinking facilitates going beyond the obvious to uncover objectives not previously considered. Additionally, obtaining perspectives from multiple decision-makers enhance the chance of widening the breadth of objectives for a given decision situation of context.
2. *Guiding information collection.* The technique guides information collection through the identification of objectives as decision-makers are able to identify what they want or desire of a given context and explain why a given objective may be important.
3. *Improving communication.* Where the opportunity exists to express the wants and needs such as in a business environment, communication and common understanding may be improved.
4. *Facilitating involvement in multiple-stakeholder decisions.* The nature of the technique and the process involved in identifying and structuring the objectives facilitates improved communication and engagement of multiple stakeholders in the decision process.
5. *Avoiding conflicting decisions.* Conflicts are a normal part of multiple stakeholder engagements however continued focus on the most desirable outcome and prioritization of objectives facilitates conflicting decisions. Further, the determination of the fundamental objectives guides the decisions and eliminates any conflicts or poorly defined decisions.
6. *Creating alternatives.* Creating alternatives is about facilitating additional considerations or ways to achieve the end objectives. This effort provides an opportunity for identifying additional objectives and uncovers solutions or alternatives that will ultimately improve the decision process.
7. *Evaluating alternatives.* Once a wider set of alternatives are created these alternatives can be examined and assessed to guide the stakeholder or decision-maker in determining the best alternatives and thereby clear the path to a more effective decision-making process (better decisions).
8. *Identifying decision opportunities.* What can I do better? This question enables the decision-maker to focus on opportunities and not be constrained by decision problems thereby possibly preventing future problems due to the attention placed on an unconstrained view of the decision situation.
9. *Guiding strategic thinking.* Any opportunity to create improved objectives and an understanding of the decision situation will likely enhance strategic insight, a necessary characteristics of successful business. Therefore, a value-focused approach to solving any given problem or opportunity enables stronger decision support.

The VFT approach has several limitations, which can be seen as challenges mainly with the level of pervasiveness in the IS field and acceptance by practitioners. Some of the main challenges are as follows:

1. Difficult process that requires hard thinking to uncover objectives
2. Most decision-makers are accustomed to the traditional approach to decision-making thus initial buy-in may be challenging
3. Its adoption in the IS field is emerging and is relatively sparse

Despite its challenges, it is apparent that this approach may have significance in identifying key organizational considerations within different contexts. VFT has been applied across a wide variety of domains such as cybersecurity/IS-Security (Dhillon & Torkzadeh, 2006; Barrett-Maitland, Barclay & Osei-Bryson, 2016), project management (Barclay & Osei-Bryson, 2010), tourism management (Kajanus et al., 2004), ERP Systems (May, Dhillon & Caldeira, 2013), tourism management (Kajanus et al., 2004), environmental risk considerations (Gregory, et al., 2001), improve watersheds (Merrick & Garcia, 2004), and to select simulation tool for the acquisition of infantry soldier systems (Boylan, et al., 2006).

10.2 Overview on Applying the VFT Methodology

VFT can be done in a top-down or bottom-up manner, with our focus in this chapter being on the former. In a top-down approach *Means Objectives* (*MO*) are obtained from *Fundamental Objectives* (*FO*), by determining for each FO all the immediate lower level things that must be done satisfactorily (i.e. *MO*) in order to achieve the given *FO*. Lower level *MO*s can be obtained for the next higher level *MO*s in a similar manner. The result is a network of objectives with the *FO*s at the root level and a subset of the *MO*s at the leaf level. Each leaf level *MO* can be considered to be equivalent to an actionable goal.

1. Frame the Decision Situation
   a. Define the Decision Context: This is framed by the associated Administrative, Political and Social structures
   b. Identify the Objectives
   c. Structure the Objectives into a Means-Ends Network
   d. Specify Attributes
2. Preference Elicitation
3. Create Alternatives
4. Recommended Decision
5. Sensitivity Analysis

In this chapter, we present a new integrated VFT methodology that will address the following issues:

■ **Decision Context**

Studies involving the application of the VFT methodology could be considered to fall into categories: (a) those that attempt to identify Fundamental *Objectives (FOs) & Means Objectives (MOs)* relevant to a given domain within specific situation organization (e.g. Barclay & Osei-Bryson, 2010); and (b) those that attempt to identify *FOs & MOs* that are generally relevant to a given domain (e.g. Dhillon & Torkzadeh, 2006). A fundamental concern with the latter approach is that VFT would be applied within a particular decision context that is determined by relevant administrative, social, cultural and political structures, and decision styles, and as such the decision contexts for a given domain (e.g. security) could vary across organizations.

■ **Types of Relationships between Objectives**

There are several types of relationships that could exist between objectives including:

– Parent-Child (PC)

– Intrinsic Conflict (IC): The objectives conflict by their very nature (i.e. the relevant desired directions of the given pair of objectives cannot be simultaneously achieved, not because they compete for the same resources but because they are intrinsically conflicting. An example of this is the intrinsic between the Confidentiality & Availability objectives of a security plan: having maximum Confidentiality results in minimum Availability, and vice versa.

– Resource Conflict (RC): The given pair of Objectives utilizes & thus competes for one or more resources, and because of this fact the relevant desired directions of the given pair of objectives cannot be simultaneously achieved. The traditional VFT process explicitly focuses on *PC* relationship types only, although both *IC* & *RC* are relevant to the Create Alternatives phase of the VFT methodology. The approach presented in this chapter will focus on both relationship types.

■ **Quality of the Description of the Objectives**

It is important that the objectives have important quality properties including *Relevance, Completeness* (i.e. for a given non-leaf objective, all of its relevant child *Means Objectives* must be specified), *Non-Redundancy* (i.e. No two objectives in the same tier should overlap), *Specificity* (i.e. *must lead to an observable action, behaviour or achievement*). With respect to leaf-level Means Objectives (MO) they should have the properties of being *Measureable, Achievable,* and *Time-bound.* These will be discussed later in the chapter.

The traditional VFT process does not explicitly focus on assessing all relevant quality dimensions.

■ **Need to Create Value-based Alternatives**
Keeney (1996) noted that

> The first alternatives that come to mind are the obvious ones … Truly different alternatives remain hidden in another part of the mind, unreachable by mere tweaking … Focusing on the values that should be guiding the decision situation removes the anchor on the narrowly defined alternatives … the means objectives are also meaningful ground to stimulate thinking about the objectives.

We adopt these insights to design a method for the automatic generation of the alternatives that factors both the relevant preference values and constraints.

10.3 Some Applications of VFT Methodology to Cybersecurity Concerns

The VFT approach has been used to elicit values and objectives that are relevant to cybersecurity/IS-security concerns. Table 10.1 presents the fundamental objectives that were elicited in three such studies. The reader may note that there are differences in the set of objectives identified in these studies. One possible reason is that they involve different decision contexts. For example, the studies of Dhillon and Torkzadeh (2006) and Drevin et al. (2007) each had organizational focus, while the study of Barrett-Maitland, Barclay and Osei-Bryson (2016) had a Social Network System (SNS) end-user focus. So objectives that appear to be organizationally inward looking (e.g. *Promote individual work ethic, Enhance integrity of business processes*) were not identified in the study of Barrett-Maitland, Barclay & Osei-Bryson (2016).

A critical phase in the VFT process involves the elicitation of the relevant values and objectives from the stakeholders. It is known from previous research (e.g. Schwenk, 1984) that there are various limitations in human decision-making processes including the effectiveness in recalling all that is highly relevant for a given decision problem. Thus the need for memory aids (e.g. Chen & Lee, 2003) has been proposed for some decision-making situations. Such memory aids are based on the premise that relevant knowledge and information might have been previously identified and recorded. With respect to a given cybersecurity/IS-security decision problem relevant objectives might have been presented in previous VFT models for the cybersecurity/IS-security domain and other domains (see Table 10.2), and so a review of such models before and during the elicitation process might be useful. Such a review would also offer the opportunity to get an understanding of relationships between context and objectives. The enhanced integrated VFT methodology that is presented in Section 10.5 includes such review.

Table 10.1   Comparison of Means-end Networks of 3 VFT-based Cybersecurity Studies

Fundamental Objectives	Dhillon and Torkzadeh (2006)	Drevin et al. (2007)	Barrett-Maitland, Barclay and Osei-Bryson (2016)
Enhance management development practices	Yes	No	No
Provide adequate human resource management practices	Yes	No	No
Develop and sustain an ethical environment	Yes	No	Yes
Maximize access control	Yes	Yes	Yes
Promote individual work ethic	Yes	Yes	No
Maximize data integrity	Yes	Yes	Yes
Enhance integrity of business processes	Yes	Yes	No
Maximizing privacy (individual)	Yes	No	Yes
Maximize organization integrity	Yes	Yes	No
Effective and efficient use of e-communication systems	Yes	Yes	No
Maximize availability of hardware and software	Yes	Yes	No
Maximize acceptance of responsibility for actions	Yes	Yes	Yes
Maximize use of resources	Yes	Yes	No
Maximize security awareness campaigns	No	Yes	Yes
Maximize individual responsibility	Yes	Yes	Yes
Maximize corporate social responsibility	No	No	Yes
Maximize security control	Yes	Yes	Yes
Maximize profile protection control	Yes	No	Yes

Source: Barrett-Maitland, Barclay and Osei-Bryson (2016)

Table 10.2   Fundamental Objectives of Some Previous VFT-based Studies

Source	Fundamental Objectives
Dhillon & Torkzadeh (2006)	Enhance Management Development Practices, Provide Adequate Human Resource Management Practices, Develop & Sustain An Ethical Environment, Maximize Access Control, Promote Individual Work Ethic, Maximize Data Integrity, Enhance Integrity of Business Processes, Maximizing Privacy, Maximize Organizational Integrity
Drevin, Kruger & Steyn (2007)	Maximize Integrity of Data, Maximize Confidentiality of Data, Effective & Efficient Use of Electronic Communication, Maximize Availability of Data & Hardware, Maximize Acceptance of Responsibility for Actions, Maximize the Use of Resources
Barrett-Maitland, Barclay & Osei-Bryson (2016)	Maximize Privacy of Individual Information, Maximize Security Control, Maximize Integrity of Social Network System (SNS), Maximize Corporate Social Responsibility, Maximize Individual Responsibility
Dhillon, Oliveira, Susarapu, & Caldeira, (2016)	Enhance System-related Communications, Improve Data Organization, Maximize Ease of Use, Maximize Standardization of System Features, Maximize System Administration Functionality, Maximize System Capability, Maximize System Integration, Maximize User Requirements Elicitation
Dhillon, Oliveira & Syed (2018)	Ensure Security of Personal Information, Increase Prevention of Fraud, Improve the Reputation of the Firm, Enhance Shoppers' Ability to Control Personal Data, Increase the Discreetness of the Transaction, Decrease Spam, Increase the Expectation of Shopping Privately, Ensure privacy is consistent with the efficiency of online shopping
Tshering & Gao (2020)	Maximize Digital Identity, Maximize **Trust** between Stakeholders, Maximize Privacy of Data, Maximize Transparency in Data & Process, Maximize **Integrity** of Data & Network, Maximize Public Service Delivery, Minimize Cost in the Long Run, Maximize *Availability* of Public Information, Maximize Individual Responsibility, Maximize **Usability of Blockchai**n
Hudgens, Hartner, Adams & Regnier (2019)	Maximizing Reliability, Maximizing Reputation, Minimizing Cost, Minimizing Casualties

(Continued)

Table 10.2 (Continued)

Source	Fundamental Objectives
Sheng, Siau, & Nah (2010)	Maximize Convenience of Education, Maximize Efficiency in Learning, Maximize Effectiveness in Learning, Maximize **Security** of Student/Instructor Information, Maximize Individual **Privacy**, Minimize Cost of Education, Ensure Academic Honesty
Gao, Li & Guo (2019)	Maximize Well-Being, Maximize Life Efficiency, Maximize **Safety**, Maximize Digital Inclusion
Rzepka (2019)	Maximize Efficiency, Maximize Ease of Use, Maximize Enjoyment, Maximize Convenience, Minimize Cognitive Effort

10.4 Overviews on Some Supporting Frameworks

There are several frameworks that could be used to enhance the VFT to allow for a more effective generation of objectives and alternatives. In this section, we present overviews of some of these frameworks.

10.4.1 The S.M.A.R.T Framework

Several frameworks have been proposed for evaluating the quality of a business objective. Among them is the *SMART* framework (Doran, 1981) which suggested the following set of criteria:

- *Specific:* It must lead to an observable action, behaviour or achievement that can be measured;
- *Measurable*: Clearly defined metrics should be available for measuring the achievement of the objective. This is particularly relevant for the MOs;
- *Achievable*: It must be achievable within the constraints of the available resources, knowledge & time;
- *Relevant:* Must be relevant to the broader goals of the organization;
- *Time-bound*: there should be specific deadlines for the achievement of the objective. This is particularly relevant for the *MOs*.

A review of previous VFT papers shows that often the *MOs* are not expressed in a manner that can be considered to be *Time-bound*. Further, the *Achievability* criterion is often not considered particularly with respect to the *Intrinsic Conflict (IC)* and *Resource Conflict (RC)* types of constraints.

10.4.2 Some Relevant Organizational Issues

The reader may recall that the Decision Context is framed by the associated Administrative, Political & Social structures. Thus, there are several types of organizational issues that have to be accommodated in the definition of the objectives. We will focus on a few of these below.

10.4.2.1 Overview on the Organizational Types

Courtney (2001) presented a set of organizational types, and corresponding organizational decision-making style. It seems reasonable to expect that the organizational decision-making style would impact on the feasibility and definition of the *MOs*.

	Leibniz	*Locke*	*Kant*	*Hegel*	*Singer*
Organizational Decision-Making Style	Formal Analytical Bureaucratic	Open Communicative Consensual	Open Analytical	Conflictual	Teleological Cooperative Ethical

10.4.2.2 Overview on Individual Decision Styles

Rowe and Boulgarides (1983) identified four major categories of individual decision styles. Martinsons and Davison (2007) observed that in different cultures, different individual decision styles are dominant. It seems reasonable to expect that in some settings the individual decision-making style would impact on the feasibility and definition of the *MOs*.

Style	*Description*
Analytical	Achievement oriented without the need for external rewards; make decisions slowly because orientation to examine the situation thoroughly and consider many alternatives systematically
Behavioural	Strong people orientation, driven primarily by a need for affiliation; typically receptive to suggestions, willing to compromise, and prefer loose controls
Conceptual	Achievement and people oriented with the need for external rewards; make decisions slowly because orientation to examine the situation thoroughly and consider many alternatives systematically
Directive	Results and power oriented but prefer to consider a limited number of alternatives

10.4.2.3 Overview on the Cultural Dimensions

Hofstede (1980) defined a set of cultural dimensions that could impact the behaviours of organizational actors that are outlined below. The characteristics of a given national culture may mean that some Means Objectives are infeasible in that context. It is therefore important that cultural issues be taken into consideration.

Dimension	Description
Power Distance	Reflects the extent to which the members of a society accept the unequal distribution of power
Individualism-Collectivism	Reflects the degree to which people are able and prefer to achieve an identity and status on their own rather than through group memberships
Masculinity-Femininity	Reflects the degree to which assertiveness and achievement are valued over nurturing and affiliation
Uncertainty Avoidance	Reflects discomfort with ambiguity and incomplete information

10.4.2.4 Overview on Organizational Perspectives

Kaplan and Norton (1992, 2001) presented the Balanced Scorecard (BSC) Model that involves 4 perspectives presented in the table below. An exploration of these perspectives could lead to the discovery of important organizational values and objectives.

Perspective	Description
Customer	How do the customers see the organization?
Internal Business	What must the organization excel at?
Financial	How does the organization look to the shareholders?
Innovation & Learning	How can the organization continue to improve and create value?

10.4.3 Assessing An Existing VFT Cybersecurity Model

In this subsection, we will use our three major criteria (i.e. *Conflict among the Objectives, Quality of the Description of the Objectives, Need to Create Values-based*

Table 10.3   Some Means Objectives of VFT Model of Dhillon and Torkzadeh (2006)

Ensure censure	**Increase trust**
Introduce a fear of being exposed or ridiculed Instil a fear of consequences Instil a fear of losing your job Instil excommunication fear	Display employer trust in employees Develop an environment that promotes a sense of organizational responsibility Maximize loyalty
Provide open communication Minimize curiosity because of lack of information Create an open-door environment within all levels of the organization Stress IT department interactiveness Develop open communication with IT department Limit 'arm's length' management	

Alternatives) to assess a well-known VFT Cybersecurity model Dhillon & Torkzadeh (2006). We will focus on a subset of the Means objectives of that model (see Table 10.3), and use material presented in Subsections 10.4.1 and 10.4.2 to guide our assessment.

1. **Conflicts among the Objectives**
   - **Intrinsic Conflicts**: 'Instil a fear of losing job' would be in conflict with 'Display employer trust in employees' and 'Maximize loyalty'
   - **Resource Conflicts**: Similar to many papers on VFT, this seemed to have not been included in the scope of the study.
2. **Quality of the Description of the Objectives**
   - **Specific**: It is not clear how an objective such as 'Introduce a fear of being exposed or ridiculed' could be accurately and ethically measured;
   - **Measurable**: It is not clear what would be the appropriate measures for an objective such as 'Introduce a fear of being exposed or ridiculed';
   - **Achievable**: It is not clear how an objective such as 'Introduce a fear of being exposed or ridiculed' or 'Instil a fear of losing your job' could be ethically achievable, particular in a society with low tolerance for an unequal distribution of power;
   - **Relevant**: It would be necessary to ensure that an objective such as 'Instil a fear of losing your job' is consistent with the organization's goals;
   - **Time-bound**: It is not clear what is the time period in which the objective 'Introduce a fear of being exposed or ridiculed' is to be achieved;

3. **Some Relevant Organizational Issues**
   ■ **Cultural Dimensions**
     – Objectives such as 'Introduce a fear of being exposed or ridiculed' or 'Instill excommunication fear' may be inappropriate in the context of some national cultures;
     – The appropriateness of the objectives such as 'Instil a fear of losing your job' may be dependent on the level of Power Distance
     – The appropriateness of the objective 'Minimize curiosity because of lack of information' may be dependent on the level of *Uncertainty Avoidance*
   ■ **Organizational Type**: For a Singerian type organization, an objective such as 'Display employer trust in employees' would be consistent with this organizational type as such organizations give high priority to ethics and cooperation; an objective such as 'Introduce a fear of being exposed or ridiculed' would not be consistent;
   ■ **Organizational Perspective – Customers**: It is not clear how an objective such as 'Introduce a fear of being exposed or ridiculed' would lead to the organization being viewed positively by its customers.
4. **Need to Create Values**-based **Alternatives**
   ■ Similar to many papers on VFT, this seemed to have not been included in the scope of the study. However, this would not be sufficient as decision-makers need to be able to identify non-trivial feasible and implementable solutions that are consistent with their set of fundamental objectives.

10.5 Description of the Integrated Extended VFT Methodology

Below we present a description of an enhanced integrated VFT methodology that could be used to address cybersecurity/IS-security decision problems. The reader should note that the first two phases (i.e. BU & DU) present probing questions that could be used to develop an in-depth understanding of the decision problem. The importance of 'probing' questions in the elicitation process has been recognized by previous VFT researchers. For example Step 1 of the research approach of Dhillon and Torkzadeh (2006) involves using '*probes to develop in depth understanding*' of the decision problem. In this subsection, we list some relevant probing questions; these questions are influenced by the material presented in Subsections 10.4.1 and 10.4.2.

10.5.1 Business Understanding (BU)

This phase is concerned with exposing and recording the organizational factors that should be included in the framing of the Decision Context. Relevant probing questions include:

■ What are the ultimate objectives for the given cybersecurity/IS-security decision problem domain? What are the previously identified Objectives for this decision problem domain?

- What are the significant concerns from a Financial perspective?
- What are the significant concerns from an External Stakeholder perspective?
- What are the significant concerns from an Internal Stakeholder perspective?
- What are the significant concerns from a Learning & Innovation perspective?
- What are the significant concerns from a Scheduling perspective?
- What are the significant concerns from a Legal perspective?

Steps in this phase would include:

1. Obtain & Review Organization Mission & Vision statements, Organization Chart/Organizational Ontology, Main Products/Services
2. Identify relevant Internal & External Stakeholders
3. Determine the Main Decision Styles of relevant Internal Stakeholders
4. Use the relevant prompting questions to identify the concerns from the 6 organizational perspectives listed above. Record these concerns

10.5.2 Domain Understanding (DU)

This phase is concerned with exposing and recording the cybersecurity/IS-security domain issues that should be included in the framing of the Decision Context. Relevant probing questions include:

- What are the perceived *Concepts* for this domain?
- What are the previously identified *Objectives* for this domain?
- What are the perceived *Best Practices* for this domain?
- What are some concerns from a *Learning & Innovation* perspective?
- What are some concerns from a *Legal* perspective?
- What are some concerns from a *Technical/Technological* perspective?

Steps in this phase would include:

1. Review relevant cybersecurity/IS-security knowledge bases such as those Best Practices for the given domain and highly related domains, previously proposed related VFT models.
2. Use the relevant prompting questions to identify cybersecurity/IS-security domain-oriented Concepts, Best Practices, Fundamental & Means Objectives, and concerns from the 4 organizational perspectives listed above. Record this information.

10.5.3 Modelling Objectives (MD)

This phase has three sub-phases as described below.

10.5.3.1 Initial Identification of Objectives

1. Use the recorded information that resulted from the *Business Understanding* & *Domain Understanding* phases to identify Objectives that meet the *Relevance* criteria.
2. Refine definition of each Objective so that it satisfies the *Specificity* property.

10.5.3.2 Classification and Refinement of Objectives

1. Classify each Objective in the current set of Objectives as being a *FO* or a *MO*, and identify the associated set of Parent-Child (*PC*) relationships. The WITI test described below could be useful here.
2. For each *FO*, determine if its current set of supporting child *MO*s is sufficient for the given *FO* to satisfy the *Completeness* property. If the *Completeness* property is not satisfied for a given *FO* then identify the remaining supporting child *MO*s so that this property is satisfied. Update the associated set of Parent-Child (*PC*) relationships.
3. For each *MO* that is a parent of other *MO*s determine if its current set of supporting child *MO*s is sufficient for the given *MO* to satisfy the *Completeness* property. If the *Completeness* property is not satisfied for a given *FO* then identify remaining supporting child *MO*s so that this property is satisfied. Update the associated set of Parent-Child (*PC*) relationships.
4. For each *MO* use the *Why-Is-It-Important (WITI)* test to determine if it has any other objective (i.e. another *MO* or a *FO*) and also its parent. Update the set of Parent-Child (*PC*) relationships.
5. Review the current set of *MO*s in order to identify the leaf-level *MO*s.
6. For each leaf-level *MO*, refine its definition so that it satisfies the **Measurability**, **Achievability** and **Time-bounded**ness properties.

The 'Why is it important?' (WITI) test is the technique used to help distinguish between the fundamental and means objectives (Keeney, 1994). For each objective, the WITI test is applied and depending on the response the type of objective is determined. Where the answer suggests that the objective is important is essential for this context and no other objectives are used as basis for its importance then the objective is at its end, i.e. end or fundamental objective. Alternatively, where the answer suggests that the objective is important as a result of another objective it means that objective is facilitating or an alternative to achieving the end i.e. means objectives.

It should be noted that after the completion of this sub-phase that the *Completeness* property and the five (5) *S.M.A.R.T.* properties would have been satisfied.

10.5.3.3 Identification of Achievement Processes (APs)

1. Define an ordered discrete set of qualitative performance levels (e.g. *High, Medium, Low*).

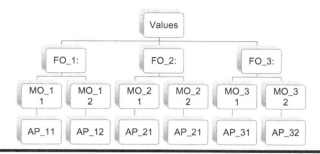

Figure 10.1   Means-objective (MO) and associated achievement process (AP)

2. For each leaf-level *MO*:
   a. Use the *Goal Question Metric* (e.g. Basili, Caldiera, & Rombach, 1994) method to identify relevant performance measures (i.e. attributes);
   b. For each corresponding qualitative performance level ℓ of the *MO*, identify the combinations of levels of the attributes of the *MO* that are associated with level ℓ. Let $\cap_{j\ell}$ be the corresponding set of attribute level combinations;
   c. Identify a set of *Achievement Processes (APs)* that could be used to realize the various performance levels of the given leaf-level *MO* (Figure 10.1).
   d. Estimate the cost and requirements of each depletable resource necessary for a given *AP* to realize each performance level of the given *MO*.
   e. Identify any additional constraints (e.g. *Legal, Technological, Scheduling*) based on the Concerns/Issues identified in BU and DU phases that relate to the achievement of relevant performance levels.

It should be noted that while an *MO* describes *WHAT* is desired, a corresponding *Achievement Process* (*AP*) would describe *HOW* the given *WHAT* could be achieved. Description of an *AP* includes its method as well as a description of the resources that are required to achieve the relevant performance levels of the *MO*. It should be noted that resource requirements that are estimated in this sub-phase could be used for the identification of Resource Conflict (*RC*) relationships. Further, the fact that at this stage each *FO* & *MO* satisfies the *Specificity* property then relevant information is also available to identify any Intrinsic Conflict (*IC*) relationship between performance levels of pairs of Objectives.

10.5.4 Elicit Preference Information

1. Use a pairwise comparisons approach such as that used in the AHP to determine, w_i, the relative importance of each *FO* 'i'.
2. For each *FO* 'i', use a pairwise comparisons approach to determine the relative value v_{ik} of each possible score level k.

10.5.5 Generate and Evaluate Alternatives

This phase has two sub-phases. The first sub-phase focuses on the formulation of a mathematical programming problem (MPP) that would be used for generating the alternatives that are reflective of the preference values and also relevant constraints. This MPP could also be used to do *What-If* and sensitivity analyses. The second sub-phase outlines the procedure for formulating & solving the MPP to generate and evaluate alternate solutions, including 'near optimal' ones. To not overburden the reader who is not mathematically inclined we have placed the details of these sub-phases in the appendix along with an illustrative example.

10.6 Conclusion

The cybersecurity/IS-security decision problem is a complex one in which the multiple concerns of multiple stakeholders must be taken into consideration. A useful resource to consider in addressing this problem is the Value Focusing Thinking (VFT) methodology as at a minimum it can be used to elicit the relevant solution objectives. However, the traditional VFT approach has several limitations, including not explicitly providing guidance on generating non-trivial solution alternatives. In this chapter, we presented an enhanced, integrated VFT methodology that takes context into consideration and also allows for the generation of feasible non-trivial alternatives that are consistent with the elicited objectives.

Appendix: Details of Generate and Evaluate Alternatives Phase

A1: Mathematical Programming Formulation Sub-Phase

- I is the set of Objectives; I_{FO} is the subset of Fundamental Objectives (FO); I_{MO} is the subset of Means Objectives (MO); $I = I_{FO} \cup I_{MO}$; $I_{FO} \cap I_{MO} = \emptyset$.
- v_{ik} is the value associated with FO 'i' being achieved at level $k \in K_i$.
- x_{ik} is a binary variable such that $x_{ik} = 1$ indicates that Objective 'i' has been achieved at level 'k'; and $x_{ik} = 0$ otherwise.

Parent-Child Constraints on Achievement of Performance Levels

- M_{ik} is the set of combinations of MOs each at a specified performance level ℓ, such that each combination in M_{ik} would result Objective i being achieved at performance level k.
  - For each $m \in M_{ik}$, J_{ikm} is a set of MOs, each a child of Objective *i* and each at a performance level that taken together would result in Objective *i* being achieved at level k.

- z_{ikm} is a binary variable such that $z_{ikm} = 1$ indicates that each MO 'j' in J_{ikm} is at the relevant performance level ℓ; and $z_{ikm} = 0$ otherwise.

  1a: $z_{ikm} - x_{j\ell} \leq 0 \ \forall \ m \in M_{ik}, (j, \ell) \in J_{ikm}$

  1b: $\Sigma_{(j,\ell) \in Jikm} \ x_{j\ell} - z_{ikm} \leq (|J_{ikm}| - 1) \ \forall \ m \in M_{ik}$

- Objective 'i' is achieved at level 'k' only if at least one combination in M_{ik} is realized:

  2: $x_{ik} - \Sigma_{m \in Mik} \ z_{ikm} \leq 0 \ \forall \ i \in I, k \in K_i$

- Each objective 'i' achieves exactly one of its allowable levels $k \in K_i$

  3: $\Sigma_{k \in Ki} \ x_{ik} = 1 \ \forall \ i \in I$

Resource Conflicts

- $q_{rj\ell}$ is the minimum amount of depletable resource 'r' that is required in order for MO 'j' to be achieved at level 'ℓ', and $q_{r\bullet\bullet}$ be the total available amount of resource 'r':

  4: $\Sigma_{j \in IMO} \ \Sigma_{\ell \in Ki} \ q_{rj\ell} x_{j\ell} \leq q_{r\bullet\bullet} \ \forall \ r \in R$

Intrinsic Conflicts

- P is the set of pairs of Objectives, (i_1, i_2) that have Intrinsic Conflicts where $i_1 \in I$ & $i_2 \in I$ such that if $i_1 \in I$ achieves level k_1 then $i_2 \in I$ cannot achieve level k_2.

  5: $x_{i1,k1} + x_{i2,k2} \leq 1 \ \forall \ (i_1, k_1, i_2, k_2) \in P$

Integer Programming Problem (MPP) to Generate Alternatives

IP_{GenAlt}: Max $\{\Sigma_{i \in IFO} \ \Sigma_{k \in Ki} \ w_i v_{ik} x_{ik} \ | \ (1) - (5), \ \&$ binary restriction on all variables$\}$

A2: Procedure for Generating Alternatives Sub-Phase

1. Formulate & Solve problem P_{GenAlt}.
2. Given the initial optimal solution to problem P_{GenAlt}, generate other alternate optimal solutions if they exist.
3. Use What-If and/or Sensitivity Analysis to generate other alternate though *near* optimal solutions to problem P_{GenAlt}.

A3: Illustrative Example

In this section, we present an illustrative example that applies the procedure for Generating & Evaluating Alternatives that satisfy the three types of constraints. Figure A1 displays the Means-Ends Objective Network (a hierarchy in this case) for an IS-security decision problem.

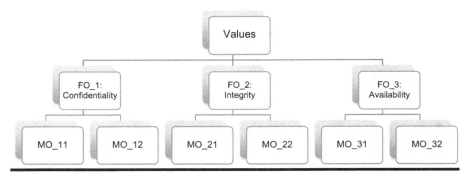

Figure A1   Means-ends objectives network

There are three possible performance levels (i.e. *High* (3), *Medium* (2), and *Low* (1)) for each Objective. It should be noted that for each Objective, exactly 1 qualitative Performance Level can be achieved. Table A1 displays the constraints that represent these facts, where the e variable name the variable that represents each Means Objective (MO) level begin with 'M', and the variable name that represents each Fundamental Objective (FO) level begin with 'F', and where each variable is a binary variable (i.e. 0 or 1).

Table A1   Select One Performance Level for Each Constraint

Type	Objective	Constraint	Explanation
Means	MO_11	M111 + M112 + M113 = 1	Ensures that for Means Objective *MO_11* only 1 level (i.e. *High* (M113 = 1), *Medium* (iM112 = 1), or *Low* (iM111 = 1)) is selected. Similarly for the other Means Objectives below.
	MO_12	M121 + M122 + M123 = 1	
	MO_21	M211 + M212 + M213 = 1	
	MO_22	M221 + M222 + M223 = 1	
	MO_31	M311 + M312 + M313 = 1	
	MO_32	M321 + M322 + M323 = 1	

(Continued)

Table A1   (Continued)

Type	Objective	Constraint	Explanation
Fundamental	FO_1	F11 + F12 + F13 = 1	Ensures that for Fundamental Objective *FO_1* only 1 level (i.e. *High* (F13 = 1), *Medium* (i.e. F12 = 1), or *Low* (i.e. F11 = 1) is selected. Similarly for the other Fundamental Objective below.
	FO_2	F21 + F22 + F23 = 1	
	FO_3	F31 + F32 + F33 = 1	

Tables A2–A4b displays the various other types of constraints: *Parent-Child Constraints on Achievement of Performance Levels* (Table A2), *Intrinsic Conflict* (Table A3), and a financial *Resource Conflict* (Tables A4a & A4b). Table A5a displays the Weight for each Fundamental Objective (FO) and the Value associated with achieving each performance level of each FO. The value of the highest level (i.e. Level 3) of each Fundamental Objective is set to 100, with the value of its lower levels be

Table A2   Parent-child Constraints

If MO_11 & MO_12 are both at *Level 3* then FO_1 is at *Level 3*; If MO_11 & MO_12 are both at *Level 1* then FO_1 is at *Level 1*;	M113 + M123 − F13 <= 1 F13 − M113 <= 0 F13 − M123 <= 0 M111 + M121 − F11 <= 1 F11 − M111 <= 0 F11 − M121 <= 0
If MO_21 & MO_22 are both at *Level 3* then FO_2 is at *Level 3*; If MO_21 & MO_22 are both at *Level 1* then FO_2 is at *Level 1*;	M213 + M223 − F23 <= 1 F23 − M213 <= 0 F23 − M223 <= 0 M211 + M221 − F21 <= 1 F21 − M211 <= 0 F21 − M221 <= 0
If MO_31 & MO_32 are both at *Level 3* then FO_3 is at *Level 3*; If MO_31 & MO_32 are both at *Level 1* then FO_3 is at *Level 1*;	M313 + M323 − F33 <= 1 F33 − M313 <= 0 F33 − M323 <= 0 M311 + M321 − F31 <= 1 F31 − M311 <= 0 F31 − M321 <= 0

relative to the value of the highest level. Methods such as the Analytic Hierarchy Process (e.g. Saaty (1980), Bryson (1995), Osei-Bryson (2006)) could be used to both derive the relative weight of each FO as well for each FO the relative value of its lower performance levels with respect to its highest performance level. In Table A5b, the coefficient of each variable is its weighted Value.

In Table A6 we display the results of solving the IP problem under three scenarios: *None* (i.e. no additional constraint), *Confidentiality* must be at its top performance level (i.e. Set FO_1 to Level 3), and *Integrity* must be at its top performance level (i.e. Set FO_2 to Level 3). For scenario, the performance levels of the *FO*s and *MO*s are provided. Since for each MO, its corresponding *Achievement Process* would have previously been identified then results generated by the *Procedure for Generating Alternatives* could be used to identify the performance levels of the relevant *Achievement Process* that corresponds to the given set of *MO*s performance levels.

Table A3   Intrinsic Conflict Constraint

Confidentiality (FO_1) & *Availability* (FO_3) cannot both be at Level 3	F13 + F33 <= 1

Table A4a   Objective Level Achievement Costs

Fundamental	Means	Level	Cost
Confidentiality(C)	MO_11	3	110
		2	80
		1	60
	MO_12	3	85
		2	75
		1	55
Integrity(I)	MO_21	3	85
		2	75
		1	65
	MO_22	3	80
		2	70
		1	60

(Continued)

Table A4a (Continued)

Fundamental	Means	Level	Cost
Availability (A)	MO_31	3	105
		2	90
		1	65
	MO_32	3	110
		2	85
		1	70

Table A4b   Financial Resource Constraint

110M113 + 80M112 + 60M111 +
85M123 + 75M122 + 55M121 +
85M213 + 75M212 + 65M211 +`
80M223 + 70M222 + 60M221 +
105M313 + 90M312 + 65M311 +
110M323 + 85M322 + 70M321

Table A5a   Weights & Achievement Level Values

Fundamental Objective	Weight	Level	Value
Confidentiality (C)	0.37	3	100.00
		2	85.00
		1	65.00
Integrity (I)	0.30	3	100.00
		2	88.00
		1	75.00
Availability (A)	0.33	3	100.00
		2	76.00
		1	55.00

Table A5b   Objective Function of IP Problem

37.00F13 + 31.45F12 + 24.05F11 + 30.00F23 + 26.40F22 + 22.500F21 + 33.00F33 + 25.08F32 + 18.15F31

Table A6   Description of the Generated Alternatives

Restriction	Value	Fundamental		Means	
		Obj	*Lvl*	*Obj*	*Lvl*
None	90.85	FO_1	2	MO_11	2
				MO_12	1
		FO_2	2	MO_21	1
				MO_22	3
		FO_3	3	MO_31	3
				MO_32	3
Set FO_1 to Level 3	88.48	FO_1	3	MO_11	3
				MO_12	3
		FO_2	2	MO_21	3
				MO_22	1
		FO_3	2	MO_31	2
				MO_32	1
Set FO_2 to Level 3	87.05	FO_1	1	MO_11	1
				MO_12	1
		FO_2	3	MO_21	3
				MO_22	3
		FO_3	3	MO_31	3
				MO_32	3

Acknowledgement

This chapter includes material that previously appeared in Osei-Bryson, K. M. (2018). An Integrated Framework for The Value Focused Thinking Methodology. *Proceedings of the 51st Hawaii International Conference on System Sciences*. 1473–1481.

References

Barclay, C., & Osei-Bryson, K. M. (2010). Project performance development framework: An approach for developing performance criteria & measures for information systems (IS) projects. *International Journal of Production Economics, 124*(1), 272–292.

Barclay, C. (2014). Overview of the Value-focused Thinking methodology. In K.-M. Osei-Bryson & O. Ngwenyama, (Eds) *Advances in Research Methods for Information Systems Research* (pp. 183–196). US: Springer.

Barrett-Maitland, N., Barclay, C., & Osei-Bryson, K. M. (2016). Security in social networking services: A value-focused thinking exploration in understanding users' privacy and security concerns. *Information Technology for Development, 22*(3), 464–486.

Basili, V., Caldiera, G., & Rombach, H. (1994). The goal question metric approach. *Encyclopedia of Software Engineering*, 528–532.

Boylan, G. L., Tollefson, M. E. S., Kwinn, L. C. M. J., & Guckert, R. R. (2006). Using value-focused thinking to select a simulation tool for the acquisition of infantry soldier systems. *Systems Engineering, 9*(3), 199–212.

Bryson, N. (1995). A goal programming method for generating priority vectors. *Journal of the Operational Research Society, 46*(5), 641–648.

Bryson, N. (1996). Group decision-making and the analytic hierarchy process: Exploring the consensus-relevant information content. *Computers & Operations Research, 23*, 27–35.

Chang, J. C. J., Torkzadeh, G., & Dhillon, G. (2004). Re-examining the measurement models of success for Internet commerce. *Information & Management, 41*(5), 577–584.

Chen, J. Q., & Lee, S. M. (2003). An exploratory cognitive DSS for strategic decision making. *Decision Support Systems, 36*(2), 147–160.

Courtney, J. (2001). Decision making and knowledge management in inquiring organizations: Toward a new decision-making paradigm for DSS. *Decision Support Systems, 31*, 17–38.

Doran, G. (1981). There's a S.M.A.R.T. aay to write management goals and objectives. *Management Review, 70*(1), 35–36.

Dhillon, G., & Torkzadeh, G. (2006). Value-focused assessment of information system security in organizations. *Information Systems Journal, 16*(3), 293–331.

Dhillon, G., Bardacino, J., & Hackney, R. (2002). Value Focused Assessment of Individual Privacy Concerns for Internet Commerce. *ICIS 2002 Proceedings.* Paper 67. http://aisel.aisnet.org/icis2002/67

Dhillon, G., Oliveira, T., Susarapu, S., & Caldeira, M. (2016). Deciding between information security and usability: Developing value based objectives. *Computers in Human Behavior, 61*, 656–666.

Dhillon, G., Oliveira, T., & Syed, R. (2018). Value-based information privacy objectives for iInternet commerce. *Computers in Human Behavior, 87*, 292–307.

Drevin, L., Kruger, H. A., & Steyn, T. (2007). Value-focused assessment of ICT security awareness in an academic environment. *Computers & Security, 26*(1), 36–43.

Gao, Shang, Li, Ying, & Guo, Hong. (2019).Understanding the Value of Using Smartphones for Older Adults in China: A Value-Focused Thinking Approach. In *Conference on e-Business, e-Services and e-Society*, pp. 533–544. Cham: Springer.

Gregory, R., Arvai, J., & McDaniels, T. (2001). Value-focused thinking for environmental risk consultations. *Research in Social Problems and Public Policy, 9*, 249–273.

Hofstede, G. (1980). *Culture's Consequences: International Differences in Work-Related Values*. Beverly Hills, CA: Sage Publications.

Hudgens, B., Hartner, C., Adams, B., & Regnier, E. (2019, January). Investing in Cyber Defense: A Value-Focused Analysis of Investment Decisions for Microgrids. In *Proceedings of the 52nd Hawaii International Conference on System Sciences*, pp. 2384–2841. Maui, Hawaii.

Kajanus, M., J. Kangas, & Kurtilla, M. (2004). The use of value focused thinking and the A'WOT hybrid method in tourism management. *Tourism Management, 25*(4), 499–506.

Kaplan, R. S., & Norton, D. P. (2001). *The Strategy-Focused Organization: How Balanced Scorecard Companies Thrive in the New Business Environment.* Cambridge, Massachussets, Harvard Business Press.

Kaplan, R. & Norton, D. (1992). The balanced scorecard: Measures that drive performance. *Harvard Business Review, 70*(1), 71–79.

Keeney, R. L. (1992). *Value-Focused Thinking: A Path to Creative Decision Making.* Cambridge, Massachussets: Harvard University Press.

Keeney, R. L. (1994). Creativity in decision making with value-focused thinking. *Sloan Management Review, 35*, 33–33.

Keeney, R. L. (1996). Value-focused thinking: Identifying decision opportunities and creating alternatives. *European Journal of Operational Research, 92*, 537–549.

Keeney, R. L. (1999). The value of Internet commerce to the customer. *Management Science, 45*(4), 533–542.

Martinsons, M., & Davison, R. (2007). Strategic decision making and support systems: Comparing American, Japanese and Chinese management. *Decision Support Systems, 43*, 284–300.

May, J., Dhillon, G., & Caldeira, M. (2013). Defining value-based objectives for ERP systems planning. *Decision Support Systems, 55*(1), 98–109.

Merrick, J. R., & Garcia, M. W. (2004). Using value-focused thinking to improve watersheds. *Journal of the American Planning Association, 70*(3), 313–327.

Nah, F., Siau, K., & Sheng, H. (2005). The value of mobile applications: A utility company study. *Communications of the ACM, 48*(2), 85–90.

Neiger, D., & Churilov, L. (2004). Goal-oriented business process modeling with EPCs and value-focused thinking. In J. Desel, B. Pernici & M. Weske (Eds) *Business Process Management* (pp. 98–115). Berlin Heidelberg: Springer.

Orfelio, G. (1999). Value-focused thinking versus alternative-focused thinking: Effects on generation of objectives. *Organizational Behavior and Human Decision Processes, 80*(3), 213–227.

Osei-Bryson, K. M. (2006). An action learning approach for assessing the consistency of pairwise comparison data. *European Journal of Operational Research, 174*(1), 234–244.

Park, R. (2008, January). Measuring Factors that Influence the Success of E-Government Initiatives. In *Hawaii International Conference on System Sciences, Proceedings of the 41st Annual* (pp. 218–218). IEEE, Waikoloa, Big Island, Hawaii.

Rowe, A. J., & Boulgarides, J. D. (1983). Decision styles - A perspective. *Leadership & Organization Development Journal, 4*(4), 3–9.

Rzepka, C. (15–17 August 2019). Examining the Use of Voice Assistants: A Value-Focused Thinking Approach. In *Proceedings of the 25th Americas Conference on Information Systems, AMCIS 2019*, Cancun, Mexico.

Saaty, T. (1980) *The Analytic Hierarchy Process: Planning, Priority Setting, Resource Allocation.* NY: McGraw-Hill.

Schwenk, C. R. (1984). Cognitive simplification processes in strategic decision-making. *Strategic Management Journal, 5*(2), 111–128.

Sheng, H., Siau, K., & Nah, F. F. H. (2010). Understanding the values of mobile technology in education: A value-focused thinking approach. *ACM SIGMIS Database, 41*(2), 25–44.

Sheng, H., Nah, F. F. H., & Siau, K. (2005a). Strategic implications of mobile technology: A case study using value-focused thinking. *The Journal of Strategic Information Systems, 14*(3), 269–290.

Sheng, H., Nah, Fiona F.-H., & Siau, K. (2005b). Values of Silent Commerce: A Study Using Value-Focused Thinking Approach. In *AMCIS 2005 Proceedings*. Paper 192. http://aisel.aisnet.org/amcis2005/192. Omaha, Nebraska.

Siau, K., Sheng, H., & Nah, F. (2003, December). Development of a Framework for Trust in Mobile Commerce. In *Proceedings of the Second Annual Workshop on HCI Research in MIS*, pp. 85–89, Seattle, Washington.

Torkzadeh, G., & Dhillon, G. (2002). Measuring factors that influence the success of Internet commerce. *Information Systems Research, 13*(2), 187–204.

Tshering, G., & Gao, S. (2020). Understanding security in the government's use of blockchain technology with value focused thinking approach. *Journal of Enterprise Information Management 33*(3), 519–540.

Chapter 11

Values of Optimizing Cyber-Hygiene Practices in MSMEs

11.1 Introduction

Micro small and medium enterprises (MSMEs) play a significant role in the economic diversity and development of a country. According to the Tax Administration Jamaica (TAJ), close to 97% of all classified and registered enterprises in Jamaica are MSMEs (GOJ, 2018). Interestingly, these figures coincide with other countries and more developed economies, as according to the World Bank (2021), these types of businesses account for the majority of businesses worldwide in that they represent about 90% of businesses and more than 50% of employment worldwide. However, despite their economic significance, MSMEs face challenges that hinder their growth and development (GOJ, 2018). A scan of the environment confirms that cybersecurity is one of the biggest challenges facing businesses and other stakeholders. Notably, the FBI Internet Crime Report (FBI, 2020) reveals that the reported incidents and losses associated with cybercrime continue to increase annually. The data also show that business email compromise (BEC), ransomware, data breach and other compromises account for billions of dollars in losses. A McAfee Security Report (Smith & Lostri, 2020) further highlights that businesses suffer significant hidden economic costs associated with cybercrime such as system downtime, reduced efficiency, incidence response costs, brand damage among others. It is reasonable to conclude that given the current cybersecurity landscape, challenges in

DOI: 10.1201/9781003028710-14

minimizing cybersecurity risks and maintaining good cyber hygiene (as evidenced by the annual reports on cybersecurity breaches) have stymied the growth and developments of MSMEs, in the Caribbean, other developing economies and the rest of the world.

Undoubtedly, the continued reports of high incidences of cybercrimes and breaches demonstrate that businesses, particularly MSMEs are experiencing difficulties in effectively managing their cyber hygiene. Hence, adopting good cyber hygiene is good business practice. Cyber hygiene consists of conditions and practices that promote the prevention or minimization of cyber threats, breaches and risks thereby presenting a healthy cyber environment or robust cybersecurity posture. Poor cyber hygiene leads to greater cybersecurity risks associated with breaches, threats and attacks which further leads to greater economic costs associated with investigations and remediation. Further, the Centre of Internet Security highlights that cyber hygiene is important for protecting businesses from common cyber threats and for keeping the systems and data secure (Centre of Internet Security, 2021). They also emphasize that most attacks take advantage of poor hygiene conditions such as poor management procedures, poor configuration management, and poor management of administrative privilege.

A report on cyber-hygiene practices in the EU notes that despite businesses recognizing that cyber hygiene is important, it is generally a low priority for most businesses unless there is a pressing, external need to comply (ENISA, 2016). The report further highlights that small businesses experience significant risks regarding their cyber-hygiene practices and generally believes that cybersecurity risks do not affect them due to their size. Similar experiences are anecdotally observed in the Caribbean region. It therefore appears that these small businesses are faced with even greater difficulties in prioritizing cyber hygiene, as according to Such, Ciholas, Rashid, Vidler, & Seabrook (2019), the resources required to establish and maintain cybersecurity often results in smaller businesses being left unprotected. These difficulties extend beyond resource concerns; however, as ENISA (2016) observes, these businesses struggle to have the resources, access or knowledge to undertake cyber-hygiene practices properly (ENISA, 2016). These experiences can have a wide-reaching impact as the security risks are not just their own but also the supply chain of other larger organizations (Such et al., 2019).

This chapter seeks to identify key considerations on what MSMEs consider as important (i.e. stakeholder values) in adopting or improving cyber-hygiene practices for their businesses.

Values-based decision-making is found to be important (Keeney, 1996) and has been successfully relied on in diverse security contexts (e.g. Barrett-Maitland, et al., 2016). The research addresses a gap in the current literature since no known study focuses on examining the cyber hygiene of MSMEs or has applied a values-based approach analysis.

This study is further motivated by the fact that developing economies and MSMEs continue to be underrepresented in the studies associated with cybersecurity and cyber hygiene. Moreover, cybersecurity solutions are not a one size fits all, and thus require solutions that are suited to the contexts and experiences of these forms of businesses. The study therefore offers important research contributions. As governments design cybersecurity strategies, policies and schemes to promote cyber hygiene, an understanding of the values of MSMEs and the factors that can influence their decisions are imperative. This study also therefore offers practical implications as the results can help to guide policy directions for setting cybersecurity and cyber-hygiene baseline standards for MSMEs, other businesses and other stakeholders.

11.2 Good Cyber-Hygiene Practices

Cyber-hygiene practices are seen as a means to improve cybersecurity resilience. The concept of hygiene is analogous in its purpose in both cyber and personal contexts. This purpose is to promote good health through commonly accepted standards and practices that are routine. Cyber hygiene seeks to address minimum standards or practices that are deemed necessary for maintaining good 'cyber health'. As with personal hygiene, these standards and practices are recommended to be routinely and pervasively adopted to minimize risks and vulnerabilities. Therefore, it is reasonably expected that with good cyber hygiene, businesses will experience fewer cybersecurity breaches and risks to their assets. This is consistent with ENISA (2016), which recommends that cyber hygiene should be properly integrated into an organization and involve 'simple daily routines, good behaviours and occasional check-ups to make sure the organization's online health is in optimum condition'.

A review of academic and practitioner-based literature reveals that cyber-hygiene practices can be broadly categorized into standards and practices geared towards end-users and businesses. While there may be overlaps in certain practices, such as using safe passwords or implementing appropriate endpoint protection, there are sufficient distinctions and demands that businesses will have which would make end-user cyber practices insufficient for businesses' good practices. In addition, cyber-hygiene practices should include not only technical measures but also include people and business process considerations. This perspective accords with Donalds and Barclay's (2021) study that found that risk mitigation, people, technical and organisational factors are essential in improving organizational cybersecurity practices.

Within the last decade, countries, particularly the more developed ones (e.g. US, UK, Canada), have developed cybersecurity guides geared at assisting businesses, including small businesses to secure their data, systems, devices (including mobile devices), networks and employees. The data has shown that the emphasis has been on the use of technical controls complemented with employee awareness and training in some instances. Over time, the considerations have also extended to include protecting the supply chain, controlling physical access and proper use of the cloud (e.g. ENISA (2016)). Further, proper disposal of devices is also essential to assuring

Table 11.1 Cyber-Hygiene Practices for Businesses

Practices by PPT categories
People
Raise awareness/conduct training of employees
Process
Conduct security audits
Control physical access to assets
Control access to systems – access control and authentication
Back up data
Use strong passwords
Secure payment processing
Activate incident response in the event of an incident
Patch and update software regularly
Technology
Use firewalls
Use endpoint security
Protect devices (e.g. mobile, interconnected) e.g. secure configuration
Use technologies securely (e.g. cloud)

Sources: (Agence nationale de la sécurité des systèmes d'information, n.d.); Canadian Centre for Cyber Security, 2021); (ENISA, 2016); (National Cyber Security Centre, 2021); U.S. Small Business Administration, n.d.)

robust security practices despite the current lack of attention to this subject. A summary of cyber-hygiene practices recommended by these agencies, categorized by the people, process and technology (PPT) framework are presented in Table 11.1. Arguably, any business decision can be broadly categorized into people, technology or process as means to improve business understanding.

11.3 Understanding Values

Understanding values or what is important to stakeholders is an important strategy in devising organizational solutions. The Value-focused Thinking (VFT) approach is commonly used to determine stakeholders' value-based objectives (see Table 11.2).

Table 11.2 Sample of VFT Literature

Literature	Objectives	Findings
Barrett-Maitland et al. (2016)	To identify individual objectives that are important in addressing end-users' security and privacy concerns in social networking services environments.	Security and privacy objectives of end-users include: user privacy, integrity of social networking sites, enhanced security controls, corporate social responsibility, individual responsibility.
Barclay and Logan (2013)	To investigate short and long-term objectives that are essential to successfully implementing and adopting MOOCs in developing economies.	Objectives to manage MOOCs' implementation and adoption include: maximize preparedness for work; maximize satisfaction with the learning experience; maximize the viability of MOOC offering, maximize access to learning; and maintain a reputation for quality.
Barclay and Osei-Bryson (2009)	Identify values to support the design and evaluation of organizational programmes based on a derived conceptual framework.	Design and demonstrate the application of a programme evaluation framework to include identification, definition, analysis and realization processes.
Barclay and Osei-Bryson (2010)	To investigate how practitioners can better account for and identify performance criteria that are aligned to project stakeholders' perspectives and how practitioners can identify suitable measures for performance criteria.	Objectives to consider in determining project performance criteria include: enhancing customer experience, maximizing the use of the projects' product or outcome, profit and efficiency.
Keeney (1999)	Identify categories of objectives influenced by customers' Internet purchases.	Objectives that influence Internet purchases include: product quality, costs, time to receive product, convenience, time spent, privacy, shopping enjoyment, safety, environmental impact.

The VFT comprises identifying, articulating and organizing the objectives of the stakeholders to guide all facets of the decision process (Keeney, 1996, 1999).

11.4 Values for Good Cyber Hygiene

According to Keeney (1996), value-focused thinking (VFT) is concerned with first deciding on what you want and then figuring out how to get it. Keeney (1996) further reiterates that values are principles used for evaluation. Thinking about values has many benefits including uncovering hidden objectives, guiding information collection and strategic thinking and facilitating decisions in multiple stakeholder decisions. The steps outlined by (Keeney (1996, 1999) are adapted to this study:

1. Develop a list of MSME values
2. Express each value in a common form
3. Organize the values to indicate their relationship

The first step involves ascertaining from MSMEs what they care about in optimizing cyber hygiene. For the purposes of this study, a single MSME, a project consulting business, is used for the purpose of identifying values and objectives for this study. The second step involves converting the elicited values into objectives in a consistent manner. The third step involves identifying the means objectives and fundamental objectives based on the standard of determining why the objective is important (WITI test).

11.4.1 Identify Values

In seeking to understand the values of Internet commerce, Keeney (1999) recommends that the purpose of interviews is to establish, ascertain from the stakeholders the set of values that would influence behaviours and thereafter stimulate thinking on specific scenarios, pros and cons of the decision context until additional values are no longer obtained. This protocol was applied through the engagement of the MSME case study. The purpose was established to be about obtaining an appreciation of factors that would enhance cyber-hygiene practices in MSMEs. The stakeholder (business owner) was asked a series of questions to include a wish list of cybersecurity and cyber-hygiene ideals for their business, challenges, hindrances and supporting conditions to implementing cyber-hygiene practices. The stakeholder was also asked to consider the concerns of other MSMEs and their likely situations and responses. A summary of the questions is as follows:

a. what do you want or wish to achieve in improving your cyber-hygiene practices?
b. what do you value in cyber hygiene?

c. what values are not negotiable?

d. what do the other MSME value in improving their cyber hygiene?

e. what are some of the current good cyber-hygiene practices that your business has adopted?

f. What are some of your ultimate objectives in improving cyber-hygiene practices?

Values such as no security breaches, safe systems, secured data, ability to quickly fix vulnerabilities, better awareness and easily accessible guidance that *will not break our pockets* were identified.

11.4.2 Convert Values to Common Form

The values expressed are converted to objectives. An objective is something to strive towards and includes a decision context, an object and a direction of preference (Keeney, 1999). The research context is analogous to the decision context i.e. to improve cyber-hygiene practices in MSMEs, the object encapsulates the general intent of each objective statement and the direction of preference is the associated actions necessary in relation to the specific object. Therefore, to reduce security breach is one objective derived from the MSME indicating that they wish for *no security breaches*. The value of better awareness is converted into objectives to improve employee awareness and to improve executive (employer) awareness. The value of quickly fixing vulnerabilities upon further probing resulted in improving incident response capabilities, minimizing malware, etc. The completion of this step resulted in 22 objectives relating to technical, management and operational consideration in improving cyber-hygiene practices.

11.4.3 Organize Values

The objectives were evaluated and organized into logical groups and the Why Is That Important? (WITI) test was applied to determine the means–ends relationship. Each objective is evaluated against the WITI question and if an objective is found to be important because it helps achieve another objective, it is categorized as a means objective; otherwise, it is a fundamental objective. For example, improving fraud detection is important because the MSME wishes to improve compliance and improve business reputation. This illustrates that fraud detection is a means to fundamental objectives of improving compliance and business reputation, within the decision context of improving cyber-hygiene practices. The means objectives are those which will influence achieving the other objectives, including fundamental objectives while the fundamental objectives refer to the objectives that represent the essential reasons for addressing the decision context. Tables 11.2 and 11.3 show the means and fundamental objectives, which are combined to show their means–end relationship in Figure 11.1.

Table 11.3 Means Objectives Related to Cyber-Hygiene Practices

Maximize security awareness	Maximize systems checks	Maximize access and availability of affordable resources
■ Improve employee awareness ■ Improve executive (employer) awareness	■ Routinize updates and systems checks ■ Conduct periodic security audits	■ Access cyber standards for businesses ■ Increase access to affordable tools (e.g. antivirus software, firewalls) ■ Access funding to support cyber-hygiene practices ■ Access pool of cyber talent
Develop security expertise ■ Improve investigative capabilities ■ Improve knowledge and learning about cyber threat and incidences	**Maximize secured process improvements** ■ Maximize secure transactions ■ Manage online transactions ■ Use secure mechanisms for transactions	**Improve awareness of support resources and services** ■ improve knowledge on where to get support
Maximize enterprise security ■ Improve security of data assets ■ Improve security of systems ■ Improve security of networks	**Maximize security investments** ■ Invest in appropriate cyber-hygiene standards ■ Invest in cybersecurity solutions (e.g. firewalls, endpoint solutions)	**Minimize fraud** ■ Avoid unverified correspondences
Maximize software security ■ Increase use of secured software ■ Increase software IP compliance ■ Improve software configuration & management	**Minimize security breaches** ■ Reduce insider threats ■ Reduce supply chain threats ■ Reduce ransomware attacks	**Maximize physical security** ■ Leverage efficient offline processes ■ Manage access to physical location

(Continued)

Table 11.3 (Continued)

Maximize knowledge about standards	Maximize incidence response capabilities	Maximize device security
■ Improve knowledge about relevant laws, rules and standards	■ Efficiently fix vulnerabilities ■ Minimize malware contagion ■ Improve recovery/ remediation	■ Improve access control ■ Improve device configuration & management ■ Maximize secure disposal of devices
	Improve defence capabilities ■ Improve detection of threats ■ Improve detection of crimes ■ Successfully defend against cyberattacks	

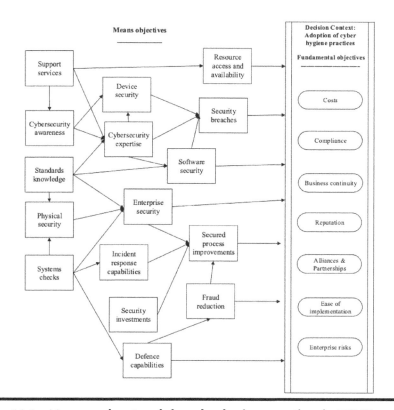

Figure 11.1   Means–ends network for cyber-hygiene practices in MSMEs

11.5 Discussion

Fifteen means objectives and six fundamental objectives were identified. Tables 11.3 and 11.4, respectively, show the means and fundamental objectives in maximizing cyber-hygiene practices in MSME. Each table also presents the sub-objectives that constitute each objective based on the process of reducing the related values to a common form.

There are 15 means objectives: *maximize security awareness; maximize systems checks; maximize access and availability of affordable resources; develop security expertise; maximize secured process improvements; improve awareness of support resources and services; maximize security investments; minimize fraud; maximize software security; maximize enterprise security; minimize security breaches; maximize knowledge about standards; maximize enterprise security; maximize incidence response capabilities; maximize device security; and improve defence capabilities.* These means objectives may be described as facilitating objectives necessary to advance the end objectives within the decision context of maximizing cyber-hygiene practices in MSMEs. Maximizing security awareness entails a comprehensive process that includes all levels of the organizations including the owners, especially where cybersecurity is not their core business. Maximizing security checks comprises undertaking regular and routine updates on systems and software. Implicit in this is the need to have licensed products and robust service agreements with hardware and software vendors. Regular security audits are also necessary to identify security risks and vulnerabilities and address

Table 11.4　Fundamental Objectives to Cyber-Hygiene Practices

Manage enterprise risks	Build reputation	Maximize ease of implementation of practices
▪ Minimize vulnerabilities ▪ Maximize lessons learnt	▪ Maintain business reputation ▪ Build reputation of strong security	▪ Minimize effort to implement security controls
Improve regulatory compliance ▪ Reduce risk of liabilities ▪ Adhere to industry/ MSME standards on security	**Maximize business continuity** ▪ Minimize system outages ▪ Maximize data back-up	**Maximize partnerships** ▪ Leverage business alliances ▪ Improve inter-MSME cooperation in cybersecurity ▪ Share cybersecurity knowledge
	Minimize costs ▪ Reduce security costs	

the same. Maximizing access and availability of affordable resources resonate with MSMEs given limited resources. This may be addressed through cooperation and partnerships to support the strengthening of cybersecurity posture, including at a sectoral level partnerships among members. For example, the manufacturing or legal sector may establish committees responsible for assisting their members in audits, awareness programmes and other initiatives. The other means objectives shown in Table 11.3 provide clarity on the composition of each mean objective.

Figure 11.1 shows the relationships between the means objectives and the means and fundamental objectives by highlighting the means objectives that facilitate another and the means objectives that facilitate the fundamental objectives. For example, the findings indicate that cybersecurity awareness facilitates improved security expertise which in turn reduces the likelihood of security breaches.

The 7 fundamental objectives are: *manage enterprise risks; build reputation; maximize ease of implementation of security practices; improve regulatory compliance; maximize business continuity; maximize partnerships; and minimize costs*. These fundamental objectives are considered the critical objectives necessary in achieving a high level of adherence to cyber-hygiene practices. The fundamental objectives highlight the main objectives of decision-makers in their strategy for improving cyber-hygiene practices in their organizations. Each fundamental objective is hereinafter discussed.

11.5.1 Manage Enterprise Risks

Enterprise risks pertain to managing uncertainty, which in this context relate to minimizing cyber threats and security breaches. According to the business owner:

> managing risks is the hallmark of meeting security standards.

The expert further highlights the importance of reducing the risk of minimizing vulnerabilities with examples such as undertaking hygiene practices such as regular system updates and ensuring that applications are licensed. This is with the intent to manage enterprise risks. The business owner also notes that:

> being able to learn from each experience puts the business in a better position to be able to respond to and recover from security incidents.

This statement underlines that learning from one's own experience is an essential requirement for MSMEs in their journey to improving cyber-hygiene practices. Arguably, within the MSME context, the ability to learn from others is also critical since larger and more experienced businesses may have more experience in managing security breaches or responding to security incidences. Learning from these experiences can allow the MSME to increase their adoption of cyber-hygiene practices and better manage their enterprise risks.

11.5.2 Build Reputation

"*In a competitive environment, reputation matters. If customers believe that the business is not serious about security, there is a high likelihood that they will take their business elsewhere*", the business owner observes.

Consequently, MSMEs may be at a distinct disadvantage especially when compared with larger businesses, if the MSME security maturity is low. Therefore, the importance of building a reputation of a good security profile is underlined. Further, it is reasonable to assert that an improved security posture has a strong positive relationship with the reputation of the organization.

11.5.3 Maximize Ease of Implementation

According to the business owner, "*operating a small business with limited resources it is important that anything we invest in is not expensive or onerous to implement.*"

Ease of implementation comprises the level of complexity in implementing security controls and programmes within an organization. It takes into account the available resources at the organization and the requisite effort and time required to operationalize those security controls and programmes.

11.5.4 Improve Regulatory Compliance

Adherence to industry and regulatory standards pertaining to cybersecurity is essential for good business practice. An MSME may be required to comply with credit card standards, i.e. Payment Card Industry Data Security Standard (PCI-DSS) or to data protection legislation if that MSME is engaged in the processing of the personal information of individual customers. In that regard, standards relating to the security of processing or the safeguarding of cardholder's information are a crucial part of daily operations and engender trust. The business owner notes that:

> actively engaging in compliance activities helps us to identify good security practices that must be sustained in the business.

11.5.5 Maximize Business Continuity

According to Smith and Lostri (2020), system downtime is the normal result of an IT security incident. Therefore, a security event can cause substantial downtime, particularly where there is a significant reliance on IT-enabled services. This may result in significant economic costs for an MSME, including loss of business as a result of customer's inability to access services, or cost of remediation. Reputational damage is also a concern, particularly where there is the perception of the frequency of downtime or poor security management by customers and the business community. The business owner states that:

in the end, adopting cyber hygiene practices will help us to ensure that we not only minimise cyber risks to give ourselves a chance to operate our business successfully.

11.5.6 Maximize Partnerships

"Learning from each other and supporting each other to become more security conscious is beneficial to the whole community", the business owner shares.

Within the cybersecurity landscape, establishing or maintaining partnerships is typically identified as a key standard in determining cybersecurity maturity (e.g. Barclay, 2014) or as a measure to improve cybersecurity at the national level. In that regard, it is reasonable to support the notion that coalescing support to promote cyber-hygiene practices, awareness of cybersecurity standards and good posture among the MSME community can yield beneficial results.

11.5.7 Minimize Costs

The business owner asserts that:

> working with limited resources, limiting costs has to be a key part of our strategy.

This underlines the necessity of cost considerations in cybersecurity initiatives. Smaller organizations, in particular, may feel added pressure given fewer financial resources; however, a risk-based approach can help in the prioritization of controls and practices.

11.6 Implications for Practice

The study has a number of implications for practice. The study identifies the essential needs of MSMEs both in terms of their values in relation to cyber-hygiene practices that could bolster their cyber resilience and the factors that could influence the adoption of these practices. The means objectives highlight the technical and organizational priorities that organizations can adopt that can improve their capabilities and cybersecurity posture. The fundamental objectives comprise both technical and management or strategic considerations necessary for ensuring the effective implementation and adoption of cyber-hygiene practices. Issues such as ease of implementation and minimizing costs bring to attention the resource limitations that MSMEs experience. Additionally, the study highlights that addressing improved adoption requires a collaborative effort at the macro level to include partnerships and business alliances and support to promote adoption. This coincides with the standard of cooperation and partnerships required at the national and international levels in devising cybersecurity priorities.

The study confirms that value-focused decision-making enables better decisions through the identification of the priorities of the stakeholders. It consequently provides a platform to reflect the values of the stakeholders regarding good cyber-hygiene practices, which contemplates the technical and non-technical measures required for successful adoption and implementation.

11.7 Conclusion

The rising cybersecurity threats pose a significant risk to MSMEs. One approach to managing this risk is through the adoption of cyber-hygiene practices. The study examines the values that are important in improving cyber hygiene in MSMEs. The 15 means objectives reflect technical and organizational practices needed to improve cyber hygiene such as security awareness, systems checks, security investments, software and device security. The 7 fundamental objectives reflect important management considerations in ensuring that cyber-hygiene goals are met such as ensuring ease of implementation of cyber-hygiene initiatives, business continuity, managing enterprise-wide risks, regulatory compliance, fostering partnerships, managing costs and building business reputation.

The study focuses on a single MSME case and can be extended to additional MSMEs within the country and within the region to obtain a richer understanding of these stakeholder values. Thus, future research includes extending the number of participants across multiple sectors and to investigate cyber-hygiene adoption in larger organizations and government agencies. Despite the current limitation, the research offers a solid contribution to the cybersecurity literature with empirical values associated with improving cyber-hygiene practices. The findings provide decision-makers with a baseline of cyber-hygiene practices to consider in bolstering their cybersecurity posture and offer policy-makers insights into values that are important to MSMEs as they try to balance their operational and cybersecurity priorities.

References

Agence nationale de la sécurité des systèmes d'information. (n.d.). *40 Essential Measures for a Healthy Network*. Retrieved from https://www.ssi.gouv.fr/uploads/2013/01/guide_hygiene_v1-2-1_en.pdf

Barclay, C. (2014). Sustainable security advantage in a changing environment: The Cybersecurity Capability Maturity Model (CM2). In *Proceedings of the 2014 ITU kaleidoscope academic conference: Living in a converged world-Impossible without standards?* (pp. 275–282). IEEE.

Barclay, C., & Logan, D. (2013). Towards an Understanding of the Implementation & Adoption of Massive Online Open Courses (MOOCs) in a Developing Economy Context. In *Proceedings Annual Workshop of the AIS Special Interest Group for ICT in Global Development*, Milano, Italy, (Vol. 6, pp. 1–14).

Barclay, C., & Osei-Bryson, K. M. (2009). Toward a more practical approach to evaluating programs: The multi-objective realization approach. *Project Management Journal, 40*(4), 74–93.

Barclay, C., & Osei-Bryson, K.-M. (2010). Project performance development framework: An approach for developing performance criteria & measures for information systems (IS) projects. *International Journal of Production Economics, 124*(1), 272–292.

Barrett-Maitland, N., Barclay, C., & Osei-Bryson, K.-M. (2016). Security in social networking services: A value-focused thinking exploration in understanding users' privacy and security concerns. *Information Technology for Development, 22*(3). doi:10.1080/02681 102.2016.1173002

Canadian Centre for Cybersecurity. (2021). *Cyber hygiene*. Retrieved from https://cyber.gc.ca/en/guidance/cyber-hygiene

Centre of Internet Security. (2021). *Getting a Grip on Basic Cyber Hygiene with the CIS Controls*. Retrieved from https://www.cisecurity.org/blog/getting-a-grip-on-basic-cyber-hygiene-with-the-cis-controls/

Donalds, C., & Barclay, C. (2021). Beyond technical measures: a value-focused thinking appraisal of strategic drivers in improving information security policy compliance, *European Journal of Information Systems*, doi:10.1080/0960085X.2021.1978344

ENISA. (2016). *Review of Cyber Hygiene Practices*. Retrieved from https://www.enisa.europa.eu/publications/cyber-hygiene

FBI. (2020). *2020 Internet Crime Report*. Retrieved from https://www.ic3.gov/Media/PDF/AnnualReport/2020_IC3Report.pdf

GOJ. (2018). *Government of Jamaica's MSME and Entrepreneurship Policy*. Retrieved from https://www.miic.gov.jm/content/updated-msme-entrepreneurship-policy-2018

Keeney, R. L. (1996). *Value-Focused Thinking*. USA: Harvard University Press.

Keeney, R. L. (1999). Value of internet commerce to the customer. *Management Science, 45*(4), 533–542. doi:10.1287/mnsc.45.4.533

National Cyber Security Centre. (2021). *Cyber Essentials*. Retrieved March 30, 2021, from https://www.ncsc.gov.uk/cyberessentials/advice

Smith, Z. M., & E. Lostri. (2020). *The Hidden Costs of Cybercrime*. Retrieved from https://www.mcafee.com/enterprise/en-us/assets/reports/rp-hidden-costs-of-cybercrime.pdf

Such, J. M., Ciholas, P., Rashid, A., Vidler, J., & Seabrook, T. (2019). Basic cyber hygiene: Does it work? *Computer, 52*(4), 21–31. doi:10.1109/MC.2018.2888766

U.S. Small Business Administration. (n.d.). *Stay safe from cybersecurity threats*. Retrieved from https://www.sba.gov/business-guide/manage-your-business/stay-safe-cybersecurity-threats

World Bank. (2021). *Small and Medium Enterprises (SMEs) Finance Improving SMEs' Access to Finance and Finding Innovative Solutions to Unlock Sources of Capital*. Retrieved from https://www.worldbank.org/en/topic/smefinance

Chapter 12

Towards a Cybercrime Classification Ontology: A Knowledge-based Approach

12.1 Introduction

Cybercrimes are considered global crimes; they transcend geographical boundaries and can be perpetuated from anywhere against any individual and any technology. While there is no single definition of the term 'cybercrime', the term is generally used to cover/describe a wide variety of illegal crimes or what is considered illicit conduct by individuals/groups against computers, computer-related and other devices, information technology networks; or traditional crimes, as well as actions targeting individuals, supported by the use of the Internet and/or technology. However, the International Telecommunications Union (ITU) cautions that the fact that there is no single definition of 'cybercrime' need not be important (2011). According to the United Nations (2005), what is important is the alarming trends in the use of technology in the commission of illicit or illegal acts.

Recent reports note that cybercrimes will continue to be endemic in society, disrupting businesses, governments, damaging citizens' lives and having negative impacts on economies (e.g. Blythe & Coventry, 2018). The WannaCry ransomware attack demonstrates this claim. In May 2017, the WannaCry attack affected more than 300,000 computers in over 150 countries within less than 24 hours,

DOI: 10.1201/9781003028710-15

with the software demanding US$300 or more in bitcoins (per device) to release encrypted files (McAfee Labs, 2017; United States Computer Emergency Readiness Team, 2017). As reported by the Washington Post, WannaCry encrypted students' in Chinese universities graduation theses and projects, caused widespread disruptions and interruptions of medical procedures across hospitals in Britain; further, Russia's Health Ministry, the state-run Russian Railways, Russia's telecom company Megafon, Spanish telecom giant Telefónica, the French carmaker Renault, systems for Brazil's social security administration and FedEx were all affected (Dwoskin & Adam, 2017).

Moreover, the financial impacts of cybercrimes are considerable and are worsening. Cybercrimes cost organizations, on average, US$11.7 million in 2017, which represents a 23% increase over 2016, according to the Ponemon Institute and Accenture (Accenture, 2017). Trend Micro is predicting that global losses from business email scams alone will exceed US$9 million in 2018 (Trend Micro, 2017). Observers suggest that cybercrime is a problem of considerable magnitude and all the signs are that the situation will deteriorate even further. One country, in its National Security Policy, describes cybercrimes as Tier 1 threats, which 'are clear and present dangers, and are therefore the top priority; they require an active response' (Government of Jamaica, 2014, p. 11). Europol has also described the WannaCry attack as one of the biggest cybersecurity attacks in recent history (Dwoskin & Adam, 2017) and Trend Micro reports that ransomware incidents like WannaCry are anticipated to make further rounds in 2018, even as other types of digital extortion become more prevalent (Trend Micro, 2017).

In response to these present and ever-increasing threats, governments worldwide have taken actions, such as enacting legal frameworks and establishing Computer Security Incident Response Teams (CSIRTs, also commonly referred to as CERTs or CIRTs), to better respond to, investigate and prosecute illicit cyber activities involving the use of information and communication technologies (ICTs) (Organization of American States, 2014). While these initiatives are important in the fight against cybercrimes, one important element remains outstanding; that is, a holistic and accepted cybercrime classification scheme. According to Ngafeeson (2010), the classification of cybercrime is one of three important elements (the others being, identification and effective counter-measures) for combating cybercrime; however, same has been grossly limited. Other scholars too advocate for agreed-upon definitions and a well-formed classification scheme to improve our understanding of cybercrimes. For instance, Barn and Barn (2016) argue that a better understanding of cybercrime is a necessary condition to develop appropriate legal and policy responses to cybercrime and for more accurate estimates of the economic costs of cybercrime on society to be provided. They argue further that 'one possible factor leading to the difficulties of estimation is the lack of well-formed definitions and classification schemes able to account for the range of cybercrimes' (Barn & Barn, 2016, p. 1). Stabek et al. (2009) also propose that a consistent classification scheme is needed for cross-jurisdictional cooperation, information sharing and for the successful prosecution of cybercriminals. Ngo and Jaishankar (2017), who in their recent cybercrime research agenda publication, indicate that a universally agreed-upon classification scheme is not only necessary to advance our knowledge and the scholarship of cybercrime, but is also needed to (i) facilitate effective collaboration and meaningful discussions between scholars and practitioners because agreed-upon definitions provide a common language for stakeholders; (ii) help researchers and practitioners determine the scope of the problem to be addressed; (iii) assist law enforcement to investigate, combat and prevent cybercrimes by improving their understanding of the different aspects of cybercrime; and (iv) enable researchers and practitioners to predict the direction of future cybercrimes as well as formulate novel and timely solutions. Like others, we also argue that a consensual, holistic, accepted cybercrime classification scheme or ontology (e.g. Château et al., 2012; Garbacz et al., 2012; Miranda et al., 2016; Ruiz-Martínez et al., 2016), specifically, a cybercrime classification ontology, is essential in the fight against cybercrime.

Despite the raisons d'être for a uniform cybercrime classification scheme, only recently/relatively recently there has been a push to develop any such classification schemes. However, the schemes are presented as taxonomies (see, for example, Applegate & Stavrou, 2013; Donalds & Osei-Bryson, 2014; Kjaerland, 2005; Simmons et al., 2009) and not ontologies. Only the study by Barn and Barn (2016) presents an ontology for cybercrime classification. Albeit, the classification schemes in prior works are insufficient, narrow in scope as each addresses only a few perspectives, fragmented and often incompatible since each focuses on different perspectives (e.g. role of the computer, attack, attacker's or defender's viewpoint), or use varying terminologies to refer to the same thing, making consistent cybercrime classifications improbable. Further, they are unable to effectively classify the range of and ever-changing types of cybercrimes. However, we argue that consistent and repeatable classification is salient to the problem domain as the same cybercrime could be classified differently by investigators, resulting in inaccurate identification of cybercrime trends and patterns. This study aims to overcome these limitations by developing a comprehensive cybercrime classification ontology that incorporates multiple perspectives (e.g. *Attack_Event, Attacker, Impact, Objective, Victim, Target, Complainant, Vulnerability, Tool and Technique, Location* and *Offence*). These perspectives are included in the ontology as they would provide pertinent information that would be beneficial for police organizations to classify day-to-day cybercrimes, identify trends and patterns, and issue releases for public education. In this chapter, we have designed a more complete cybercrime classification scheme. It should be noted that our proposed ontology integrates and extends prior cybercrime classification schemes by incorporating previously proposed perspectives as well as adding new perspectives, respectively.

Our work offers several contributions including:

1. An explicitly integrated conceptualization of cybercrime classification for use by researchers and cybercrime investigators.

2. A comprehensive and holistic, multi-perspective cybercrime classification and analysis model that involves a parsimonious set of relevant concepts and direct relationships.
3. A flexible artefact that is better able to classify current and future cybercrime attacks.
4. A formal Cybercrime Classification Ontology that could allow cybercrime agents (human or artificial) to share knowledge.
5. An extensible artefact that can easily accommodate new concepts and potential new relationships.

The next section discusses cybercrime classification schemes, knowledge, knowledge-based system (KBS), crime and ontology. Other works related to this study are subsequently presented. The Design Science Research Methodology (DSRM) is then described and its application to the study elucidated. Then, the conceptual model of our cybercrime ontology is presented. The following section presents our ontological representation and the demonstration and evaluation of our artefact by using it to classify and store two real-world cybercrimes. The conclusion and future work section concludes the chapter.

12.2 Background

12.2.1 Summary of Existing Cybercrime Classification Schemes

While there is a vast amount of literature in the cybercrime domain, a review of same reveals that research focusing on cybercrime classification is relatively limited. Furthermore, most cybercrime classification schemes are presented as taxonomies (Alkaabi et al., 2010; Applegate & Stavrou, 2013; Barn & Barn, 2016; Donalds & Osei-Bryson, 2014; Furnell, 2001; Gordon & Ford, 2006; Kjaerland, 2005; Moitra, 2004; Ngafeeson, 2010; Simmons et al., 2009), not ontologies. Moreover, a commonplace approach used to classify cybercrimes generally, and used in some of the cited studies, is to focus on the role technology plays in the commission of the crime (see, Alkaabi et al., 2010; Furnell, 2001; Gordon & Ford, 2006; Smith et al., 2004). In this commonplace approach, cybercrimes are classified as one of two top-level dichotomies: 'computer-assisted crimes' or 'computer-focused crimes'. According to Furnell (2002), 'computer-assisted crimes' are those crimes that pre-date the Internet but take on a new life in cyberspace, e.g. fraud, theft, money laundering, sexual harassment, hate speech and pornography, while 'computer-focused crimes' are those crimes that have emerged in tandem with the establishment of the Internet and could not exist apart from it, e.g. hacking, viral attacks and website defacement. While this top-level dichotomy may be socio-technically helpful, it has limited utility for crime stakeholders such as CSIRTs and cybercrime scholars and does not help to reduce the phenomena to a more systematic observation, therefore they are not considered further.

While acknowledging the role of technology as an enabler or as a contingent tool, Ngafeeson (2010) makes the case that cybercrime classification could be improved by incorporating additional perspectives. However, only few studies have attempted any such classification (see, for example, Applegate & Stavrou, 2013; Barn & Barn, 2016; Donalds & Osei-Bryson, 2014; Kjaerland, 2005; Simmons et al., 2009). Since our intent is to propose a holistic cybercrime classification ontology, we reviewed the literature for prior ontological contributions. However, the review revealed that cybercrime classification ontology research is scant. In fact, to the best of the researchers' knowledge only the study by Barn and Barn (2016) has offered an initial cybercrime classification ontology, expressed in Protégé OWL.

12.2.2 Knowledge, Knowledge-Based System, Crime and Ontology

Police work has been established as 'knowledge centric'. For instance, criminal investigations typically include crime scene processing, evidence collection, investigative report writing, interviewing of victim(s), arresting and interviewing of suspect(s), assisting prosecutor with indictment, etc., all requiring a wide range of knowledge and skills. Luen and Al-Hawamdeh (2001) found that police officers require vast knowledge to carry out their normal duties. In fact, Holgersson and Gottschalk (2008) identified at least 30 categories of knowledge in use in the police practice. Gottschalk (2007) categorized the types of knowledge needed in police work as administrative, policing, legal, procedural and analytical.

Recent decades have seen several shifts in the primary approaches to crime-fighting, each emphasizing the critical role of knowledge in achieving effective policing. For instance, Problem Oriented Policing (POP), coined by Herman Goldstein, has four basic steps (acronymized 'SARA' by John Eck and William Spelman) that require police to use knowledge to: (1) scan the environment for problem selection; (2) analyse the problem selected; (3) respond to the problem in a new and different way and (4) assess the results of the new response (Eck et al., 1987). Intelligence-led policing (I-LP), while building on the paradigm of POP, is a more recent, popular crime-fighting approach based on what Ratcliffe (2008) refers to as 'new' knowledge. Ratcliffe (2008) argues that this 'new' kind of knowledge has evolved due to the rapid digitization in the last 20 years and is represented by a broader interpretation of intelligence, which incorporates approaches such as crime mapping, trend and demographic analysis. According to the Bureau of Justice Assistance (2005), intelligence is what is produced after collected data are evaluated and analysed. For law enforcement 'information is compiled, analyzed, and/or disseminated in an effort to anticipate, prevent or monitor criminal activity' (IALEIA, 2004, p. 33). Therefore, I-LP has a significant information processing requirement and is usually supported by ICTs.

In support of their crime-fighting activities, more police organizations are implementing ICTs and other KBSs or technologies to assist in identifying crime trends and the corresponding knowledge about detection and prevention of crimes. The term KBS is broad and refers to different types of organizational information technologies that are used to manage organizational knowledge, such as Expert Systems, Decision Support Systems and Groupware (Laudon & Laudon, 2002). For instance, the Jamaica Constabulary Force (JCF) has in recent years implemented ICTs and/or KBS, such as Integrated Ballistics Identification System (IBIS), Automated Palm and Fingerprint Identification System (AFIS), Sardonyx Criminal Intelligence Management System and Govcheck (designed for JCF members to view information on motor vehicle, traffic tickets and drivers licence) (Ministry of National Securiy, 2008; Planning Research & Development Branch, 2016). COPLINK Connect (Chen et al., 2002) and POLNET (Gultekin, 2009) are examples of knowledge-based solutions implemented in other jurisdictions to assist in the fight against crime. Indeed, the adoption of these and other technologies in policing indicate the recognition that police work is knowledge centric.

While the adoption of technologies has created new opportunities for police to better understand crime, crime patterns and trends, it has simultaneously increased opportunities for, and methods of criminality. Criminals are now committing traditional and new crimes (cybercrimes) via technology. According to Wall (2005), the Internet has three levels of impact on criminal opportunity: (1) more opportunities for traditional crime, such as fraud, money laundering, pyramid schemes, stalking and trading of sexual materials; (2) new opportunities for traditional crime, such as Hacktivism, organized pedophile rings, identity theft and 419 scams; and (3) new opportunities for new types of crime, such as e-auction scams, spam, DoS, DDoS, cybersex, hate speech and intellectual property piracy.

Being one of the most difficult challenges facing law enforcement today, new knowledge and skills are essential to effectively fight cybercrimes. In fact, police investigators make the case that police need to learn vast new skills, such as intrusion detection and computer forensics, and accumulate much knowledge to effectively fight cybercrimes (Chang & Chung, 2014). The knowledge-centric nature of policing cybercrimes clearly establishes the need for KBSs and applications. However, there is a dearth of knowledge-based developments to address the phenomenon of cybercrime. Our work is a step in that direction. In this chapter, we present our knowledge-based artefact and our cybercrime classification ontology.

An ontology is a mechanism used to capture knowledge about a problem domain and is described as 'an explicit specification of a conceptualization' (Gruber, 1995). According to Gruber (1995), a conceptualization is an abstract, simplified view or model of a domain of interest which captures objects, concepts, entities and the relationships that hold among them (e.g. Château et al., 2012; Garbacz et al., 2012; Gil et al., 2015; Labib et al., 2017; Miranda et al., 2016; Ruiz-Martínez et al., 2016). Thus, in this study we capture knowledge about cybercrimes by explicitly identifying pertinent cybercrime classification concepts, entities and their relations identified by police practitioners and researchers. Our ontology then formally represents (1) knowledge as a set of concepts in the domain and (2) the relationships between the concepts.

An ontology is also described as a conceptualization of a domain into a human-understandable, but machine-readable format consisting of entities, attributes, relationships and axioms (Guarino & Giaretta, 1995). It is the basic structure or armature around which a KBS can be developed. In fact, Kharbat and El-Ghalayin (2008) assert that ontologies have become the backbone technology in most knowledge-based applications. However, it is not a programmatic representation, but rather, it addresses domain conceptualizations, free of technical requirements. It provides the means for describing explicitly the conceptualization behind the knowledge represented in a knowledge base (Bernaras et al., 1996). Ontologies have been identified as important in the development of knowledge-based crime systems. For instance, Donalds and Osei-Bryson (2012) make the case that before beginning the elaboration of a KBS for criminal investigations, it is necessary to define the ontological entities and the relationships among them. Similarly, Dzemydiene and Kazemikaitiene (2005) maintain that the development of an application ontology helps create the framework that ensures the collection, accumulation, storage, treatment and transmission of, in proper form, important crime investigation information; pre-requisites to make optimal decisions in the investigation of crimes by a knowledge-based crime system. In developing the Integrated Crime Emergency Response System (iCERS), a system which integrates all sorts of crime emergency service resources, the Crime Emergency Event Model (CE2M) ontology was developed as an effective means to implement semantic level integration (Wang et al., 2005).

We therefore assert that future cybercrime systems/applications for police organizations should be knowledge-based, incorporating a shared conceptualization that an ontology-based approach provides. We note, however, that while knowledge-based developments are not sufficient, they are necessary and will prove useful to stakeholders in the fight against cybercrime.

12.3 Related Works

While research focusing on cybercrime classification is scant, studies that have incorporated additional perspectives other than the role technology plays in cybercrime and studies focused on network and computer-related attacks that have influenced our work, are now discussed. Network and computer-related attacks are described as types of cybercrimes, i.e. attacks against computer systems, networks and infrastructure (Council of Europe, 2001; Jamaica Houses of Parliament, 2015).

Hansman and Hunt (2005) proposed a computer and network attack classification taxonomy consisting of four dimensions. The first dimension covers the attack vector and the main behaviour of the attack; the second dimension allows for the classification of the attack targets; vulnerabilities and payloads are classified in the third and fourth dimensions, respectively. This taxonomy has proved valuable in that it identifies a vulnerability dimension as well as the classification of attack targets, which we adopt in our ontology. Further, it classifies attacks based on dimensions; a similar approach is used in this study. However, the taxonomy is not practical for classifying cybercrimes since it cannot classify blended attacks and other pertinent dimensions are omitted, rendering same incomplete. A blended attack utilizes a technique to include a combination of semantic and syntactic attack methods against the victim (Choo, 2011). A syntactic attack exploits a technical vulnerability in the system such as a virus transmitted via email while a semantic attack exploits human vulnerabilities, such as social engineering, to obtain personal information.

Kjaerland (2005) proposed four faucets with which to classify cybercrimes: source sector, impact, target and method of operation. Using these faucets Kjaerland (2005) analysed cyberattacks against entities in the commercial and government sectors reported to one CSIRT. Kjaerland's taxonomy proves useful in several ways: (1) it classifies cyber incidents using faucets/characteristics; and (2) it also identifies new characteristics pertinent for cybercrime classification. For instance, the characteristic 'source sector' is incorporated in our ontology; specifically, we relate it to the market sector to which the victim belongs. Notwithstanding its usefulness, this taxonomy is limited in that it focuses on only few characteristics, thus lacking the details needed for thorough insight into and complete classification of cybercrimes.

Simmons et al. (2009) proposed a cyberattack taxonomy called AVOIDIT to characterize the nature of an attack using five characteristics: Attack Vector, Operational Impact, Defence, Information Impact, and Target. This taxonomy is informative and proves useful in many ways: (1) it examines relationships between access path, targets, hosts and the impacts of attacks on targets, which we believe should improve our understanding of the phenomenon under investigation; (2) unlike previous efforts, it allows for the classification of blended attacks, which is now commonplace in cyberattacks; (3) it has the ability to classify cyberattacks from multiple taxonomic perspectives, an improvement over some previous works; and (4) its overall style of classifying cyberattacks, based on characteristics, is useful and is consistent with the approach used in this work. Further, we adopt the *Operational* and *Information Impact* concepts in this study. However, the AVOIDIT taxonomy is limited. For instance, it does not allow for the classification of attacks by attacker, objective or motive of the attacker nor identifies the victim, perspectives we argue can improve the classification of cybercrimes.

van Herdeen et al. (2012) offered a taxonomy of computer network attacks which formed the basis of their proposed ontology framework with which to classify network attacks. van Herdeen et al.'s ontological framework allows for the classification of network attacks with classes: attack scenario, actor, actor location, aggressor, attack goal, motivation, scope size, scope, target, vulnerability, asset, sabotage, effect, phase, attack mechanism and automation level. Within each class additional information is provided to classify network attacks. While this ontological framework focused exclusively on computer network attacks, its style and structure have proven useful to this study in that it identifies additional classes/characteristics not previously identified that can now be used for classifying cybercrimes. For instance, in this study we adopt vulnerability and aggressor classes and propose an attack_event class, which is comparable to the attack scenario class proposed by van Herdeen et al. Since van Herdeen et al.'s ontology framework focuses exclusively on computer network attacks, it has limitations for the classification of cybercrime. For instance, it cannot handle the range of cybercrimes, in particular those committed against individuals and, it too cannot classify blended attacks.

Applegate and Stavrou (2013) proposed a cyber conflict taxonomy to describe cyber conflicts events and is divided into two main groups, categories and subjects. Subjects are either entities or events and represent the actual real-world cyber conflict events and their participants (i.e. individuals, organizations, states). Categories are used to classify subjects via two subcategories, actions and actors, with each subcategory being further subdivided into increasing specific subcategories used to describe subjects. Like few prior works, Applegate and Stavrou's taxonomy employs multiple taxonomic perspectives (i.e. characteristics) to classify cyber events. Additionally, its refinement of previously proposed characteristics proves particularly useful to this study. For instance, Applegate and Stavrou (2013) adapted and extended Simmons et al. (2009) operational and informational impacts, which we have adopted in this study. Moreover, our work draws on the approach used by Applegate and Stavrou's which seeks to explore relationships that may exist between actors, attacks, vectors used and the impacts associated with cyber events. Although Applegate and Stavrou's present a useful cyber conflict taxonomy it lacks details needed for thorough insight into a cybercrime. For example, the objective of the attacker, the complainant and offence committed are all information we argue would be beneficial for classifying cybercrimes by police practitioners and for issuing advisories.

Based on the concept of characteristic structure Donalds and Osei-Bryson (2014) proposed a taxonomy that classifies properties about cybercrimes and not the actual cybercrimes themselves. Specifically, *victim, attacker, objective, tool & tactic, impact, result, relationship, target* and *offence* are proposed as the characteristics with which to classify cybercrimes. The proposed taxonomy is useful in several ways: (1) it classifies cybercrimes using multiple characteristics; (2) it attempts to identify links that potentially exist between taxonomic characteristics; (3) it classifies cybercrimes using characteristic structure, the approach adopted in this study; and 4) it adapts, integrates and extends prior cybercrime classification schemes. From the Donalds and Osei-Bryson (2014) study we adopt the concepts *victim, objective, attacker* and *attacker classification*. It should be noted that although it offered improvements over prior works, the taxonomy of Donalds and Osei-Bryson (2014) is limited as other pertinent characteristics with which to classify cybercrimes were not included in the taxonomy. For instance, *attack_event, vulnerability* and the different types of *impacts* were not considered.

Barn and Barn (2016) proposed a taxonomy that was then developed as an ontology and implemented in Protégé OWL, for classifying cybercrimes. The main concepts presented in the ontology are action, agent, contact, external observer, impact, location, motivation, social engineering act, target, technology role and viewpoint. The presented ontology is informative as it offers several characteristics with which to classify cybercrimes, attempting an integrated view of cybercrimes. Further, additional characteristics that can be incorporated in future works and their relationships are formally identified. We adopt the *Geopolitical* and *Psychological* classification of *Impact* from this study. However, a drawback to the ontology is that it does not appear to have been created for police organizations and knowledge bodies such as CSIRTs, since it includes 'viewpoint of external observers' and aims to classify their perceptions of the actions executed. We posit that the viewpoint class would not be useful for police organizations, our target constituency. Further, the ontology delineates traditional crime vs. cybercrime. We contend that an ontology for the classification of cybercrimes should exclude traditional crimes. While we understand that the authors wish to capture whether the crime is technology enabled or technology dependent, we suggest that the technology role subclass captures the data relevant to infer such information. Additionally, other pertinent cybercrime concepts, such as vulnerability, operational and informational impacts are not incorporated.

While previous attempts at cybercrime classification have proved useful, the above discussion shows that the various taxonomies address various aspects of cybercrime, thereby, offering different concepts with which to classify cybercrimes. Moreover, these works use varying terminologies interchangeably, even though they sometimes refer to the same thing. While we admit that most of the taxonomic frameworks can be used to classify cybercrimes, we argue that none offer a holistic framework with which to effectively classify these crimes. Consequently, they are unable to account for the range of and ever-changing types of cybercrimes. Further, most of the previous taxonomic frameworks are unable to effectively illustrate complex interactions between attackers, victims, impacts, locations, motivations, actual cybercrimes and other potential pertinent concepts.

12.4 Methodology

This research adopts a design science (DS) research paradigm in developing our formal cybercrime classification ontology (CCO). DS is described as a problem-solving paradigm that is used to create and evaluate innovative IT artefacts intended to solve organizational problems (Hevner et al., 2004; Simon, 1996). Moreover, DS is considered the link between information system (IS) research and practice (Peffers et al., 2007). According to Gregor and Hevner (2013, p. 337), 'in IS, DS research involves the construction of a wide range of socio-technical artifacts such as decision support systems, modeling tools, governance strategies, methods for IS evaluation, and IS change interventions'. We argue that this approach is particularly suited to address our research objective because it allows us to produce an innovative IS artefact to address a real-world problem, cybercrime classification. In this study, our IS artefact then is our formal knowledge-based CCO, expressed in Protégé OWL.

In constructing our CCO IS artefact, we were guided by the steps outlined in the DSRM proposed by Peffers et al. (2007). According to Peffers et al. (2007), the DSRM emphasizes the design and construction of applicable artefacts that could potentially contribute to the efficacy of IS in organizations. We chose the DSRM for several reasons: (1) it accommodates the construction of practically useful artefacts since its focus is on artefact development (Peffers et al., 2018); (2) it does not demand that the artefact evaluation involve a formal process embedded in the design effort (Peffers et al., 2018); (3) it builds on the strengths of prior efforts that focused of DS research guidelines; and (4) we concur with other researchers that it provides a useful synthesized general model (Gregor & Hevner, 2013). The steps in the DSRM methodology and how each is applied in this research are now discussed.

Problem identification and motivation – this step involves defining the specific research problem and justification of the value of the solution. We have defined our problem, established its relevance and importance as well as justified the value of the CCO artefact in prior sections.

Define the objectives for a solution – objectives of a solution are to be inferred from the problem definition. As stated previously the objectives of our solution is to address current research gaps as identified above by designing: (1) An explicit integrated conceptualization of cybercrime classification for use by researchers and cybercrime investigators; (2) A comprehensive and holistic, multi-perspective cybercrime classification and analysis model that involves a parsimonious set of relevant concepts and direct relationships; (3) A flexible artefact that is better able to classify current and future cybercrime attacks; (4) A formal cybercrime classification ontology that could allow cybercrime agents (human or artificial) to share knowledge; and 5) An extensible artefact that can easily accommodate new concepts and potential new relationships.

Design and development – create the artefact which can be constructs, models, methods, instantiations or new properties of technical, social, and/or informational resources. Our cybercrime classification ontology conceptual model as well our knowledge-based CCO artefact, implemented in Protégé OWL, are discussed in subsequent sections.

Demonstration – demonstration shows whether the artefact works as intended in one instance (Peffers et al., 2018). In a subsequent section, we demonstrate our CCO by using it to classify two real-world cybercrime cases that occurred in multiple jurisdictions.

Evaluation – observe and measure how well the artefact supports a solution to the problem. This activity involves comparing the objectives of a solution to actual observed results from use of the artefact in the demonstration; our results are presented in Table 12.4.

Communication – communicate the problem and its importance, the artefact, its utility and novelty, the rigor of its design, and its effectiveness to researchers and other relevant audiences, such as practicing professionals. This is attempted in this chapter through the presentation of the research problem and its importance, the artefact's design, utility and effectiveness.

12.5 Conceptual Model and Classification Concepts

12.5.1 Our Conceptual Model

Drawing on prior works, we present the conceptual model of our proposed CCO in Figure 12.1. This model identifies the main characteristics for cybercrime classification and the relationships among them. The conceptual model characteristics are discussed below. Note that since the CCO is designed to be extensible, additional characteristics and relationships may be added in the future as necessary. Also below is a table that presents the classification concepts covered in this chapter and prior works.

Attack_Event. An *Attack_Event* is an actual real-world cybercrime or nefarious cyber action committed by an *Attacker*. Examples of *Attack_Event* are: EmailHacked_NudePhotosUploaded and LulzSecAssoicateIndicted. Other pertinent metadata such as start and end dates of the *Attack_Event* will be captured, if known. These kinds of metadata could aid police practitioners identify cyber trends/patterns over time.

Vulnerability. A *Vulnerability* is a flaw or a weak point in the system that is exploited by an *Attacker* in a cyber *Attack_Event*. *Vulnerability*, would therefore

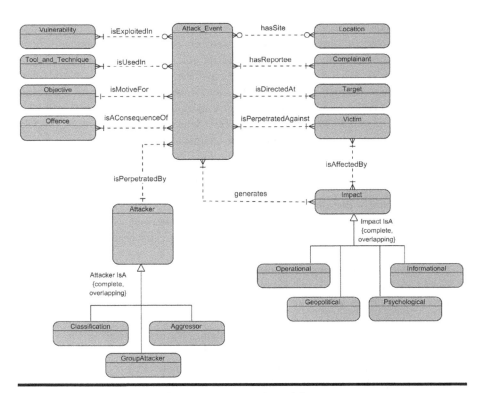

Figure 12.1   Our proposed CCO conceptual model

only be applicable in a cyber ***Attack_Event*** committed against ICTs. Howard (1997) suggests three types of vulnerabilities: implementation vulnerability, design vulnerability, and configuration vulnerability. Simmonds et al. (2004) suggest security policy vulnerabilities and technology vulnerabilities. While technology vulnerabilities are generally 'weaknesses' in the technology, security policy vulnerabilities are weaknesses of security policy such as poor planning and control. In this study, we categorize vulnerabilities as ***Implementation Vulnerability***, ***Design Vulnerability***, ***Configuration Vulnerability*** and ***Security Policy Vulnerability***.

Tool_and_Technique can be thought of as the 'means' (i.e. tool and/or technique) used by an ***Attacker*** to execute a cyber ***Attack_Event***. The categories of ***Tool_and_Technique*** proposed by Donalds and Osei-Bryson (2014) are adopted in this study (***Tool***, ***SocialEngineering***, ***IllicitCollusion*** and ***AttackVector***).

Objective. An ***Objective*** can be thought of as the main purpose, motive or end goal of an ***Attacker*** for committing a cyber ***Attack_Event***. Mostly, we have adapted the classification of attackers' objectives by Donalds & Osei-Bryson (2014) and have added new ones based on empirical data of cybercrime cases in the trade press. For instance, we have incorporated ***SelfPreservation*** and ***Moral*** to be able to classify these types of ***Objectives***.

Offence. An ***Offence*** can be described as an illicit cyber action or ***Attack_Event*** that has been perpetrated by an ***Attacker*** and is punishable by law. An example is 'unauthorised access to computer program or data' (Jamaica's Cybercrimes Act, 2015 – Jamaica Houses of Parliament, 2015).

Location. *Location* addresses five concepts: ***Attacker***, ***Attack_Event***, ***Victim***, ***Complainant*** and ***Target***. *Location* refers to the country (generally) and/or specific address of an individual/group ***Attacker***, the ***Victim*** and/or ***Target*** that experiences the ***Attack_Event***, the ***Complainant*** who reports the ***Attack_Event*** and where the ***Attack_Event*** is launched from. We note, however, that while it may be possible to identify the ***Location*** of a computer involved in a cyber ***Attack_Event***, that ***Location*** may not necessarily correspond the attacker's ***Location*** since the attack occurs in cyberspace or the ***Attack_Event*** can be launched from multiple sources.

Complainant. A ***Complainant*** is one who reports a cyber ***Attack_Event***, making the authorities aware of the illicit activity. A ***Complainant*** can be of type ***Individual*** or ***Group***. Further, a ***Complainant*** may or may not be a ***Victim***. For instance, an individual notices that his/her home computer is involved in a cybercrime, this individual will perhaps be the ***Victim*** as well the ***Complainant***. If however, in an organization an employee is unable to access/retrieve emails due to hacking of the email server, the employee in question may contact the Information Technology (IT) department to report the matter and would thus be a ***Complainant***, not a ***Victim***. While the employee would be affected by the cybercrime, the ***Victim*** would be the organization.

Victim. A ***Victim*** is an entity that is affected in some way by a cyber ***Attack_Event***. Since a ***Victim*** can be of type ***IndividualVictim***, ***GroupVictim***, ***OrganizationVictim***, ***GovernmentVictim***, we propose a ***VictimType*** to capture the type of ***Victim*** involved in a cyber ***Attack_Event***. A ***Victim*** may or may not be the specific *Target* of a cyber *Attack_Event*. When the *Victim* is specifically targeted, then the *Victim* and the *Target* are the same. On the other hand, if for instance, an *Attacker* mass distributes a virus, the *Victim* is not necessarily the specific *Target*, but becomes a *Victim* based on opportunity (*Vulnerability* in the specific system).

Target. A *Target* is an entity that a cyber *Attack_Event* is specifically directed at. Hansman and Hunt (2005) identify hardware, software and network as types of *Target*. Simmons et al. (2009) identify a *Target* as operating system, network, local [computer], user and application. Personal computer, network infrastructure device, server and industrial equipment are proposed as types of *Target* by van Herdeen et al. (2012). Barn and Barn (2016) propose TargetIndividual, TragetTechnology, State and Organization as *Target* types. We propose *TargetType*, which identifies the type of *Target* involved in a cyber *Attack_Event* and are: *TargetInfrastructure*, *TargetPersonalDevice*, *TargetNetworkDevice*, *TargetOrganization*, *TargetIndividual*, *TargetGovernment*, *TargetGroup*, *TargetSoftware* and *TargetSite*. Of note, an *Attack_Event* may involve one or multiple targets which may be any of or a combination of *TargetType*.

Impact. An *Impact* can be defined as the direct effect caused by a cyber *Attack_Event* on a *Victim*. Prior works have classified *Impact* as operational impact and informational impact (Applegate & Stavrou, 2013; Simmons et al., 2009) as well as economic, psychological and geopolitical (Barn & Barn, 2016). Since economic impact overlaps with operational impact, in this study, we propose *Operational*, *Informational*, *Psychological* and *Geopolitical* as types of *Impact*.

Attacker. An *Attacker* can be defined as an entity that attempts or commits a cyber *Attack_Event* to achieve an *Objective*. We adapt and extend the *Classification* values of *Attacker* proposed by Donalds and Osei-Bryson (2014).

An *Attacker* may be a group. Choo (2008) proposes three types of criminal groups that exploit the advances of ICTs to infringe legal and regulatory controls: (1) traditional organized criminal group whose primary motivation is for profit or to increase their wealth; (2) organized cybercriminal groups which operate exclusively online; and (3) organized groups of ideologically and politically motivated individuals. van Herdeen et al. (2012) propose organized criminal group, protest group and cyber army. StateAgent and OrganizationAgent are proposed by Barn and Barn (2016) as types of group attacker (termed Agent in the study). We propose four *GroupAttacker* types: *OrganizedCriminalGroup* – which includes both traditional and exclusively online organized criminal group that commits a cyber *Attack_Event* for financial or other material gains; *StateGroup* – refers to a nation state or its proxy that commits a cyber *Attack_Event* that is for intelligence gathering, stealing of intellectual property and/or identity, financial gain or political motivations; *SexualGratificationGroup* – refers to a group that commits a cyber *Attack_Event* for sexual delight; *IdeoliticalGroup* is a group that commits a cyber *Attack_Event* for ideological, political, ethical or moral reasons.

An *Attacker* may be an *Aggressor*. According to van Herdeen et al. (2012) *Aggressor* describes the association with the *Attacker* rather than the type of *Attacker* and is one that may be hired or sanctioned to perform a cyber ***Attack_Event***. In this study an ***Aggressor*** may be *StateAggressor, CommercialAggressor, IndividualAggressor, SelfInstigator* or *UnknownAggressor*. Of note, when the ***Attacker*** and ***Aggressor*** are the same, *SelfInstigator* is applicable.

12.5.2 Structural Comparison of Cybercrime Classification Models

In this subsection, we address the novelty of our cybercrime classification model in the context of prior studies. We first examine the similarities and differences in the concepts covered in the various models. In Table 12.1 we present the concepts that are addressed in a given study using checkmarks; each main concept is presented in bold and its set of subtypes appearing immediately after in italicized font. It should be noted that though in some cases a prior study may have used a different name for an equivalent concept in our model we consider that concept to also be included in the model of that prior study. Concepts that are not addressed in a given study remain unchecked/blank.

A review of Table 12.1 shows that our conceptual model includes more cybercrime classification concepts than any other prior works, supporting our claim that our classification scheme is a more holistic scheme with which to effectively classify cybercrimes. It should also be noted that of the studies referenced in Table 12.1, all except one (i.e. Barn & Barn, 2016) present taxonomies only. Now, by its nature, a taxonomy would only represent parent–child (i.e. One-to-Many) relationships and so would exclude relevant Many-to-Many relationships necessary for the classification of cybercrimes. An ontological-based approach, as is used in our work, overcomes this challenge.

We will now consider some of the relationships that are present in our model but not present in others. Relationships are important as they form the basis for whether a query involving two or more concepts is answerable. Obviously, if for a given pair of concepts that is present in our model but at least one concept of the pair is not present in the other model, then any query involving that pair of concepts would not be answerable in the other model. However, there are other cases where a pair of concepts are present in both models but only one model could answer a specific query. For example, though the pair of concepts of *Attacker* and *Attack_Event* are covered in our ontology as well as that of Barn and Barn's, given Barn and Barn's ontology it would be unsuccessful in finding out which *Attacker* is associated with a given *Attack_Event*, yet our ontology could be successfully queried for same. Similarly, Barn and Barn's model does not allow for querying what *Tool and Technique* is most frequently used by a given *Attacker* because there is no formal relationship between *Attacker* and *Tool and Technique* even though the concepts are included in their model. On the other hand, our ontology would be able to generate such information because of the explicit logical link between *Attacker* and *Tool and Technique* in our chapter.

Table 12.1 Cybercrime Classification Concepts Covered in this Study and Prior Works

Concept	This Study	Hansman and Hunt (2005)	Kjaerland (2005)	Simmons et al. (2009)	van Herdeen et al. (2012)	Applegate and Stavrou (2013)	Donalds and Osei-Bryson (2014)	Barn and Barn (2016)
Attack_Event	✓			✓		✓		✓
Vulnerability	✓	✓			✓	✓		
:Categorization	✓							
Tool_and Technique	✓	✓	✓	✓	✓	✓	✓	✓
:Categorization	✓						✓	
Objective	✓				✓		✓	✓
:Classification	✓				✓		✓	✓
Offence	✓				✓		✓	
Location	✓							✓
Complainant	✓							
:Type	✓							
Victim	✓		✓				✓	

	1	2	3	4	5	6	7	8
:Type	✓							
:MarketSector	✓							
Target	✓	✓		✓	✓	✓	✓	✓
:Type	✓		✓					✓
Impact	✓			✓	✓	✓	✓	✓
:Operational	✓			✓		✓		
:Geopolitical	✓							✓
:Psychological	✓							✓
:Informational	✓			✓		✓		
Attacker	✓		✓		✓	✓	✓	✓
:Classification	✓				✓	✓	✓	
:Aggressor	✓				✓			
:GroupAttacker	✓				✓			

12.6 Ontological Representation, Classification, Comparison and Evaluation

12.6.1 Our Cybercrime Classification Ontological Representation in Protégé OWL

In this section, we translate our conceptual model (Figure 12.1), to our CCO, implemented in Protégé OWL (http://protege.stanford.edu/). The conceptual model is a straightforward translation into OWL classes, as shown in Figure 12.2. Object

Figure 12.2   The class hierarchy and object property hierarchy for our ontological artefact

properties used to link instances of classes together are also shown. Our CCO arte-fact is the explicit formal specification of the characteristics with which to classify cybercrimes and the relationships among them.

12.6.2 Classifying and Storing Two Real World Cyber Attack Events

In the following sub-sections, we demonstrate the utility of our artefact by using our Protégé OWL CCO to store and classify two real-world cybercrimes: *EmailHacked_NudePhotosUploaded* and *LulzSecAssoicateIndicted*. Also in this section, we compare how the previously identified classification schemes and this study's classification scheme would classify the cybercrimes.

12.6.2.1 Details of Attack_Event 1 – EmailHacked_NudePhotosUploaded – and its classification in Protégé OWL

A synopsis of **Attack_Event** 1, *EmailHacked_NudePhotosUploaded*, is presented in Figure 12.3. Using our Protégé OWL CCO we show the **Attack_Event** from two perspectives; one view with the **Attack_Event** as the central instance (Figure 12.4) and the other from the perspective of the alleged **Attacker** (Figure 12.5). Each view shows different characteristics of the **Attack_Event** and illustrates relation-ships between the **Attack_Event** and other characteristics in the CCO. Additionally, Figure 12.5 shows some inferred relationships (highlighted in yellow at the bottom right-hand side).

Emails Hacked: Nude Photographs Uploaded (Jamaica Information Service, 2012; The Gleaner, 2012):

On Monday August 27, 2012 the police arrested and charged Ronald Oates, a 27-year-old man of a Kingston address, with unauthorised access, unauthorised obstruction and unlawfully making available data for the commission of an offence. It is alleged that Mr. Oates hacked into the email accounts of his victims, gaining access to their nude photographs. He would either upload the photographs to a local website then demand money from the victims for them to be removed or contacted the women threatening to upload the photographs if they di not pay. According to the police, Mr. Oates demand between $10,000 and $20,000 from his victims. The police says those targeted were mainly from St. Catherine and Kingston & St. Andrew.

The arrest of Oates provided some relief for popular entertainer Denyque, one of the first women to come forward with claims of being extorted by operators of a website that had obtained nude photographs of her. Bianca Bartley, one of the complainants in the matter involving Oates, reported that passwords to two of her email accounts were changed without her consent, preventing her access and, her nude photographs were published on several websites including one operated by the accused, "Jamaicagirlsexposed.blogspot.com".

Figure 12.3   Excerpt for Attack_Event 1: EmailHacked_NudePhotosUploaded

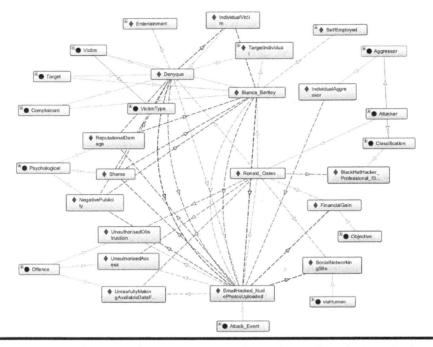

Figure 12.4 The 'Attack_Event' perspective of EmailHacked_NudePhotos Uploaded

Figure 12.5 The 'Attacker' perspective of EmailHacked_NudePhotosUploaded

12.6.2.2 Classification Schemes' Comparison of Attack_Event 1 – EmailHacked_NudePhotosUploaded

Using the details of *EmailHacked_NudePhotosUploaded*, we show how our CCO compares with some previously proposed classification schemes discussed above, for classifying the **Attack_Event**. Classification schemes proposed for computer/network attacks are omitted since they cannot classify *Attack_Events* perpetrated by individuals. Table 12.2 shows the result of classifying *EmailHacked_NudePhotosUploaded*.

Table 12.2 shows that Kjaerland's cyber incident taxonomy does provide some important information about the *Attack_Event*, however, its lacks pertinent characteristics such as *Objective*, *Victim* and the specific *Attacker* involved. Similarly, Simmons et al.'s and Applegate and Stavrou's taxonomies omit characteristics pertinent for cybercrime classification. While Donalds and Osei-Bryson's taxonomy does improve on previous works in some key areas such as *Objective* and the specific *Attacker* involved in the *Attack_Event*, it does not differentiate between the different types of *Impact* and excludes other pertinent characteristics such as *Vulnerability*. Using Barn and Barn's ontology we were unable to differentiate between *Victim* and *Target* and it cannot classify a *Vulnerability* that may have been exploited in an *Attack_Event*. However, our CCO is able to thoroughly classify the *Attack_Event* and further, potential blended attacks, since it allows for the classification of *Vulnerability* that may be exploited.

12.6.2.3 Details of Attack_Event 2 – LulzSec Associate Indicted – and its classification in Protégé OWL

A synopsis of *Attack_Event* 2, *LulzSecAssoicateIndicted*, is presented in Figure 12.6. In Figure 12.7 we show some of the relationships between the *Attack_Event* *LulzSecAssoicateIndicted* and other individuals by class in the CCO.

12.6.2.4 Classification Schemes' Comparison of Attack_Event 2: LulzSecAssociateIndicted

Using the excerpt in Figure 12.6, we demonstrate how previously proposed classification schemes as well as our CCO would classify *LulzSecAssociateIndicted*. Table 12.3 shows the results. Of note is that the results of the classification of the *Attack_Event* *LulzSecAssociateIndicted* is similar to the classification of *EmailHacked_NudePhotosUploaded* in that all the previously proposed classification schemes are limited; that is, they do not capture important information deemed relevant for cybercrime classification. For instance, Kjaerland's classification scheme does not capture information with regards to *Attacker*, *Victim*, *Impact*, among others. Similarly, Donalds and Osei-Bryson's taxonomy as well as Barn and Barn's ontology do not capture *Vulnerabilities* that may have been exploited in the *Attack_Event* nor do the schemes differentiate between *Victim* and *Complainant*. On the other hand, by comparison our CCO is able to comprehensively classify *LulzSecAssociateIndicted*.

12.6.3 Evaluating Our CCO

To evaluate our CCO, as per the recommendation of Peffers et al. (2007), we compare the solution objectives with results of the artefact demonstration, shown in Tables 12.2, 12.3 and 12.4.

Table 12.2 Classifying EmailHacked_NudePhotosUploaded Using Previously Proposed Classification Schemes and Our Proposed CCO

KJAERLAND

Name	Source Sectors	MO	Impact	Target Sectors
EmailHacked_NudePhotosUploaded		Social Engineering	Disrupt Disclosure	

SIMMONS ET AL

Name	Attack Vector	Operational Impact	Defence	Informational Impact	Target
EmailHacked_ NudePhotosUploaded	Social Engineering			Disrupt Disclosure	Email Server

APPLEGATE & STAVROU

Name	Vector	Informational Impact	Operational Impact	Systems Impact	Defence	Actors
EmailHacked_ NudePhotosUploaded	Social Engineering	Deny Disclose				Ronald Oates Denyque Bianca Bartley

DONALDS & OSEI-BRYSON

Name	Victim	Attacker	Attacker: Category	Objective	Tool & Tactic	Impact	Result	Relationship	Target	Offence
EmailHacked_ NudePhotos Uploaded	Denyque Bianca Bartley	Ronald Oates	Black Hat Hacker_ Professional_ Elite	Financial Gain	Social Engineering	Loss of access	Negative Publicity Shame Reputational Damage	External	Denyque Bianca Bartley	Unauthorized Obstruction Unauthorized Access Unlawfully making available data for the commission of an offence

BARN & BARN

Name	Action	Agent: Individual Agent	Contact	External Observer	Impact: Psychological	Location: Cyberspace	Motivation: Extrinsic	Social Engineering Act	Target: Target Individual	Technology Role	Viewpoint
EmailHacked_ NudePhotos Uploaded	Cybercrime	Ronald Oates	Cyberspace		Negative Publicity Shame Reputational Damage		Financial Gain	Yes	Denyque Bianca Bartley	Enabler	

(Continued)

Table 12.2 (Continued)

				Our CCO					
Attack_Event	*Location (Attack_Event)*	*Objective*	*Impact: Psychological*	*Target*	*Complainant*	*Complainant: Complainant Type*	*Victim*	*Victim: Victim Type*	*Victim: Victim Market Sector*
EmailHacked_NudePhotos Uploaded	Kingston	Financial Gain	Negative Publicity Shame Reputational Damage	Denyque	Denyque	Individual Complainant	Denyque	Individual Victim	Entertainment
				Bianca Bartley	Bianca Bartley	Individual Complainant	Bianca Bartley	Individual Victim	Self Employed

Attacker	*Attacker: Classification*	*Attacker: Aggressor*	*Offence*	*Tool and Technique*	*Vulnerability*
Ronald Oates	Black Hat Hacker_Professional_Elite	Self-Instigator	Unauthorized Obstruction Unauthorized Access Unlawfully making available data for the commission of an offence	Social Engineering	

Note: **Class: Subclass** Details of Attack_Event 2 – LulzSec Associate Indicted – and its classification in Protégé OWL.

LulzSec Associate Indicted (Arthur, 2013; Romero, 2012; The FBI, 2012):

On June 12, 2012 a Los Angeles (USA) federal grand jury indicted Ryan Cleary, a 20-year-old resident and citizen of the United Kingdom, with one count of conspiracy and two counts of the unauthorized impairment of protected computers. The indictment alleges that Cleary and other co-conspirators used a botnet to launch DDoS attacks on several entities as well as hacked into several businesses to steal data. The indictment further alleges that Cleary would even rent out his botnet to fellow hackers so they could use them to coordinate their own attacks. According to the indictment Cleary targeted Fox, where he went after the information of people who wanted to audition for The X-Factor; PBS, which saw its News Hour show site defaced; and, hacked Sony Pictures' website to steal sensitive personal data including emails, online passwords and credit card details of users registered there. According to federal investigators, Cleary and his co-conspirators then published information he got from Fox and Sony on a lulzsecurity.com site he helped set up.

It is alleged that Cleary is an associate of the hacking group LulzSec, a known affiliate of the international hacking group Anonymous. According to The Guardian, the intention of Cleary and his co-conspirators was to gain attention, embarrass website owners and ridicule security measures.

Figure 12.6   Excerpt for Attack_Event 2: LulzSecAssociate indicted

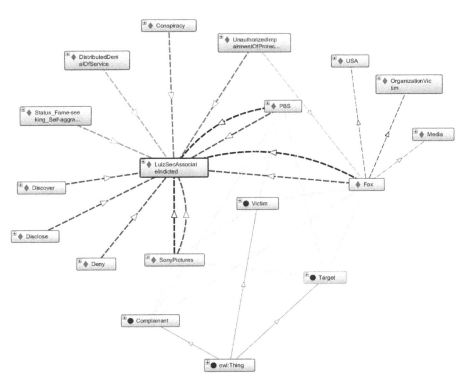

Figure 12.7   The LulzSecAssociate indicted Attack_Event perspective and some associated relationships

Table 12.3 Classifying LulzSecAssociateIndicted Using Previously Proposed Classification Schemes and Our Proposed CCO

KJAERLAND

Name	Source Sectors	MO	Impact	Target Sectors
LulzSecAssociateIndicted		DDoS	Disrupt Disclosure	COM

SIMMONS ET AL

Name	Attack Vector	Operational Impact	Defence	InformationalImpact	Target
LulzSecAssociateIndicted	Design Flaws	DDoS		Disrupt Disclosure	Network

APPLEGATE & STAVROU

Name	Vector	Informational Impact	Operational Impact	Systems Impact	Defence	Actors
LulzSecAssociateIndicted	Technology	Deny Discover Disclose	Organizational Disruption	Denial of Service		Ryan Cleary Fox PBS Sony Pictures

DONALDS & OSEI-BRYSON

Name	Victim	Attacker	Attacker: Category	Objective	Tool & Tactic	Impact	Result	Relationship	Target	Offence
LulzSecAssociateIndicted	Fox PBS Sony Pictures	Ryan Cleary	Cyber-punks_ Coders_ Writers	Status_ FameSee-king_ SelfAggran-dizement	Attack Vector	Organizational Disruption	Financial loss Reputational Damage	External	Fox PBS Sony Pictures	Conspiracy Unauthorized Impairment of Protected Computers

BARN & BARN

Name	Action	Agent: Individual Agent	Contact	External Observer	Location: Cyberspace	Impact: Economic	Motivation: Extrinsic	Social Engineering Act	Target: Organization	Technology Role	Viewpoint
LulzSecAssociateIndicted	Cybercrime	Ryan Cleary	Cyberspace	Cyberspace		Financial Loss	Mischief		Fox PBS Sony Pictures	Contingent	

(Continued)

Table 12.3 (Continued)

					Our CCO					
Attack_Event	Location (Attack_ Event)	Objective	Impact: Operational	Impact: Informational	Target	Complainant	Complainant: Complainant Type	Victim	Victim: Victim Type	Victim: Victim Market Sector
LulzSec AssociateIndicted	USA	Status_ FameSeeking_ SelfAggran- dizement	Organizational Disruption	Deny Discover Disclose	Fox PBS Sony Pictures	Fox PBS Sony Pictures	Organizational Complainant	Fox PBS Sony Pictures	Organizational Victim	Media
Attacker	**Attacker:** *Classification*			**Attacker:** *Aggressor*		**Offence**		**Tool and Technique:***Attack Vector*		**Vulnerability**
Ryan Cleary		Cyber-punks_Coders_Writers		Individual Aggressor		Conspiracy Unauthorized Impairment of Protected Computers		DDoS		Design Vulnerability

Note: **Class: *Subclass***

Table 12.4   Evaluation of Our Artefact – Comparing the Solution Objectives with Our Artefact's Demonstration Results

Solution Objective	Artefact Demonstration Result
An explicit, shared conceptualization of cybercrimes classification for use by crime stakeholders	In developing our artefact, potential cybercrime classification characteristics and relationships were identified by police practitioners and researchers, representing a shared conceptualization of cybercrime classification. Since an ontology is a formal explicit specification of characteristics/ concepts in a domain and the relationships that hold among them, our artefact then is an explicit, shared conceptualization of cybercrime classification.
A more comprehensive and holistic artefact that incorporates multiple cybercrime perspectives	Since our artefact consists of a more extensive set of cybercrime classification characteristics than prior works, and same successfully and accurately classified an *Attack_Event*, we argue that our artefact is more comprehensive and holistic. In fact, the results from sub-Section 6.2, Classifying and storing two real-world cyberattack events, support our claim.
A flexible artefact, better able to classify current and future *Attack_Events*	We use the characteristic structure design approach when developing our artefact. This permits the characterizing/classifying of any *Attack_Event* without regard for changing conditions and evolving technology, thus, is not easily outdated. Further, our artefact can easily and tidily classify blended *Attack_Events*, a limitation of some previously proposed classification schemes.
A formal CCO that could allow cybercrime agents (human or artificial) to share knowledge	An ontology facilitates knowledge sharing between human and artificial agents by providing a consensual and formal conceptualization of a given domain. *Formal* refers to the fact that an ontology should be machine-readable. Our artefact: (1) consists of a set of consensual characteristics that describe the cybercrime classification domain; (2) specify the semantics of the domain in terms of the conceptual relationships between characteristics; and (3) is formal, since it is implemented in Protégé OWL.

(Continued)

Table 12.4 (Continued)

Solution Objective	Artefact Demonstration Result
An extensible artefact that can easily accommodate new concepts and potential new relationships	As above, our artefact's design is based on the characteristic structure design approach, which classifies properties about the **Attack_Event** and not the actual **Attack_Event** itself. Characteristic structure is analogous to the nucleotides of deoxyribonucleic acid (DNA) in that one or more of the characteristics of the **Attack_Event** can be linked together to describe the item that is being placed in a ontology. Thus, our artefact is extensible; new characteristics and potential new relationships are easily incorporated.

12.7 Conclusion and Future Work

It is anticipated that cyber **Attack_Events** will become more prevalent in the future, thus every contribution towards improving our understanding of **Attack_Events** is critical. In this chapter, we present a knowledge-based artefact for classifying **Attack_Events**. Our CCO provides an explicit, formal specification of a shared conceptualization of cybercrime classification. We propose that any **Attack_Event**, known or new, can be successfully classified using these characteristics: **Attacker**, **Vulnerability**, **Tool_and_Technique**, **Objective**, **Offence**, **Location**, **Complainant**, **Target**, **Victim** and **Impact**.

While prior works have proposed classification schemes, our work offers improvement in several key areas, including: (1) it is flexible and extensible; (2) it offers a more robust classification scheme; (3) it effectively illustrates complex interactions between the ontological characteristics via associations that formally describe their relationships; and (4) because our artefact is ontological, it supports inferencing of new knowledge relating to cybercrime classification.

We have successfully demonstrated how our CCO can be used to classify and store two real-world **Attack_Events**. Our demonstration shows that all previously proposed classification schemes are able to classify cybercrimes but the classifications are incomplete. That is, they do not capture all pertinent information required to completely and effectively classify cybercrimes, however, ours do. Further, we show that given the same pair of concepts in our classification model and another study's model, ours is able to answer queries relating to the concepts, yet, the others could not.

While we have designed a more robust cybercrime classification scheme, there are several issues that should be addressed in future research including:

- ■ The veracity of our artefact could be further validated by classifying additional cases of **Attack_Events**, of different types. For instance, **Attack_Events** involving groups as well as those exploiting vulnerabilities could be classified.

- Also while we have applied the guideline of the DSRM to evaluate our arte-fact, it would be useful to conduct a more robust evaluation that involves implementing a prototype in a police organization for use by its CSIRT to classify reported cyber *Attack_Events.*
- Further evaluation might also involve other researchers using measures such as those discussed in Maes and Poels (2006) and Rao and Osei-Bryson (2007) to assess stakeholders' perceptions of the quality of the CCO; such studies could be done in various organizational settings.
- The use of text mining and artificial intelligence technologies for automatic or semi-automatic instantiation of the contents of our CCO ontology as well as enrichment of our CCO ontology using news reports and other data (e.g. social media data) could also be explored by other researchers since various ontology population and enrichment methods have for some time been sug-gested (Richard Gil & Martin-Bautista, 2014; Petasis et al., 2011).

Our work has implications for both research and practice. Our work can facilitate effective collaboration and meaningful discussions between scholars and practitio-ners of the domain since consensual definitions provide a common language; an agreed-upon classification scheme can improve cross-jurisdictional cooperation, information sharing and support the prosecution process of cyber criminals; assist law enforcement to investigate, fight and prevent cybercrimes by improving their understanding of the different aspects of cybercrime; and, disaggregating *Attack_Events* can invoke different policy responses, thereby, assisting policy makers to develop appropriate cyber policies and legal responses. Our ontology then should prove to be a more useful tool for cybercrime stakeholders.

Acknowledgement

The material in this chapter previously appeared in Donalds, C., & Osei-Bryson, K. M. (2019). Towards a cybercrime classification ontology: A knowledge-based approach. *Computers in Human Behavior*, *92*, 403–418. doi:https://doi.org/10.1016/j.chb.2018.11.039

References

Accenture. (2017). *2017 Cost of Cyber Crime Study*, 54. Retrieved from https://www.accen-ture.com/t20170926T072837Z__w__/us-en/_acnmedia/PDF-61/Accenture-2017-CostCyberCrimeStudy.pdf Accessed January 7, 2018.
Alkaabi, A., Mohay, G. M., McCullagh, A. J., & Chantler, A. N. (2010, October 4–6). Dealing with the Problem of Cybercrime. *Paper presented at the 2nd International ICST Conference on Digital Forensics & Cyber Crime*, Abu Dhabi, United Arab Emirates.

Applegate, S. D., & Stavrou, A. (2013, June 4–7). Towards a Cyber Conflict Taxonomy. *Paper presented at the 5th International Conference on Cyber Conflict*, Tallinn, Estonia.

Arthur, C. (2013). LulzSec: What they did, who they were and how they were caught. *The Guardian*. Retrieved from https://www.theguardian.com/technology/2013/may/16/lulzsec-hacking-fbi-jail Accessed April 9, 2017.

Barn, R., & Barn, B. (2016, June 12–15). An Ontological Representation of A Taxonomy for Cybercrime. *Paper presented at the 24th European Conference on Information Systems (ECIS)*, İstanbul, Turkey.

Bernaras, A., Laresgoiti, I., & Corera, J. M. (1996, August 11–16). Building and Reusing Ontologies for Electrical Network Applications. *Paper presented at the European Conference on Artificial Intelligence (ECAI)*, Budapest, Hungary.

Blythe, J. M., & Coventry, L. (2018). Costly but effective: Comparing the factors that influence employee anti-malware behaviours. *Computers in Human Behavior, 87*, 87–97.

Bureau of Justice Assistance. (2005). *Intelligence-Led Policing: The New Intelligence Architecture 52*. Retrieved from https://www.ncjrs.gov/pdffiles1/bja/210681.pdf Accessed March 22, 2017.

Chang, W., & Chung, P. (2014, May 13). Knowledge Management in Cybercrime Investigation – A Case Study of Identifying Cybercrime Investigation Knowledge in Taiwan. *Paper presented at the Pacific-Asia Workshop on Intelligence and Security Informatics*, Tainan, Taiwan.

Château, S. D., Boulanger, D., & Mercier-Laurent, E. (2012). Managing the domain knowledge: Application to cultural patrimony. *Knowledge Management Research & Practice, 10*(4), 312–325.

Chen, H., Schroeder, J., Hauck, R. V., Ridgeway, L., Atabakhsh, H., Gupta, H., ... Clements, A. W. (2002). COPLINK connect: Information and knowledge management for law enforcement. *Decision Support Systems, 34*, 271–285.

Choo, K.-K. R. (2008). Organised crime groups in cyberspace: A typology. *Trends in Organized Crime, 11*(3), 270–295.

Choo, K.-K. R. (2011). The cyber threat landscape: Challenges and future research directions. *Computers & Security, 30*(8), 719–731.

Council of Europe. (2001). *Convention on Cybercrime*. Retrieved from http://conventions.coe.int/Treaty/en/Treaties/Html/185.htm

Donalds, C., & Osei-Bryson, K.-M. (2012, December 16). The Construction of A Domain Ontology for Criminal Investigation: The Case of the Jamaican Constabulary Force. *Paper presented at the SIG ICT in Global Development, 5th Annual Pre-ICIS Workshop*, Orlando, USA.

Donalds, C., & Osei-Bryson, K.-M. (2014, May 21-23). A Cybercrime Taxonomy: Case of the Jamaican Jurisdiction. *Paper presented at the CONF-IRM 2014 Proceedings*. (p. 5), Ho Chi Minh City, Vietnam.

Dwoskin, E., & Adam, K. (2017, May 14). More than 150 countries affected by massive cyberattack, Europol says. *The Washington Post*. Retrieved from https://www.washingtonpost.com/business/economy/more-than-150-countries-affected-by-massive-cyber-attack-europol-says/2017/05/14/5091465e-3899-11e7-9e48-c4f199710b69_story.html?utm_term=.08d45056d139

Dzemydiene, D., & Kazemikaitiene, E. (2005). Ontology-Based Decision Support System for Crime Investigation Processes. In O. Vasilecas, W. Wojtkowski, J. Zupančič, A. Caplinskas, W. Wojtkowski, & S. Wrycza (Eds.), *Information Systems Development: Advances in Theory, Practice, and Education* (pp. 427–438). US: Springer.

Eck, J. E., Spelman, W., Police Executive Research Forum, & National Institute of Justice. (1987). *Problem-solving: Problem-oriented Policing in Newport News*. Washington DC, US: U.S. Department of Justice, National Institute of Justice. p. 136.

Furnell, S. M. (2001, November 29-30). The Problem of Categorising Cybercrime and Cybercriminals. *Paper presented at the 2nd Australian Information Warfare and Security Conference*, Perth, Australia.

Furnell, S. M. (2002). *Cybercrime: Vandalizing the information society*. London: Addison Wesley.

Garbacz, P., Kulicki, P., & Trypuz, R. (2012). A formal ontology of knowing and knowledge. *Knowledge Management Research & Practice, 10*(3), 206–222.

Gil, R., & Martin-Bautista, M. J. (2014). SMOL: A systemic methodology for ontology learning from heterogeneous sources. *Journal of Intelligent Information Systems, 42*(3), 415–455. doi:10.1007/s10844-013-0296-x

Gil, R., Virgili-Gomá, J., García, R., & Mason, C. (2015). Emotions ontology for collaborative modelling and learning of emotional responses. *Computers in Human Behavior, 51*, 610–617.

Gordon, S., & Ford, R. (2006). On the definition and classification of cybercrime. *Journal in Computer Virology, 2*(1), 13–20.

Gottschalk, P. (2007). *Knowledge Management in Law Enforcement: Technologies and Techniques*. Hershey, PA, USA: Idea Group Publishing.

Government of Jamaica. (2014). *A New Approach: National Security Policy for Jamaica*. Government of Jamaica Cabinet Office. Retrieved from http://www.cabinet.gov.jm/ files/NATSEC%20March%2025%202014%20%281%29%20%281%29.pdf.

Gregor, S., & Hevner, A. R. (2013). Positioning and presenting design science research for maximum impact. *MIS Quarterly, 37*(2), 337–355.

Gruber, T. R. (1995). Toward principles for the design of ontologies used for knowledge sharing? *International Journal of Human-Computer Studies, 45*(5–6), 907–928.

Guarino, N., & Giaretta, P. (1995). Ontologies and Knowledge Bases: Towards a Terminological Clarification. In N. J. I. Mars (Ed.), *Toward Very Large Knowledge Bases: Knowledge Building and Knowledge Sharing* (pp. 25–32). Amsterdam: IOS Press.

Gultekin, K. (2009). *Knowledge Management and Law Enforcement: An Examination of Knowledge Management Strategies of the Police Information System (POLNET) in the Turkish National Police*. Denton, USA: (PhD), University of North Texas, University of North Texas Libraries, Digital Library. Retrieved from digital.library.unt.edu/ ark:/67531/metadc11040

Hansman, S., & Hunt, R. (2005). A taxonomy of network and computer attacks. *Computers & Security, 24*(1), 31–43.

Hevner, A. R., March, S. T., & Park, J. (2004). Design science in information systems research. *MIS Quarterly, 28*(1), 75–105.

Holgersson, S., & Gottschalk, P. (2008). Police officers' professional knowledge. *Police Practice and Research, 9*(5), 365–377. doi:10.1080/15614260801980802

Howard, J. D. (1997). *An Analysis of Security Incidents On The Internet 1989–1995*. Pittsburg, Pennslyvania: (Doctor of Philosophy), Carnegie Melon. Retrieved from http://www. cert.org/archive/pdf/JHThesis.pdf

IALEIA. (2004). *Law Enforcement Analytic Standards*. Retrieved from https://www.scribd. com/document/63790140/Law-Enforcement-Analytic-Standards.

International Telecommunication Union. (2011). *Understanding Cybercrime: A Guide for Developing Countries*, 493. Retrieved from https://www.itu.int/ITU-D/cyb/cybersecurity/docs/ITU_Guide_A5_12072011.pdf. Accessed November 16, 2013.

Jamaica Houses of Parliament. (2015). *The Cybercrimes Act, 2015 (Act No.31 of 2015)*. Retrieved from www.japarliament.gov.jm/attachments/article/341/The%20Cybercrimes%20Act,%202015-final%20No.31.pdf.

Jamaica Information Service. (2012, September 3). *COPS Make Major Breakthrough in Cybercrime*. Retrieved from http://jis.gov.jm/cops-make-major-breakthrough-in-cybercrime/

Kharbat, F., & El-Ghalayini, H. (2008). Building Ontology from Knowledge Base Systems. In E. G. Giannopoulou (Ed.), *Data Mining in Medical and Biological Research* (p. 320). Vienna, Austria: InTech.

Kjaerland, M. (2005). A taxonomy and comparison of computer security incidents from the commercial and government sectors. *Computers and Security, 25*(7), 522–538.

Labib, A. E., Canós, J. H., & Penadés, M. C. (2017). On the way to learning style models integration: A learner's characteristics ontology. *Computers in Human Behavior, 73*, 433–445.

Laudon, K. C., & Laudon, J. P. (2002). *Essentials of Management Information Systems* (5th ed.). New Jersey: Prentice Hall.

Luen, T. W., & Al-Hawamdeh, S. (2001). Knowledge management in the public sector: Principle and practices in police work. *Journal of Information Science, 27*(5), 311–318.

Maes, A., & Poels, G. (2006, November 6-9). Evaluating Quality of Conceptual Models Based on User Perceptions. *Paper presented at the 25ʰ International Conference on Conceptual Modeling*, Berlin, Heidelberg.

McAfee Labs. (2017). *McAfee Labs Threat Report, September 2017* (3525_0917_rp-threats-sept). Retrieved from https://www.mcafee.com/enterprise/en-us/assets/reports/rp-quarterly-threats-sept-2017.pdf

Ministry of National Securiy. (2008). *A New Era of Policing in Jamaica: Transforming the JCF*. Retrieved from http://lib.ohchr.org/HRBodies/UPR/Documents/Session9/JM/JFJ_Jamaicansforjustice_Annex4.pdf.

Miranda, S., Orciuoli, F., & Sampson, D. G. (2016). A SKOS-based framework for subject ontologies to improve learning experiences. *Computers in Human Behavior, 61*, 609–621.

Moitra, S. D. (2004). Cybercrime: Towards an assessment of its nature and impact. *International Journal of Comparative and Applied Criminal Justice, 28*(2), 105–123.

Ngafeeson, M. (2010, March 3–6). Cybercrime Classification: A Motivational Model. *Paper presented at the 2010 Southwest Decision Sciences Institute Conference*, Dallas, Texas.

Ngo, F., & Jaishankar, K. (2017). Commemorating a decade in existence of the international journal of cyber criminology: A research agenda to advance the scholarship on cyber crime. *International Journal of Cyber Criminology, 11*(1), 1–9.

Organization of American States. (2014). *Latin America + Caribbean Cyber Security Trends*. Retrieved from http://www.symantec.com/content/en/us/enterprise/other_resources/b-cyber-security-trends-report-lamc.pdf Accessed February 17, 2015.

Peffers, K., Tuunanen, T., & Niehaves, B. (2018). Design science research genres: Introduction to the special issue on exemplars and criteria for applicable design science research. *European Journal of Information Systems, 27*(2), 129–139. doi:10.1080/0960085X.2018.1458066

Peffers, K., Tuunanen, T., Rothenberger, M. A., & Chatterjee, S. (2007). A Design Science Research Methodology for information systems research. *Journal of Management Information Systems, 24*(3), 45–77.

Petasis, G., Karkaletsis, V., Paliouras, G., Krithara, A., & Zavitsanos, E. (2011). Ontology Population and Enrichment: State of the Art. In G. Paliouras, C. D. Spyropoulos, & G. Tsatsaronis (Eds.), *Knowledge-Driven Multimedia Information Extraction and Ontology Evolution: Bridging the Semantic Gap* (pp. 134–166). Berlin, Heidelberg: Springer Berlin Heidelberg.

Planning Research & Development Branch. (2016). *Jamaica Constabulary Force Annual Report 2015*. ISSUU Retrieved from https://issuu.com/jamaicaconstabularyforce2015/docs/annual_report_final_2015.

Rao, L., & Osei-Bryson, K. M. (2007). Towards defining dimensions of knowledge systems quality. *Expert Systems with Applications, 33*(2), 368–378.

Ratcliffe, J. (2008). Knowledge Management Challenges in the Development of Intelligence-Led Policing. In T. Williamson (Ed.), *The Handbook of Knowledge-Based Policing: Current Conceptions and Future Directions*. (pp. 205–220). Chichester, UK: John Wiley & Sons, Ltd.

Romero, D. (2012, June 13). Ryan cleary indicted in L.A. For alleged LulzSec hacking of X-factor, sony, PBS. *L.A. Weekly*. Retrieved from https://www.laweekly.com/news/alex-villanueva-looks-to-become-first-democratic-sheriff-in-138-years-9903623

Ruiz-Martínez, J. M., Miñarro-Giménez, J. A., & Martínez-Béjar, R. (2016). An ontological model for managing professional expertise. *Knowledge Management Research & Practice, 14*(3), 390–400.

Simmonds, A., Sandilands, P., & van Ekert, L. (2004, October 29–31). An Ontology for Network Security Attacks. *Paper presented at the Asian Applied Computing Conference, AACC*, Kathmandu, Nepal.

Simmons, C., Ellis, C., Shiva, S., Dasgupta, D., & Wu, Q. (2009). *AVOIDIT: A Cyber Attack Taxonomy* (CS-09-003). Retrieved from http://citeseerx.ist.psu.edu/viewdoc/download?doi=10.1.1.372.4700&rep=rep1&type=pdf

Simon, H. (1996). *The Sciences of Artificial* (3rd edn.). Cambridge, MA: MIT Press.

Smith, R. G., Grabosky, P. N., & Urbas, G. F. (2004). *Cyber Criminals on Trial*. Cambridge, UK: Cambridge University Press.

Stabek, A., Brown, S., & Watters, P. A. (2009, July 7-9). The Case for a Consistent Cyberscam Classification Framework (CCCF). *Paper presented at the UIC-ATC'09. Symposia and Workshops on Ubiquitous, Autonomic and Trusted Computing*, Brisbane, Australia.

The Federal Bureau of Investigation. (2012). *Associate of Hacking Group LulzSec Indicted for Conspiracy to Conduct Cyber Attacks* Retrieved from https://archives.fbi.gov/archives/losangeles/press-releases/2012/associate-of-hacking-group-lulzsec-indicted-for-conspiracy-to-conduct-cyber-attacks Accessed July 29, 2013.

The Gleaner. (2012, September 5). Denyque praises cops on porn hacker case. *The Gleaner*. Retrieved from http://jamaica-gleaner.com/gleaner/20120905/lead/lead6.html

Trend Micro. (2017, March 10, 2018). *Paradigm Shifts: Trend Micro Security Predictions for 2018*. Retrieved from https://documents.trendmicro.com/assets/rpt/rpt-paradigm-shifts.pdf

United Nations. (2005). Report of the Eleventh United Nations Congress on Crime Prevention and Criminal Justice, 97. Retrieved from https://www.unodc.org/documents/congress/Documentation/11Congress/ACONF203_18_e_V0584409.pdf Accessed June 19, 2017.

United States Computer Emergency Readiness Team. (2017, May 19, 2017). *Alert (TA17-132A): Indicators Associated With WannaCry Ransomware*. Retrieved from https://www.us-cert.gov/ncas/alerts/TA17-132A

van Herdeen, R., Irwin, B., Burke, I. D., & Leenen, L. (2012). A computer network attack taxonomy and ontology. *International Journal of Cyber Warfare and Terrorism, 2*(3), 12–25.

Wall, D. S. (2005). The Internet as a Conduit for Criminal Activity. In A. Pattavina (Ed.), *Information Technology and the Criminal Justice System*. (pp. 77–98). USA: Sage Publications.

Wang, W., Guo, W., Luo, Y., Wang, X., & Xu, Z. (2005, September 14–16). The Study and Application of Crime Emergency Ontology Event Model. In R. Khosla, R. J. Howlett, & L. C. Jain (Eds.), *Knowledge-Based Intelligent Information and Engineering Systems: 9th International Conference, KES 2005, Melbourne, Australia, September 14-16, 2005, Proceedings, Part IV* (pp. 806–812). Berlin, Heidelberg: Springer Berlin Heidelberg.

Chapter 13

An Integrated Framework for Developing and Implementing a National Cybersecurity Strategy for Global South Countries

13.1 Introduction

It is established and accepted that information and communication technologies (ICTs) are ubiquitous, permeating every aspect of human life. ICTs have been playing salient roles in businesses, education, entertainment, and socialization, even more so during the COVID-19 pandemic. In fact, the United Nations (UN), on its website, in elaborating one of its sustainable development goals 'SDG 9: Build resilient infrastructure, promote sustainable industrialization and foster innovation', reports that the pandemic 'has accelerated the digitalization of many businesses and services, including teleworking and video conferencing systems in and out of the workplace, as well as access to healthcare, education and essential goods and services' (https://www.un.org/sustainabledevelopment/infrastructure-industrialization/). However, the use of ICTs is not without peril; private, public and government agencies are often confronted by ever-increasing and more sophisticated cyberse-curity (CS) attacks that often challenge the confidentiality, integrity and availabil-ity of their ICT systems and infrastructures. Therefore, the transformational power of ICT as a catalyst for socio-economic development, and as espoused in some Caribbean countries (such as Jamaica and Barbados) National Development Plans (e.g. Planning Institute of Jamaica, 2009; Research and Planning Institute, 2005), may not be realized, due in part to CS incidents.

To fully realize the potential of ICTs, according to the International Telecommunication Union (ITU) and other intergovernmental organizations (IGOs), entities must align their national economic objectives and their national security priorities (ITU, The World Bank, Commonwealth Secretariat (ComSec), Commonwealth Telecommunications Organisation (CTO), & NATO Cooperative Cyber Defence Centre of Excellence (NATO CCD COE), 2018). The argument is that if countries do not balance CS risks with comprehensive national CS strategies, it is unlikely that they will achieve the socio-economic growth and development and the national security goals they seek.

In fact, it is reported that entities in the Latin America and the Caribbean (LAC) region and in other developing state's jurisdictions are not immune to CS challenges. According to the Inter-American Development Bank (IDB) and the Organisation of American States (OAS), cyberattacks in the LAC region are increasing, especially targeting financial institutions (IDB & OAS, 2020). Statistica reports that in the first half of 2020 the LAC region recorded the world's highest cyberattack rates relative to the global average; specifically, mobile browser attacks exceeded 8% while the global average was 2.4%, the desktop attack rate surpassed a 6% rate against an average of 1.7% in the world (Statista Research Department, 2021).

The trade press also reports some cyber incidents in the LAC region however, incidents in the region are generally underreported (GLACY+, 2019). Examples of reported cyber incidents in the region include the theft of US$150 million from the Bank of Nova Scotia in 2014; the hacking of Caribbean government websites in 2015; tax authorities' systems were infected with malware, preventing legitimate users from accessing their accounts and money demanded from them to regain access; a security breach of Jamaica National Group (a large financial institution in Jamaica) by way of a cyberattack, which resulted in members' and customers' data being stolen and disruptions in operations for weeks; a ransomware attack on ANSA McAl in Barbados and Trinidad and Tobago, which resulted in the shut-down of Tatil and Tatil Life's information technology (IT) systems; and the breach of the Jam-COVID web portal, which exposed local and international travellers' personal and travel data (Caricom Caribbean Community, 2016; Newsday, 2020; The Gleaner, 2020, 2021a, 2021b). Belize also reports a significant increase in cybercrimes; a massive 50% over the five-year period 2013–2018 (Government of Belize, 2020). Elsewhere, in other developing jurisdictions, there are reports of a continued spike in cyber threat events. For instance, the National Kenyan CIRT report that it detected a staggering 56,206,097 in cyber threat events during the fourth quarter alone (October–December) of 2020; with approximately 82% of the total threat events accounting for malware threat events, 4% distributed denial of service (DDoS)/Botnet threat events, approximately 14% Web application attack events and the remaining percentage attributable to system vulnerabilities (Communications Authority of Kenya, 2021).

Despite these reported and other unreported incidents, governments in the LAC region are not adequately prepared to handle these attacks. The IDB and OAS report that the region possesses limited ability to identify and respond to attacks as, out of the 32 countries in the region, only 20 countries have established Cyber Incident Response Teams (CIRTs/CSITRs/CERTs), 22 countries are considered to have very low capacities to investigate and prosecute cybercrimes, one-third of the counties do not have a legal framework to deal with cybercrimes and only 5 have ratified the Budapest Convention, the leading framework for international cooperation in dealing with cybercrimes (IDB & OAS, 2020).

It is proposed that GS countries such as those in the LAC region develop and implement national CS strategies (NCSSs) which establish government priorities and policies as a response to potential CS threats to national and individual security. According to the ITU et al. (2018), a NCSS can help nations in the fight against cybercrimes as it can improve the protection of the country's digital infrastructure and ultimately contribute to its broader socio-economic aspirations, when implemented. The goal of the NCSS is the alignment of the whole government efforts to achieve or improve CS (Newmeyer, 2015) and to provide a clear indication of the country's intent with regard CS to other countries and interested parties (Luiijf, Besseling, & Graaf, 2013). However, many countries in the Global South (GS) do not have critical infrastructure plans nor approved national CS strategies. The IDB and OAS (2020) report that in the LAC region only 7 countries have critical infrastructure (CI) plans and 12 have approved national cybersecurity strategies. These statistics highlight the low rate of adoption of NCSSs in the LAC region, for instance.

A NCSS is regarded as a tool to improve the security and resilience of national infrastructures and services (ENISA, 2012). It is also described as a government's vision, principles and priorities that guide it in addressing CS; it typically includes the steps, programmes and initiatives that should be put in place, the resources required for those efforts as well as how the resources could be used (adapted from the ITU et al., 2018). Further, a NCSS should reflect the unique national interests of the country contextualized to the global cyber environment. Ron, Ninahualpa, Molina, and Diaz (2020) note that the NCSS should be a useful, flexible and easy-to-use framework which takes into account the cultural and social-economic contexts of the country as well as its current situation with CS.

In this chapter, we propose a NCSS framework for consideration by developing or GS countries. This framework aims to provide a useful and practical guide for policy-makers in formulating and implementing their national cybersecurity strategies to protect the confidentiality, integrity, availability and improve the resilience of IT infrastructure and systems. In subsequent sections, some proposed best practice NCSS development guides and as well as previously published NCSS guides by GS countries are reviewed. The subsequent two sections present the proposed framework for developing a NCSS and a Cybersecurity Strategy (CSS) Implementation framework, respectively. The chapter ends with a Conclusion section.

13.2 Select National Cybersecurity Strategy Development Guides

In this section, we focus on some proposed practice guides for developing CS strategies by international agencies and IGOs such as the National Institute of Standards and Technology (NIST), the International Organization for Standardization and the International Electrotechnical Commission (ISO/IEC), ITU, and The European Union Agency for Network and Information Security (ENISA). The aim of this section is to highlight what international bodies propose as strategic areas to be considered for the successful development of a NCSS.

13.2.1 NIST Framework for Improving Critical Infrastructure Cybersecurity

The NIST critical infrastructure (CI) CS framework (NIST, 2018) utilizes a risk-based approach to improve the management of or to reduce CS risks to stated security and other related objectives. The Framework proposes a set of best practices, standards and recommendations that when adopted, should help entities improve their cybersecurity measures. The NIST Framework is based on a collaborative model to include input from industry, academia and government. According to the developers of the Framework, it provides a common taxonomy and mechanism for entities to: describe their current cybersecurity posture; describe their target state for cybersecurity; identify and prioritize opportunities for improvement within the context of a continuous and repeatable process; assess progress towards the target state; and communicate among internal and external stakeholders about cybersecurity risk (NIST, 2018). The Framework proposes a set of activities across five key functions that entities should focus on to improve cybersecurity or when building a cybersecurity strategy. The Functions provide a high-level, strategic view of the lifecycle of an entity's management of cybersecurity risk. The following briefly describes the five key functions:

    i. **Identify**: This function is considered foundational for an effective CS strategy and aims to help an entity develop an understanding to manage CS risk to systems, people, assets, data and capabilities. Activities include risk assessment, inventorying IT assets and formulation of a risk management strategy. The idea is that by identifying risks and documenting where sensitive data are stored, appropriate controls can be implemented to protect the most valuable data and critical processes.

ii. **Protect**: This function involves both human, technological and process solutions to ensure the entity's data protection and continued service delivery. Activities are geared towards supporting the ability to limit or contain the impact of a potential cybersecurity event and include user awareness training, access controls, information protection processes and procedures, maintenance and the implementation of protective technological solutions such as intrusion detection systems, malware and antivirus software.

iii. **Detect**: This function includes the implementation of appropriate activities to identify the timely occurrence of a cybersecurity event such as continuous monitoring and review of anomalies and events.

iv. **Respond**: This function includes controls that ensure that the entity has the ability to quickly and efficiently contain/respond to a CS incident and include activities such as response planning and communication strategy.

v. **Recover**: This function includes controls to support the timely recovery to normal operations to reduce the impact from a cybersecurity incident. Some activities to achieve the stated objective include testing recovery processes, recover planning and improvement.

In addition to these five core functions, the Framework identifies 'Tiers', which provide context on how an entity views CS risks and the processes in place to manage those risks. Ranging from Partial (Tier 1) to Adaptive (Tier 4), Tiers describe an increasing degree of rigor and sophistication in cybersecurity risk management practices. Tiers help determine the extent to which cybersecurity risk management is informed by business needs and is integrated into an entity's overall risk management practices.

13.2.2 ISO/IEC 27110: 2021 Standard

Recognizing that business groups, government agencies and other organizations produce documents and tools called CS frameworks to help them organize and communicate cybersecurity activities of organizations, which are often diverse and varied, the ISO (the International Organization for Standardization) and IEC (the International Electrotechnical Commission) created the ISO/IEC TS 27110: 2021, to harmonize the different lexicons and conceptual structures existing in the various CS frameworks. Moreover, according to the ISO/IEC, the goal of the ISO/IEC TS 27110: 2021 is to ensure a minimum set of concepts are used to define cybersecurity frameworks across entities and to help ease the burden of cybersecurity framework creators and cybersecurity framework users (ISO/IEC, 2021). The ISO/IEC TS 27110: 2021 lists the minimum set of concepts a CS framework should have. These concepts parallel those identified in the NIST CS Framework (NIST, 2018) and are identify, protect, detect, respond and recover. Moreover, the activities related to these concepts mirror those in the NIST CS Framework.

i. **Identify**: This concept is foundational and considers the ecosystem of CS. When defining the scope of activities associated with this concept, entities should address people, policies, processes and technology. The CS creator should consider activities related to the business environment, risk assessment, risk management strategy, governance, asset management, laws, regulations, business context analysis and supply chain considerations.

ii. **Protect**: This concept relates to an entity developing appropriate safeguards to protect the entity's cyber persona (i.e. the digital representation of an individual or organization necessary to interact in cyberspace), to ensure preventative controls are working so as to produce the desired readiness of the organization to deliver critical services and maintain its operations and security of its information. In developing the protect concept, the CS creator should consider protection for people, process and technology. Activities relevant to the protect concept include access control, awareness and training, data security, information protection processes and procedures, maintenance, protective technology, traffic filtering, cryptography, and identity and access management.

iii. **Detect**: This concept develops the appropriate activities to discover CS events and include activities related to anomalies and events, security continuous monitoring, detection process, logging, log correlation and analysis, threat hunting, anomaly detection and operational baseline creation.

iv. **Respond**: This concept develops the appropriate activities regarding the response to cybersecurity events. The activities related to the respond concept allow an entity to qualify the cybersecurity events in their environment (i.e. categorize and evaluate the events) and react to/remediate them based on their specific needs, resources, stakeholders and requirements. Additional activities can include the communication to and from external parties relating vulnerability disclosures, threat reports or other information provided by external sources.

v. **Recover**: The activities in the recover concept define the restoration and communication-related activities after a cybersecurity event. The recovery concept is not only a reactive concept, but also a proactive concept. Effective and efficient planning and execution of the activities in the Recover concept should minimize damage and help organizations resume operations.

13.2.3 ENISA Cybersecurity Guide

The European Union Agency for Network and Information Security (ENISA) offers a NCSS Good Practice Guide to EU Member States in their efforts to develop and update their NCSS. The guide presents six steps for the design and development of a NCSS (ENISA, 2016):

i. **Set the vision, scope, objectives and priorities:** Setting clear objectives is paramount for achieving this step. Tasks that are typically included in this step include: define the vision and scope that set the high-level objectives to be accomplished in a specific time frame; define the business sectors and services in scope for the strategy; prioritize objectives in terms of impact to the society, economy and citizens; and, define a roadmap for the implementation of the strategy.

ii. **Follow a risk assessment approach**: Conduct a national risk assessment with a specific focus on critical information infrastructures. Tasks in this step include agreeing on what risk assessment methodology to use; task a national authority with conducting the risk assessment; design and follow an approach to risk identification and assessment; and develop a method for the identification of critical (information) infrastructure.

iii. **Take stock of existing policies, regulations and capabilities**: The aim of this step is to align the NCSS with international standards and to identify important gaps. Tasks in this step include: establishing existing policies developed over the years in the area of cybersecurity; identifying all regulatory measures applied in different sectors and their impact in improving cybersecurity (e.g. mandatory incident reporting in the electronic communications sector); identifying existing soft regulatory mechanisms (e.g. public and private partnerships) and assessing the extent to which these have achieved their goals; analysing the roles and responsibilities of existing public agencies mandated to deal with cybersecurity policies, regulations and operations; and when updating the NCSS make the strategic evolution transparent: What kind of new/updated objectives are part of the new NCSS and why?

iv. **Set a clear governance structure**: The cybersecurity strategy will succeed only if a clear governance framework is in place. A governance framework defines the roles, responsibilities and accountability of all relevant stakeholders. It provides a framework for dialogue and coordination of various activities undertaken in the lifecycle of the strategy. Some tasks include: defining who is ultimately responsible for the management and evaluation of the strategy; defining the management structure; defining the mandate (e.g. roles, responsibilities, processes, decision rights) and tasks of this advisory body; and properly analysing and defining the role of existing, national cybersecurity and incident response teams (CERT).

v. **Identify and engage stakeholders**: A successful cybersecurity strategy requires proper cooperation between public and private stakeholders. Identifying and engaging stakeholders are crucial steps for the success of the strategy. Selected private entities should be part of the development process because they are likely the owners of most of the critical information infrastructures and services.

vi. **Establish trusted information-sharing mechanisms**: Information-sharing is a form of strategic partnership among key public and private stakeholders. Owners of critical infrastructures could potentially share with public authorities their input on mitigating emerging risks, threats, and vulnerabilities while public stakeholders could provide on a 'need to know basis' information on aspects related to the status of national security, including findings based on information collected by intelligence and cybercrime units. Some tasks in this step include: properly defining information-sharing mechanisms and the rules governing the mechanisms; encouraging cross-sector communication; providing appropriate incentives for stakeholder (mostly private entities) to participate and share sensitive information; and updating the national risk registry and distributing the collected information in an anonymous way to appropriate targeted entities/users through early-warning systems.

13.2.4 *ITU National Cybersecurity Strategy Guide*

The ITU proposes a NCSS good practice guide, which they propose include elements that can make the Strategy comprehensive and effective while allowing for tailoring to the national context (ITU et al., 2018). The good-practice elements are grouped into seven distinct focus areas, which serve as the overarching themes for a NCSS. The following briefly describes the focus areas:

i. **Governance**: The NCSS should indicate the government's CS vision and outline the roles and accountabilities required to ensure its implementation. The NCSS should also have the formal endorsement of the highest level of government, identify a dedicated national-competent CS authority who is a high-level government official to provide direction, coordinate action and monitor the implementation of the strategy.

ii. **Risk management in national CS:** Since CS risks cannot be fully eliminated, a risk management approach should be adopted. This ensures that a country has a good understanding of the protentional risks to which it may be exposed and allow it to effectively manage the risks. A risk management approach should be defined and adopted by government agencies and CI operators. Additionally, the establishment of additional CS policies, such as mandating reporting of cyber incident and CS procurement, are highlighted as important.

iii. **Preparedness and resilience:** This focus area highlights good practices that support the establishment and sustainability of effective national capabilities to prevent, detect, mitigate and respond to major cybersecurity incidents, and to improve a country's overall cyberresilience. CERTS are emphasized as important in this focus area along with contingency planning for CS crisis management and information-sharing mechanisms between and amongst public and private sectors.

iv. **Critical infrastructure services and essential services:** In this area, the NCSS should focus on practices to protect the country's CIs and critical information infrastructure (CII). CI can be described as assets that are essential to the functioning and security of a society and economy and CIIs are the IT and ICT systems that operate key functions of the CI in the country. To increase the security of CIs and CIIs, the guide emphasizes the need for formal public–private partnerships, given CIs and CIIs are usually not owned nor controlled by the government.

v. **Capacity and capability building and awareness training:** This area focuses on the human element of CS to include activities to establish CS curricula and awareness-raising programmes, workforce training schemes and development programmes, adoption of international certification schemes and promotion of research and development (R&D) clusters.

vi. **Legislation and regulation:** The development of a legal and regulatory framework to protect society against cybercrime and promote a safe and secure cyberenvironment, is the focus of this area. The legislative framework should promote the adoption/development of legislative frameworks that defines what constitutes illegal cyberactivity, recognition of individual rights and civil liberties such as due process rights (i.e. criminal investigation and prosecutions), data protection and privacy, freedom of expression, establishment of compliance mechanisms, development of cyber-law-enforcement capacity (e.g. lawyers, judges, forensic specialists), international cooperation to fight cybercrimes and the institutionalization of critical entities.

vii. **International cooperation** Since cybercrimes are borderless crimes, there is need for cooperation nationally and internationally. The NCSS should express a commitment to international cooperation on CS and recognize cyber issues as an integral component of the country's foreign policy. Participation in international fora is another mechanism to engage diplomatically on cyber-related issues.

13.2.5 Cybersecurity Development Guides Best Practices

Based on the foregoing it is evident that the international CS development guides highlight the importance of a multifaceted or holistic approach to tackle CS. In fact, the international organizations such as NIST, ISO/IEC, ITU and ENISA present a set of comprehensive recommendations on the development of a national CS strategy. Table 13.1 presents a side-by-side comparison of the recommended elements of a NCSS offered by the various international agencies. Taken as a whole, these elements comprise the core of international best practices in the field.

Table 13.1 Recommended Elements or Best Practices of a NCSS

Recommendation/Element	*NIST*	*ISO/IEC*	*ENISA*	*ITU*
Risk management approach	•	•	•	•
Multi-stakeholder collaboration	•		•	•
Establish governance framework	•		•	•
Develop and implement technical standards	•	•		
Implement technical controls	•	•		
Set CSS scope, vision, objectives and priorities			•	•
Align business/sector/national objectives with CS framework	•	•	•	•
Identify CI/assets/systems/process	•	•	•	•
Public–private partnership			•	•
Continuous monitoring	•	•		
Legal and regulatory requirements	•		•	•
Establish supporting policies	Implied	Implied	•	•
CS awareness and education programme	•	•	•	•
Regional/international cooperation			•	•
Articulate CS outcomes	•			•
CS workforce-development programmes	Implied		•	•
Law enforcement and judicial capacity building			•	•
Support fundamental freedoms and privacy	•		•	•
Establish communication framework	•	•	•	
Recovery planning framework	•	•		
Incident response management	•	•		

(*Continued*)

Table 13.1   (Continued)

Recommendation/Element	NIST	ISO/IEC	ENISA	ITU
Establish CSS implementation framework	•		•	
Top-level business/government support	•		•	•
Appoint national CS coordinator			•	•
Implement national CERT			•	•
Trusted information sharing framework & mechanism			•	•
Communicating CSS to supply chain		•		
Develop cyber-contingency plan and cyber exercises			•	•
Incident reporting mechanism	•		•	
Maintain risk and incident registry			•	
Foster R&D in CS			•	•
Incentivize CS participation			•	•

13.3 Select National Cybersecurity Strategies

In this section, we review some published NCSS of GS countries. This section does not present an exhaustive review but instead aims to review a sample of published national cybersecurity strategies including from several regions. Specifically, Africa, i.e. South Africa and the Federal Republic of Nigeria and the LAC region. Recall, in the LAC region a substantial number of countries have yet to document and/or publish national cybersecurity strategies (IDB & OAS, 2020).

13.3.1 South Africa National Cybersecurity Policy Framework

Following the precepts of then published strategy guides, the national CS policy framework (NCPF) for South Africa emphasizes the important role of government in meeting the increased risk of evolving cyber threats. The key strategic objectives of the NCPF of South Africa are: (i) **facilitate the establishment of relevant** structures in support of cybersecurity; (ii) **ensure the reduction of cybersecurity threats and vulnerabilities**; (iii) **foster cooperation and coordination between government and private sector**; (iv) **promote and strengthen international cooperation on cybersecurity**; (v) **build capacity and promoting a culture of cybersecurity**; (vi) **promote compliance with appropriate technical and operational cybersecurity standards**; and (vii) **establishing/strengthening legal framework and compliance with technical and operational cybersecurity standards** (State Security Agency, 2012). While the policy framework was brief, it meets the essentials recommended by international guidelines. Moreover, the policy framework serves to promote an explicit national vision of establishing confidence in a safe and secure cyberspace.

13.3.2 Jamaica National Cybersecurity Strategy

The Jamaican NCSS (JNCSS) recognizes that cybercrimes are a real and present threat to the stability of any society, Jamaica being no exception (Government of Jamaica, 2015). The Strategy also recognizes that ICTs are necessary tools for development however, with their increased use are increased risks that have the potential to erode confidence and trust in the economy, thereby impeding national development (Government of Jamaica, 2015). According to the JNCSS, its ultimate objective is to 'engender confidence in cyberspace such that Jamaicans can continue to achieve their full potential' (Government of Jamaica, 2015, p. 6).

The JNCSS is built around four key areas: (i) **technical measures**; ii) **human resource and capacity building**; (iii) **legal and regulatory**; and (iv) **public education and awareness** (Government of Jamaica, 2015). The main focus of the **technical measures** area is to ensure that network infrastructure and in particular critical infrastructure systems are resilient to cyber threats. The **human resource and capacity building** area recognizes that establishing and sustaining a pool of trained information security (InfoSec) professionals will ensure there is national capacity to detect, respond to and recover from cyber incidents as well encourage collaboration and research and development in InfoSec in Jamaica. The **legal and regulatory** efforts focus on examining and undertaking legislative reforms to promote a safe and healthy cyber business environment and recourse to all stakeholders should they fall victims to cybercrime. **Public education and awareness** seek to develop targeted campaigns to elucidate and improve stakeholders' understanding of potential cybercrime threats and risks they may face and the appropriate action they can take to protect themselves. The strategy also establishes clear roles and responsibilities within government for CS activities and establishes a risk-based approach in establishing IT and InfoSec standards, policies and guidelines for ICT infrastructure and cybersecurity governance. It also promotes leveraging regional and international cooperation and mechanisms for secure information sharing with regional and international stakeholders.

13.3.3 Trinidad and Tobago National Cybersecurity Strategy

The Trinidad and Tobago NCSS (TTNCSS) emphasizes the need for improved CS strategy as a key component of economic development (Inter-Ministerial Committee for Cyber Security, 2012). The TTNCSS highlights five key focus areas: (i) **governance**: emphasizes the establishment of a T&T Cyber Security Agency (TTCSA) as the main body responsible for all CS-related matters and the coordinating centre for all CS operations; (ii) **incident management**: recognizes the importance of establishing a CSIRT as a national focal point for incident reporting, incident management and incident response; (iii) **collaboration**: the Framework emphasizes the need for of public–private/civil society partnership in securing the country's cyberinfrastructure and for the promotion of cooperation with international organizations; (iv) **culture**: the emphasis is to raise awareness, increase training and education in CS throughout the country; (v) **legislation**: in this area the Strategy focuses on the drafting and enactment of relevant cybercrime legislation that criminalizes offences, protects citizens and prosecutes offenders (Inter-Ministerial Committee for Cyber Security, 2012). The Strategy also provides a series of operational goals coupled with requisite implementation actions required to achieve those goals.

13.3.4 Columbia National Cybersecurity Strategy

The overarching objective of the Columbian NCSS (CNCSS) is to 'strengthen the capabilities of the state to confront threats that undermine its security and defense in cyberspace (cybersecurity and cyberdefense), creating the necessary environment and conditions to provide protection therein' (Republic of Columbia, 2011). In order to achieve its CS objective, the CNCSS emphasize three main focus areas: (i) the role of government in establishing appropriate bodies to prevent, provide assistance, control, produce recommendations and issue rules on cyber incidents or emergencies, in order to confront threats and risks to national CS and cyberdefence; (ii) provide specialized training in InfoSec and broaden lines of investigation in CS and cyberdefence; and (iii) strengthen the CS and cyberdefence laws, bolster international cooperation. The CNCSS is heavily aligned with the country's national security approach with much of the focus of the strategy being placed on the development of a national CERT, colCERT, to be domiciled in the Ministry of Defense with clear lines of coordination between the military Joint Cyber Command and the Police Cyber Center. Interestingly, the Strategy presented timelines for implementation and allocated funding for the various focus areas (Republic of Columbia, 2011).

13.3.5 Belize National Cybersecurity Strategy

Developed in collaboration with government and stakeholders, the Belize NCSS (BNCSS) strategic vision is: 'recognizing the benefits that technologies in this new digital age can bring, the people of Belize will work together to create a safe and trusted digital environment that will promote economic growth and social inclusion for all' (Government of Belize, 2020, p. 12). The following principles guided the development of the strategy: (i) **respect for and the promotion of fundamental rights**: the strategy highlights that human rights not only apply offline but also online, thus protecting and promoting fundamental human rights such as the right to privacy, freedom of expression, freedom of association and assembly with others; (ii) **government led**: this area highlights the imperative that government leads by example in adopting CS best practices in its operations, given it is one of the largest consumers of IT services; (iii) **risk-based approach**: the strategy seeks to mitigate cybersecurity risks to acceptable levels with regards CI; (iv) **shared responsibility**: cybersecurity affects everyone and as a result it is a shared responsibility for all to exercise cybersecurity best practices. This is to be accomplished through targeted awareness-raising initiatives to enable and empower end-users to keep themselves and their organizations safer online; (v) **fostering an environment for economic growth and innovation**: recognizing the importance of innovation and business development to the national economy, a cyberenvironment that is safe and conducive to such development will be promoted; and (vi) **international cooperation**: the strategy recognizes the need for comprehensive stakeholder partnership as well as the need to leverage international partnerships to investigate criminal activities, build capacity and protect Belize's cyberspace (Government of Belize, 2020).

13.3.6 Nigeria National Cybersecurity Policy and Strategy

The Federal Republic of Nigeria (FRN) NCS Policy and Strategy (NCSPS) aims to 'provide a safe and secure digital community that provides opportunities for its citizenry and promote peaceful and proactive engagements in cyberspace for enhanced national prosperity' (Federal Republic of Nigeria, 2021, p. xi). Based on the precepts of the previously discussed strategy guides, the FRN national CS programme has a strategic focus on eight key areas (Federal Republic of Nigeria, 2021):

i. **strengthening CS governance and coordination**: establishment of a national CS coordination centre, a National Coordinator and roles and responsibilities of all stakeholders clearly outlined;

ii. **fostering protection of critical national information infrastructure** (CNII): development of necessary cohesive measures and strategic actions towards assuring the security and protection of national CI and systems and the establishment of effective collaborative partnership with CI owners and operators;

iii. **enhancing CS incident management**: ngCERT is the focal point of the national cyber incident management and should possess the capability to pre-empt, respond and expeditiously mitigate the potential consequences of cyberattacks, while minimizing the impacts; develop frameworks for international, multinational and bilateral collaborations towards cyber incidents and management, incident reporting and sharing;

iv. **strengthening legal and regulatory framework**: the NCSPS highlight the need to improve, update and enact federal laws to combat cybercrimes, ensure harmonization of provisions in other legislations relating to cyberspace and strengthen Data Governance and Protection of Digital Intellectual Property;

v. **enhancing cyber defence capability**: this area focuses on developing the capability of the military and defence establishments to identify, detect and effectively deter any form of organized cyberattack launched on the nation and to defend the military networks and systems, government ICT assets and the country's CNII domiciled with the private sector against national cyberattacks;

vi. **promoting a thriving digital economy**: the aim is to use CS as a catalyst to promote the use of the Internet and social media for increased commercial, financial and related government activities, fostering a thriving digital economy and engendering trust and confidence in the FRN's cyberspace;

vii. **assurance monitoring and evaluation**: the implementation of high quality, robust CS technologies, along with adopting good CS practices, processes and standards for the CS technologies are highlighted as important in this strategic focus area; and

viii. **enhancing international cooperation**: the objective of this focus area is to strengthen relationships with regional and global partners, participate in international CS forum, strengthen information sharing and promote ratification of CS conventions.

Additionally, the FRN NCSPS recognizes the importance of availability of substantial financial resources to actualize its National CS programmes. The strategy also provides an action plan with associated actions, timelines and key performance indicators (KPIs) required to achieve the strategic objectives.

13.3.7 Comparison: Published National Cybersecurity Strategies and Best Practices

Table 13.2 presents a side-by-side comparison of published NCSSs in GS countries with the recommended NCSS best practices proposed by the various international agencies. Table 13.2 also includes additional element(s) at the end of the table that may be presented in a published NCSS but not proposed as a recommended best practice.

Table 13.2 Comparison of Published NCSS in GS Countries with Recommended Best Practices

Recommendation/Element	SA	JM	T&T	CL	BL	FRN
Risk management approach	•	•			•	•
Multi-stakeholder collaboration	•	•	•		•	•
Establish governance framework	•	•	•	•	•	•
Develop and implement technical standards	•	•	•	•	•	•
Implement technical controls	•	•	Implied	•		•
Set CSS scope, vision, objectives and priorities	•	•	•	•	•	•
Align business/sector/national objectives with CS framework			•	•		•
Identify CI/assets/systems/process	Implied	Implied	Implied	Implied	•	•
Public–private partnership	•	•	•	•	•	•
Continuous monitoring	•	•	•	•	•	•
Legal and regulatory requirements	•	•	•	•	•	•
Establish supporting policies	•	•	Implied	•	•	•
CS awareness and education programme	•	•	•	•	•	•
Regional/international cooperation	•	•	•	•	•	•
Articulate CS outcomes	•		•	•	•	•
CS workforce-development programmes	•	•	•	•		•

Criterion	SA	JM	T&T	CL	BL	FRN
Law enforcement and judicial capacity building	•	•	•	Implied	•	•
Support fundamental freedoms and privacy	•	•	•		•	•
Establish communication framework		•	Implied	Implied	•	
Recovery planning framework	•	•	Implied	Implied	•	•
Incident response management	•	•	•	Implied	•	•
Establish CSS implementation framework	•	Implied	•	•	•	
Top-level business/government support	•	•	Implied	•	•	•
Appoint national CS coordinator	•	•				•
Implement CIRT/CERT/CSIRT	•	•	•	•	•	•
Trusted information sharing framework & mechanism	•	•				•
Communicating CSS to supply chain		Implied				
Develop cyber-contingency plan & cyber exercises						Implied
Incident reporting mechanism					•	
Maintain risk & incident registry			•			
Foster R&D in CS	•					•
Incentivize CS participation						•
Indicate budgetary requirements[a]		Implied	•		Implied	Implied
Develop a CS knowledge management system[a]			•	•		
Establish redundancy for CI[a]						•

[a] Note: – additional element; SA – South Africa; JM – Jamaica; T&T – Trinidad and Tobago; CL – Columbia; BL – Belize; FRN – Federal Republic of Nigeria

13.4 Proposed Framework for Developing a National Cybersecurity Strategy

In this section, we advance a framework for developing an NCSS that GS countries can consider, which is presented in Figure 13.1. The framework is informed by best practice guides proposed by international entities, IGO's, already published NCSS frameworks in GS countries and prior research in the discipline. It is imperative that a NCSS framework consider the protection of people, CI and other technology and processes to include critical supply chain. Thus, the framework consists of three sections: (i) at the top is the 'Vision, Scope, Objectives and Priorities' section; (ii) in the middle is the **Supporting Columns** category; and (iii) at the bottom the **Foundational** category. The Supporting Columns and Foundational categories consist of varying strategic focus areas that a nation should address when developing its NCSS. While each strategic focus area associated with the two categories will be discussed in subsequent sections, in the 'Vision, Scope, Objectives and Priorities' section, the adopting nation should clearly articulate the aim of the CSS as well as its objectives and priorities. The nation should set the high-level objectives to be accomplished in a specific time frame, define the business sectors and services in scope for the strategy and prioritize objectives in terms of impact to the society, economy and citizens (ENISA, 2016). While not addressing all the areas as indicated above, the Belize's NCSS highlights its strategic vision as 'recognizing the benefits that technologies in this new digital age can bring, the people of Belize will work together to create a safe and trusted digital environment that will promote economic growth and social inclusion for all' and .... 'the strategy addresses three priorities pillars and includes actionable objectives to be realized over a period of three (3) years' (Government of Belize, 2020, p. 8 & 12). The Columbian Policy

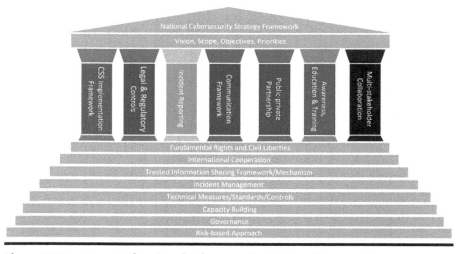

Figure 13.1 Integrated national cybersecurity strategy framework

Guideline on CS indicates the overarching objective of the policy as 'the strengthening of the state's capacity to confront cyber threats to its security and defense' (Republic of Columbia, 2011, p. 2).

13.4.1 Foundational Strategic Focus Areas

Like that of a building, the Foundational strategic focus areas, en bloc, can be described as the bedrock of the NCSS or the elements that are core to the strategy, providing the ground structure/support on which the NCSS is built.

13.4.1.1 Risk-Based Approach

Risk management is an ongoing process of identifying, assessing and responding to risk (NIST, 2018). Recognizing that since technology constantly evolves, and associated risks are increasingly sophisticated, as well as the tactics of potential cybercrime perpetrators, CS risks cannot be fully eliminated. Thus, a risk management approach in developing its CSS is appropriate in helping a nation understand potential risks to which it may be exposed. A risk-based approach, then, is also useful in aiding the nation to effectively manage such risks. Therefore, a risk management approach should be adopted/adapted by government agencies and operators of CIs.

13.4.1.2 Governance

A governance framework defines the roles, responsibilities and accountability of all relevant stakeholders. The NCSS is likely to fail without a clear governance framework. The NCSS should have formal endorsement from the highest level of government and identify a dedicated national-competent CS authority (individual/entity) who is at the highest level of government also to manage all aspects of the NCSS development and implementation plans. Additionally, the role of CERTs/CSIRTs should be clearly defined.

13.4.1.3 Capacity Building

The NCSS should highlight the steps (such as development of CS curricula, certification of professionals, formal internships) to develop and sustain a trained pool of CS and InfoSec professionals that will assist in ensuring that there is national capacity to deter & protect, detect, respond and recover from cyber incidents. These professionals include Red, Blue and Purple Teams. Another key area of capacity building is that of continual and specialized training for law enforcement, judiciary and judiciary staff. CS innovation and research and development are also highlighted in this Foundational strategic focus area. Further, to improve capacity, baseline requirements for public and private entities are to be developed and then existing capabilities evaluated in order to identify gaps. Where existing capabilities are insufficient, same should be enhanced or developed.

13.4.1.4 Technical Measures/Standards/Controls

Technical measures include security controls that safeguard the confidentiality, integrity and availability of CI and other information assets (Dennis, Jones, Kildare, & Barclay, 2014). Government agencies should implement government-wide international IT, InfoSec and CS standards, policies and guidelines, that are to be monitored and enforced when implemented. CI operators, organizations and individuals should also be encouraged to adopt the government's established technical standards, policies and guidelines to ensure delivery of services.

13.4.1.5 Incident Management

For managing CS incidents, a CS Incident Management Framework (CSIMF), as shown in Figure 13.2, should be adopted. The CSIMF is cyclical, indicating that CS incident management is a continuous process. When addressing incident management, the areas of deter & protect, detect, respond and recover should be considered.

    i. **Deter and Protect** involve first assessing current CI and Information assets technical controls as well 'human element' threats. This step also involves conducting national CS assessments such as Cyber Hygiene: Vulnerability Scanning, Risk and Vulnerability Assessment and Phishing Campaign Assessments. Identified vulnerabilities and/or weaknesses should be remediated to strengthen the entity's security posture. Additionally, mandatory adoption of international CS standards should be enforced in government agencies.
    ii. **Detect** is continuous and appropriate activities should be developed and implemented to identify the occurrence of a CS event. These activities should

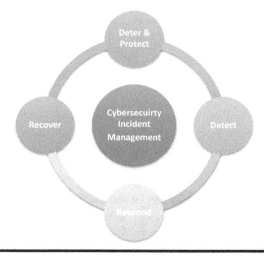

Figure 13.2   Cybersecurity incident management framework

enable the timely discovery of cyber events. Logging, log correlation and analysis, threat hunting, anomaly detection and security continuous monitoring are some asset monitoring attack detection activities that can be employed.

iii. **Respond** involves the implementing of national capabilities to address CS incidents which is often the mandate of specialized, dedicated national security teams or CERTs/CSIRTs. Responding to CS incidents could include following formally approved response procedures and plans, conducting forensic investigations, environment sterilization and removal of malware. Respond can also include managerial procedures such as what is communicated about the CS incident to external parties.

iv. **Recover** involves the restoration of affected information assets/systems to normal operations as well as post-incident management activities. To fully restore systems may involve the assistance of or information from local, regional and/or international partners. Recovery should not be just reactive but should also be proactive. The NCSS should emphasize the adoption of business continuity measures, to include incident crisis management and recovery plans. Recovery management may also include the analysis and documenting/reporting of incident details. This can play an important role in enhancing future recoveries as the more security specialists know about major incidents, the better they can understand the security threat environment. This information can then be used to improve existing security measures, strengthening the entity's security capability to **Deter & Protect** against other vulnerabilities/threats.

13.4.1.6 *Trusted Information Sharing Framework/Mechanism*

The NCSS should encourage the establishment of trusted information sharing mechanisms between and amongst private, public, regional and international partners to gain/share actionable intelligence and threat information that can counter/mitigate cyber threats and improve cyber resilience. As CS incidents may be as a result of criminals residing in other jurisdictions, interagency cooperation between and among CERTs/CSIRTs, law enforcement and the judiciary should be emphasized to ensure information sharing to assist with arresting and prosecuting is facilitated. Furthermore, the ITU et al. (2018, p. 41) note that

> formal and informal information-sharing frameworks/mechanisms can help foster effective coordination and consistent, accurate and appropriate communications during incident response and recovery activities; facilitate rapid sharing of threat and intelligence information among affected parties and other stakeholders; help improve the understanding of how and which sectors have been targeted; disseminate information on the methods that can be used to defend and mitigate damage on the affected assets; and ultimately reduce vulnerabilities and exposure along with their attendant risks.

13.4.1.7 International Cooperation

In the digital era, the saying that 'no man is an island' has taken on new life and the need for comprehensive cooperation has never been greater, especially given the 'borderless' nature of cybercrimes and CS incidents. Engaging in information sharing with international partners can improve the understanding of and response to the changing cyber landscape (ENISA, 2016). Ultimately, international cooperation can enable and increase combatting transnational electronic crimes. It is typical for CERTs/CSIRTs to be tasked with the responsibility for cooperation with other national/government teams in other jurisdictions. Another mechanism through which international cooperation to protect society against cybercrimes globally can be demonstrated by ratification, such as ratifying the Budapest Convention, the leading framework for international cooperation in dealing with cybercrimes. The ITU et al. (2018) espouse the virtues of international cooperation as being key in facilitating constructive dialogue, developing trust and cooperation mechanisms, finding mutually acceptable solutions to common challenges and creating a global culture of CS.

13.4.1.8 Fundamental Rights and Civil Liberties

Rights that individuals have offline should also be observed and protected online. The NCSS should reflect this and should also emphasize the importance of and respect for universally agreed fundamental rights. For instance, the NCSS should observe individuals' rights to freedom of expression, privacy of communications and personal data protection and privacy. Unlawful interception of communication and/or data as well as surveillance should be guarded against in the NCSS.

13.4.2 Supporting Columns Strategic Focus Areas

Continuing with the building analogy, Supporting Columns strategic focus areas, en bloc, like columns in a building, are used for structural reinforcement of the NCSS. In other words, Supporting Columns are strategic focus areas that strengthen or provide support for the successful achievement of the objectives and priorities of the NCSS as well as those related to the foundational strategic areas.

13.4.2.1 Multi-stakeholder Collaboration

It is without question that the digital economy has become critical to all, individuals, businesses and governments alike. Each group, individually and collectively, is faced with CS risks and the responsibility in managing those risks. All users, enjoying the benefits of ICTs and Internet-based services, should take reasonable steps to secure their IT systems and exercise care in the communication and storage of personal and sensitive data electronically. This NCSS framework encourages a multi-stakeholder collaborative approach to assure shared responsibility for a secure cyber environment. Additionally, different stakeholder groups may face different CS challenges or have different CS imperatives, therefore it is essential to engage relevant stakeholders for the development and successful implementation of a NCSS. It is with a view that engaging different stakeholders, should improve the understanding of stakeholder needs and their unique knowledge and expertise, thus facilitating cooperation towards achieving the objectives of the NCSS.

13.4.2.2 Awareness, Education and Training

Research has shown that awareness, education and training positively influence users' CS behaviour (see Chapter **5**, *Cybersecurity Policy Compliance Assessment: Findings from Government Agencies in the Global South*). Thus, increasing public awareness of CS threats and vulnerabilities and their possible impact, as well as best practices for countering them, is an imperative for achieving CS initiatives. CS awareness programmes could include awareness-raising campaigns targeting the general public, children and digitally challenged individuals. Additionally, best practice recommends partnering with universities to develop CS curricula with the aim of accelerating cybersecurity skills development and awareness throughout the formal education system (ITU et al., 2018). The NCSS should also emphasize the development of CS training and skills development schemes for experts and non-experts in both public and private sectors, through mechanisms like formal internships and traineeships and certification of security professionals.

13.4.2.3 Public–Private Partnership

In many countries, including those of the GS, CI and critical services are often owned and provided by private companies. For instance, financial services infrastructure, ICT, Internet and telephony systems and infrastructure, transportation (air, road, rail) and power and energy systems and infrastructure are examples of critical national infrastructures that may not be owned nor operated by government. However, CS protection of these CI and critical services is paramount to the proper functioning of the society and economy. The recent Colonial Pipeline ransomware cyberattack in the United States, which led to a complete shutdown of delivery of fuel services across the nation, long lines at gas stations, many of which ran out and higher fuel prices (Turton & Mehrotra, 2021), demonstrates the impact that a disruption in such CI and critical services can have. Therefore, it is imperative that the NCSS encourage the creation of formal public–private partnerships to increase the protection and resilience of CI and critical services. It is espoused that key to the protection of CI and critical services in the short and long term are public–private partnerships, which are also essential for boosting trust amongst and between the industry and the government (ITU et al., 2018).

13.4.2.4 Communication Framework

Based on reports discussed in an earlier section, it is evident that cyberattacks can and have been costly in that they can invariably lead to market disruptions such as decrease in sales revenue, higher expenses, decrease in dividends, reduction in market value, decline in profit, negative impact on operational activities and reputational damage and, direct and substantial financial loss such as paying ransomware for the restoration of systems to normal operations, as in the case of Colonial Pipeline in May 2021. To mitigate such reputational damage, this NCSS framework encourages the establishment of a Communication Framework to include what is communicated to and from external parties related to a major CS incident. For instance, the communications could be vulnerability disclosures, threat reports or other information provided by external sources. This framework also recommends that a competent authority (e.g. a national CS Coordinator) is tasked with the responsibility for transmitting accurate and actionable information among the national CS community, including the public and private sectors and also general information to the public at large. Accurate, timely and relevant communication can, among other things, engender trust.

13.4.2.5 Incident Reporting

Incident reporting, and even more so, the timely reporting of CS incidents can play an important role in enhancing national security. It is a reasonable argument that incident reporting can improve incident analysis, which in turn should help CS authorities determine what should be the focus of their security measures to inform national preparedness, response and recovery efforts. It is typical that this responsibility would be the remit of a national CERT/CSIRT. Incident reporting can improve the issuing of timely alerts on emerging threats to ensure the integrity of systems that may be at risk, as well as build collaborative relationships with all sectors to, among other things, foster trust.

13.4.2.6 Legal and Regulatory Controls

Even if all the technical measures and other initiatives such as awareness campaigns are to be implemented but there are no comprehensive criminal legislation that addresses the prosecution of cybercrimes such as hacking, ransomware, website defacement, electronic fraud, unauthorized access and social engineering, the national CS efforts would not be effective. Dennis et al. (2014) highlight that there needs to be continuous assessment of the relevant laws to ensure that existing and emergent cybercrimes are prosecutable. The legal and regulatory controls should also address legislation related to ICTs, privacy and data protection, human rights as well as a substantive and procedural cybercrime law.

13.4.2.7 CSS Implementation Framework

A general weakness relating to CS in the GS is that even when a NCSS has been adopted, many remain largely unimplemented (see the 2020 Global Cybersecurity Index) (ITU, 2020), rendering these countries vulnerable to cyberattacks. In this

Figure 13.3   National CSS implementation framework

section, we propose a NCSS implementation framework, as shown in Figure 13.3, for governing a NCSS. In keeping with best practices, we recommend applying a lifecycle approach to check and continuously improve the strategy and related policies as well as its implementation through measures, actions and processes.

The proposed NCSS implementation framework consists of five (5) major phases: Planning & Initiation, Analysis, Development, Implementation and Monitoring & Maintenance. Each phase can be expanded into steps detailing the activities that occur within each. A brief discussion of each phase is discussed hereafter. It is important to note that the NCSS is a policy and policy development is an iterative and continuous process. Since technology constantly changes, the business environment and legal compliance requirements, the CSS implementation phase is followed by the maintenance and monitoring phase which incorporates these and other changes and ensures that the directives of the policy are operationally executed. At the bottom of the five phases are feedback loops, emphasizing that phases are not static and that information from a subsequent phase can be used to adjust the previous phase.

- **Phase I: Planning and Initiation:** This phase includes the initial activities necessary for the successful development of the NCSS. It typically focuses on timelines, processes and the key stakeholders that will be involved in the development of the NCSS. At the end of this phase, a plan for developing the National Cybersecurity Strategy is drafted and submitted to the project's Steering Committee and top-level government official for approval. Of note, the draft plan should include major steps, and activities, timelines, human and financial resources needed and where same can be procured.
- **Phase II: Analysis:** In this phase CI and assets that the policy will address are identified. Vulnerabilities and threats to those assets and CIs are also identified. Risk assessment is conducted, and possible measures and controls are evaluated. The results of these steps are used to decide the scope of the NCSS to ensure that identified risks are mitigated. A risk assessment report is generated, providing an overview of the national CS posture and risk landscape, to be submitted to the Steering Committee.
- **Phase III: Development**: Through a series of consultations with public and private sectors, academia and working groups a preliminary NCSS is generated. This preliminary document should consider in its development the CSS best practices such as those proposed in the NCSS framework presented

in Figure 13.1. The preliminary document is subsequently disseminated, soliciting recommendations from stakeholders and the public at large. Recommendations received are used to revise the preliminary NCSS and submitted for official approval by the top-level government official. The official NCSS is a public document and should be made readily available.

■ **Phase IV: Implementation**: After developing the NCSS, it is time to implement the new CS document. A detailed implementation plan is usually required to translate the CSS into reality. The initiatives to be implemented are identified and the required human and financial resources for the implementation are allocated. Key performance indicators and development metrics to assess each of the initiatives undertaken, such as implementing CS training and awareness campaigns, are also identified.

■ **Phase V: Monitoring and Maintenance**: In this phase a formal process is devised to monitor and maintain the NCSS. Appropriate monitoring mechanisms should be in place to ensure that the CSS is implemented according to the implementation plan. Since technology and associated risks constantly changes, periodic reviews of the strategy should be conducted to assess whether it remains relevant and whether it continues to reflect the government's objectives and the necessary adjustments.

13.5 Conclusion

Governments in GS countries recognize the importance of information and communications technologies (ICTs) as powerful tools for sustainable socio-economic development. However, CS risks continue to threaten the benefits that may accrue from these technologies. To mitigate these CS risks, it is important to understand that CS is not only a technical challenge but a complex and multi-faceted issue to include areas such local and international cooperation, legislative controls, awareness and capacity building, public-private collaboration, communication framework and research and development. To improve the resilience of CIs and critical services, nations have adopted and implemented national CS strategies. However, many nations in the GS have not yet begun the process of documenting a NCSS. In this chapter, a NCSS framework has been proposed that can be considered by these GS nations. The NCSS framework is informed by CSS best practices, other published national CS strategies by GS countries and prior research.

The NCSS framework proposed in this chapter emphasizes three categories, vision, scope, objectives and priorities, foundational, and supporting columns. Foundational strategic areas can be considered as the bedrock of the NCSS or the elements that are core to the strategy, providing the ground structure/support on which the NCSS is built. Examples of foundational strategic areas include Governance, Capacity Building, Incident Management and Fundamental Rights and Civil Liberties. On the other hand, supporting columns are used for structural reinforcement of the NCSS and include such strategic areas as Multi-stakeholder

Collaboration, CSS Implementation Framework, Awareness, Education and Training, and Legal & Regulatory Controls. This chapter provides a significant contribution to research and practice. The development of an integrated national cybersecurity strategy framework, that incorporates the most recent CSS best practices is an important contribution. Additionally, the framework can be adopted by GS countries, an important contribution to national development.

References

Caricom Caribbean Community. (2016). *Caribbean to Tackle Escalating Cybercrime with Regional Approach.* Retrieved from https://caricom.org/communications/view/caribbean-to-tackle-escalating-cybercrime-with-regional-approach

Communications Authority of Kenya. (2021). *October - December 2020 Communications Authority of Kenya National KE-CIRT/CC Cybersecurity Report.* Retrieved from https://ca.go.ke/wp-content/uploads/2021/01/Cyber-Security-sector-statistics-Report-Q2-FY-2020-2021.pdf

Dennis, A., Jones, R., Kildare, D., & Barclay, C. (2014). Design science approach to developing and evaluating a national cybersecurity framework for Jamaica. *The Electronic Journal of Information Systems in Developing Countries, 62*(6), 1–18.

ENISA. (2012). *National Cyber Security Strategies - Setting the Course for National Efforts to Strengthen Security in Cyberspace.* Retrieved from https://www.enisa.europa.eu/publications/cyber-security-strategies-paper

ENISA. (2016). *NCSS Good Practice Guide - Designing and Implementing National Cyber Security Strategies* (ISBN: 978-92-9204-179-3 DOI: 10.2824/48036). Retrieved from https://discoveryproject.eu/wp-content/uploads/2016/11/Updated-Good-Practice-Guide-on-NCSS-1.pdf

Federal Republic of Nigeria. (2021). *National Cybersecurity Policy and Strategy 2021.* Retrieved from https://cert.gov.ng/ngcert/resources/NATIONAL_CYBERSECURITY_POLICY_AND_STRATEGY_2021.pdf

GLACY+. (2019). *Regional Conference on Cybercrime Strategies and Policies and features of the Budapest Convention for the Caribbean Community,* 24. Retrieved from https://rm.coe.int/3148-1-1-3-final-report-dr-reg-conference-cy-policies-caribbean-comm-1/168098fb6c

Government of Belize. (2020). *National Cybersecurity Strategy - Towards a Secure Cyberspace 2020-2023.* Retrieved from https://www.pressoffice.gov.bz/wp-content/uploads/2019/12/belize-cybersecurity-strategy-2020-2023.pdf

Government of Jamaica. (2015). *Jamaica National Cyber Security Strategy.* Ministry of Science, Technology, Energy and Mining Retrieved from http://www.mstem.gov.jm/sites/default/files/documents/Jamaica%20National%20Cyber%20Security%20Strategy.pdf.

IDB & OAS. (2020). *2020 Cybersecurity Report: Risks, Progress, and the Way Forward In Latin America and the Caribbean.* Retrieved from Inter-American Development Bank: https://publications.iadb.org/publications/english/document/2020-Cybersecurity-Report-Risks-Progress-and-the-Way-Forward-in-Latin-America-and-the-Caribbean.pdf

Inter-Ministerial Committee for Cyber Security. (2012). *Government of the Republic of Trinidad and Tobago: National Cyber Security Strategy.* Retrieved from http://www.nationalsecurity.gov.tt/Portals/0/Pdf%20Files/National_Cyber_Security%20Strategy_Final.pdf

ISO/IEC. (2021). *ISO/IEC TS 27110: 2021 Information Technology, Cybersecurity and Privacy Protection — Cybersecurity Framework Development Guidelines*. Retrieved from https://www.iso.org/standard/72435.html

ITU. (2020). *Global Cybersecurity Index 2020*. Retrieved from https://www.itu.int/en/ITU-D/Cybersecurity/Documents/GCIv4/New_Reference_Model_GCIv4_V2_.pdf

ITU, The World Bank, Commonwealth Secretariat (ComSec), Commonwealth Telecommunications Organisation (CTO), & NATO Cooperative Cyber Defence Centre of Excellence (NATO CCD COE). (2018). *Guide to Developing a National Cybersecurity Strategy – Strategic Engagement in Cybersecurity*. Retrieved from https://www.itu.int/dms_pub/itu-d/opb/str/D-STR-CYB_GUIDE.01-2018-PDF-E.pdf

Luiijf, E., Besseling, K., & Graaf, P. D. (2013). Nineteen national cyber security strategies. *International Journal of Critical Infrastructures, 9*(1), 3–31.

Newmeyer, K. P. (2015). Elements of national cybersecurity strategy for developing nations. *National Cybersecurity Institute Journal, 1*(3), 9–20.

Newsday. (2020). *Responding to the Cybersecurity Threat*. Retrieved from https://newsday.co.tt/2020/10/22/responding-to-the-cybersecurity-threat/

NIST. (2018). *Framework for Improving Critical Infrastructure Cybersecurity*. Retrieved from https://nvlpubs.nist.gov/nistpubs/CSWP/NIST.CSWP.04162018.pdf

Planning Institute of Jamaica. (2009). *Vision 2030 Jamaica: National Development Plan (978-976-8103-28-4)*. Retrieved from Planning Institute of Jamaica: http://www.vision2030.gov.jm/Portals/0/NDP/Vision%202030%20Jamaica%20NDP%20Full%20No%20Cover%20(web).pdf

Republic of Columbia. (2011). *Conpes 3701: Policy Guidelines on Cybersecurity and Cyberdefense* Retrieved from https://www.itu.int/en/ITU-D/Cybersecurity/Documents/National_Strategies_Repository/Colombia_2011_articles-3510_documento.pdf

Research and Planning Institute. (2005). *National Strategic Plan of Barbados 2005-2025*. Retrieved from Ministry of Finance and Economic Affairs, Barbados: http://www.sice.oas.org/ctyindex/brb/plan2005-2025.pdf

Ron, M., Ninahualpa, G., Molina, D., & Diaz, J. (2020). How to develop a national cybersecurity strategy for developing countries. Ecuador case. In Á. Rocha, C. Ferrás, M. C. Montenegro, & G. V. Medina (Eds.), *Information Technology and Systems. ICITS 2020. Advances in Intelligent Systems and Computing* (Vol. 1137, pp. 553–563). Cham: Springer.

State Security Agency. (2012). *National Cybersecurity Policy Framework for South Africa*. Retrieved from https://www.gov.za/sites/default/files/gcis_document/201512/39475gon609.pdf

Statista Research Department. (2021). *Latin America: Cyber Attack Rate Compared to Worldwide 2020*. Retrieved from https://www.statista.com/statistics/1180143/latin-america-cyber-attack-rate-compared-worldwide-channel/

The Gleaner. (2020). *Jamaica National Hit by Major Cyber Attack*. Retrieved from https://jamaica-gleaner.com/article/news/20200320/jamaica-national-hit-major-cyber-attack

The Gleaner. (2021a, February 15, 2021). Data breach blowback - JAMCOVID exposure a treasure trove for scammers, says expert. *The Gleaner*. Retrieved from http://jamaica-gleaner.com/article/lead-stories/20210218/data-breach-blowback-jamcovid-exposure-treasure-trove-scammers-says

The Gleaner. (2021b). Prosecution threat for JAMCOVID breach. *The Gleaner*. Retrieved from http://jamaica-gleaner.com/article/lead-stories/20210219/prosecution-threat-jamcovid-breach

Turton, W., & Mehrotra, K. (2021). *Hackers Breached Colonial Pipeline Using Compromised Password*. Retrieved from https://www.bloomberg.com/news/articles/2021-06-04/hackers-breached-colonial-pipeline-using-compromised-password

Index

Pages in *italics* refer figures and **bold** refer tables.